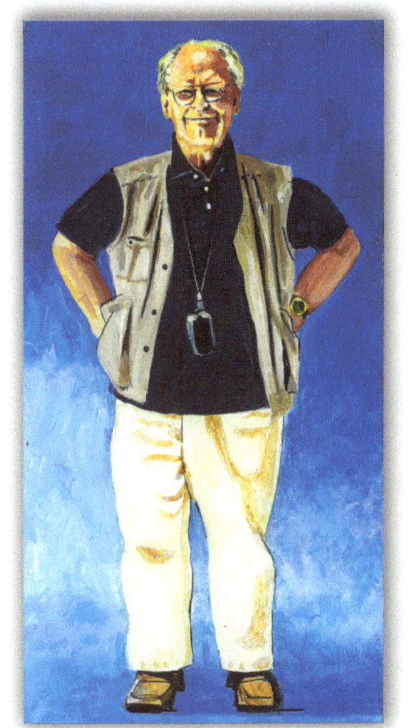

Bob Miller

ALWAYS WORKING

Art & Words by Bob Miller

Composed & Created by Bob Androvich

FEATURING CONTRIBUTIONS FROM

STAN ATKINSON

DON CHANDLER

MICHAEL DUNLAVEY

BRUCE MARWICK

BOB MATSUMOTO

CHRIS MCGLASSON

TOM MILLER

BOB RAKELA

BURT WILSON

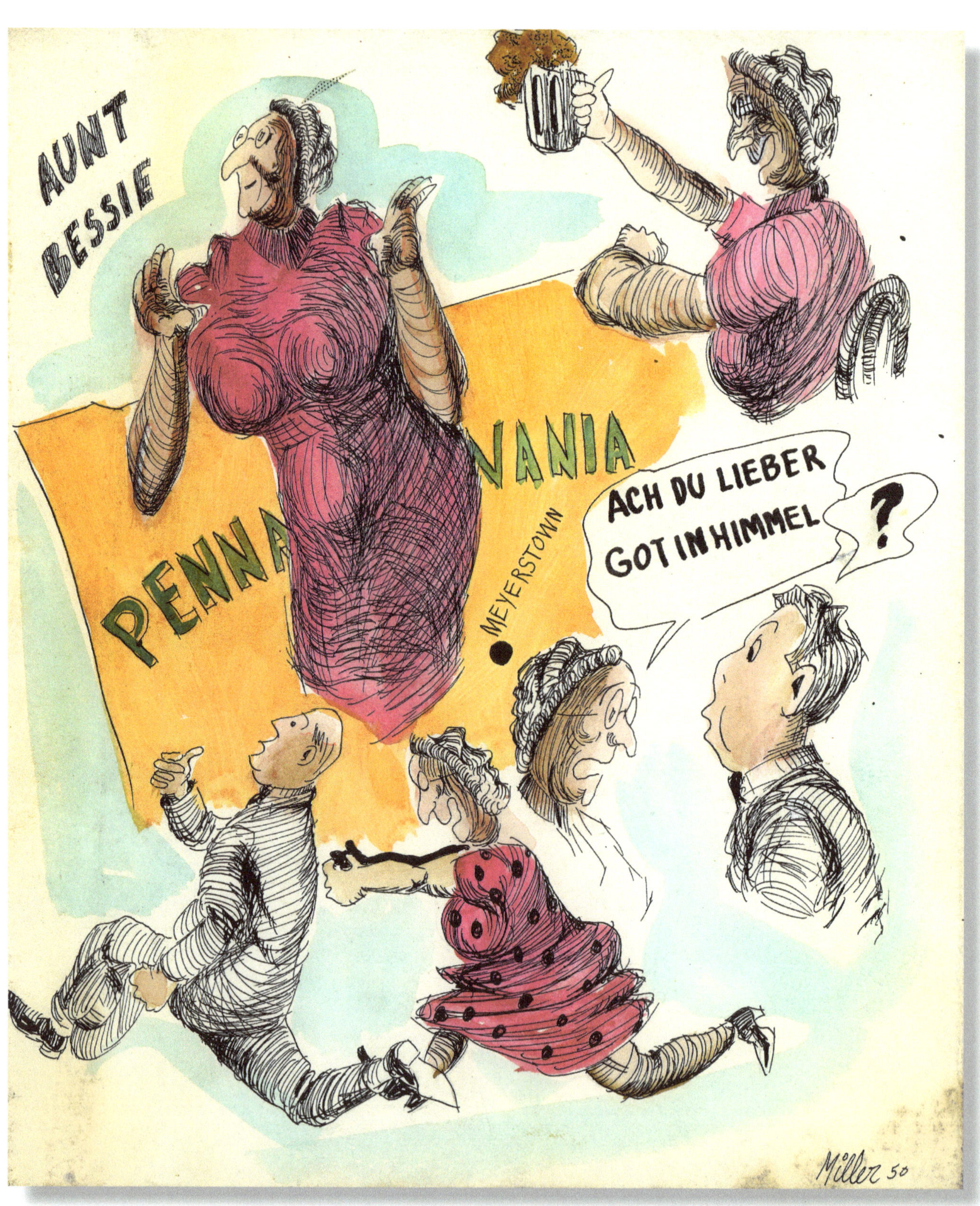
AUNT BESSIE
PENNA
NANIA
MEYERSTOWN
ACH DU LIEBER GOTINHIMMEL
?
Miller 50

Introduction by Bob Androvich

This is a book about Bob Miller.

Every word in it was written or spoken by Bob Miller.
It is his story as he chose to tell it.

Every image was created by Bob Miller.

I was just lucky enough to meet him and talk him into allowing me to put it together for him.

The title was a natural.
If you know Bob Miller, you know he is
Always Working.

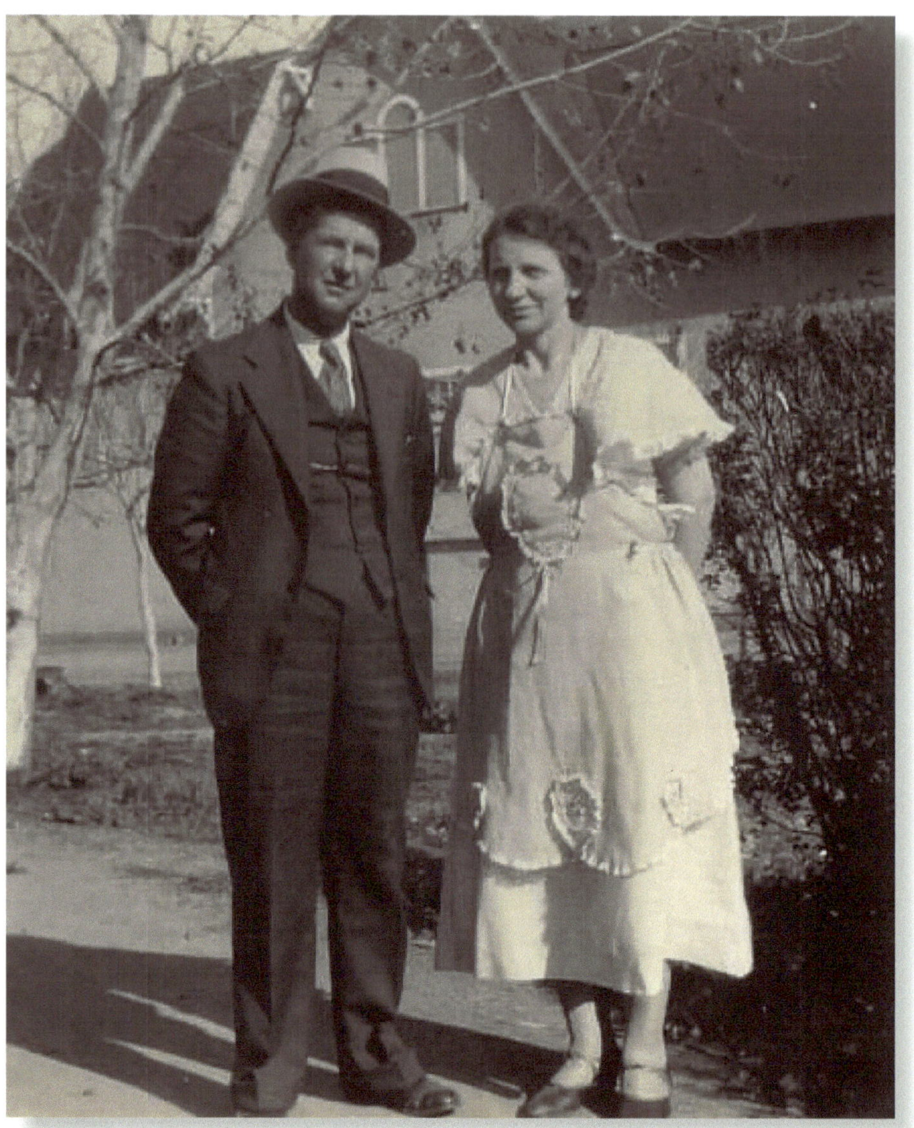

My parents lived on a farm near Hughson, California, a small town about 10 miles southeast of Modesto. My father, Pierce Alan Miller, was a peach farmer. In the late 1920's he developed a method of pruning peaches which doubled the yield of an orchard. He raised more peaches per acre than any other peach farmer in California. He was an orphan and raised by aunts: sisters named Deck. He left school in the third or fourth grade. He was a hard worker and in spite of his lack of education he embraced new ideas.

As a young man--probably in his early twenties--he went to Arizona to homestead land the government offered for free, but it was too hot. He moved from there to Los Angeles. He owned a dairy farm at the corner of Vermont and Slausen (I'm not sure where he got the money to fund his enterprises). Apparently the dairy was a success, but in 1915 he sold it, went to Pennsylvania and married my mother.

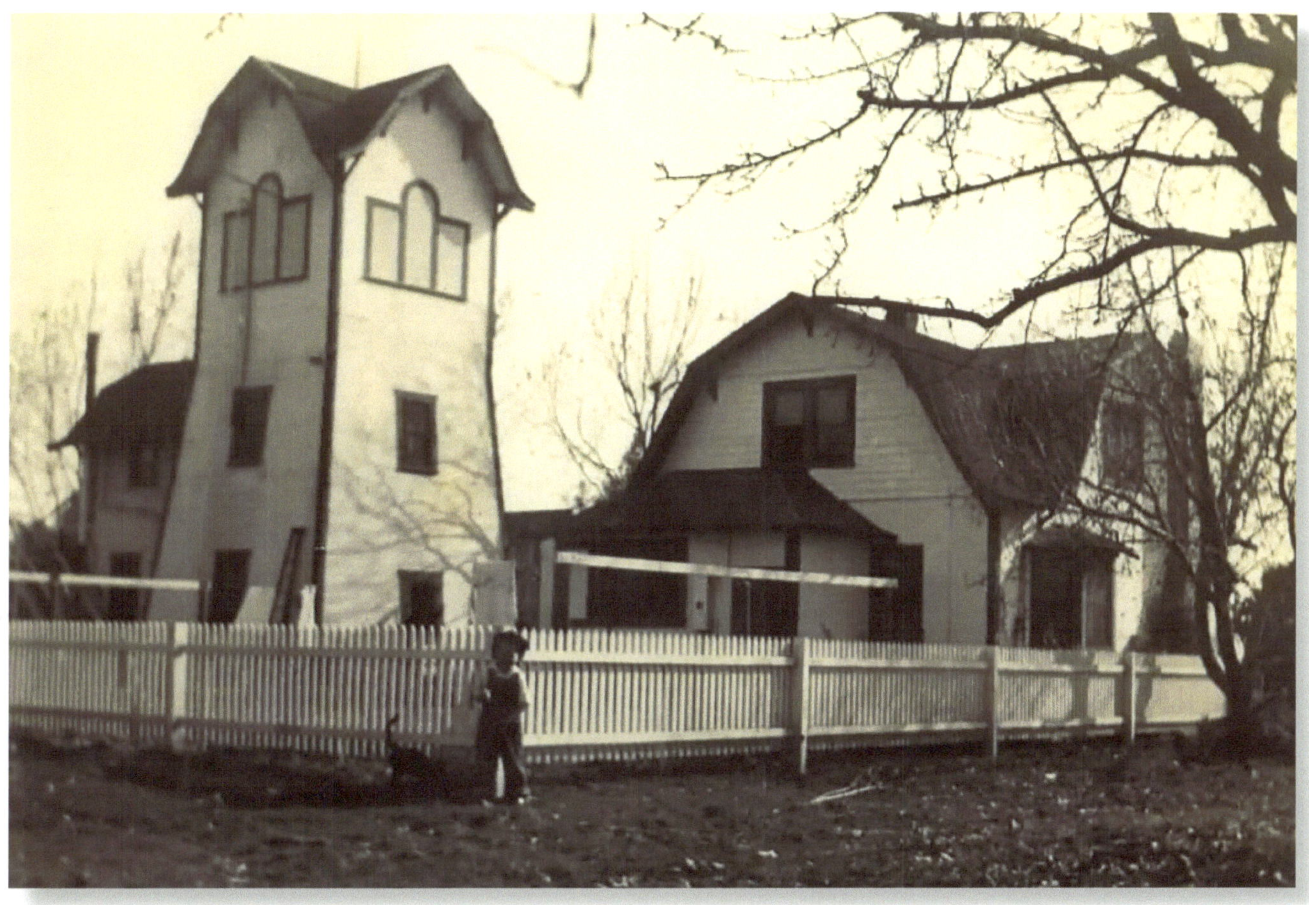

My brother Billy in front of the tank house about 1934. Any pre-war farm had a tank house. Water was stored in a tank at the top of the structure and was gravity fed. Postwar farms utilized mechanical pumps.

He brought her to Hughson. He seems to have been fascinated by the new irrigation system installed in that area. He worked hard. He bought a peach farm and had interest in a livery stable as well as a blacksmith shop. He was also a Star Route mail man (Star Routes were postal routes turned over to private contractors) as well as a school bus operator for the Hughson School District. He used old Greyhound buses and a Fageol truck converted to a school bus with a wooden body.

His friends told him he was crazy. The soil was considered not good for peaches, but Dad knew better. He planted Halford cling peaches. They thrived. In a few years the ranch was paying handsomely.

" In the late 1920's my father signed a ten year contract with a cannery in Santa Clara. By the early 1930's, because of the depression, most farmers were getting less than $10 a ton for their fruit.
My father was getting $50."

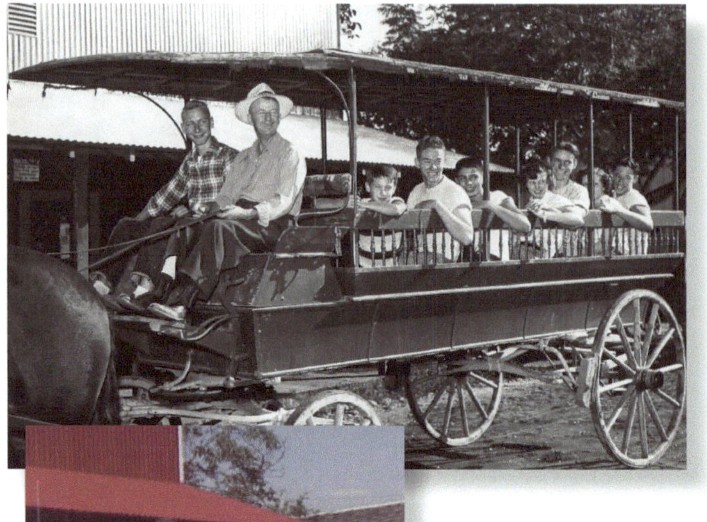

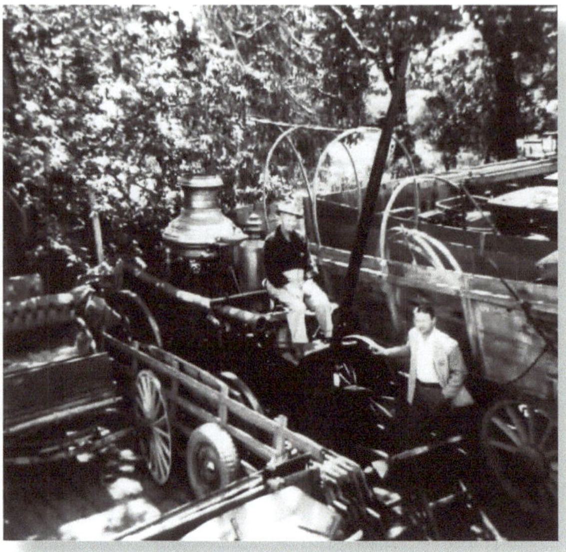

My father driving a hotel bus: Hotels used buses like this to attract clients at train stations. That's my brother riding shotgun. • My father collected all kinds of old wagons. He is in the driver's seat of an old fire engine stored at the farm. • My mother always wanted a Cadillac. This was the last one my father bought her: a pink, 1956. It is now in an auto museum in Sweden.

In the late 1920's he signed a 10-year contract with Pratt-Low Cannery in Santa Clara. By the early 1930's, because of the Depression, most farmers were getting less than $10 a ton for their fruit. My father was getting $50. Pratt-Low thought so much of my father's peaches they honored the contract throughout its duration.

In the early 1930's he started collecting horse-drawn buggies. He thought at first he would collect a few to use in parades and special events. They were pulled by Mae and Jim, our team of horses. The collection became an obsession. In 1933 we moved from Hughson to an 80-acre ranch on Highway 132 (Yosemite Boulevard) about 5 miles east of Empire. On the ranch was a huge hipped-roof, Indiana style barn, just right to hold his buggies.

Because of his collection my father met some unusual, quirky and therefore interesting people. One of the most intruiging was Walter Nilsson. Nilsson had been on the vaudeville circuit in the 1930's; he rode in a production called "Hells-A-Poppin." He was a star. His act consisted of a series of stunts on bicycles or unicycles. But by the time my father met him around 1946, vaudeville was virtually dead. Nilsson had accumulated a collection of unusual and historic bikes. My father was just beginning his bicycle collection. He probably had ten or so: double bikes; a triple bike and a wooden bike or two. Along came Nilsson with about forty bicycles of every description. He needed money and wanted to sell.

In Nilsson's collection were bikes that went all the way back to the beginning of pedalling.

A wooden "Boneshaker;" a four-seated bike; bikes with driveshafts instead of chain drives; and one of the stars, a double bike inlaid with mother-of-pearl, given to Lillian Russell by Diamond Jim Brady.

My father paid Nilsson $20,000 for the whole bunch, lots of money in 1946. The transaction occurred in our family dining room at our big dining table. Nilsson was a bigger-than-life character. He brought with him a gorgeous, red-headed showgirl from Las Vegas. She wore a very tight, dark green knit dress. I'll swear you could see her nipples through the knit! My brother Bill and I were very intrigued. You didn't see this sort of thing often in Waterford.

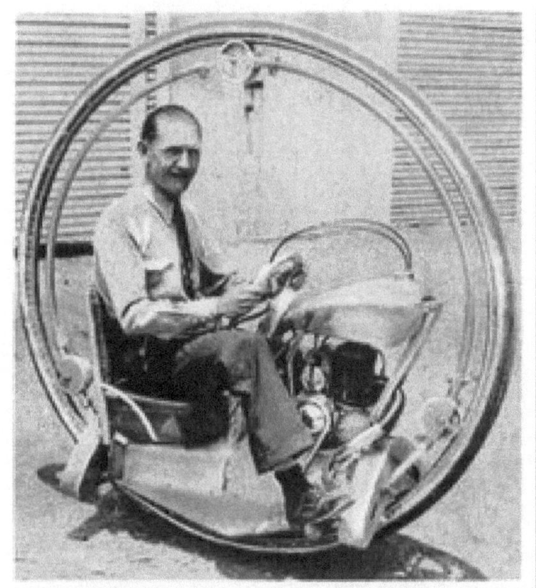

High speeds with perfect safety are claimed for this gravity defying unicycle. Walter Nilsson, the inventor, is shown at the wheel of his machine after a conclusive demonstration.

My mother offered everyone coffee, so there were paper napkins on the table. Just before my father handed the check to Nilsson a huge fly started buzzing around the table--the kind that if you try to swat it, it just takes off in front of the swatter. Nilsson watched it circle around for a few moments, then reached out and grabbed it in his hand! It was alive and buzzing around in his loose fist. Then he took a napkin and with his other hand tore a strip of napkin less than a quarter of an inch wide and about six inches long. He wet one end of the strip with his tongue and attached it to the fly. The fly flew around the room trailing the strip of napkin. The whole procedure took only a few seconds, it was so deft and such a surprise. My brother and I thought it was absolutely wonderful. I have forgotten what happened to the fly. I think Bill and I made sure it had a long and fruitful fly's life and had stories to tell his children.

After Mr. Nilsson left with his check, my mother said, "I don't want to ever see that man in my house again!" Bill and I looked at each other in disbelief! We thought he was fantastic!

It took about 20 years for him to fill the barn with buggies, the sheds with old automobiles and, in an old style general store he built, vintage bicycles. By the time he was done collecting it was the biggest of its kind in the west, maybe even in the country.

He was a remarkable man. Although he collected the past he embraced new farm equipment and new technology. His 1919 Fageol truck was the first balloon-tired truck in Stanislaus County. I can remember, even in the 1930's you could hear a truck with solid rubber tires beating on the highway from a mile away. He also owned the first balloon-tired tractor, a 1929 Minneapolis and Moline. It was the first vehicle I was to drive.

He died in 1965. I still miss him. As I get older there is more and more I would like to share with him.

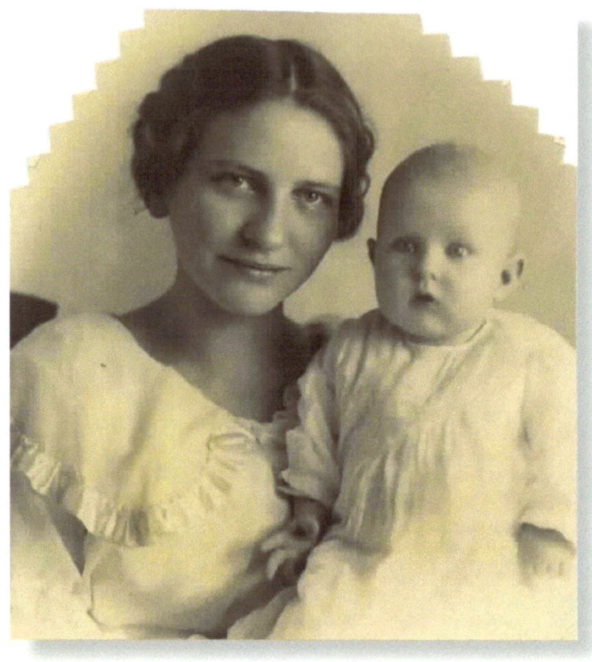

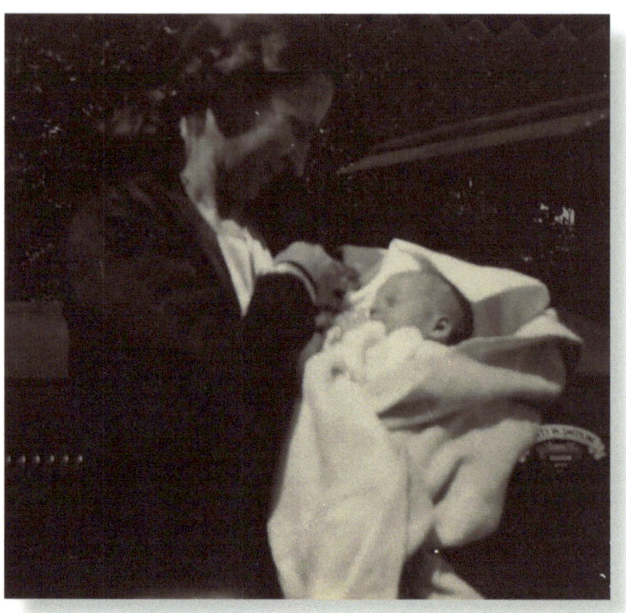

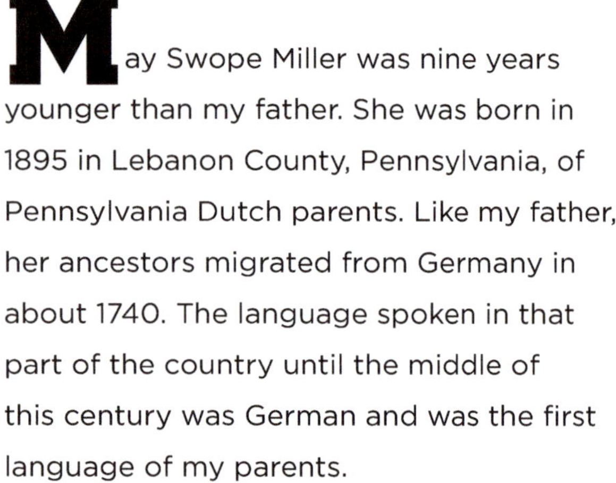

May Swope Miller was nine years younger than my father. She was born in 1895 in Lebanon County, Pennsylvania, of Pennsylvania Dutch parents. Like my father, her ancestors migrated from Germany in about 1740. The language spoken in that part of the country until the middle of this century was German and was the first language of my parents.

I visited Lebanon County in 1946 when I was 15. Everybody spoke German. In deference to me they would speak English, but when they got into animated conversation, it was German. My parents chose not to teach us the language because they didn't want us to have accents. When they were young an accent of any kind might make it difficult to be placed in a good job.

At night my mother would read to my brother Bill and I before we went to bed. She read not only children's books, but novels. She belonged to the Book of the Month Club. By the time we were six or seven years old she was reading us books like Gone With The Wind and Pearl Buck's The Good Earth. We loved it. We hated for the chapters to end.

She was educated. She went to school in Pottstown and taught grade school for a year before she married my father. My father was very proud that he married someone who had an education. He constantly reminded my brother and I of how lucky we were to have a mother who was so smart. My mother believed in education and insisted that all of her children attend college.

She outlived my father by almost 30 years. When she was near 90 Anita and I took her and her sister Emily to Europe. It was a great trip. In England we picked up Isabel Wilcock, an old friend of ours in her 80's. Three women in their 80's: it sounds like a burden but it was wonderful. They were energetic and interested in everything.

We visited very distant cousins in Germany. Mother had her very first sip of wine in Paris. She was a teetotaler. Because alcoholism ran rampant in the Pennsylvania Dutch community my parents took a vow of abstinence. She sipped a little at an outdoor cafe. A little sip was enough. She didn't like it much, but she was a good sport.

She watched over my father's collections after he died, but it was almost too much for her. My brother Tom moved to the ranch to help her maintain it and to help her live an independent life until she died. But when my father died, the heart of the collection of old vehicles died with him. During a Saturday or Sunday afternoon when my father was alive, more than a hundred people might come to visit the old things. He gave buggy rides and let them ride his double bicycles. It was great fun. He loved to be with people. My mother was more private. She would have the occasional school group visit, but people finally stopped coming.

She died in 1994. She was gardening from her golf cart. She used a golf cart to get around the farm yard. She apparently slipped and fell and died from the trauma. The night before she called me and asked how much my line of credit interest was. In those days it was high, around 12%. I told her and she said. "I'll give it to you for 9%." Some annuities had come to fruition and she wanted to help me. She loaned money to my children when they needed it. She didn't give money, she felt that bred irresponsibility, but she was generous.

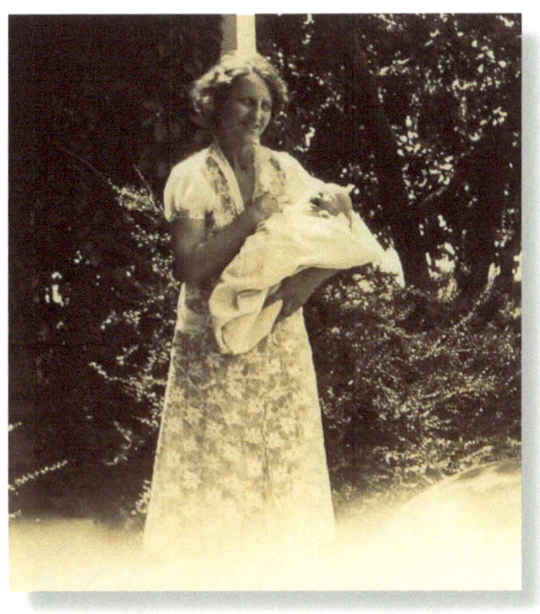

"My father constantly reminded us of how lucky we were to have a mother that was so smart."

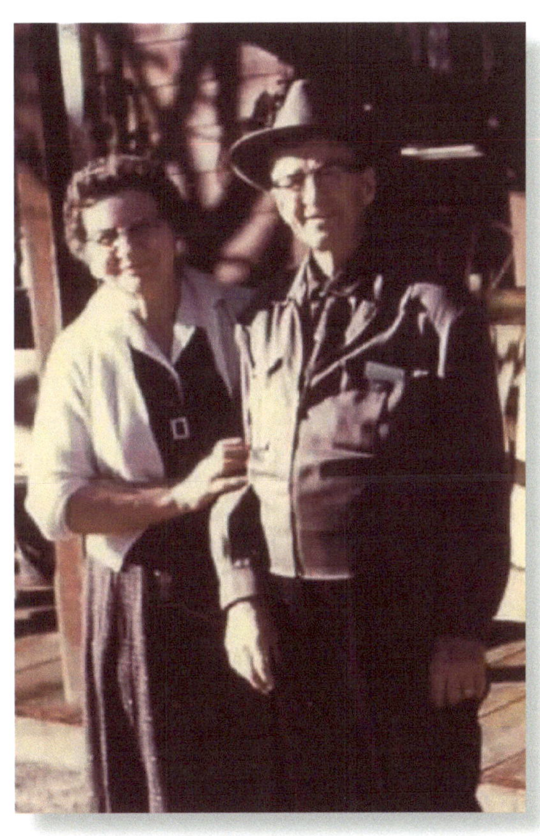

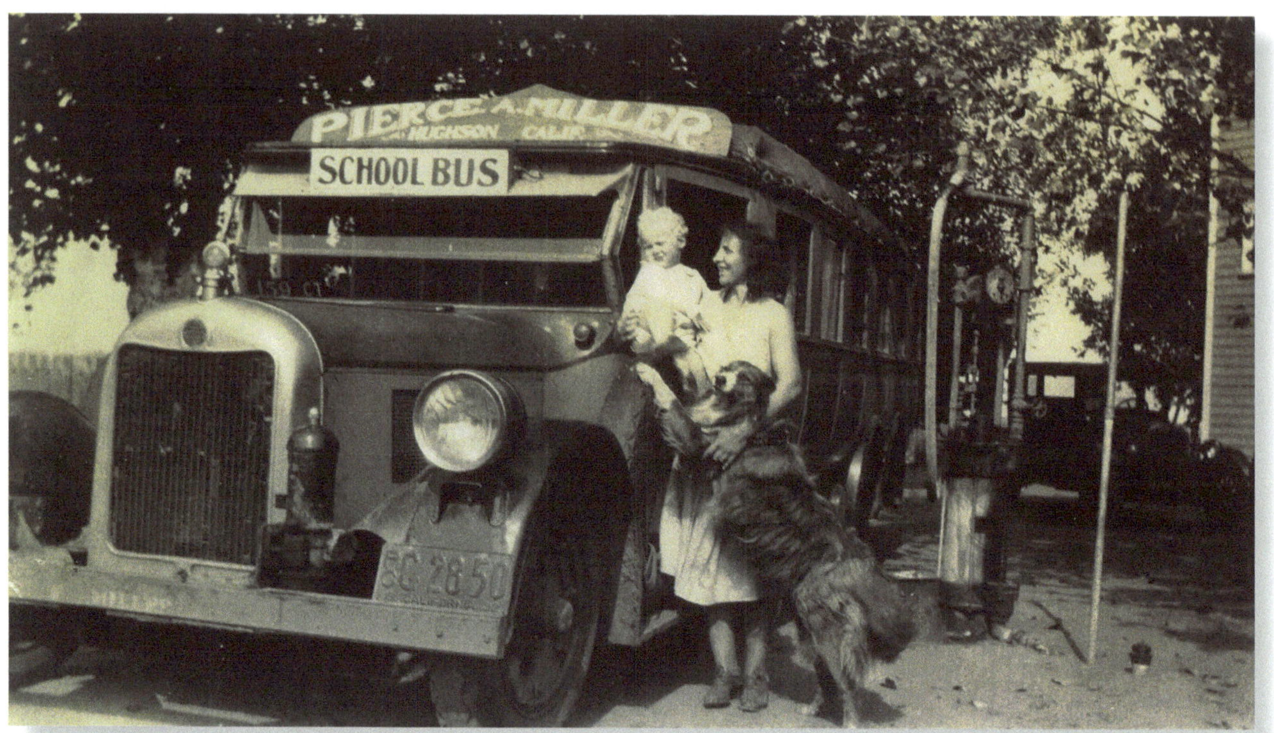

Aside from being a successful farmer, my father also had a contract to haul school children. My father bought a couple of old Greyhound buses and designated them school buses. In the photo above are my mom and me with family dog Queenie.

I was born in St. Mary's Hospital in Modesto, March 28, 1931. My first memory was when I was probably about two. We lived on a peach ranch near Hughson. Through the ranch ran an underground canal. We had a long driveway that ran through a vineyard. About halfway to the house, next to the driveway was a ditch box, an open area about six feet square surrounded by a cement barrier that couldn't have been more than eighteen inches high. The box was open at the top. You could look in and see the underground water rushing through. I don't know what the ditch box was for but it fascinated me, all that rushing water. Somehow I had escaped the house and was drawn to the mesmerizing sound of the swiftly flowing water. I could have easily fallen in. I had no clue as to the danger. I remember my mother screaming up the driveway telling me to get away from that dangerous place. I think she may have spanked me. It wasn't long before my father built a barrier around the box.

Another early memory was riding in the Fageol truck. It was loaded with household goods and I was sitting next to my father with the wind rustling through my blond curls--and no seat belts!

I also remember--it might have been the same day--playing with the Boone boys on the lawn of our new home. My father had just bought the ranch from the boys' father. I remember them as dirty little snot nosed kids wearing overalls and no underpants.

The new ranch was wonderful with its huge barn and many outbuildings. There were plenty of places for good hide and seek games or kick the can (not the political kind!).

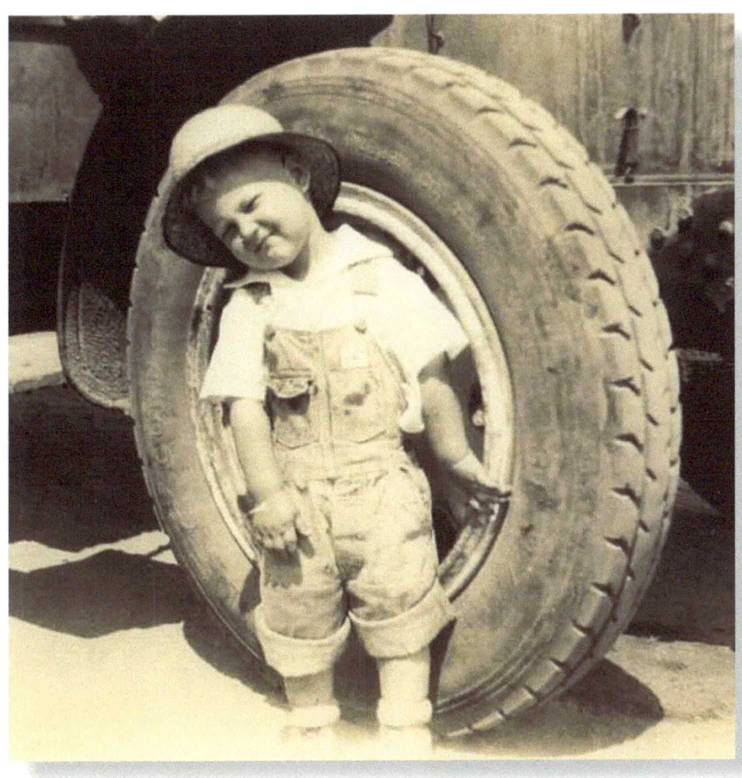

I had an overactive pituitary gland (not thyroid) and grew very fast from the time I was about five until about seven. By the time I was six years old I was five feet, four inches tall (at 85 years old, I've shrunk to about five feet!).

My parents made arrangements in the mid-1930's to have me examined at the University of California hospital in San Francisco. I remember going from Modesto to San Francisco with my mother on a brand new Greyhound bus. It was clean and modern. We crossed the Bay Bridge entering San Francisco. It was like a fantasy land: glowing lights, the shimmering bay and the big San Francisco skyline.

The hospital stay lasted for about a week. I was in a children's ward. The other children did not believe I was just 6 years old. They thought I was lying and made fun of me. I don't remember the results of the tests except that my growth was attributed to the pituitary gland. Somewhere, misplaced in my files, I have a folder with that information.

Because I was so large, my parents--at my brother Tom's encouraging--enrolled me in the first grade when I was five. Empire Grammar School, the closest, would not take me because I was too young and in those days there was no kindergarten. My parents knew the principal of Hickman Grammar School. Hickman was a small settlement south of Waterford about ten miles from our ranch. My mother enrolled me.

The first day was not pleasant. The principal asked a student to take me to the first grade classroom. Instead he took me to the boy's bathroom and left me there. I had not been in a public bathroom quite like that. I was bewildered. Someone finally rescued me!

Although I was in the body of a 12 year old I was still only 5 and I started school long after the fall session had started. I was completely lost. I was in the last reading group. I felt really dumb. After a month or so at Hickman my mother was able to transfer me to Empire Grammar School. The school bus picked me up in front of our house.

Mrs. Webb was my first grade teacher. She was severe. I was still in the last reading

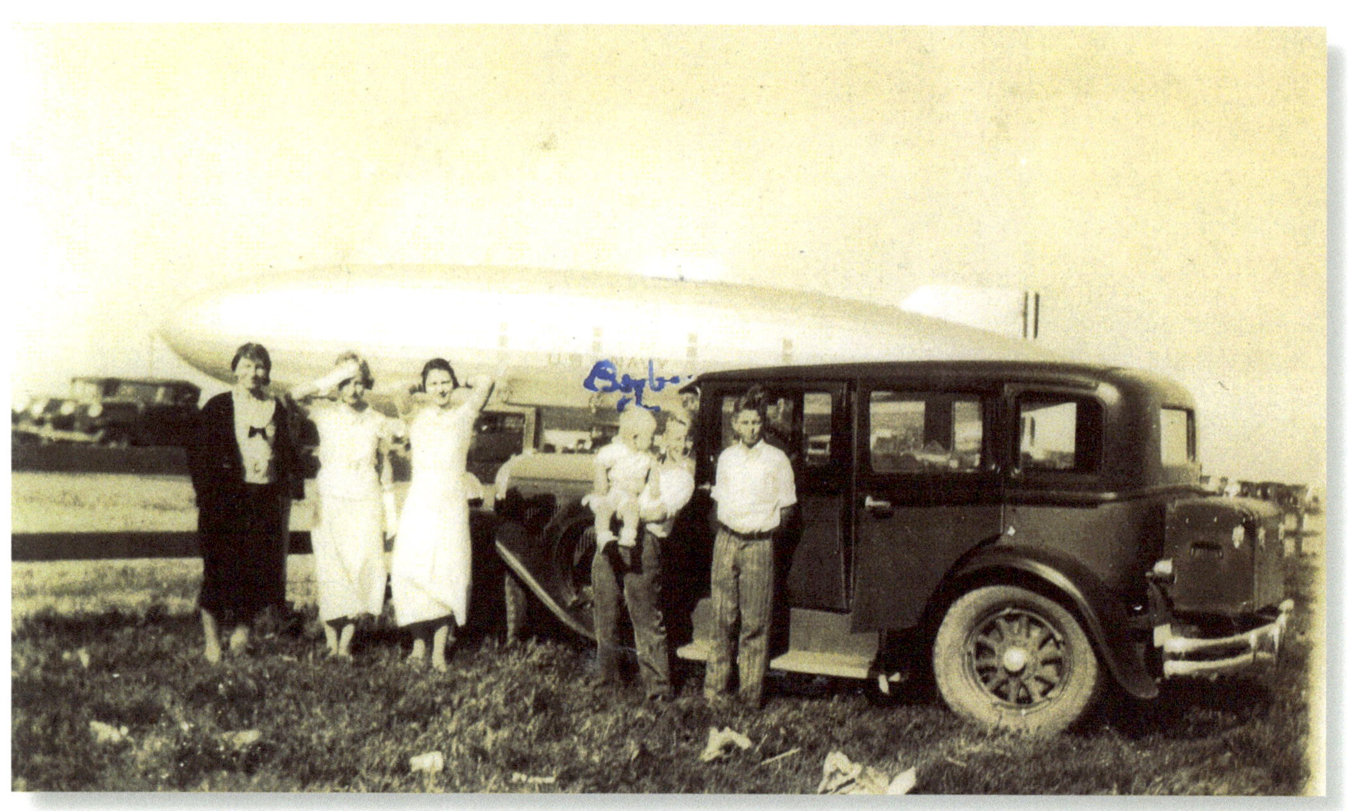

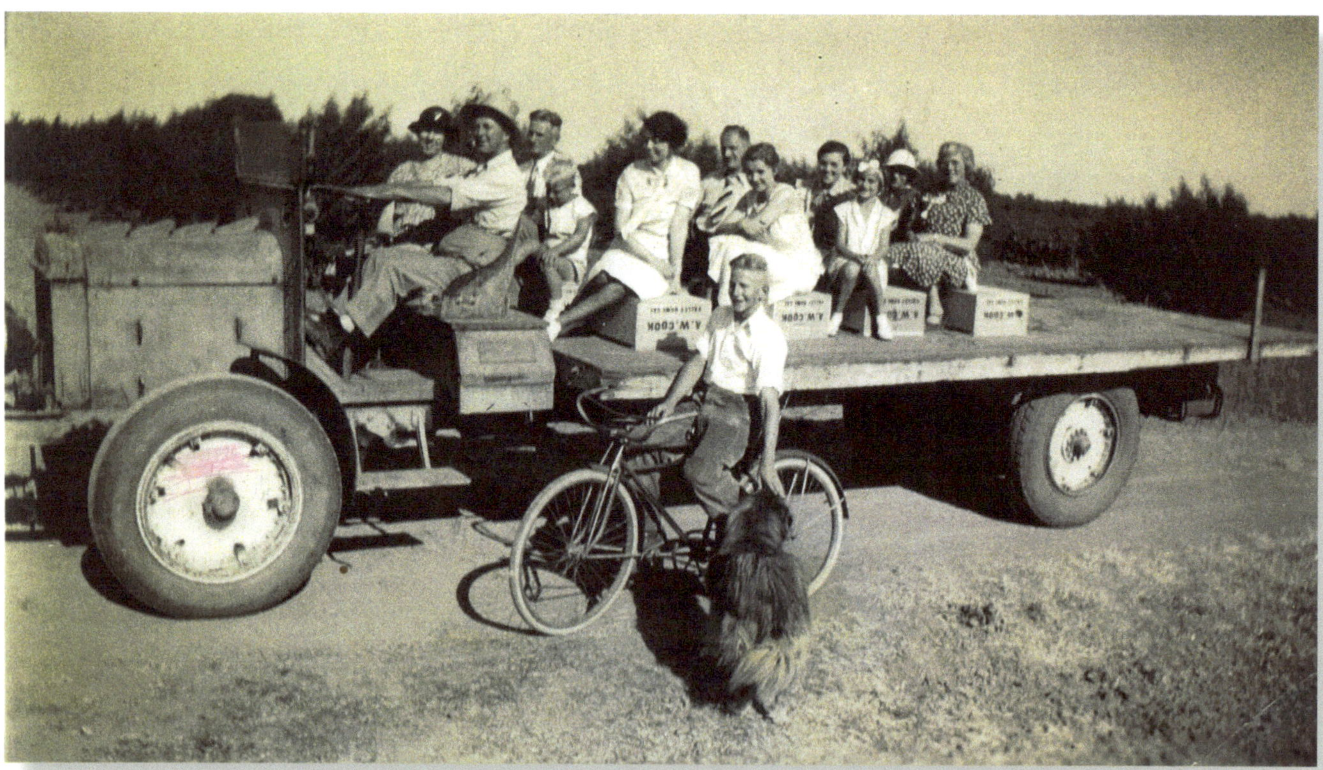

A U.S. Navy zeppelin at Moffett Field in Sunnyvale, 1933. I have always been intrigued by zeppelins. Maybe it stems from visits like this . My mother, sister, a friend of Mary's, Tom holding me in his arms, and a friend of Tom's.

In the bottom photo, my father is taking us all on a tour of the farm showing off his trees. We are sitting on fruit crates on the bed of his 1919 Fageol truck. Brother Tom is on the bicycle with family dog Queenie.

" Since I was very young I liked to draw. I copied Disney characters out of children's books and drew airplanes."

group. When it came to read aloud I simply hung my head in silence until someone else was called on to read. It was humiliating. It went on like that until after third grade. I was popular because I was such a good athlete. In those days we played rough and tumble tackle football. Every time I got the ball I made a touchdown or at bat I always hit a home run. I was always the first one chosen for any team. I was like the stupid giant.

But then, in the third grade it all came together. My intellect caught up with my body. My mother gave me a book, The Boy Allies in the Baltic. I read it. I'll never forget that transporting sense of adventure. It was about two boys who were on their uncle's submarine during World War I. Their uncle cruised around the Baltic Sea sinking German boats. I wished I had an uncle like that! What an adventure.

I have read ever since. I became a good student and moved from the third reading group to the first. School became much more pleasant after the first few grades. I became a leader not just in sports, but in classroom activities. In the fifth grade, our teacher Mrs. Johnson devised a broadcast. It was like a radio program with

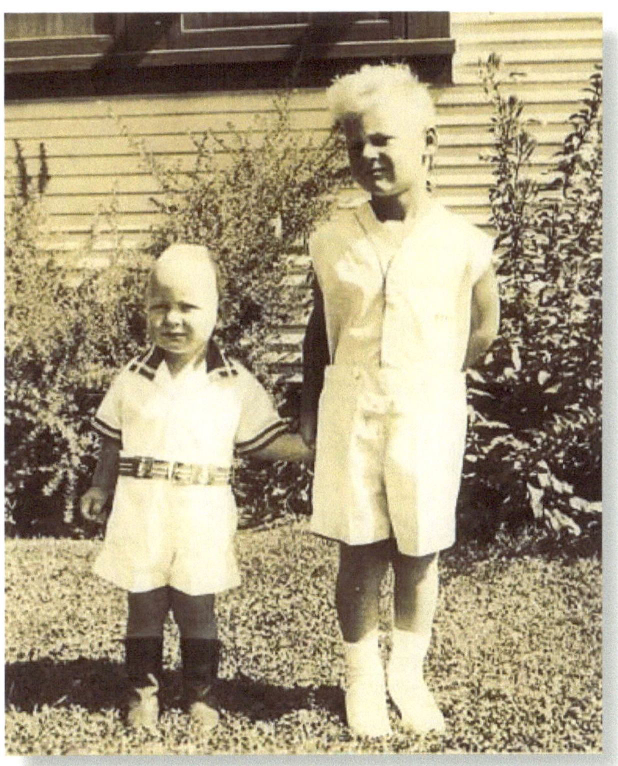

With brother Billy, 1936.

a dummy microphone that didn't work, but we pretended it did. I was the announcer. We did it several days a week in the morning. Students would bring tidbits of news about current projects, club activities or sports.

I had crushes on girl friends Loybeth Bawman, Joyce Dooley, Donna Valpey and Margaret Pettit. Most didn't know how much I liked them although I did go hunting with Margaret Pettit's brother Kenneth.

The Pettit family rented a big house on the Triangle Ranch. At 1,000 acres it was by far the largest farm in the area. Mr. Pettit was a Safeway Stores executive and worked in Oakland. Somehow I managed to develop a friendship with Kenneth, who loved to hunt.

At 12 years old I hitchhiked into Modesto, went to Valley Sporting Goods and paid $12 for a Remington over-under rifle.

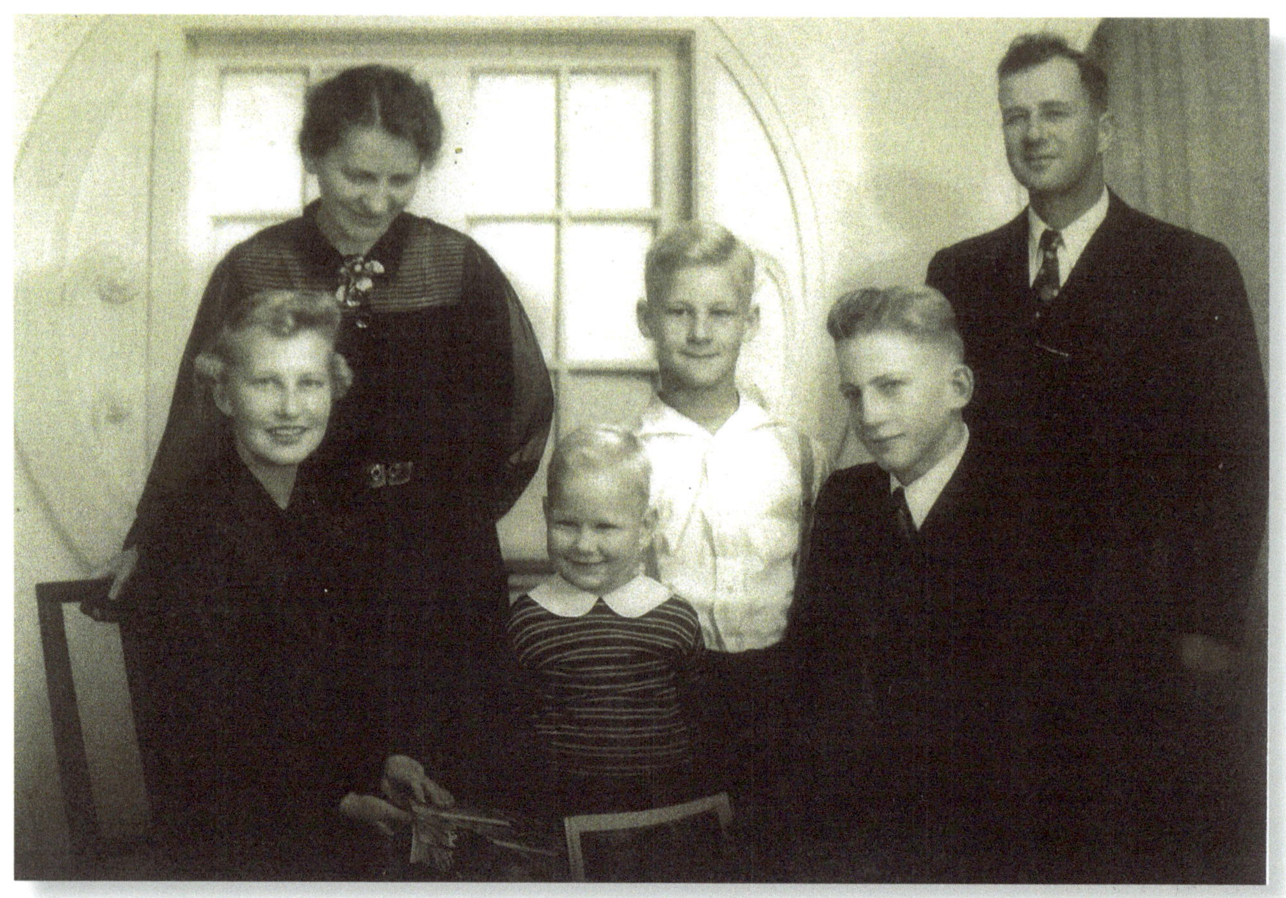

The family portrait. Mary, my mother, Mae, Billy, Me, Tommy and my father, Pierce.

It had two barrels: one was a .410 gauge shotgun; the other was a 22-caliber rifle. After buying it I hitchhiked home, rifle in hand, and was picked up. Those were the days when almost everyone had guns but they seldom killed each other.

I hunted with Kenneth. The Triangle Ranch was bordered on the south side by the Stanislaus River. It was swampy. There was a small flat-bottomed boat available. I have no idea who owned it but we poled around the swamp looking for ducks. Kenneth was able to shoot one or two. I was not a good shot. I always missed.

One day after duck hunting on our way back to Kenneth's house I shot and killed a jack rabbit. Holding it by the ears we were met by Mrs. Pettit, Kenneth's mother. She said something like, "Bobby, you should be ashamed of yourself. That poor creature is dead. They are not good to eat. You took a life just for the fun of it. Shame on you!" I have not hunted since.

Since I was very young I liked to draw. I copied Disney characters out of children's books and drew airplanes. I loved airplanes and hoped that one day I would learn to fly one. That never happened, but I can probably still draw from memory fairly accurate pictures of the most well known aircraft from World War II: The Bell AirCobra, Curtiss P-40, Lockheed Lightning P-38,

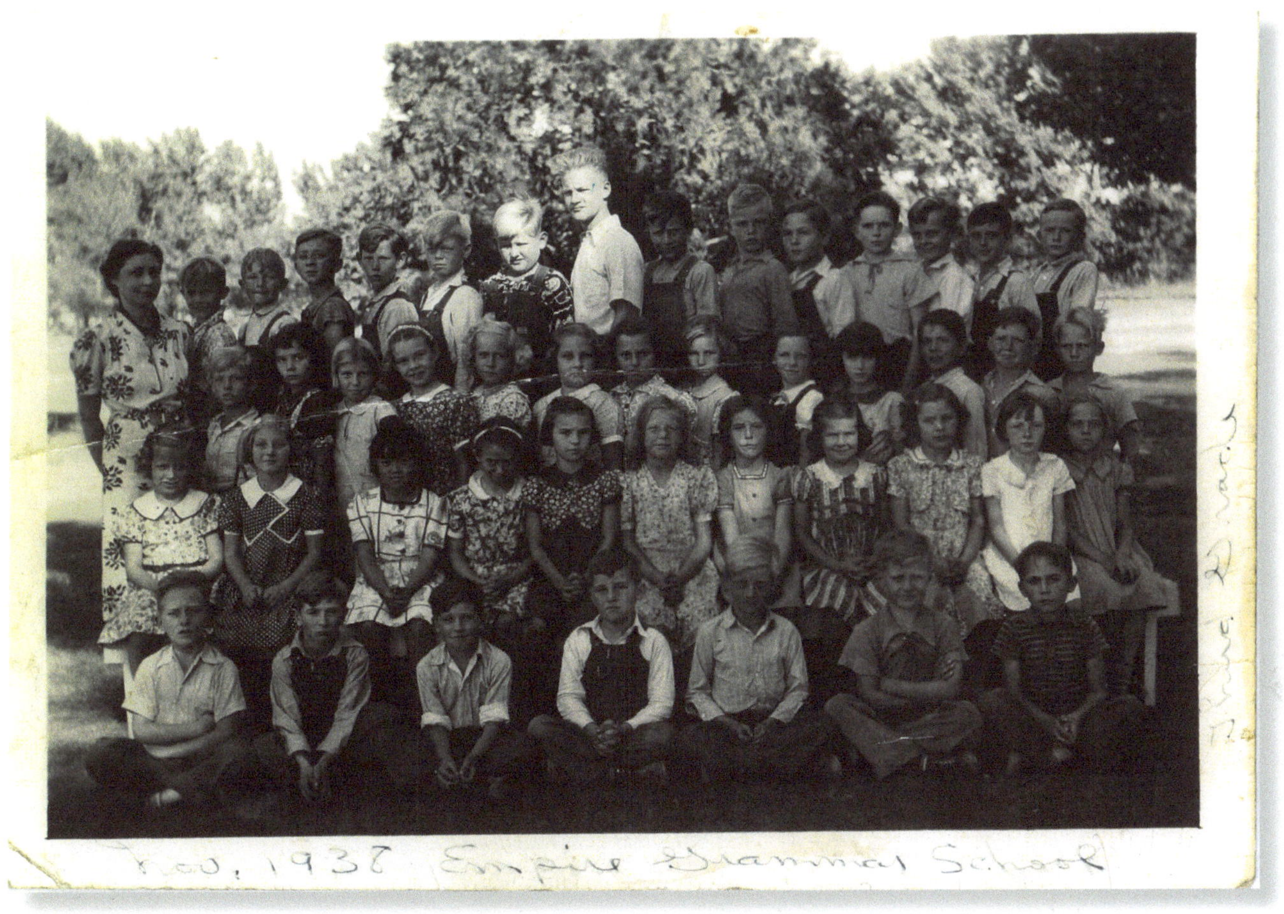

I am the giant in my class photo. I'm the one in the sun. "I'm anointed. I'm anointed!"

Republic's Thunderbolt and many more.

My parents were very involved in our education. My father was on the Empire School Board and my mother did substitute teaching. During the war she taught full time at Milne School, a little one-room schoolhouse near Riverbank.

Dad would hitch up buggies to give rides at school carnivals. I can still smell the mixture of cotton candy and horse manure in the air.

My sixth grade teacher was Hubert Rae. He was handsome and in his early 20's. He taught for a few months and then Pearl Harbor happened. Within a few weeks, he was gone. He enlisted in the Navy and served in the South Pacific. After the war he moved to Sacramento where he taught school. We reconnected and had lunch together from time to time. He was a good educator and became a good friend. He died several years ago. I still miss him.

Halloween was always a big deal. In those days we did not trick or treat. We did mischief. Wilbur Wiemer was one of the few in the neighborhood who still had an outhouse. We would wait in the dark for Wilbur to come to the little shack and then tip it over onto the door. Poor Wilbur. Fred Little had a Model T Ford with no fenders or top. We would putt-putt to Empire and throw rotten eggs at the one bar in town and

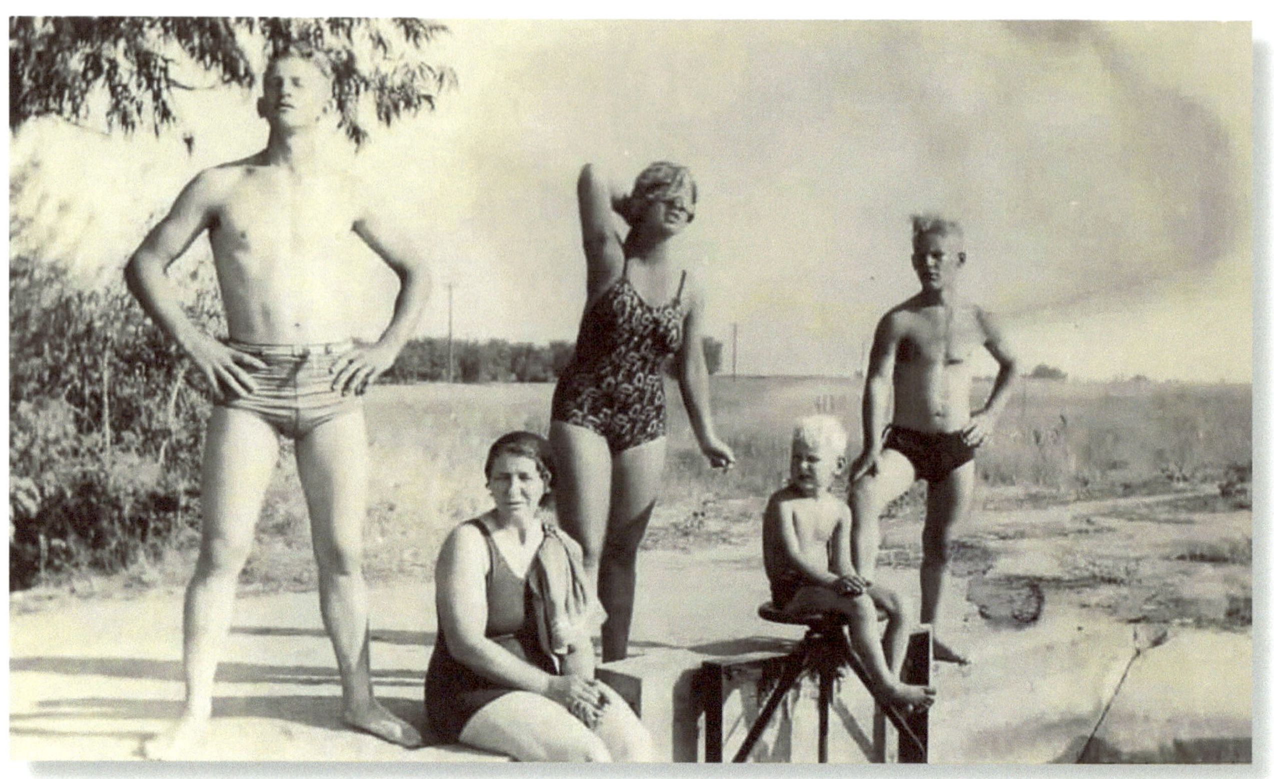

Swimming at a canal in 1937. Tommy, mother, Mary, Billy and me. Wow. I wish I had that tummy now!

let the air out of tires of cars in the parking lot. Then we'd go to the grammar school and cut hookers on the lawn. Fred got in serious trouble for that because his Model T tires were easily traceable. One year we even managed to get an old buggy up on to the roof of the school. It's a wonder we didn't all end up in Juvenile Hall.

During summer vacation we worked for our father or for Bess Fike, who lived next door. Bess had a dry yard. Before dehydrators cured fruit for drying, fruit was cut by hand in cutting sheds and placed on large trays. The trays were then taken to what was called a dry yard. They were laid out on the ground to be dried in the sun. Before about 1948 you could drive all over Stanislaus County during the summer and see field after beautiful field of orange colored peaches or apricots toasting under the sun's rays...and boy, did those dried fruits taste good.

Bess Fike was an interesting person. She defined the term "a good Christian." She was very religious and put her religion to good purpose. She farmed with the help of her brother Rob, but she also took in welfare children. Sometimes they were orphans or occasionally almost incorrigable. She was paid for her service, but more importantly, she felt it was her Christian duty. She put the children to work, taught them self esteem and how to be good citizens. I remember one family especially. Their name was Miller, like mine. Their parents had been killed in an automobile accident. There were three

> **“ Before the internet there was the Party Line. It is hard to imagine with the instant, private communication that is now available, but in the 1920’s and the 1930’s we had telephones that were inter-connected, with as many as ten households on the same line. One would pick up the phone to make a call and hear another conversation, of someone else’s on the line.”**

boys and two girls. Of the boys, one was killed on D-Day in June, 1944; the oldest became a successful contractor in Waterford; and the youngest, George, grew up on the ranch, worked hard and as Bess grew older, bought the ranch from her. He now owns more than 400 acres in Stanislaus County, a very successful farmer. The two girls both married doctors.

During the time that I lived next door to Bess she must have raised as many as 20 children, maybe more. Later in her life as the children grew into adulthood and had families of their own, dozens and dozens of cars would arrive to visit for the holidays. The children she had raised came home to Bess with their families. Bess never married but she had the largest, most loving family I have ever known.

Before the Internet there was the Party Line. It is hard to imagine with the instant, private communication that is now available, but in the 1920’s through the 1930’s we had telephones that were interconnected, with as many as ten households on the same line. One would pick up the phone to make a call and hear another conversation, from someone else on the line. You might have to wait ten or fifteen minutes, maybe longer until the line was open and free to make a call. However, you knew all the subscribers on the party line. If it was a true emergency they would get off the line so you could make your call. You could also listen to that conversation to pick up gossip. I can remember my mother shushing me to be quiet while she was eavesdropping. When I talked to girlfriends on the phone, everyone knew what was going on.

The party line also served as an answering service. If my mother or father was leaving the farm to run errands or to be gone for a length of time, they would call Bess and ask her to pick up the phone and take messages. Our ring was four “shorts”: ring ring ring ring. Bess’s was three shorts and a “long”: ring ring ring riiiiiiiing. Wilbur Wiemer was three shorts.

When Bess delivered the messages there was frequently editorial comment. “It was someone you didn’t want to talk to anyway,” or “It was the Fuller Brush man; I told him you weren’t interested.”

My mother and father also took messages for Bess and other subscribers on the line. The phone company was owned by the farmers. It was called The Farmer's Line. Our phone number was 110F4. The "F" stood for Farmer. If you wanted to make a call, you picked up the receiver (ours was a stand-up "candlestick" phone) and clicked the prongs that held the receiver. A voice, a woman called "Central" answered. You gave her the number you wanted to reach and she would connect the call. It wasn't until the 1950's that my parents got a rotary dial telephone and much, much later a push-button phone.

I got my first bicycle for Christmas when I was in the fourth grade. It was an Iver Johnson one-speed, balloon tired beauty. Although I rode my brother Tom's bike for a long time before I got my own, having your own bike gave you freedom never known before. My parents gave us more freedom than most. We could ride as far as we wanted or could. We rode 10 miles to Modesto or to the Turlock reservoir where we sometimes camped overnight. I don't think I have ever felt more free than when I got my first bike.

In the cupola on the top of our family's huge barn my father put in a floor so my brother and I could use it as a clubhouse. The space was about ten feet square. We brought our set of Thorton Burgess books and an assortment of other adventure books to read in our high flying clubhouse. From our 30 foot high vantage point we could see for miles. Dad nailed footsteps to the side of the barn and roof to gain access to the cupola. We also played tag up there around the cupola. There was no protection: if we slipped or fell there was a thirty foot drop to the yard below. For some reason it never occurred to us that that could even happen.

Years later I thought I'd go up to the cupola to see what childhood memories I could kindle. I got about halfway up and was scared to death! I have developed a fear of heights in my adulthood that I did not have when I was younger. It was dangerous, but as children we simply didn't recognize it.

Bill Kline and I were hunting specimens for our biology class. The teacher gave extra points for the delivery of live snakes and lizards. I found a great little harmless snake about 12 inches long. I put it in a shoebox I found in Bill's car. When I got home I put the shoebox on my father's desk on our back porch. I was dirty from our field trip so I went upstairs to the bathroom to bathe. Within about fifteen minutes I heard screams from downstairs. My father burst into the bathroom and pulled me from the tub. He was furious. He had never been physical with me except for this moment. After I had drawn my bath the phone had rung. My mother went to my father's desk to answer it. She reached for the old candlestick phone. My snake had escaped its shoebox cell and had wrapped itself around the phone like a caduceus. My mother was deathly afraid of snakes and was sobbing uncontrollably in the bedroom. My father destroyed my specimen: so much for extra credit. Outside of being pummeled by my father I have forgotten my punishment, but I never brought a snake home again.

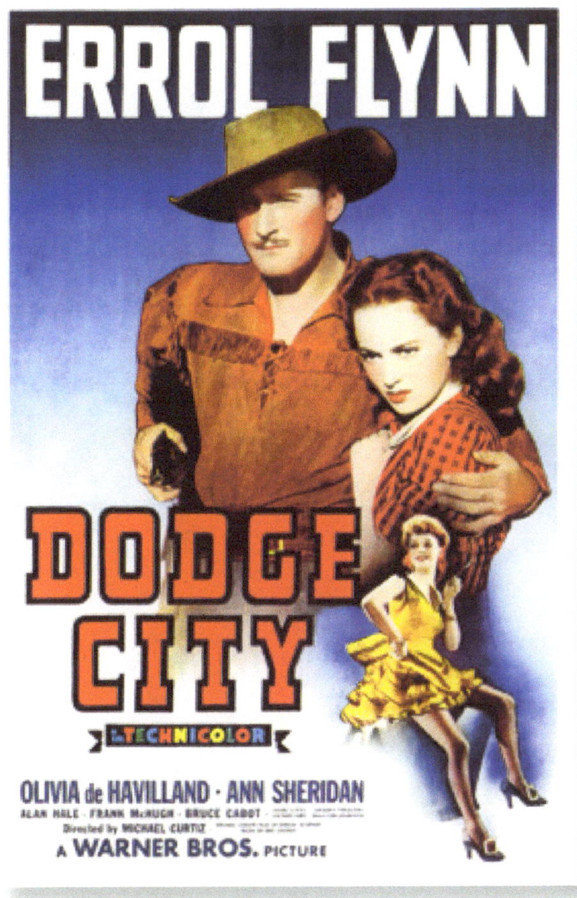

"Errol Flynn! Wow! He was my hero!"

In 1938 Warner Bros. came to the Sierra foothills near La Grange, about 20 miles from our ranch on Yosemite Boulevard, to make movies. In quick succession they made "Dodge City" and "Virginia City." The Warner Bros. equipment trucks with their lights, cameras and cranes would drive by our house twice every day. They were followed a short time later by the actors, lesser knowns, in buses, then finally by the stars in their limousines. Errol Flynn was my hero. I would climb to a branch in a sycamore tree along the highway and wait for the entourage to pass just to get a glimpse of Errol and hopefully, Olivia DeHavilland. I begged my father to take me to see the movie being made. Finally he did. I don't know if we needed permission or not but we stood about 50 feet from where Olivia was standing under a tree. After a few minutes Errol Flynn came galloping over a hill on a beautiful horse. He galloped up to Olivia, jumped off his horse and gave her a great big hug and a very passionate kiss. Then they stood around and smoked for about ten minutes. Errol crushed out his cigarette, got back on his horse, trotted over the hill and then came galloping back, jumped off the horse and gave Olivia another big hug and kiss. Then they took another cigarette break. Then he got on his horse, trotted over the hill, turned around and galloped back, got off again, and hugged and kissed her again.

I was so disappointed! In my young mind I thought that movies were an extension of life and by some miracle that I did not understand cameras followed real live people around while the people did their exploits. Movies and Errol Flynn were never the same to me after that. It was all fake, just good looking people pretending to be heroes. I have often thought about John Wayne and his war heroics. I think some believe him to be a real life action hero because of his many war movies as he pretended to storm Iwo Jima and Okinawa...and we named an airport after him.

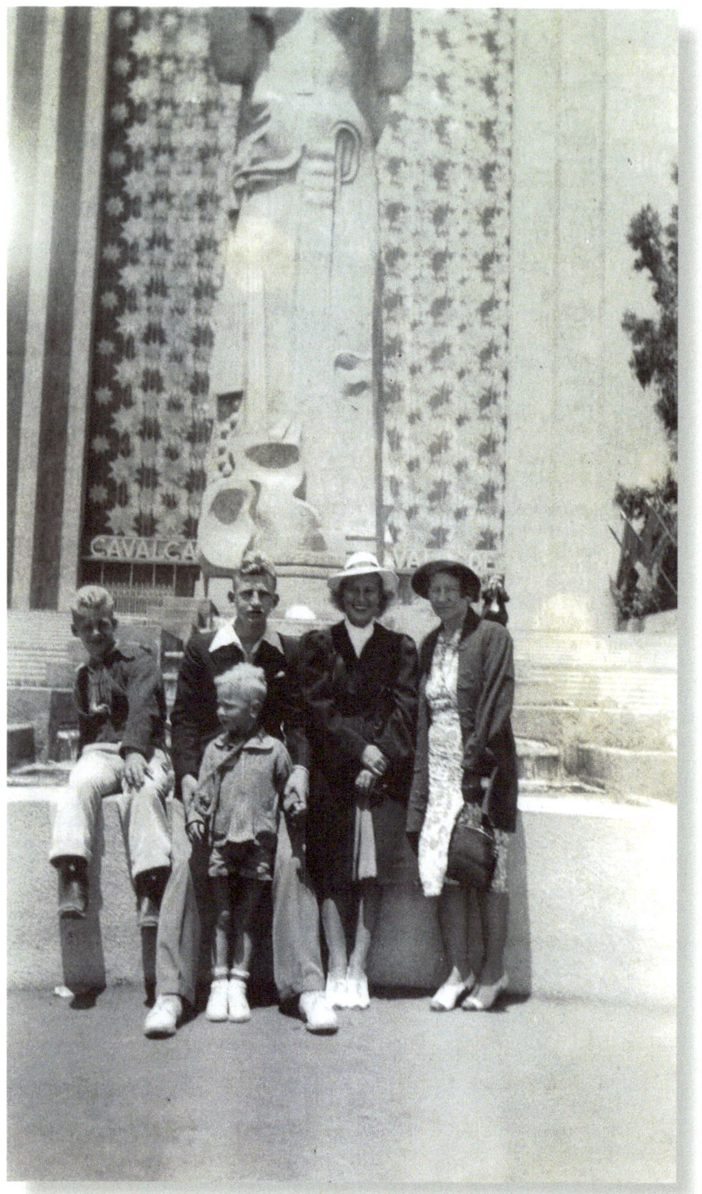

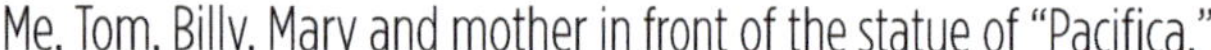

Me, Tom, Billy, Mary and mother in front of the statue of "Pacifica."

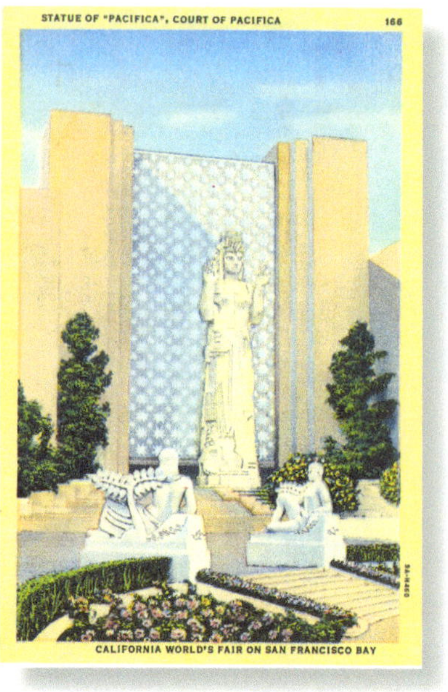

" ... I had passes to everything. That included Sally Rand and her Nude Ranch! I took advantage of that and watched the near naked ladies play badminton!"

Although it was during the Depression of the 1930's, money was found to put on World's Fairs, both in San Francisco and New York. San Francisco's Fair took place on man-made Treasure Island, in the middle of the bay. It opened in February of 1939. It was to commemorate the construction and opening of the two new bridges, the Golden Gate and the Bay Bridge. It was a fantasyland with Art Deco structures everywhere: The Tower of the Sun; the big stucco statue of Pacifica; The Court of Reflections; The Avenue of the Seven Seas; and more and more glittering extravaganzas.

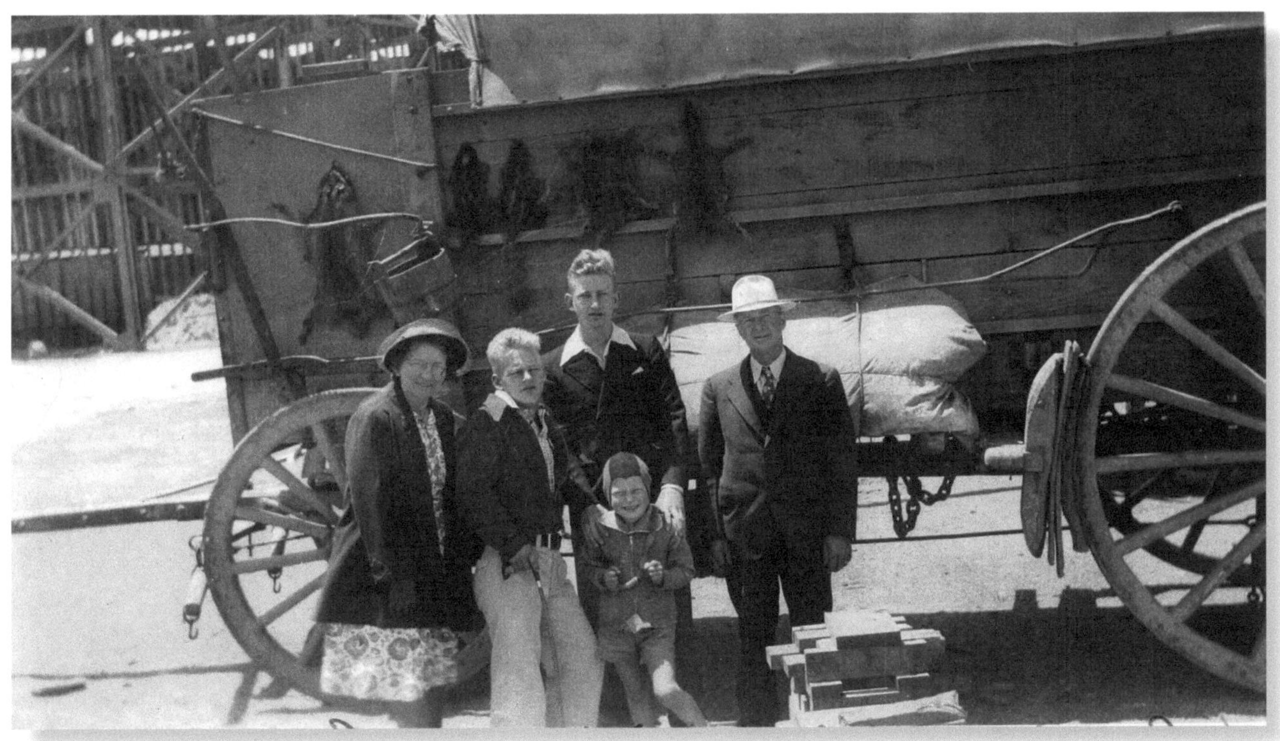

The family at The Cavalcade of the Golden West in front of one of the many wagons owned by my father used at the fair.

There was an outdoor show called "The Cavalcade of the Golden West." It was on a huge outdoor stage, maybe a hundred yards wide. The show described the settling of the West, featuring such events as Custer's Last Stand; wagon trains; the driving of the Golden Spike completing the transcontinental railroad; and the San Francisco earthquake of 1906.

They needed scores of buggies and wagons. They came to my father to supply them. My brother Tom was a gifted athlete and horseman. He was 19 at the time. Tom insisted if my father rented buggies to the cavalcade that he be hired to ride in the show! So he was hired. In some scenes he became an Indian, in others a cavalryman or a gandy dancer on the railroad.

During that summer he invited me to stay with him in San Francisco. He lived in a small apartment across from Treasure Island on the waterfront. Every morning we went to a small cafe and ate breakfast, then got on a ferry and crossed the bay to the fair. Tom would go to work and I was set free to do whatever I wanted! I was 8 years old and had passes to everything.

In the General Motors exhibit there was a clear plastic car. I think it was a Chevrolet. You could see all the moving parts, even the cylinders, moving up and down in the engine block and the driveshaft powering the rear wheels.

Bell Telephone--there was only one telephone company--had an exhibit where you could call anywhere in the world for free. Unfortunately I didn't know anybody anyplace further than Modesto.

A B-17 bomber was on display and the Pan American Airways China Clipper was

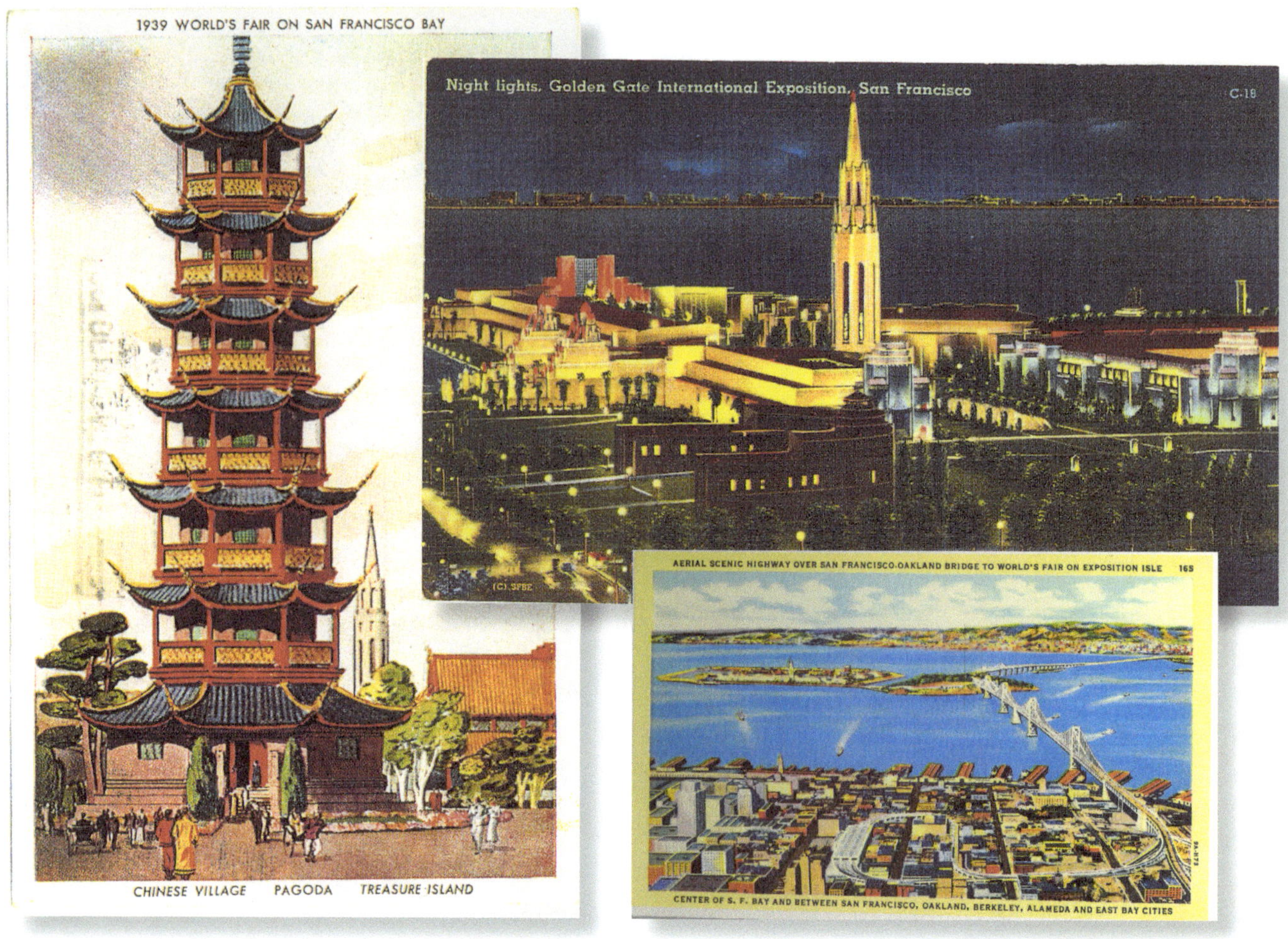

The 1939 World's Fair. Wow. That was MY fair!

based there. It was said that when the Clipper took off it flew under the Bay Bridge then out over the city to the Pacific Ocean. When I first saw it I was surprised at how small it was.

Although at war in some areas of the world, Germany and Japan both had exhibits. We were not at war yet.

The carnival was called "The Gayway." It had nothing to do with homosexuality, of course. In those days "gay"meant fun and hilarity.

At the Cavalcade I would sit in the front row. I watched Tom ride. I was so proud of him. The stage and show were so big it was impossible to have curtains between the scenes. They cleverly solved that problem by creating a curtain of water! After a scene ended a huge sheet of water--with different colored lights playing on it--shot up twenty feet or more, obscuring the stage.

I said I had passes to everything. That included Sally Rand and her Nude Ranch! I took advantage of that and watched the near naked ladies playing badminton.

The fair was so popular it was extended into a second year's run in 1940. I did not attend the World's Fair in New York although my younger brother went with my parents. I was SO jealous. The New York fair featured the Trylon and the Perisphere. Inside the Perisphere

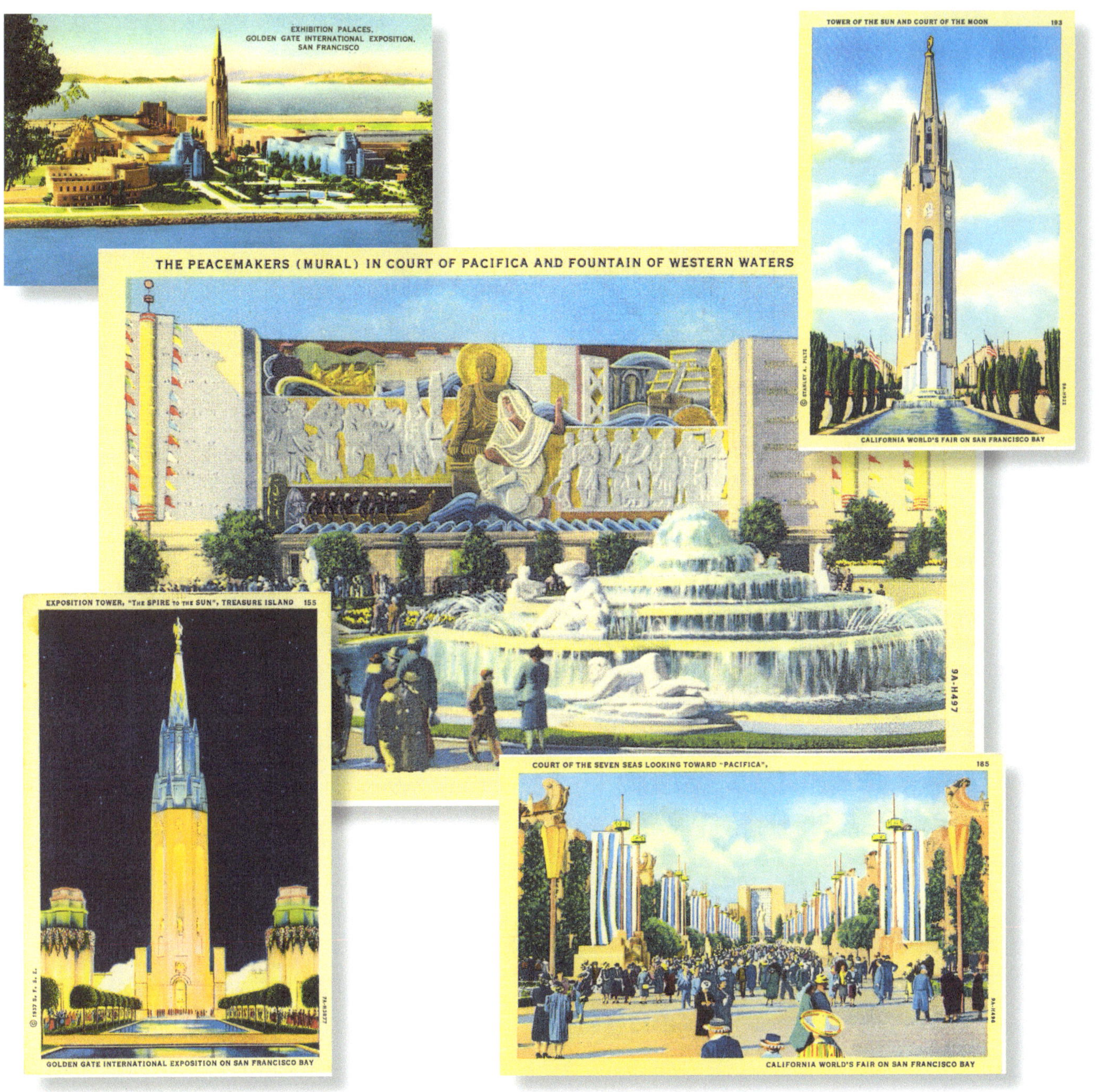

"In GM's exhibit The World of Tomorrow, tomorrow was 1960.

In 1939 I wondered if I'd ever see 1960 and all its wonders."

General Motors created "The World of Tomorrow"--tomorrow was 1960. It had slow moving, comfortable, loge-style seating that revolved around a model of this beautiful well ordered fantasyland. It was designed by one of my heroes Norman Bel Geddes. I was intrigued by design even then. In 1939 I wondered if I'd live to see 1960 and all its wonders.

The San Francisco World's Fair was my Disneyland. Even though war was imminent there was a sense of hope and optimism about the future.

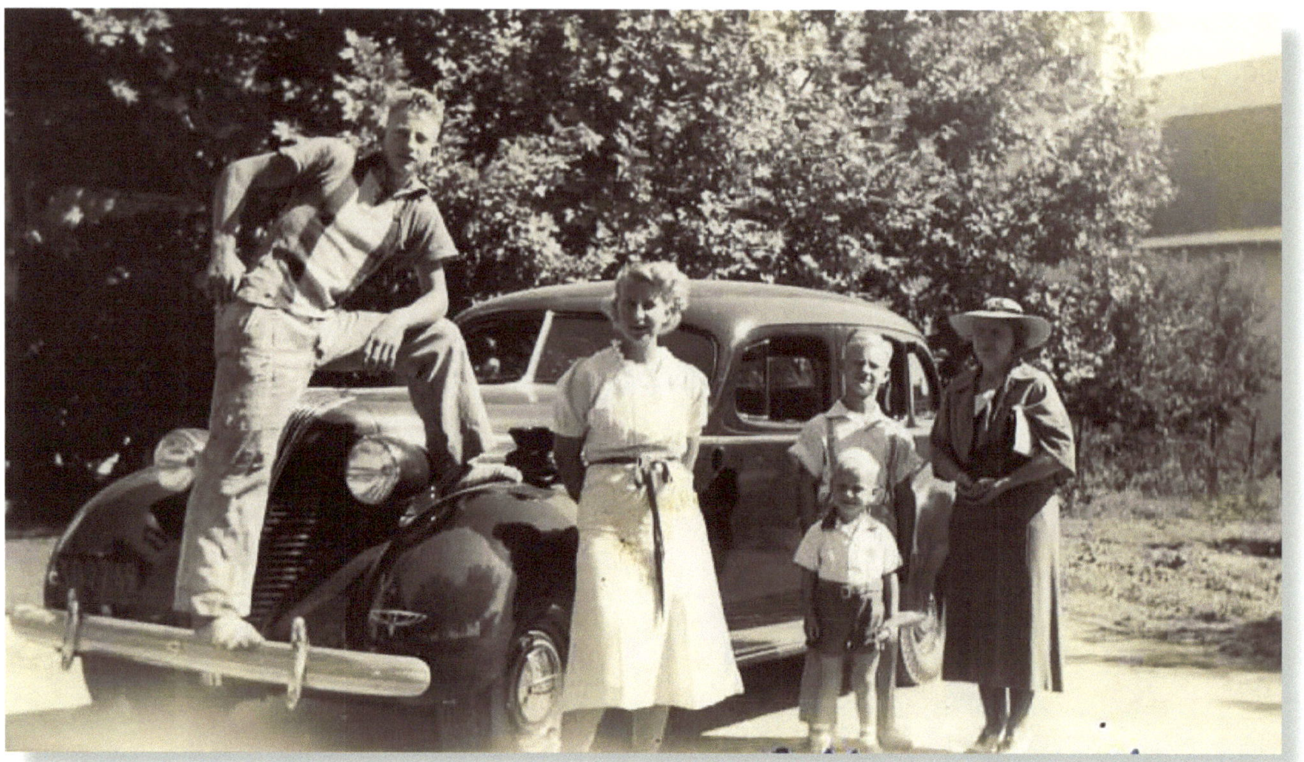

After the World's Fair closed in 1940 my brother Tom left San Francisco and moved to Santa Monica, the center of the nation's aircraft production. The Douglas Aircraft plant was in Santa Monica as was North American Aviation. Scattered through other areas of the Los Angeles basin were Lockheed, Hughes, Consolidated, Northrup, Ryan and countless others I have forgotten. Sadly they are are all gone now.

Tom got a job with Douglas as a painter on an assembly line that produced their DB-7 aircraft (Douglas Bomber Number 7). At that time most were sold to Britain's Royal Air Force. The DB-7 was known as "The Boston" in England. In the Army Air Corps it was the A-20 Havoc. It was a fast and efficient twin engine attack bomber. I was very patriotic and even at 10 or 11 years old followed the war very closely. I was very proud of Tom: I felt he was doing his bit for the war against the Nazis.

Tom lived in a small apartment on the Santa Monica waterfront near the Santa Monica Pier. Several summers during the war years he invited me to stay with him. I was 12-13 years old. During the day when Tom worked I had the freedom to visit the entire Los Angeles area. Most have forgotten--or don't know--that in those days Southern California had one of the best public transit systems in the country. In the various cities there were streetcars that took residents from their homes to downtown to shop. To get from community to community one took the big inter-urban Pacific Electric Red Cars. For about 25¢ I could get on a Red Car and go from Santa Monica to San Bernardino or Long Beach. With a transfer I could get off a Red Car and catch a streetcar to a museum in Los Angeles or Whittier or any other Southern

California community.

So, while Tom worked I visited interesting places in the area. There were many to visit. In downtown LA there was "Angel's Flight," a streetcar pulled by a cable that carried passengers up Bunker Hill. The Los Angeles City Hall was open to the public and the tallest structure in the area. And the movie studios gave tours, as did Forest Lawn Cemetery, full of dead celebrities. Olivera Street was the center of the thriving Mexican community. For a little boy from Modesto it was like visiting a foreign country. It was there that I saw my first Zoot Suiters: young Latinos dressed in long sports coats and baggy, pleated pants pinched at the ankle, with long chains drooping from their trousers.

Fat Jones was a friend of my father's. He rented buggies and wagons to the movie studios. He was really nice to me and took me to see the horse races at Santa Anita.

The Los Angeles County Museum was a terrific place to visit with dioramas filled with stuffed wild animals in what appeared to be their natural habitat. I even visited the Rose Bowl and the Coliseum, as in those days I was a great football fan.

Closer to Tom's apartment was the Santa Monica Pier and about a mile away, the Venice Pier. Each had a variety of amusements: Penny Arcades (yes, a penny bought thirty seconds of a flickering moving picture of a magician doing tricks and the like); bumper cars; merry-go-rounds; and even roller coasters. There also was a show called "Sex and Sin." They wouldn't let me in, even after I'd seen Sally Rand in San Francisco!

One of the piers had a movie theater. I saw Citizen Kane, Orson Welles' classic movie there. I thought it was terrific but was too young to understand the connection with William Randolph Hearst.

In 1944 it was apparent we were winning the war. The military's need for aircraft was over. Douglas shut down its A-20 production line and my brother's job

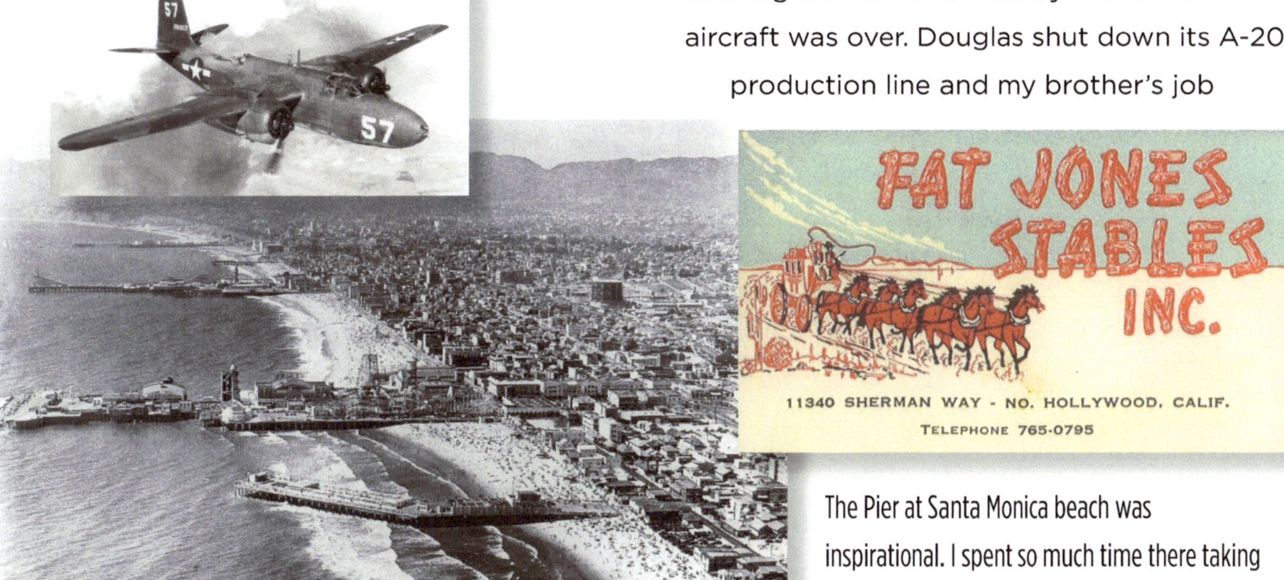

The Pier at Santa Monica beach was inspirational. I spent so much time there taking in all the incredible sights and sounds.

"In 1946 Tom bought an Army surplus Harley Davidson... and rode it all they way to South America, a trip of about nine months!"

ended. However, the draft was still in force and young men without deferments were still being taken into the service. Tom was drafted.

Something was happening to the brother I worshiped. I did not understand it but his behavior was gradually changing. He was becoming more withdrawn. He picked arguments with his friends. He didn't trust people. He found it hard to negotiate. It came to a climax a few months after entering the Army.

During basic training he was put into a mental hospital in the bay area and diagnosed as a paranoid schizophrenic, unfit for military service. Army doctors suggested he seek therapy. In those days mental ailments were viewed as a family blemish. My mother told the doctors "He'll be fine when we get him home." But he wasn't. His life after leaving the Army was not a happy one. On the surface it appeared to be a life full of adventure. He travelled all over the world, but he was never able to escape himself.

In 1946 he bought an Army surplus Harley Davidson "Scout" motorcycle for $50. He told our parents he was going to ride it to Los Angeles to visit some friends from his Douglas days. Our family didn't hear from him for several months. Finally a postcard arrived from Mexico City! We don't know many of the details of his trip, but he rode his Scout all the way to Buenos Aires, Argentina! In some places the roads were so bad he put the motorcycle on ox carts. The whole trip took about nine months. Somehow along the way Harley Davidson heard of the trip and was able to find him. They agreed to sponsor him on the adventure. They shipped Tom and the motorcycle back to the United States. They reconditioned the old Scout. It is now in the care of his son Glen in Modesto. Tom seldom rode it after his adventure and had very little to say about his journey.

After his return from his South American adventure Tom got a job driving Greyhound buses, but it didn't last long. Apparently an altercation of some sort occurred and he was fired. My father bought him a 1939 Dodge semi truck. He hauled a varity of agricultural goods up and down the San Joaquin valley. But he was bored and restless and because of his illness had few friends. In the late 1940's he joined the Merchant Marine and for a number of years sailed all over the world, but still had little to say about what he had seen.

After my father died Tom came home to live with our mother. He returned to trucking and finally in the 1990's was killed in a trucking accident. Although he was not a good custodian of my father's wonderful collection of antique vehicles he did make it possible for our mother to live independently until she died.

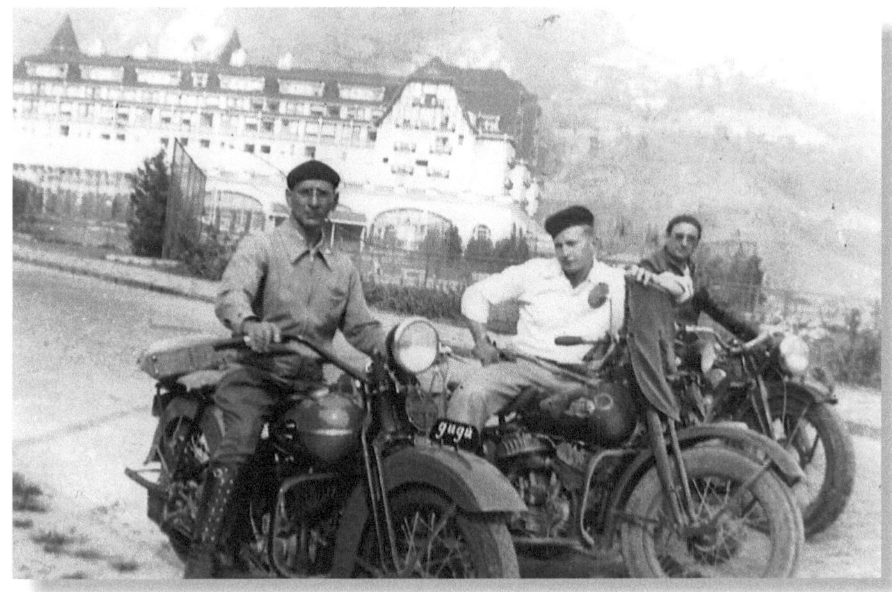

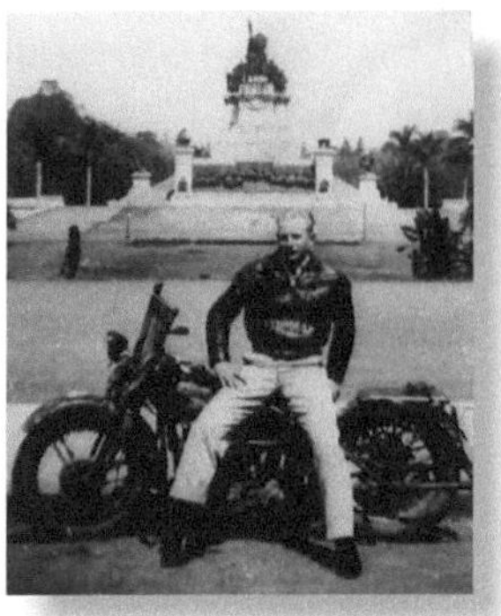

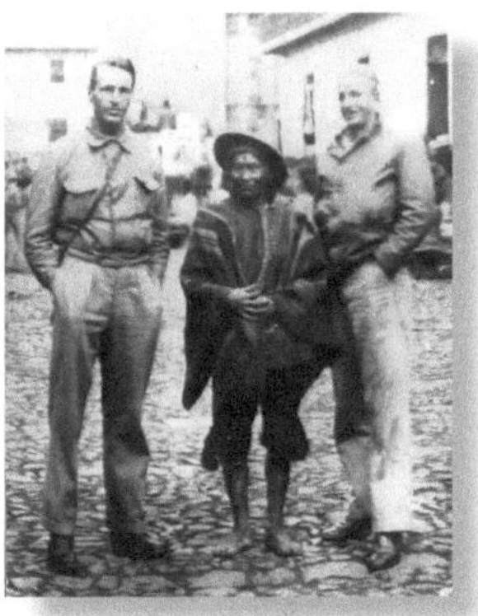

TOM'S ADVENTURE TO SOUTH AMERICA

IN HIS OWN WORDS FROM URUGUAY....

I am a farmer in my country, but I like sports a lot. I have practiced baseball, rugby and basketball. I am also an enthusiast of motorcycling. Adventures please me and one day I had the idea of a trip, a great trip. I wanted to visit Latin America.

I spoke to two friends: Byrd Nelley and Bob Harding, also motorcyclists. We planned the trip and decided to fulfill it.

We took off March 26th from Modesto, my native town. We got to Panama and Nelley desserted us. Harding and I continued through the PanAmerican Highway. We arrived at Lima and then to La Paz. He accompanied me up to here and then he returned to Lima. Do you know why? He met a beautiful Peruvian and...he got married!

It may seem curious but that's the way it is. I decided to continue myself and here I am. Now I am heading to Rio de Janiero. I leave tomorrow, Monday.

In La Paz I witnessed the political unrest that nation experienced and I saw President Villareal. As I headed to Buenos Aires, I learned about his death. I have been able to appreciate, through my passage through diverse countries that life in some of them is not like the life I have seen here.

In Uruguay everyone is the same. It seems that they are neither poor nor rich. I have also evidenced the cordiality of the Uruguayans. I had heard about them, but I never imagined that they could be so amiable. I have found true friends.

I will return to my country taking with me very pleasant memories of this great culture.

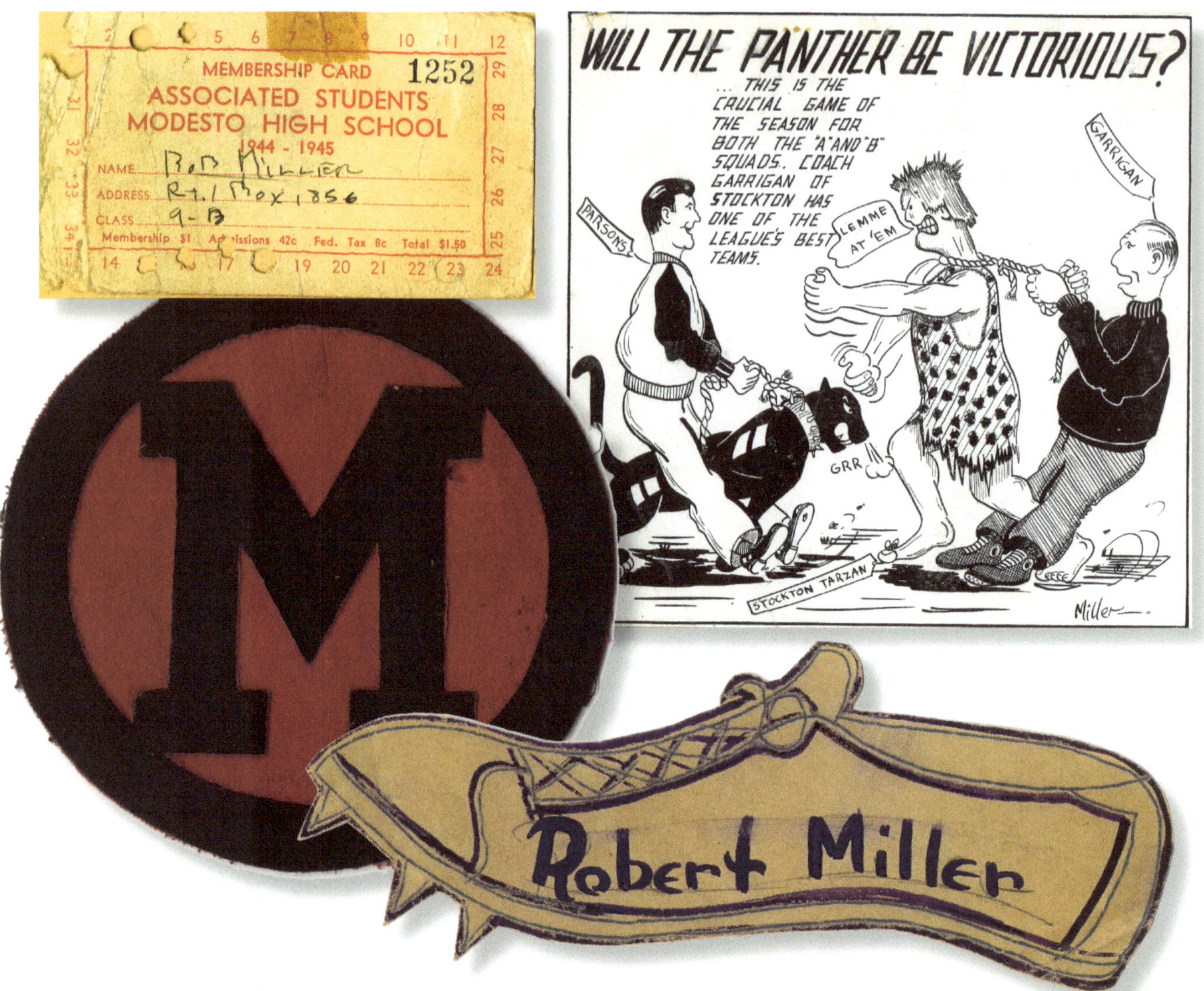

I graduated from grammar school in 1944 and started Modesto High School that fall. It was the only high school for miles around. We were picked up in front of our house by a big, snub nosed yellow school bus, just like in grammar school. The farm kids at high school were considered a bunch of hicks by the metropolitan Modesto kids who had gone to Roosevelt Junior High. It took a while to fit in but I did develop a friendship with Mac Pollock. We stayed friends until his death. He was a great guy.

It did not take long to learn the difficult social rules one plays in high school. I never felt like I quite fit in to the highest social levels.

I loved football and in spite of my ability to draw and paint, football became my passion. I played peewee football as a freshman, then the B Team as a sophomore. Our B Team played the varsity squads of some of the smaller local schools like Denair or Patterson. Finally I played varsity in my senior year, but in the last practice before the first game I was clipped behind my left knee and pulled some ligaments. I was on crutches the rest of the football season. There went my football career!

I had two really great art instructors, Mrs. Ida Gross and Jean Ariey. Jean had just started teaching. She was in her early twenties. We really liked each other. I think she was most instrumental in my becoming a professional artist.

I became the sports cartoonist for the Broadcast, our school newspaper. I learned a little about letterpress reproduction that stood me well later. I also learned several art techniques that I still use, like posterization, the simplifying of a photograph for ease of reproduction. Printing was not nearly as sophisticated as it is now, especially newspapers, so simplifying for better impact for ads appearing in newspapers was very important.

Although fraternities and sororities were outlawed in high school there were underground social clubs that existed anyway. As a sophomore I was asked to join The 36 Club. I thought it would be great for my social standing, so I joined. Of course there was a humiliating pledge time when you had to perform tasks for the older members and if you didn't do well you were paddled. I stayed in the club until early in my senior year. My brother Bill was asked to pledge. His duties on the farm interfered with some silly pledge duty he was supposed to perform and he was paddled mercilessly at the next meeting. We both realized how shallow this whole business was and quit the club. Social structure in high school can be cruel and when one realizes how unimportant it is, not just in high school, but in life, life is more comfortable. Status is earned; not gained by membership.

By the time I was a senior I realized I wanted art to be my life. I even met my my future wife Anita in Ida Gross's art class. We met in April 1947 and fell in love. In July, 1950 we married at Modesto's First Methodist Church. We are still married.

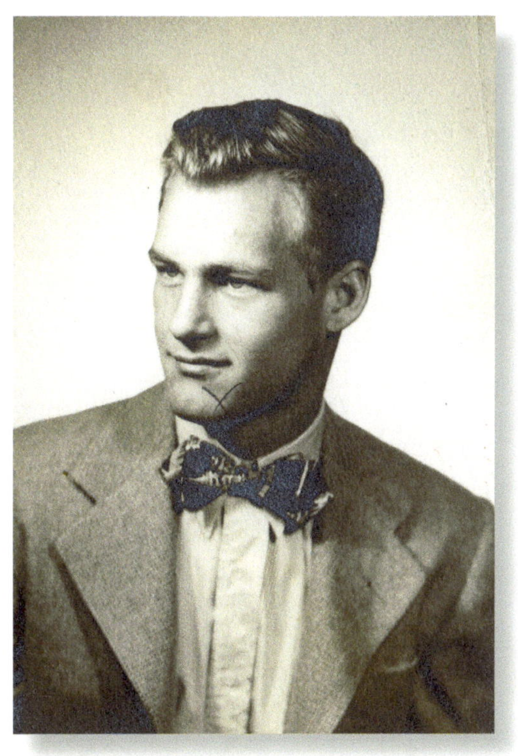

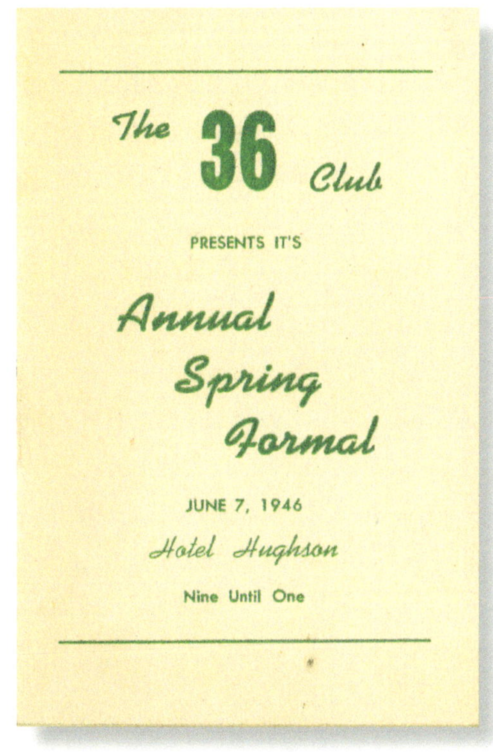

Previous page: Mementos of high school. I got the Circle 'M' as a sophomore. I don't remember if the Panthers won or not. This page: My graduation picture. A dance bid.

"My first car was a 1936 Ford. My dad paid $600 for it."

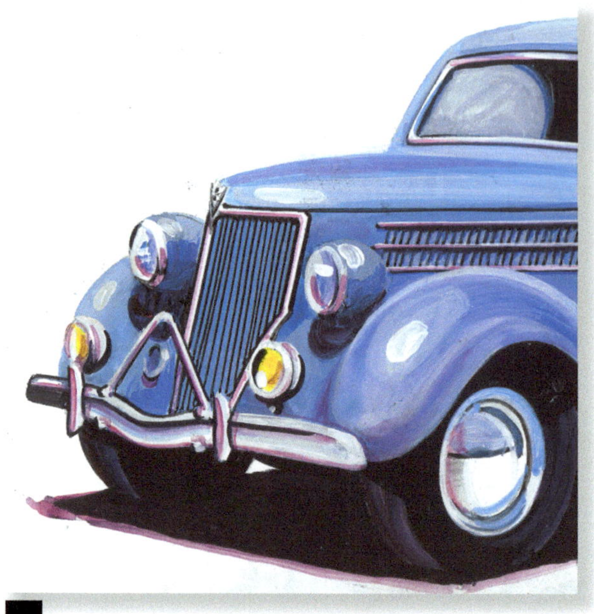

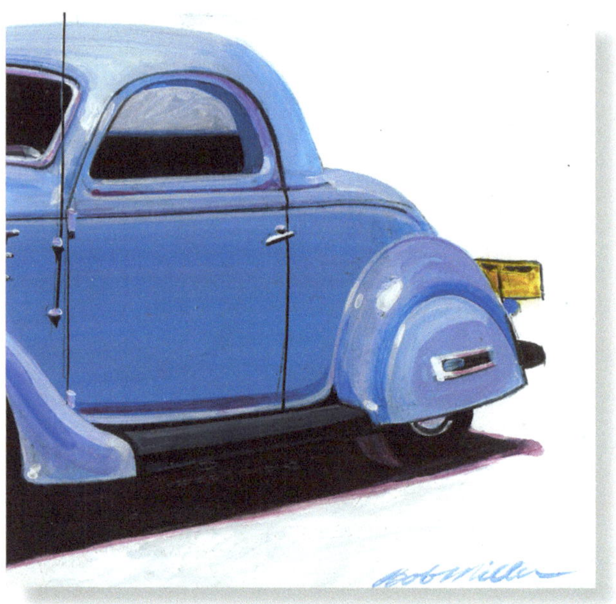

In the spring of 1947 I was voted Student Body President. I ran against Glen Sauls. I was president during the fall of 1947. My friend Robert M. Miller--who I went all the way through grammar and high school with--was president in the spring. He also ran against Glen--poor Glen!

My first car was a 1936 Ford three-window coupe. It was sky blue. My father paid $600 for it. Before the war, in 1936, the car sold new for the same price. After the war, cars were in short supply: hard to get and overpriced. It was not until the early 1950's that supply finally caught up with demand. I had the car untill 1950 when I traded it in for a Raymond Loewy designed 1947 Studebaker.

Just after I got my '36 Ford, my friends Donald and Edward Little wanted to go to Los Angeles to shop for a car. They were cheaper in L.A. I was into the trip for the adventure. We drove down to Los Angeles, arriving at night.

The Ford had a huge trunk and the seats flipped down so we could sleep in it. Very tired, we drove around and around trying to find a parking lot. At last we saw a huge expanse of lawn with a curb around it. We bumped up and over the curb into a grove of trees, parked and went to sleep. When we awoke we discovered we were in a parking lot no more than a hundred yards from the Rose Bowl.

More about The 36 Club: After meetings we would sometimes play "ditch" in our cars. A car would go ahead of the pack by a few hundred yards and try to lose the cars following. It was a dangerous teenage game. We were in and out of private property and people's driveways. I was the

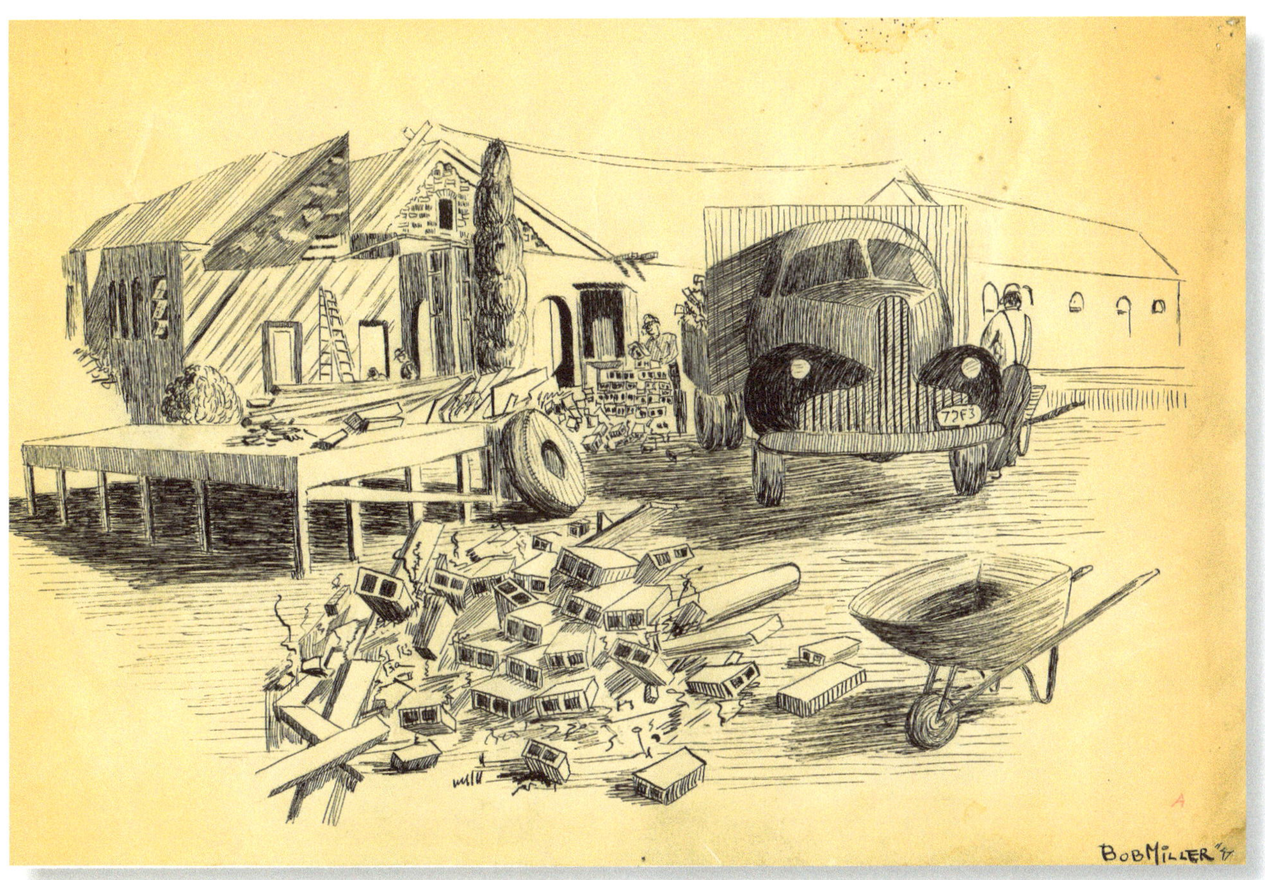

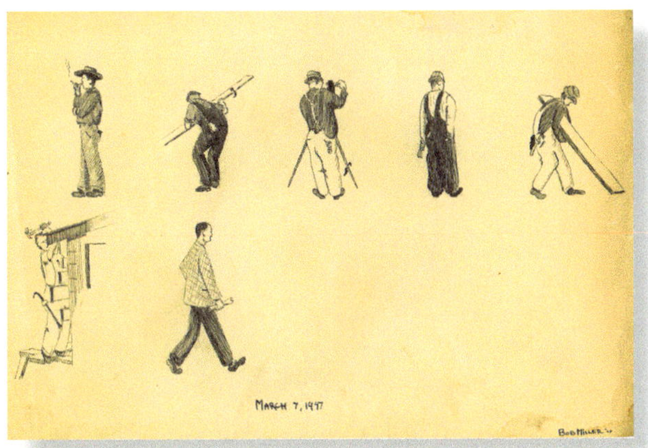

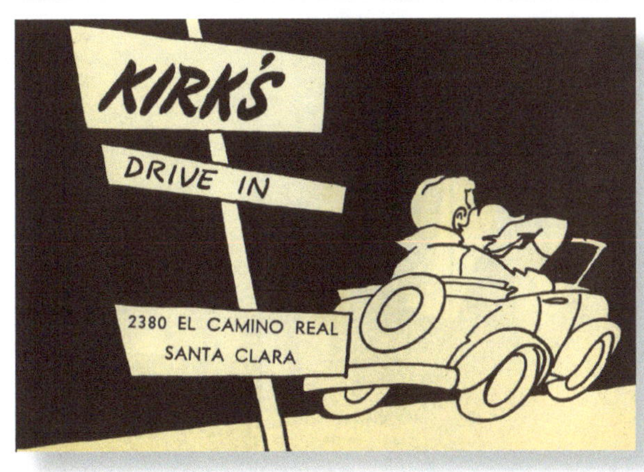

lead car one of those wild nights. I was driving my father's 1935 Ford pickup. We headed out McHenry Boulevard as fast as we could go, turned on Floyd Avenue, all vineyards then. I turned into a long driveway. At the end of the driveway was a huge trellis made of lathe with grape vines crawling through it. I caught the trellis on the back of the pickup and tore it down, carrying it out through the vineyard rows. It caught on vines and left pieces all over the vineyard. I managed to escape unscathed except for a slightly bent bumper, but I was followed by at least 10 other cars speeding down the driveway, roaring by the house and through the littered vineyard. Lights burst on all over the farm house. None of us were ever caught. It is probably the most irresponsible thing I have ever done.

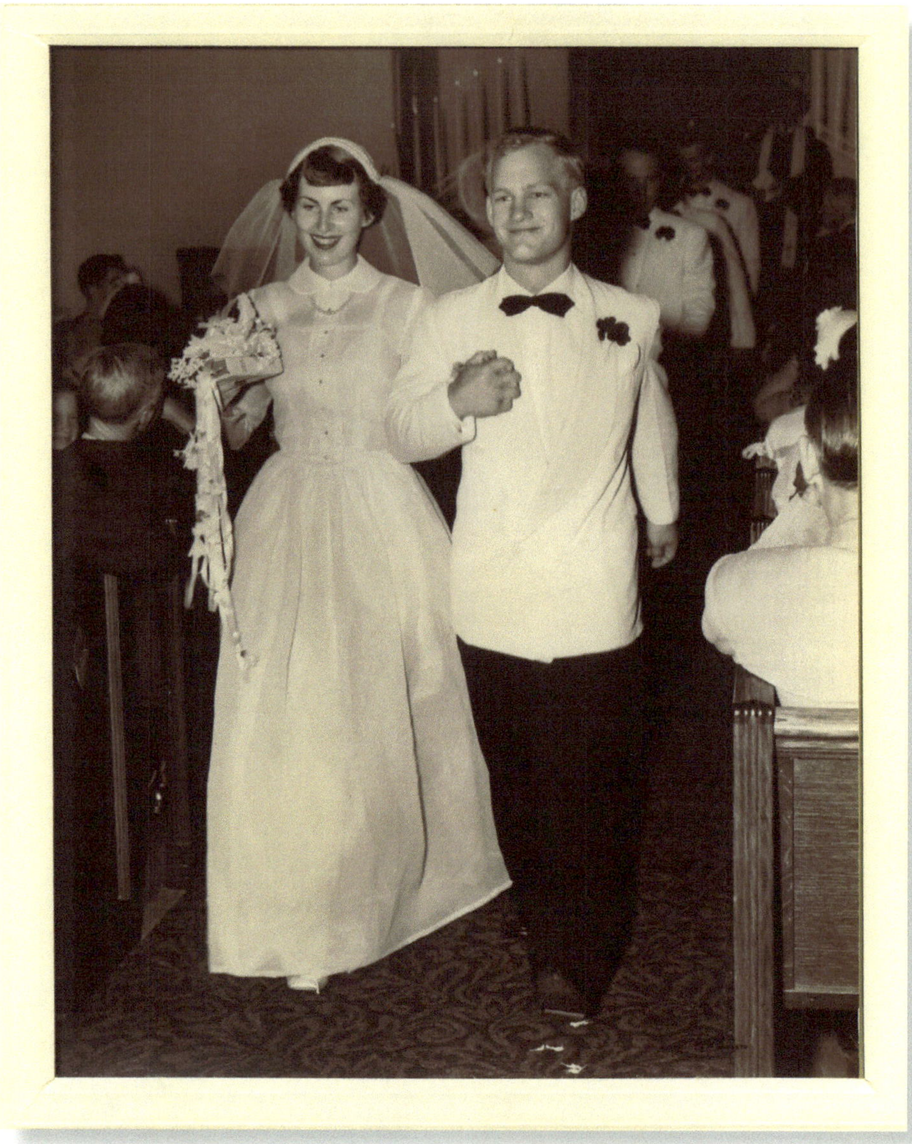

I started San Jose State College in 1948. My chosen major was Commercial Art, with a minor in History. "Commercial Art" better explains the profession than "Design." Commercial Art simply means one is doing art with sales in mind. Advertising art is a call for action, art designed to motivate people to do something.

Bill Armell, a friend from high school, and I roomed together with 20 other guys in a rooming house about 5 or 6 blocks east of the campus. Almost everyone in the house were veterans of World War Two. They meant business. All were attending school on the G.I. Bill. They wanted to get their degrees and get on with their lives. No fraternity paddles for this group. It was good for a couple of 17 year olds from Modesto to be with these hardened adults.

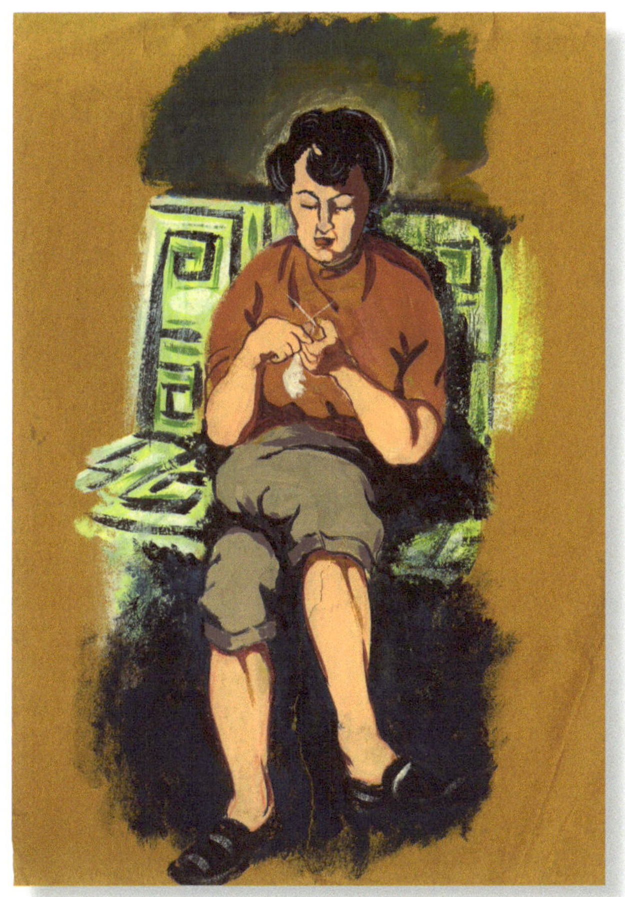

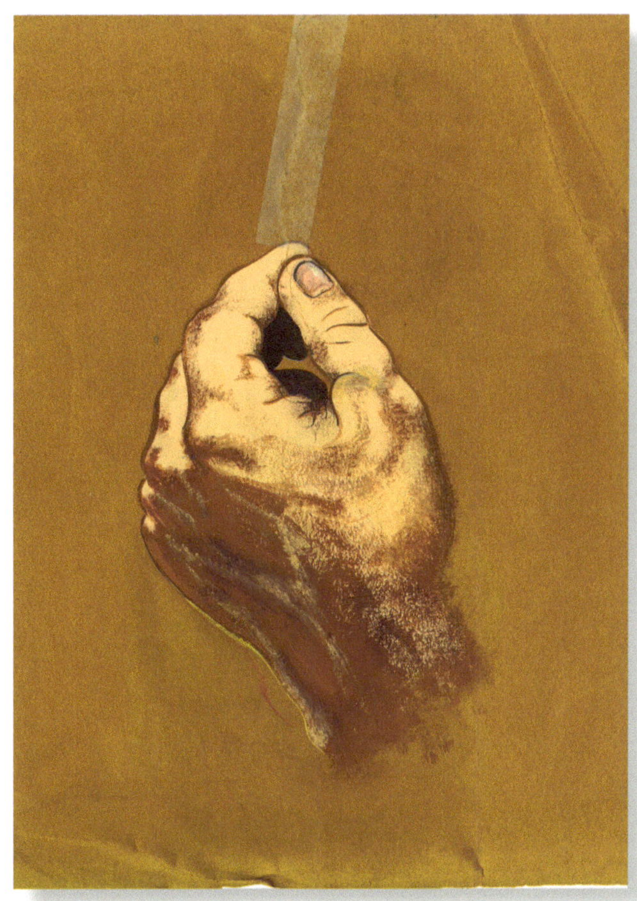

Previous page: Our wedding day, July 2, 1950. • Above left: I borrowed a hundred bucks from my friend and roommate George Ramsey to buy the sofa in the painting of Anita. That was a lot of money in those days! Above right: The Hand of God...ha ha ha!!

Every weekend I would drive my Ford back to Modesto to be with Anita. We were getting real serious.

My painting instructors were Dr. Reitzal and Ted Johnson. Johnson was a very amicable man. He had studied in Paris during the Depression and was really a good painter and instructor. I loved to paint. My commercial art instructor was Marian Moreland. She was a good, practical teacher. When I graduated I had practical skills that most art students didn't have.

Anita and I were married between my sophomore and junior years. We lived for a brief time in a house we rented on a hill above Almaden. From our deck at night we could see the lights of San Francisco. It was a small house with one bedroom, a huge living room with a fireplace. Winter came. We discovered it was a summer cabin with a very small electric wall heater that warmed about 10 cubic feet. We prowled the neighborhood and stole wood for the fireplace, but it was too much! After Christmas we moved to a small (but warm!) duplex in the Willow Glen section of San Jose, then later to a studio apartment above a garage in the same neighborhood.

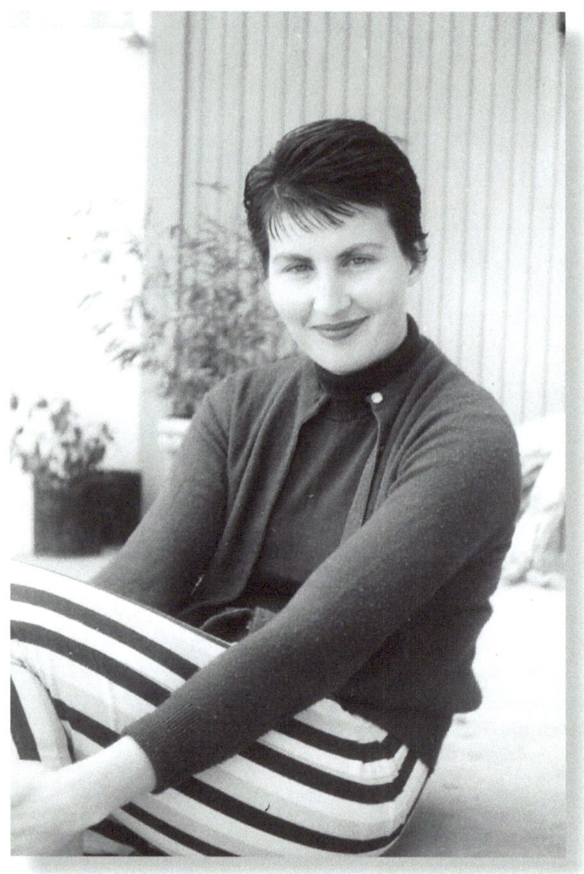

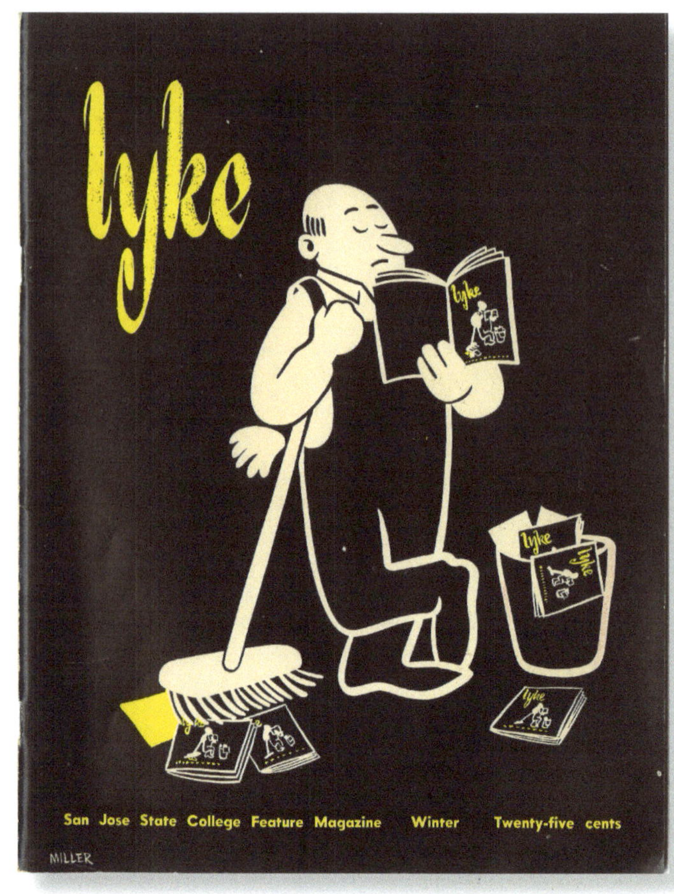

In 1951 our daughter Gayman was born. We moved to a bigger duplex on 13th Street. It was then the main street to Oakland and there was always lots of heavy traffic.

Tuition at San Jose state was $7.50 per quarter. Total for my three-quarter year was $22.50! Before I was married my father gave me the same stipend a veteran was getting: $75 per month, plus books and tuition. He made it clear if I got married I was on my own.

I worked while I was in college. As a freshman I started at Bettencourt's Busy Markets and worked there all the time I was in school. I think I made a dollar an hour. I painted big window banners on butcher paper and did "shelf-talkers": small signs that were attached to in-store displays. During my time there I painted thousands of signs, maybe tens of thousands. Ed Crandall was my boss. He had flown Curtiss P-40s during the war. Ed was a great boss and very encouraging in my career.

I was on the staff of the college humor magazine "Lyke." It was a required course. We ran the magazine like a commercial venture. It had to support itself. We sold ads, wrote copy, shot pictures, did the illustrations, as well as the actual production. In those days production was all paste-up. In my senior year I was editor of the magazine. I still have copies in my files. It

“In the middle of the silkscreen shack were two Doberman Pinscher guard dogs. All day while cutting stencils or screening, they strained at their leashes and growled at me. It was my job to give them water and clean up their shit.”

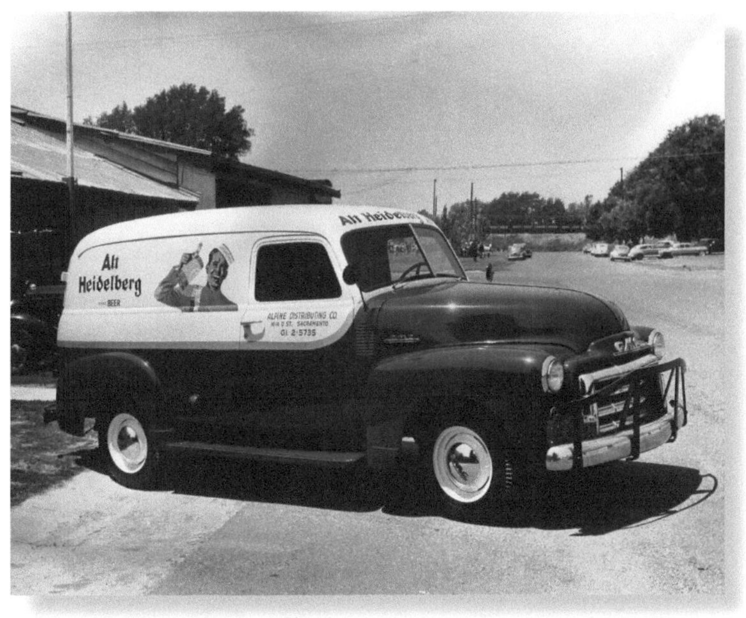

This was a typical truck sign job at Dosch in 1954. The business was housed in ramshackle structures that would never be allowed today! (Photo courtesy Ed Weidner)

was a great practical learning experience, but it also meant I was away from my little family a lot. It was a hard time for Anita.

Our second child Michael was born in 1952. His circumcision did not heal properly and he cried day and night. It was a bad time, especially for Anita. Frequently she was alone, trying to cope with the children. Both Michael and Gayman are now in their sixties and have become wonderful adults we are very proud of.

I graduated in 1953. My first job after graduation was with R&A Signs in Sunnyvale. I was making $2 an hour designing signs and cutting stencils for silkscreen reproduction. They were located across from a huge lettuce field. We had lots of free lettuce when in season.

Everything seemed secure. We put $500 down on a small house in Cupertino. The selling price of the house was $4,999. The development was called Ranch Rinconada. But R&A's business took a downturn. I was laid off. We got our $500 deposit back and decided to move to Sacramento where Anita's parents lived.

I took my portfolio around. Brown Clark and Elkus, a major advertising firm, liked it, but there were no openings and none at Chapin and Damm, a competitive agency. I landed a job as a silkscreen craftsman at Dosch Sign Company. I still made $2 an hour. Dosch was located at Second and V Streets, now underneath a freeway exchange. The company took up half a block. Dosch had a contract to de-mothball World War Two warships. There were plasticized domes all over the yard that at one time might have covered gun turrets

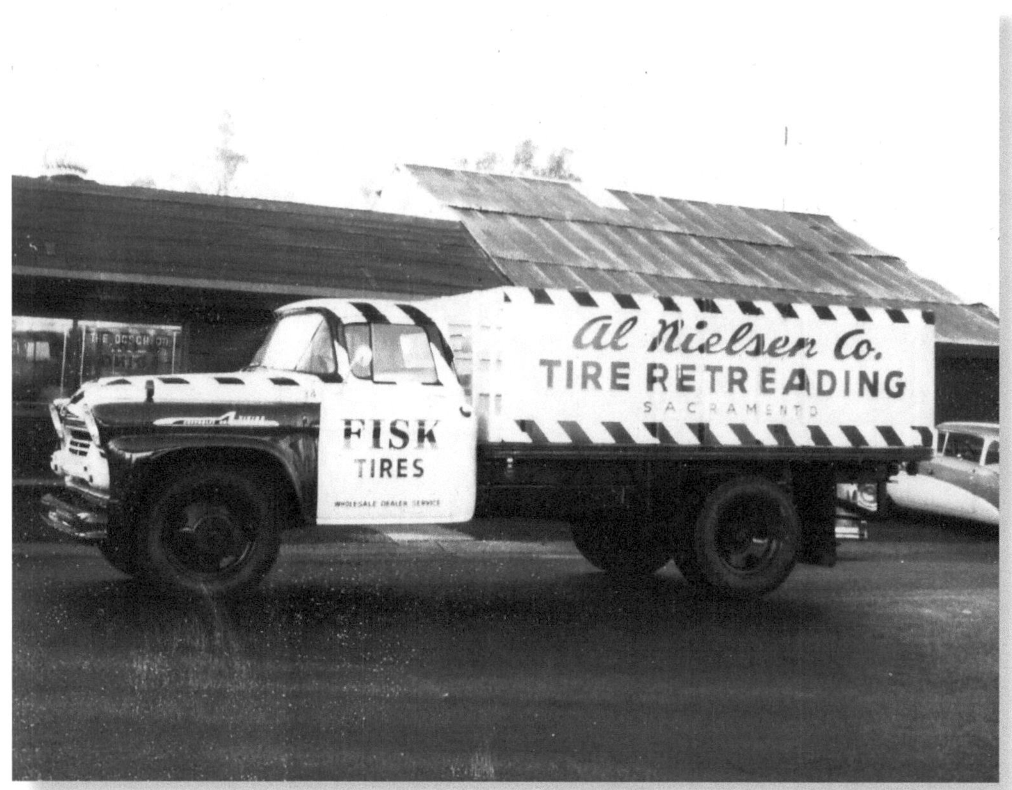

Dosch Sign Company was located at 2nd and V Streets, a site now beneath the big freeway interchange at the west end of town. You can see portions of the business office and run down shops in the background of these photos. (Photo courtesy of Ed Weidner, from his book "Watching Paint Dry").

or radar equipment on battleships. Dosch also painted Continental Trailway buses and did signage on trucks and cars for many businesses in the region. The silkscreen department was a tar paper covered shack that had once been a chicken coop. My boss was a man named George Ochikubo. He had been in the Internment Camps during the war. He did not take kindly to smart alecky, blond, white college kids.

In the middle of the shack was a 2x4 post. Attached to the post on leashes were two Doberman Pinscher guard dogs. All day while cutting stencils or screening, they strained at their leashes and growled at me. It was my job to give them water and clean up their shit.

During the summer it had to be 120° in the place and during the winter if it was 50° outside, it was 50 inside. Stencils are hard to cut wearing gloves, but it can be done.

We lived in a little duplex off Fruitridge Road near Power Inn Road. One day Mrs. Dosch came out of her office in a panic saying my wife was on the phone. Anita said, "Gayman is missing on her tricycle. I can't find her!" I got in my Studebaker and roared home. We found Gayman and her friend Patty Croy riding their tricycles on Southern Pacific's main line tracks...and just in time as trains began to come closer.

On Christmas morning Mr. Dosch came into the silkscreen department and shoved five dollars into my pocket. "There's a bonus for you," he said. "Take the rest of the day off." What a great guy. Later, when payday came, I noticed my check was short by $8. I went to the office to talk to Mrs. Dosch, the bookkeeper. She said, "Well Bob, you know you didn't work Christmas Eve."

FROM A CHICKEN COOP TO A TELEVISION STUDIO!

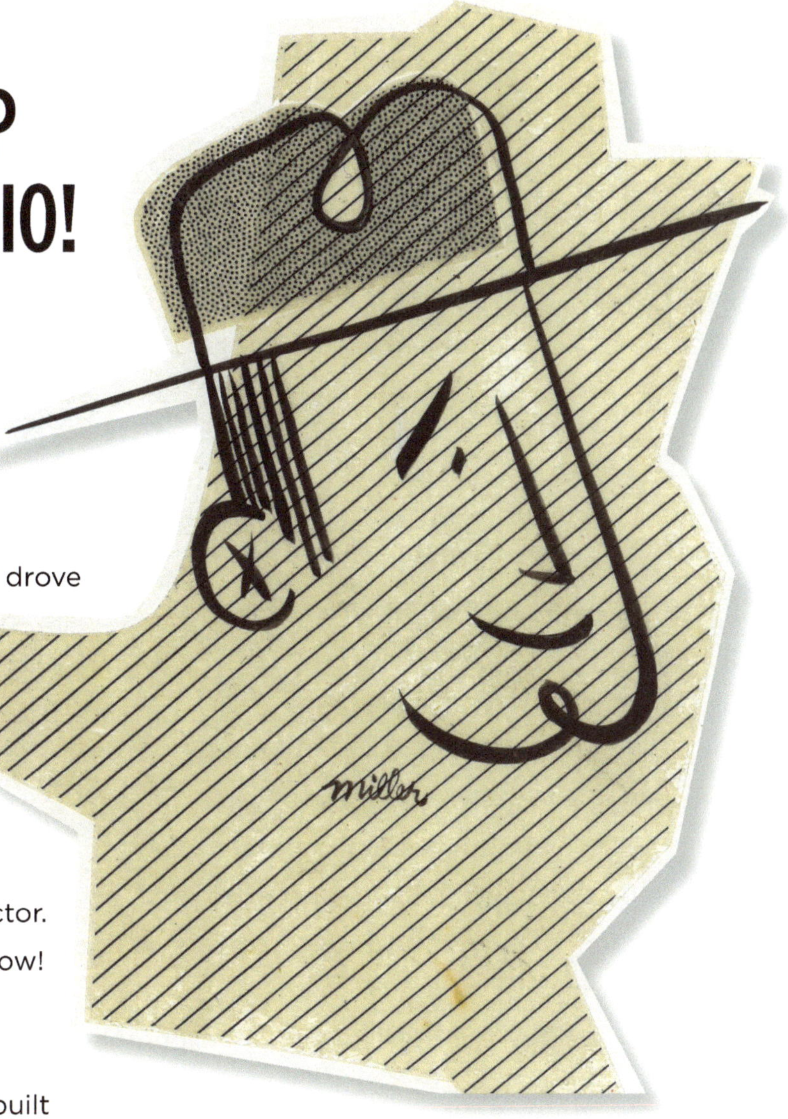

In 1954 Channel 36, KTVU went on the air in Stockton. Its artwork was lousy.

I put my portfolio in my Studebaker and drove down there. I showed them my portfolio. They liked it but Dave Hume thought I might be too short to operate the boom mike for the Milly Sullivan Show. I stood on my tippy toes and managed to move the boom around. I was hired.

From silk screen flunky to TV Art Director. From a chicken coop to a television studio. Wow! But I didn't make any more money.

KTVU was a great experience. I got to do the things I was trained to do and more. I built sets, stretched linen over frames to make eight foot high flats. I designed and produced their TV Guide ads as well as posters and brochures. And once a week I went on the air with "Magic Jeannie." Jeannie was Jean Hardie. She did a half hour children's show every weekday at five. She showed cartoons. Once a week I would appear on the show. I would show the children in the television audience how to draw a character: usually an animal like "Elmer the Elephant." Then I would tell a story about Elmer. I used lecturer's chalk on large sheets of butcher paper. We asked children in the TV audience to send in their drawings of the character. We'd get anywhere from 800 to 1,000 drawings a week! We picked the ten best and the winners would appear on the show and get prizes from "The Toy Shop," a sponsor of the show. One of our winners was Mike Dunlavey who grew up to be the owner of the Dunlavey Studio in Sacramento. He and his wife Lindy owned the studio. They recently retired and I considered theirs to be the best in the area. Mike is not only an excellent designer but also a very talented artist.

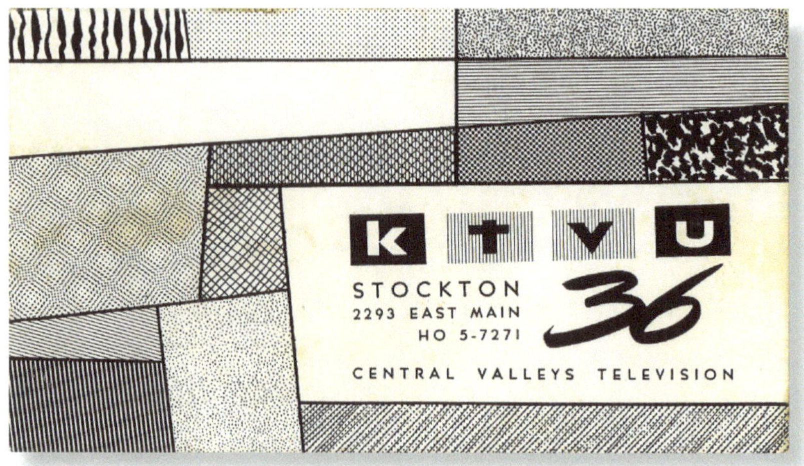

KTVU was headquartered in what had been Stockton's East Theater. It closed in the early 1950's and Channel 36 moved in in 1954. My art department was on the stage of the old theater. Sets and furniture were stored in what had been the seating area.

Everything was broadcast live and in black and white. Color and video tape recording had not been invented yet. We could have recorded using kinescopes, but they were of poor quality and too expensive for Channel 36.

Bel Lange, Harry Martin and Milly Sullivan all were on-air personalities. Bel went on to have a outdoor hunting and fishing show, The Outdoorsman, and ultimately became station manager of Channel 13. Harry moved to KCCC, Channel 40 in Sacramento where he played Bonanza Bill, then moved to KCRA TV Channel 3 in Sacramento where he became the second Captain Sacto. He ended his career after decades as Channel 3's entertainment personality. He was a Sacramento icon. Milly Sullivan did a cooking and interview show on Channel 36. She moved to Sacramento's Channel 3 to host Valley Playhouse, an afternoon show featuring older movies. She was very popular.

Being involved in the birth of television didn't seem like a big deal then, but looking back, it amazes me. Everything was so new, experimental, and LIVE! Every day was an artistic adventure. At Channel 36, I had the pleasure of working with Sam Morrison. Sam was the ugliest man in television, perhaps the ugliest man in America. I'm not making fun of him at all, just stating what I recall about him. He was so ugly people would stop and stare at him in public.

Ugliness aside, he was brilliant! He and I were always trying new stuff. One day, Sam came up with a brilliant idea. He had me paint a Channel 36 logo on a showcard. Then, with a film camera rolling, he shot the card completely full of holes with a BB rifle, shredding it to nothingness. I had no idea what he was up to. He later played the film backwards, creating the stunning special effect of the logo "reappearing" from nothingness. We experimented like that every single day.

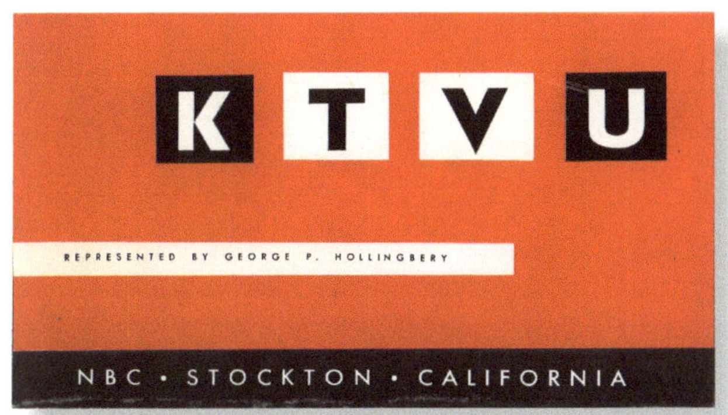

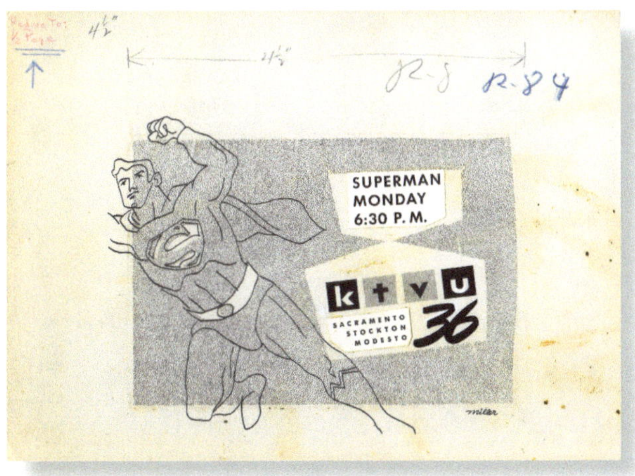

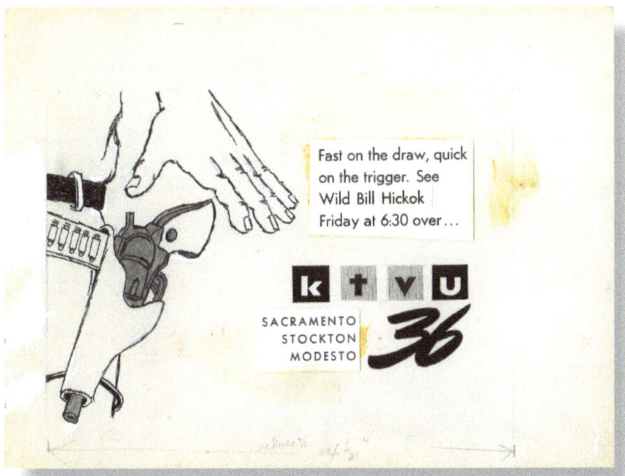

I used to sign my ads. Ha!. • Various graphics from the early days at Channel 36. Page 39: Part of a "paste-up" for a Red Rider TV show advertisement. • The ads on this page are paste-ups, too. I would have a photostatic copy shot of the art and send that to the printer. All of the paste-up lines and marks would disappear when they shot the "stat."• The other three pieces are rate cards used to sell our on-air ads.

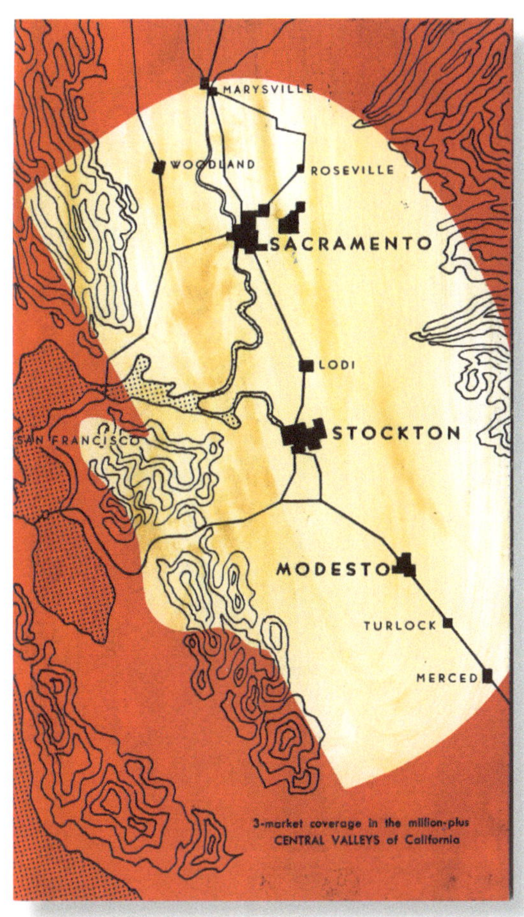

GENERAL RATE CARD NO. 3
Effective Feb. 1, 1955

CLASS A — 6:30 PM to 10:30 PM—Sunday thru Saturday

	1	13	26	52	104	156	208	260
1 hour	175.00	165.00	157.00	148.00	140.00	131.00	122.00	113.00
½ hour	105.00	100.00	95.00	90.00	85.00	80.00	75.00	70.00
¼ hour	70.00	66.50	63.00	59.50	56.00	52.50	49.00	45.50
10 Min.	60.00	57.00	54.00	51.00	48.00	45.00	42.00	39.00
5 Min.	50.00	47.50	45.00	42.50	40.00	37.50	35.00	32.50
20-60 Sec. Annc.	35.00	33.50	32.00	30.50	28.50	26.50	24.50	22.50
10 Sec. ID	17.50	16.75	16.00	15.25	14.25	13.25	12.25	11.25

CLASS B — 5:00 PM to 6:30 PM—Sunday thru Saturday

	1	13	26	52	104	156	208	260
1 Hour	125.00	119.00	112.50	106.00	99.50	93.00	86.50	80.00
½ Hour	75.00	71.00	67.00	63.00	59.00	55.00	51.00	47.00
¼ Hour	50.00	47.50	45.00	42.50	40.00	37.50	35.00	32.50
10 Min.	45.00	43.00	40.50	38.00	36.50	34.00	31.50	29.00
5 Min.	35.00	33.50	32.00	30.50	28.50	26.50	24.50	22.50
20-60 Sec. Annc.	25.00	24.00	22.50	21.00	20.00	18.50	17.50	16.00
10 Sec. ID	12.50	12.00	11.25	10.50	10.00	9.25	8.75	8.00

CLASS C — ALL OTHER TIME — Sunday thru Saturday

	1	13	26	52	104	156	208	260
1 Hour	75.00	71.00	67.00	63.00	59.00	55.00	51.00	47.00
½ Hour	45.00	43.00	40.50	38.00	36.50	34.00	31.50	29.00
¼ Hour	30.00	28.50	27.00	25.50	24.00	22.50	21.00	19.50
10 Min.	25.00	24.00	22.50	21.00	20.00	18.50	17.50	16.00
5 Min.	20.00	19.00	18.00	17.00	16.00	15.00	14.00	13.00
20-60 Sec. Annc.	15.00	14.25	13.50	12.75	12.00	11.25	10.50	9.75
10 Sec. ID	7.50	7.25	6.75	6.50	6.00	5.75	5.25	4.75

GENERAL INFORMATION

All basic charges are grouped together and include studio or transmitter, and existing film facilities and necessary technical staff. Special talent, art, props, set contruction, staging, extraordinary production services, etc., are not included in the charges.

Announcements, participations, and station ID's CAN BE COMBINED to earn frequency discounts.

Programs of varying lengths CAN BE COMBINED to earn frequency discounts, but programs and announcements CANNOT BE COMBINED for that purpose.

Announcements scheduled between time classifications take the rate of the later classification.

Announcements adjacent to a special event take the rate of the special event.

There is NO ADDITIONAL CHARGE or "premium rate" for film, slide, and/or live on-camera announcements within existing participating programs. Regular one-time announcement rates apply to the following:

3:30-4:30 PM KTVU Kitchen
4:30-5:30 PM Family Feature
5:30-6:00 PM Kids Klub
6:00-6:30 PM Super Serial

After 6:30 P. M. there is an additional charge of $25.00 for the use of one studio camera, and $40.00 for the use of two studio cameras for each live on-camera announcement, or program, regardless of length. No discounts apply for camera charge.

All rates except camera charges are subject to 15% commission to recognized agencies.

KTVU reserves the right to change its rates effective on such date as it my announce. Changes which increase rates will not apply to schedules on the air at the time the increase is announced until six months after the effective date of new rates, provided there is no interruption.

Contracts are subject to 28-day advance notice in writing for programs, 14 days for announcements.

Schedules must start within 30 days of contract date.

Closing time on all film, slides and other program material and announcements is 48 hours prior to the scheduled time of telecast, except that material for Sunday and Monday must be received no later than the prior Thursday at 6:00 PM.

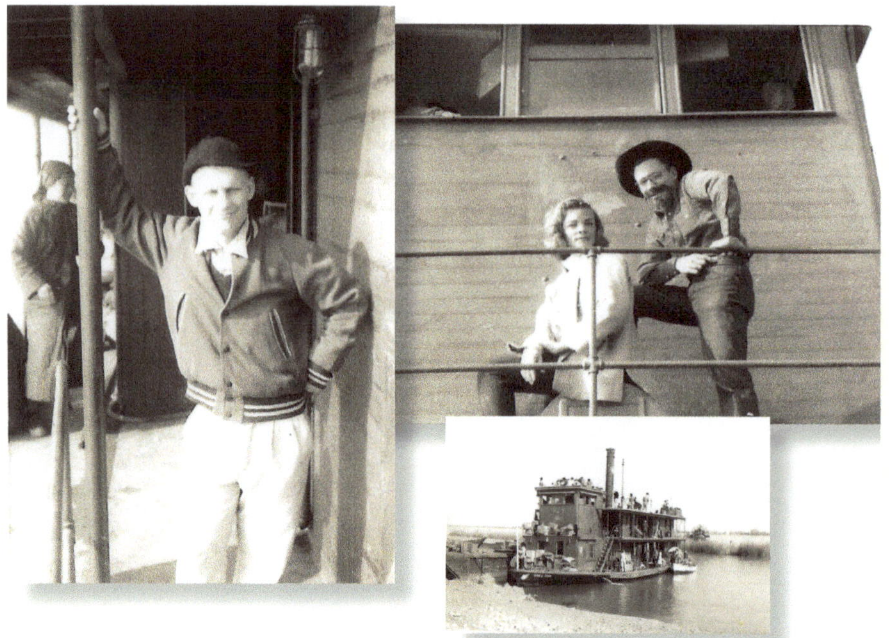

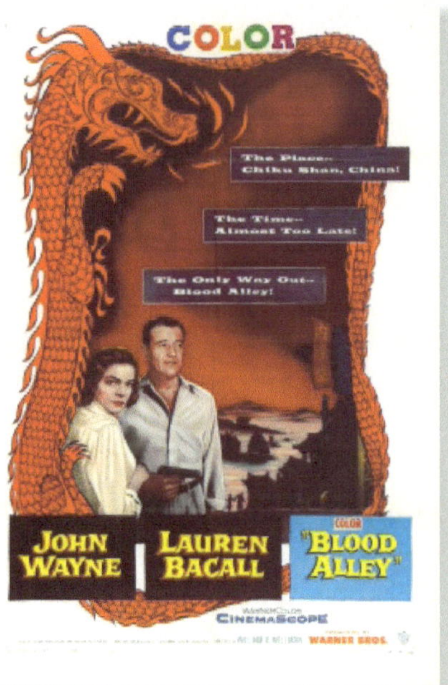

In 1954 Hollywood came to Stockton. The movie was "Blood Alley" starring John Wayne and Lauren Bacall. The plot of the movie was about refugees escaping the Chinese Communists on a paddlewheel steamer that was leaving mainland China for Taiwan. John Wayne captained the boat. It was thought the San Joaquin Delta, near Stockton, looked a little like the coast off China.

My friend Don DeGraf played "Buffalo" on one of Channel 36's children's shows. We pretended to be the news department at KTVU Channel 36. Channel 36 had no news department! I had my Argus A-2 camera loaded with black and white film (I don't know why it wasn't loaded with Kodachrome).

We drove on to the filming site early in the morning in Don's MG-TD and talked our way on board. Then we waited and waited. Finally they brought John Wayne on board. I think he had had a hard night. He stumbled up the gang plank with lots of help and was delivered to the one cabin on the little boat. That was the last we saw of John Wayne.

Then a bundle of extras dressed as Coolies jumped off the boat and pulled it away from the mooring. Don and I were offered $10 each to jump in the water as Coolies. It was tempting (I was making $2 an hour...$10 was almost a day's pay!), but the water was too cold.

We were on the boat for about two hours. We met Lauren Bacall, who was very nice to us. The boat paddled around the Delta with cameras shooting from the levee, then turned around and came back to where Don's MG was parked. It was fun to see the movie when it ultimately came out in theaters and impress our friends with, "See that boat? We are on the other side, out of sight!" Most were not impressed.

After the filming of "Blood Alley" the little paddle wheeler was brought up the river by Frank Parisi and he converted it to a restaurant on Sacramento's waterfront.

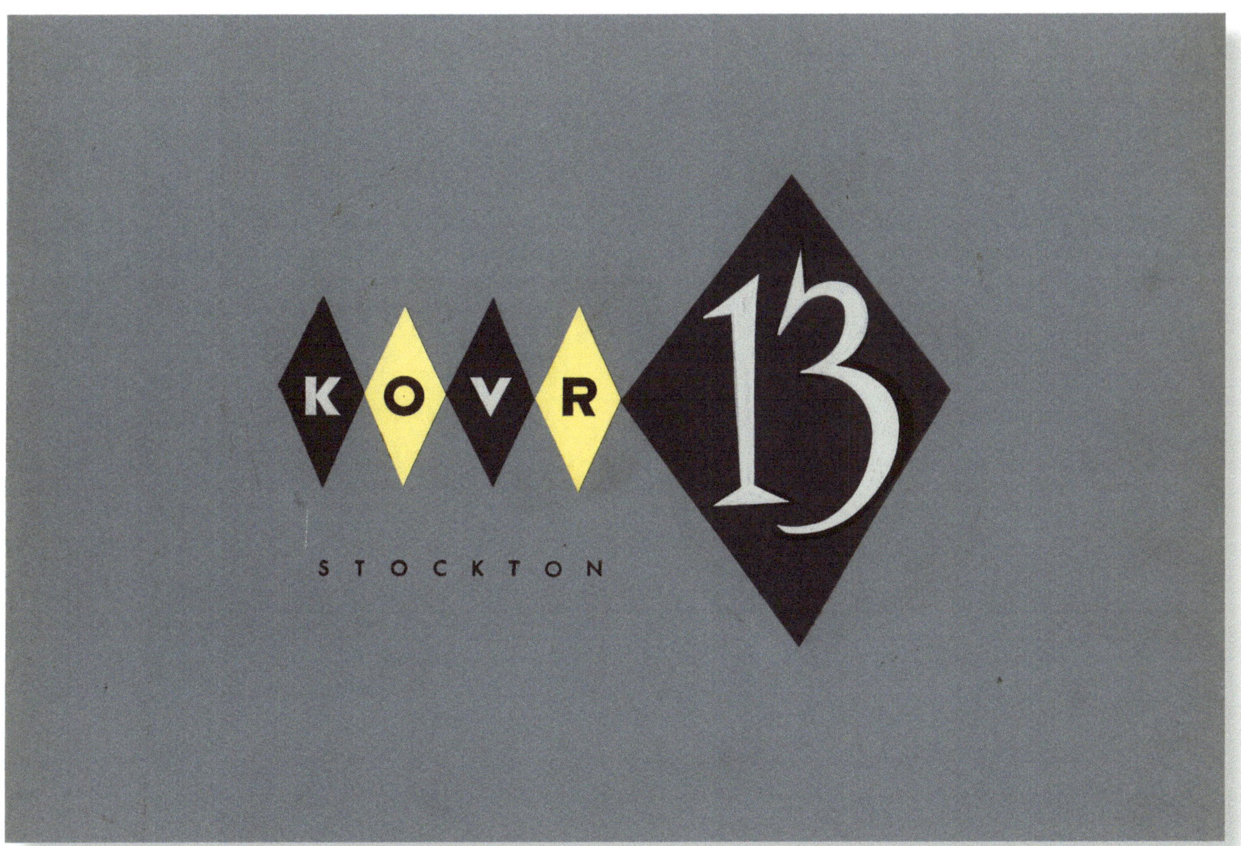

Anita and I lived in a flattop house; two bedrooms, one bath in Lincoln Village, not far from downtown Stockton. Because everything on TV was "live" I worked late, sometimes not getting home til 8 or 9 in the evening. Every day was a learning experience. It was fun.

Late in 1954 KOVR Channel 13 went on the air. TV stations were popping up all over the valley. In the late 1940's there had been a freeze on new TV station licenses. The freeze was lifted in the early fifties. Channel 13 started in Stockton. On of the first graphics on the air was misspelled: "KVOR." I don't remember who was responsible but Dick Block, who had worked at Channel 36 encouraged me to bring my portfolio to KOVR. I did. I was interviewed by the station manager, a very nice guy named Watson. He hired me for $400 a month, not bad money in those days!

My on-the-air days were over and shortly after I left Channel 36 they went bankrupt. Its call letters and channel number were picked up by stations in the San Francisco Bay Area. 13 was owned by the Hoffman Easy Vision Network. Our network was the Dumont Network. Dumont had Jackie Gleason, Bishop Fulton Sheen, Ernie Kovacs and the San Francisco 49ers, but it was weak compared to the three major networks' programming.

Locally we produced a big hour-long show called the "Hoffman Hayride." It was once a week, hosted by Cottonseed Clark, a well known western personality from the 1940's and 50's. Each show had as many as eight production numbers. Each number required a set. For example, for the song "When The Moon Came Over The Mountain" I would create a set of mountains and trees. I used huge rolls of background paper. It came in various colors. I used lecturer's chalk in a variety of colors to create the scenes. By the time I created the eight sets I was covered in chalk dust. I looked like "the decorated man."

We also covered wrestling from the Uptown Arena in downtown Modesto. I was a floorman on the show. I let the wrestlers know when it was time for a commercial. Gorgeous George was one of the stars. The fans loved it, but it was really vaudeville.

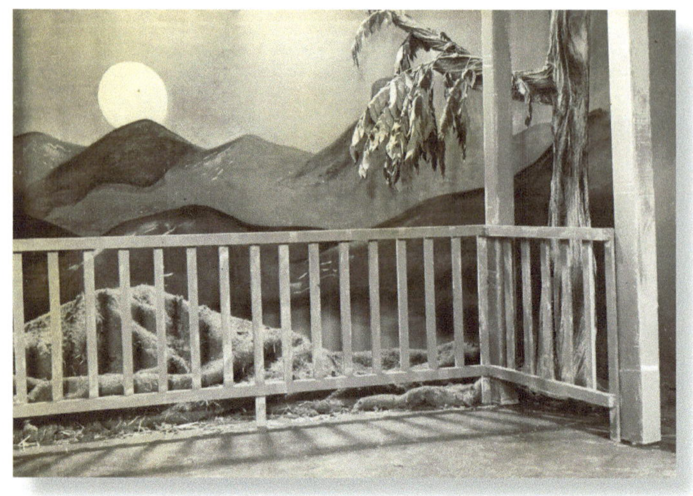

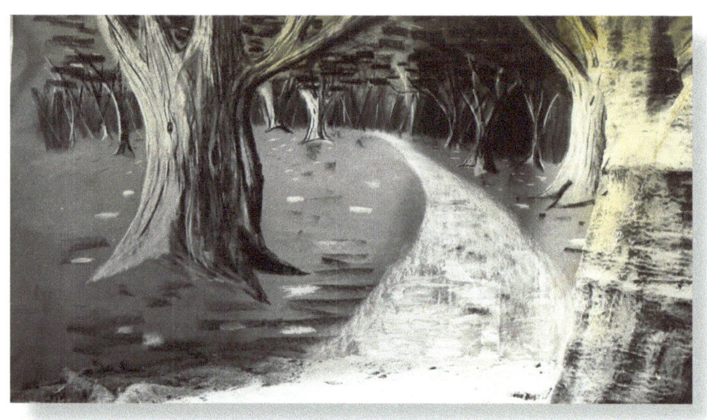

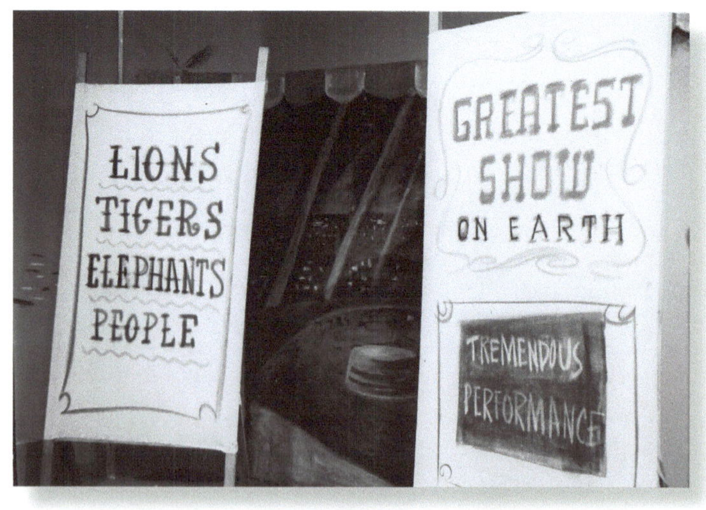

These graphics were called "production numbers." I would produce six or so in a day on seamless paper. I'd start in the morning and work until the start of the show. I'd come home looking like a clown, covered in chalk dust!

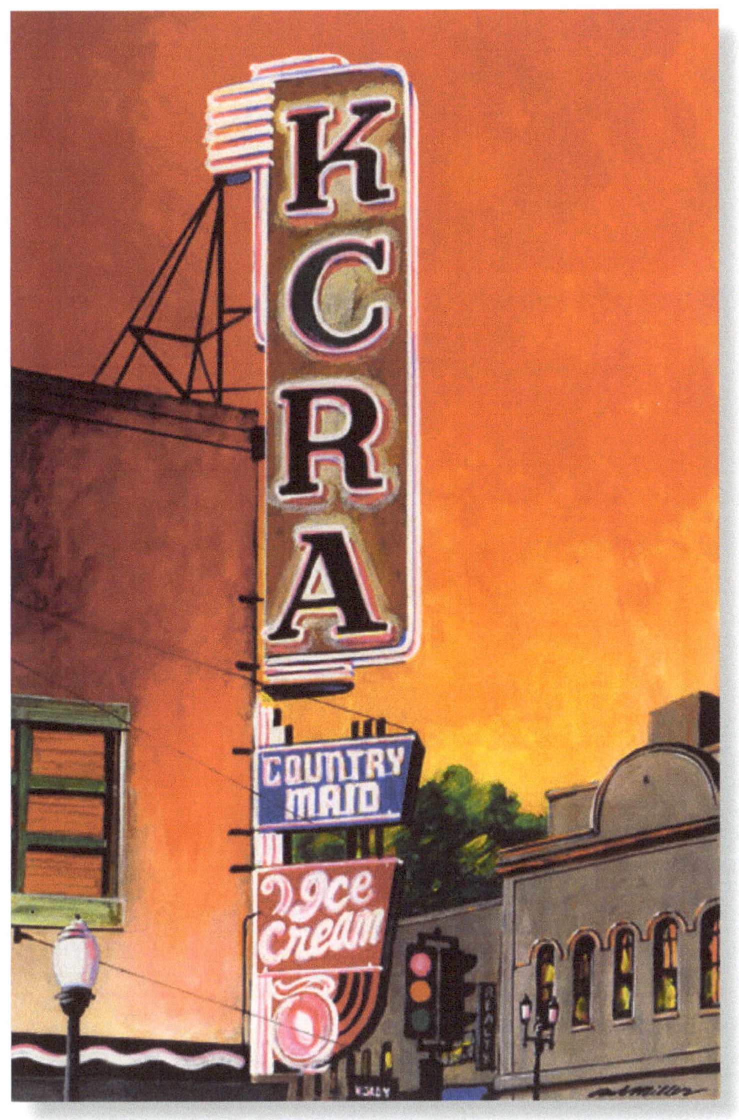

"YOU'RE HIRED, KID!"

In August of 1955 Dick Block said he was interviewing at Channel 3 in Sacramento. My interview was at the KCRA Radio station above the Country Maid restaurant at 11th and J Streets, in Gene Kelly's office. He owned KCRA in partnership with the Hansen family, owners of Crystal Creamery. The interview went well, then he said, "Let's take a walk outside." We did. Standing on the sidewalk he pointed to the the big KCRA neon sign attached to the wall outside his office. He said, "What's that typeface?" I said, "Beton Bold." His reply, "You're hired, kid." And now I was making $450 a month. I started with KCRA the day they went on the air in September, 1955.

The art department had not been planned, for it was a tar paper covered roof with no wall on one side. It had been used as a receiving dock for Crystal's delivery trucks. They added a wall and heating and air conditioning. It was very raw but very functional.

It was great. Everything was new. The original on-the-air graphics were designed by a bay area ad agency. I thought they were pretty awful. I designed a new logo using a large Clarendon type face number 3. It was used for over 20 years.

Then there were sets to build. News programs, Milly Sullivan's Valley Playhouse, Bosun Bill, Skipper Stu, Captain Sacto... and then there were commercial cards to do and TV guide ads... and then newspaper ads for ratings week. We were very productive. Later, when we went to color we invented a technique of creating color out of black and white promotional photos.

Every day there was something new. Some did not always go well. In November of 1955 there were terrible floods in the Marysville-Yuba City area. We had film to show, but we needed to superimpose copy explaining the conditions. For example, "Yuba City, 4 feet above flood stage." My sign machine, which had been ordered, had not been delivered. I was using wax-on letters for some of my graphics on the air. It was called 'Formatt.' We used a machine called a Bellopticon to put opaque graphics on the air. It took 4" x 5" cards. I used black cards and white wax-on letters to convey the information. We put them in the Bellopticon. The lights went on and all the letters fell off the cards! The heat from the lights was too much for the wax. It was Sacramento's first animation! Tom Breen, the program director was not happy with me. Shortly after, my sign machine arrived.

"Many talented people were at the station-- Stu Nahan, Harry Martin, Milly Sullivan, Betty Stanley, Bob Whitten, Bob Wilkins and Stan Atkinson."

Ken Nagle was chief floorman. He was super at building sets I designed. He stayed at the station for over 20 years. In the 1970's he opened a bookstore in Old Sacramento. Many talented people were at the station when I was there. Stu Nahan, Bill Rase, Harry Martin, Milly Sullivan, Betty Stanley, Bob Whitten, Bob Wilkins and Stan Atkinson. Of those, only Stan is alive and well....and selling hearing aids in his spare time!

There were also many talented people behind the cameras. Tom Breen was the program director. Dave Hume, the news director. Herb Hartman was chief engineer. Bill Thorpe presented the weather for many years, and was followed by Harry Geise.

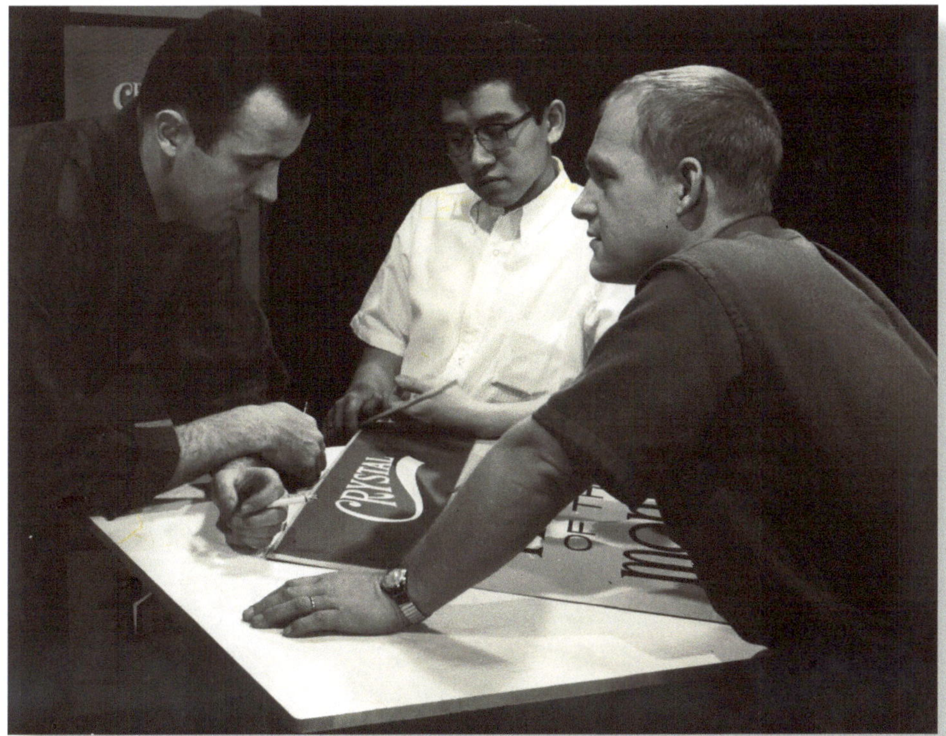

Don Chandler, Bob Matsumoto and I review art for an ad for Crystal Creamery. This piece was probably for an in-store display. When we took on a client for TV, we also provided all kinds of traditional advertising services. Once we got a client, we provided them with everything. We were a full service ad agency, and with the power of television, landing clients was easy.

I hired Don Chandler, a talented illustrator, to join me in the art department at Channel 3 in the late 1950's. Don's mother Edna Walker Chandler was a very popular childrens' book author. She wrote a series called Cowboy Sam, another called Cowboy Andy, as well as over twenty other titles.

As a favor to me for hiring her son she invited me to illustrate a new book she was writing called The New Red Jacket. I jumped at the opportunity. The book was published by Whitman. I am not positive, but I think it was the most popular children's book published in 1962. I was paid $400 for my efforts, in those days almost a month's salary! It was enough to pay for wall-to-wall carpeting in our home. The book is available in battered condition on Amazon.com for as little as $1.98.

Bob Kelly asked me to look at the portfolio of a young student from Sacramento City College. His name was Bob Matsumoto. Bob Kelly was very impressed with his work and said he would like to add him to our art department. I looked at the portfolio and was equally impressed.

I don't remember how long Bob was with us but he added new depth and style to our list of capabilities. After working with us for a while, Bob Kelly came to Bob with an offer: he would like to pay his tuition to Art Center, the most prestigious design school in America--and very expensive. There was a provision and that was, after graduation from the school when he became successful in the advertising world, that he do the same for a young, talented artist.

FROM BOB MATSUMOTO

1960. Fresh out of the Navy, I was pursuing a career in "Commercial Art." I met Bob; he reviewed my portfolio and felt very lucky to be hired as an apprentice for his KCRA art department.

Along with Bob and Don Chandler, I was given their encouragement and every opportunity to fulfill my goal of attending the prestigious Art Center College of Design.

Bob gave me assignments that challenged my learning process. Projects that inspired me to bring my limited skills to a higher professional level. On many occasions, he would take me aside and demonstrate how to make my work better. To meet the standards to help build his vision for the KCRA brand. Hearing his philosophy about life, family, raising children, accepting reality, helping me to find a path for my future. His wisdom helped me to "grow-up" during all our hours of working together. (In between his humorous stories and the laughter.)

Shortly thereafter, Bob Kelly, one of the station owners, was very generous in offering me a loan to attend Art Center. I was accepted into their program on a very high semester level, mainly because of the portfolio examples I had created at KCRA.

Upon graduating, luck entered again. I began a career at the famous creative advertising agency Doyle Dane Bernbach, during the Mad Men era. Throughout my years as a Creative Director/Art Director, Bob Miller's past influence and his work ethics were always part of the recognition that fortunately came my way. (The Permanent Collection of The Museum of Modern Art, The American Advertising Museum, a documentary exhibited at The Smithsonian.)

My huge ego treasures these honors. In another huge way, I treasure my friendship with Bob. Reflecting back, a lot of years have flowed between us since our first meeting in 1960. Somehow we've always managed to see each other via lengthy phone conversations and emails. Hearing about his latest art exhibits. His new paintings. His home plumbing problems.

Always keeping in touch with Bob. Maybe that's my way of holding onto something special. In my case, knowing I have a Special Friendship. And a Special Mentor.

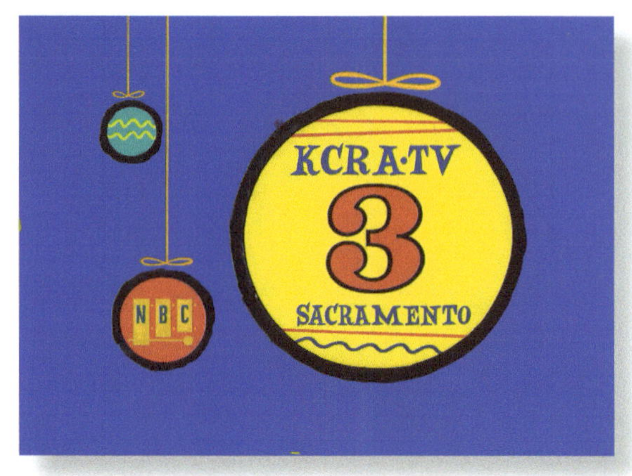

Bob Matsumoto took him up on his offer and after graduation became very successful. For a time he worked for Doyle Dane Bernbach in New York City and then he went back to Los Angeles and opened an advertising agency, Matsumoto and Herzog. Bob became the success Bob Kelly knew he would and kept his part of the bargain he made. He offered the same opportunity and aid to a young, talented (and poor) aspiring artist.

We were lucky to have Bob Kelly as an employer. He was not only a visionary but he had a remarkable eye for talent as well. Don Chandler, Bob Matsumoto and I have remained good friends for over fifty years.

FROM DON CHANDLER

My good friend Bob Miller was art director at KCRA-TV. Thanks to his decision to hire me, we have joint custody of many memorable moments. Some were cause to celebrate; others were ordinary. Then there were moments that felt like "train wrecks" in our career journey. One of the third order that Bob shared with me was instrumental in my unwarranted fear of Ewing Charlie Kelly, whom I had yet to meet. Fear was a dysfunctional companion to awe, which would eventually be dealt with in the court of time and reason. My awe for Ewing Kelly stemmed from his success in growing a small one-man advertising agency into an NBC affiliate television station to be reckoned with.

While Bob found humor in the telling of a particular story, he at the same time succeeded in instilling a wrenching trepidation that haunted my early months of employment. Whenever Ewing Kelly popped up on my radar, I would bend low over my work of the moment, the better to be overlooked.

Bob told of an encounter he had with Ewing Kelly as a young art director new to the station. Calling upon pre-KCRA experience and elements of design he had learned as a student of advertising design in college, Bob developed an ad concept to promote news. The ad began with a bold, simple headline tied to an appropriate photo image supported by minimal text and the KCRA-TV Channel 3 logo, surrounded by an abundance of white space intended to make the ad stand out on a busy newspaper page.

Inside the "oval office" of Ewing Kelly, Bob gave the ad his best sales pitch, pointing out the use of white space and its inherent value. Mr. Kelly's challenge was instantaneous.

"Why all the wasted space?"

"It's white space. It's not wasted when it isolates the message from busy surrounding copy."

"That's wasted space, kid! You know how much ad space costs?"

"A clean and succinct message gets ten times more readership than busy clutter." Bob's conviction was supported by rich vocabulary and nerves of a gladiator but served only to provoke a roar of displeasure from Mr. Kelly.

"Ten times nothing is nothing!!!" He barked. In emphasis of his point, Mr. Kelly spun Bob around, grabbed him by the seat of his pants and thrust him through his office doorway past Irma Davis' desk, into the hall.

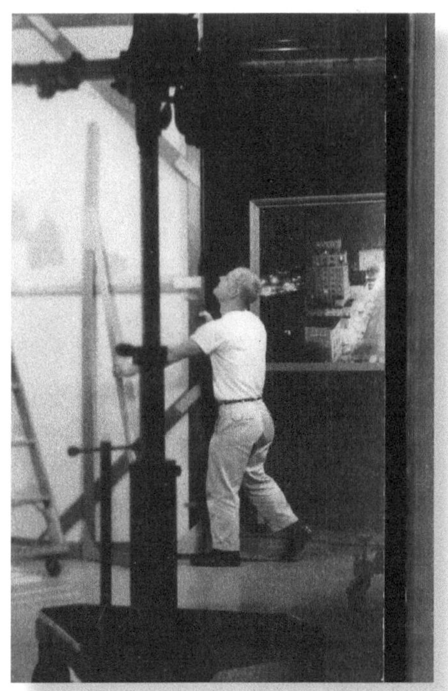

Getting a set ready for a show at KCRA.

FROM BURT WILSON

I first met Bob when I went to work at KCRA-TV in 1959 as commercial writer-producer. Bob headed the art department there and I was surprised when I made my first visit to his art habitat and couldn't see him! His head didn't stick up above the drawing table!

But the little guy turned out to be a giant in my life as I could always count on him to come up with a graphic I needed for a commercial. He only made positive suggestions and it was a pleasure to work with him.

In fact, when I opened my own advertising agency nine months later, Bob became my Art Director. My ad agency, Mediascope Advertising, Ltd., was Sacramento's first broadcast agency, but, of course I had to do newspaper ads, too, and Bob was just the guy for the job. I learned a lot from him and was even able to do a few print ads myself after awhile.

Bob and I have remained the best of friends since our salad days and now that we're way past dessert and coffee we still get together frequently. He is as much a part of my life now as ever and I can't imagine life without him.

In 1958 I was getting restless and took my portfolio to Los Angeles. My goal was "Big Time TV." In those days it was the country's third largest market and where most TV programming originated. I was offered a job as an art director on The Dinah Shore Show (See the USA in Your Chevrolet!). I was elated, but when I told Anita, she said, "I am not going to raise my children in Los Angeles." As a result we have been in the same house on Tobari Court in Sacramento's north area ever since. Who knows what might have happened to our lives had we moved south. The children are grown and live productive and fulfilling lives. Maybe Anita was right.

"Where the News Comes First," was Bob Kelly's passion. KCRA was sold to Hearst News in 1999. Gene Kelly died of a heart atttack in 1960. Bob Kelly was the President; brother Jon the General Manager.

I was at Channel 3 for ten years. It was a great opportunity to grow and learn professionally. Management gave me incredible freedom. We developed many graphic techniques that were imitated by other stations in the area and other markets.

In the early 60's I attended a conference in Phoenix. Flying in we could see a huge handpainted billboard. The TV station copied my design exactly, simply substituting their local call letters and channel number!

I recall Tom Breen telling about a PSA (Pacific Southwest Airways) flight from Los Angeles. He said on the approach to Sacramento he could see the spots of dayglo orange from my billboards all over the landscape below. In the early days of broadcasting most stations were owned locally. Channel 10 was owned by Sacramento investors when it went on the air; Channel 13 was owned briefly by the McClatchy family; and Channel 3 was owned by the Kelly Family.

The Federal Communication Commission had a restriction on how many outlets a business could own. In 1996 all that changed. The restriction was dropped and as a result a company like Clear Channel Communications can own over a thousand outlets. The ability to spread propaganda is in the hands of a few giant corporations. Local ownership has almost vanished.

Currently, there is almost no radio like the radio of the 1930's. Modesto's radio station KTRB went on the air in the early 1930's. It was owned by Bill Bates. Bill was also on the air with shows like "Auction Block." It was about as folksy as anything one can imagine. My father would call in and tell Bill he had a manure spreader for sale. Listeners would respond and finally a price was agreed on and the spreader was sold. It was talky and friendly. There was no political bellyaching, just casual conversation and give-and-take negotiating.

KTRB also featured Bob Wills and His Texas Playboys and The Maddux Brothers and Rose, all now part of the Country Western Hall of Fame. Anita went to business school with Rose Maddux. Rose was a practical person. In those days show business didn't pay too well.

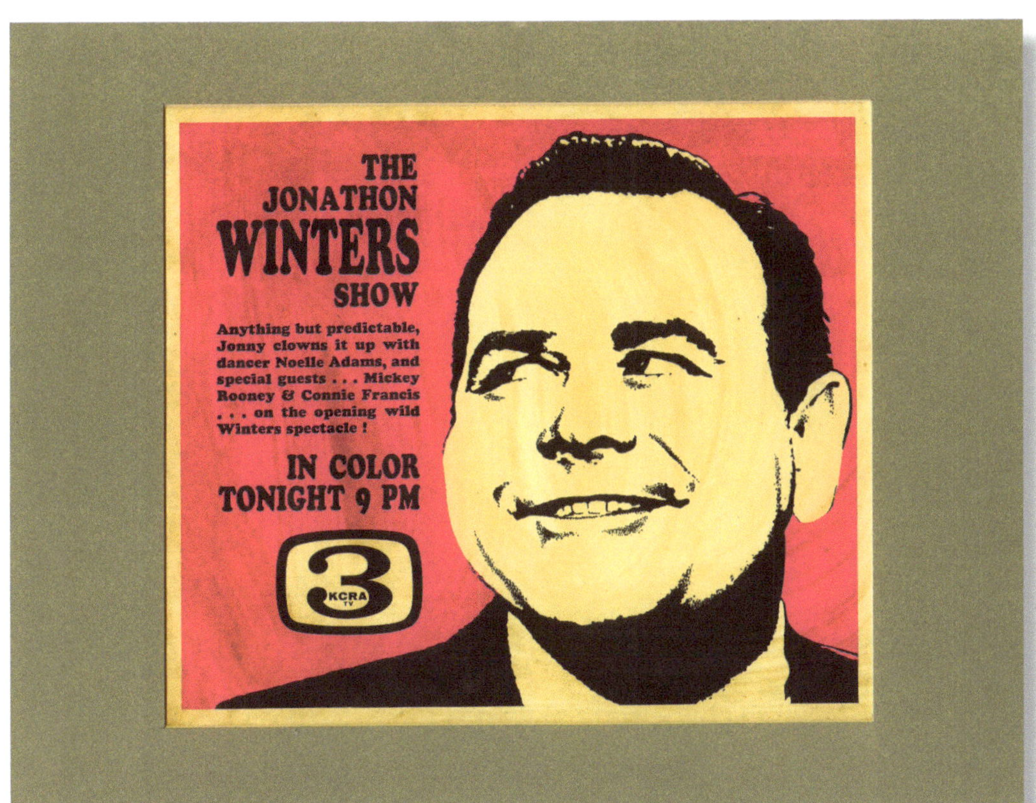

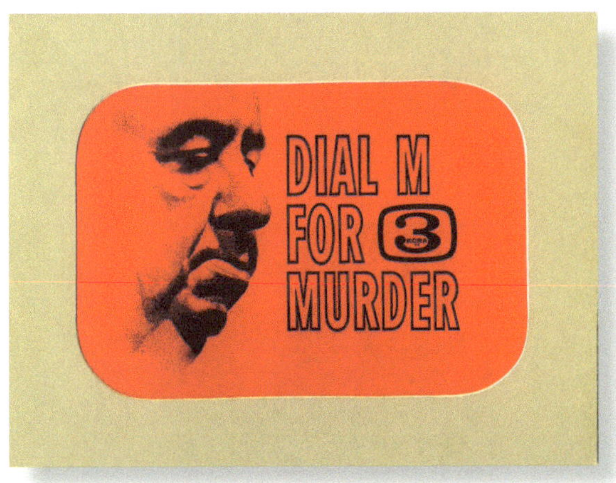

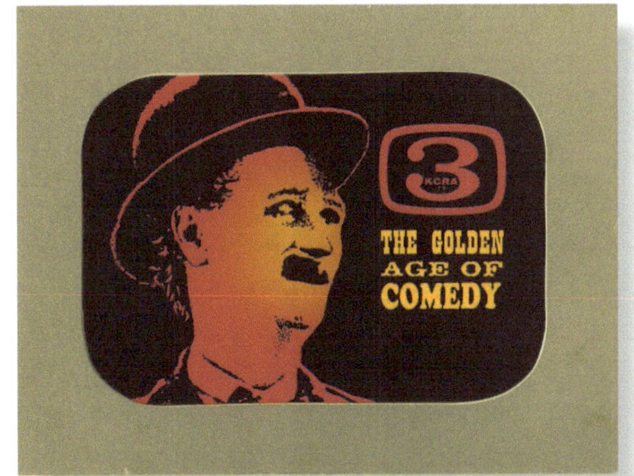

These are "promotional slides," used to promote upcoming shows. Our original paste-ups were shot onto a clear film positive. Then we colored the film using acetate, color board or spray paint and placed them in the mat designed for television. The slides were then shot on video tape for broadcast.

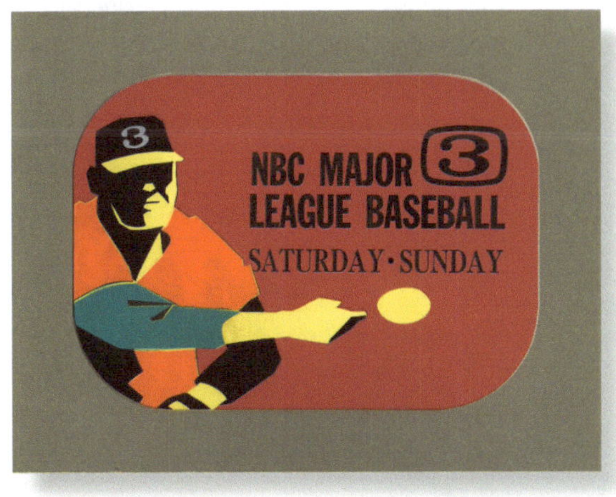

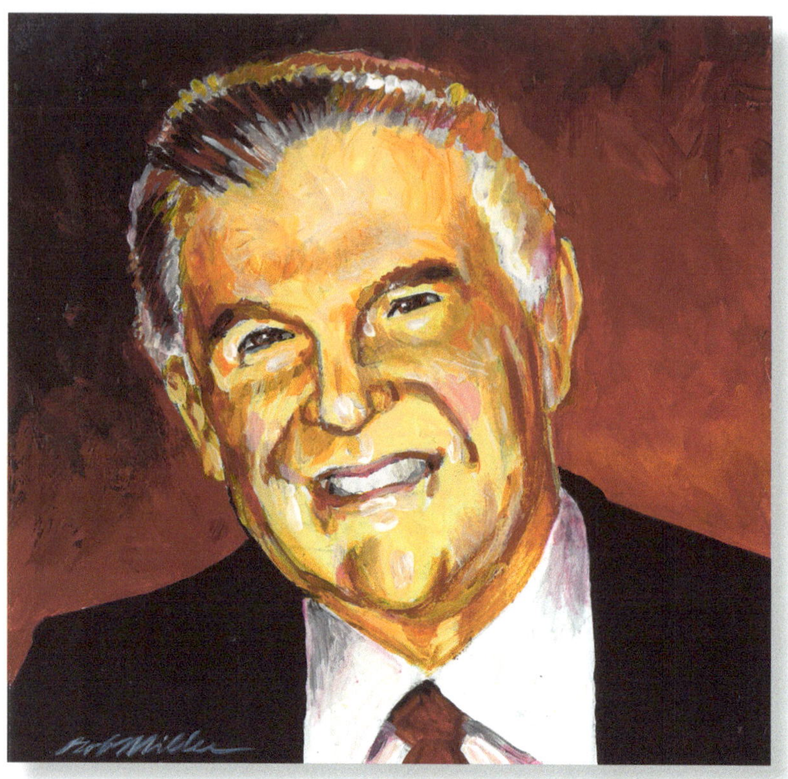

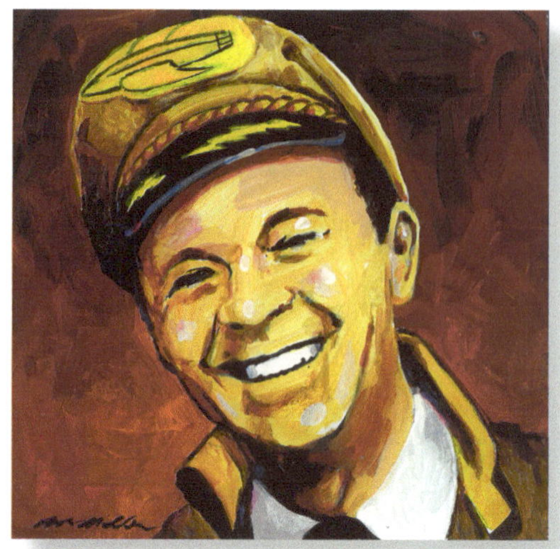

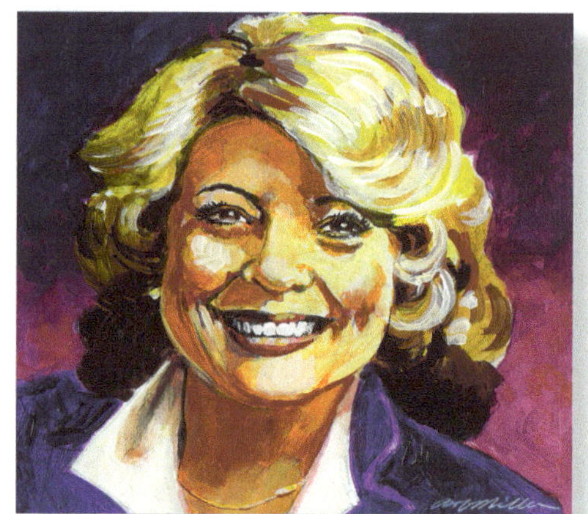

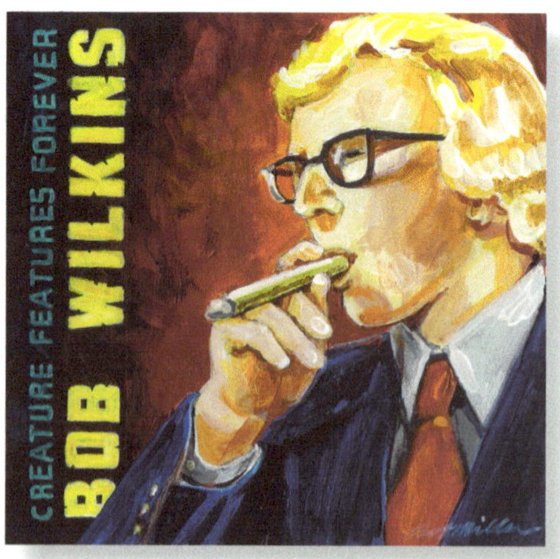

Top to bottom:
Harry Martin
Bette Vasquez
Bob Wilkins

FROM STAN ATKINSON

'Tis reaching a'ways back in the narrowing crevices of my noggin...but I do remember some imagery...and even facts.

The imagery hasn't changed that much... it's a small perpetual flash of human activity. A manner of speech that was often as rapid...and all coming from an always upbeat and positive life-force. Amazing, considering what he was always asked to do. Back in that day (the late 50's and early 60's) before the remarkable things that technology would bring into graphics et al...the tools were very basic and even by comparison... klutsy.

But Bob, as wizard of show cards and rubber cement could get virtually anything done that was needed for the TV screen. In record time and with a first Class "look."

And in the end product his immense creativity and artistic skill was always amazing. In fact, a lot of it lives on. The Channel 3 and River City Bank logos still smack of his original creations, or at least I see it. And his work today.... just WOW!

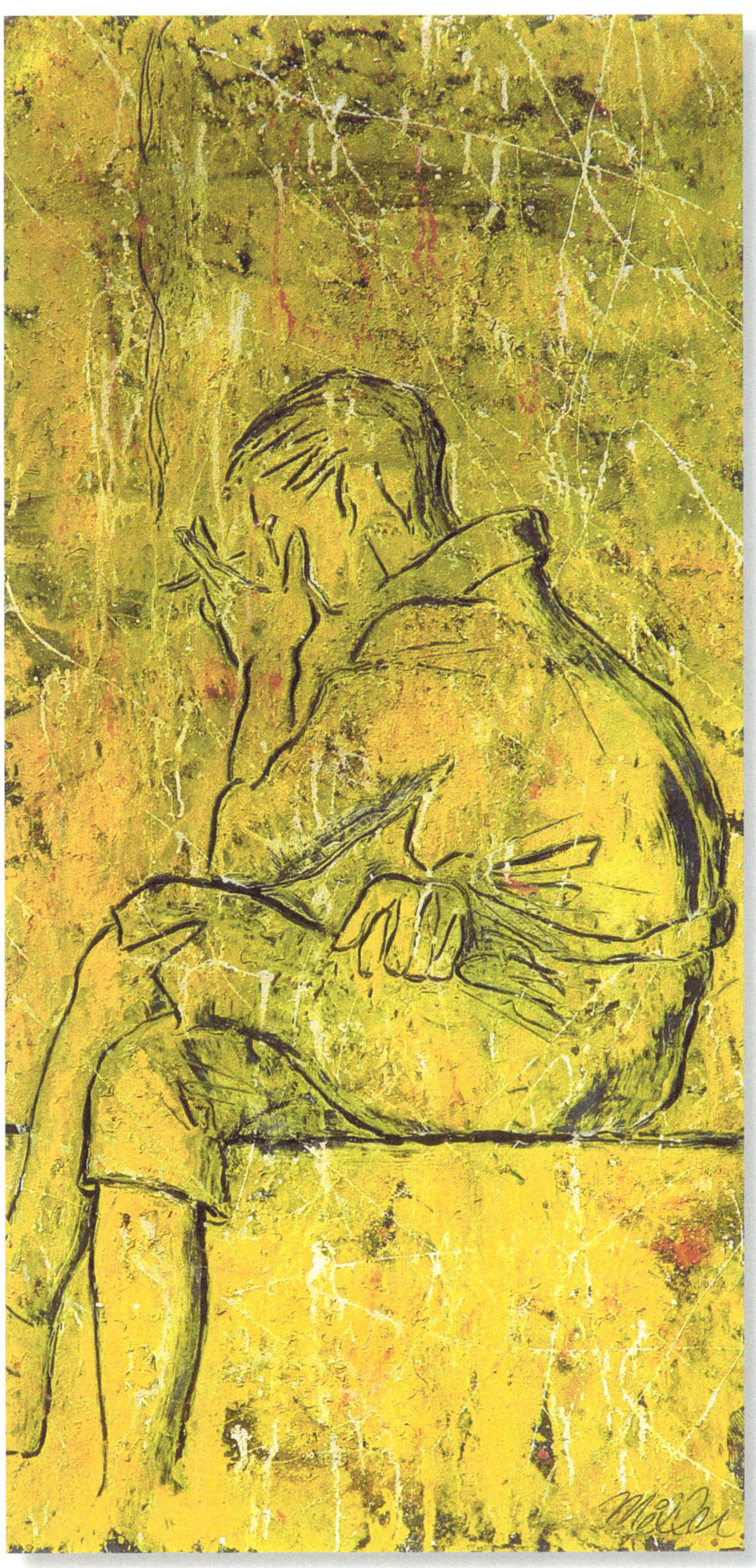

My "Artist's Statement"

I am compelled to paint and draw. The compulsion feeds no higher philosophical purpose. I simply like to do it.

I seldom miss a day of painting. I have a pleasant, but cluttered studio attached to my home. I like getting up every morning. I get my coffee, bathe, shave, read the Sacramento Bee newspaper, and then go to my studio and start painting... sometimes on a picture that is part of a theme for a particular show, or a subject that simply strikes my fancy.

Drawing and sketching enhances travel. When taking snapshops I frequently cannot remember what the subjects were when I return home. When I sketch I can remember almost every single moment. While sketching people comment on the quality of your work; once in a while even take you for a glass of wine when you are done. I have many sketchbooks filled with travel drawings and rich memories.

I also enjoy the occasional assigned projects: a wine label or a painting commission.

I look forward to going to my studio almost every day (except when I pay the monthly bills or do taxes).

My philosophy is "Life is better when you're having fun."

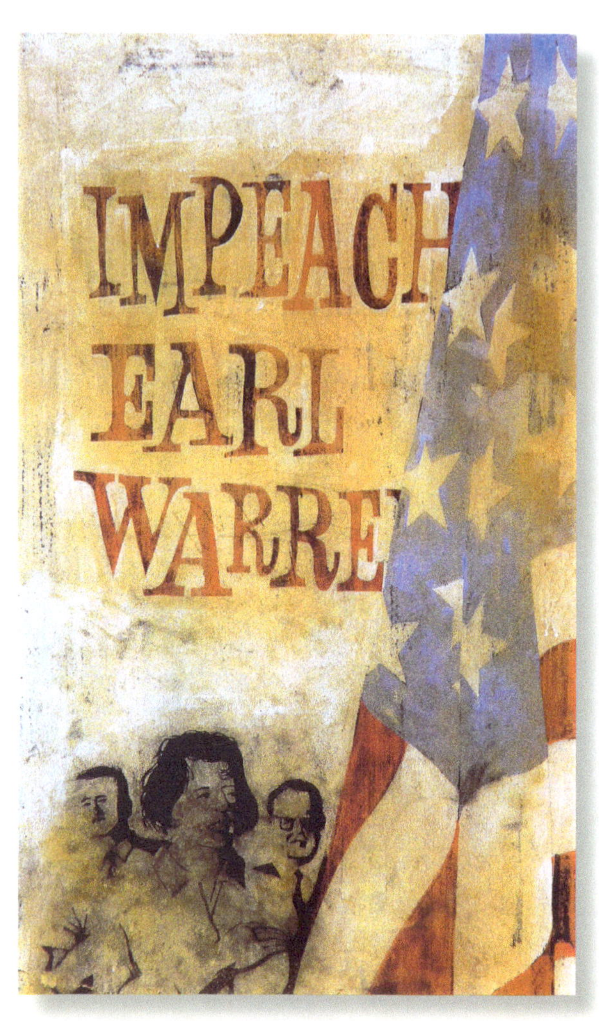
IMPEACH
EARL
WARRE

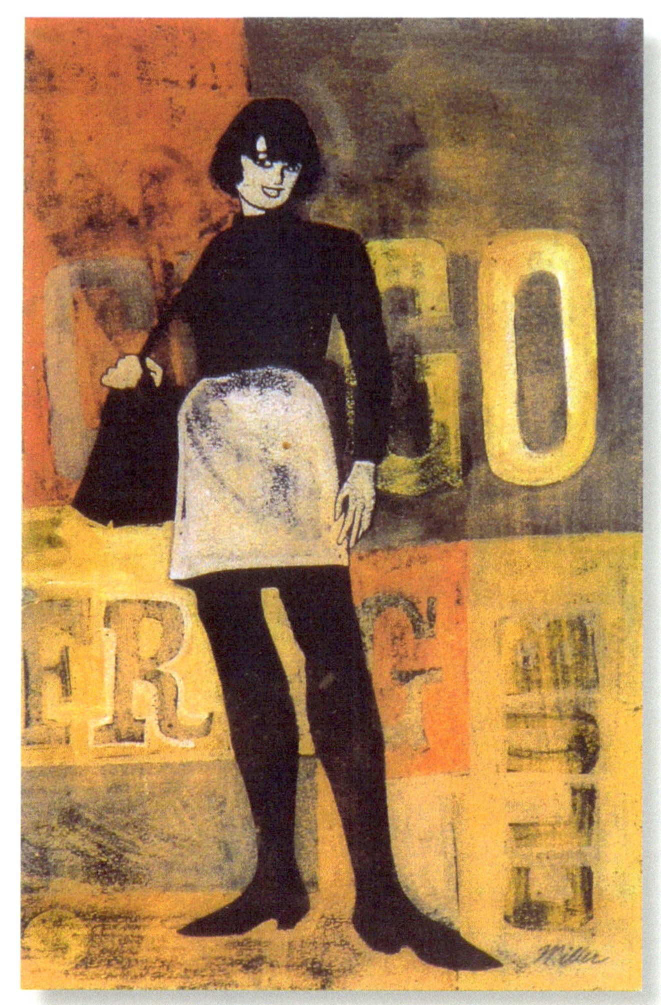
GO

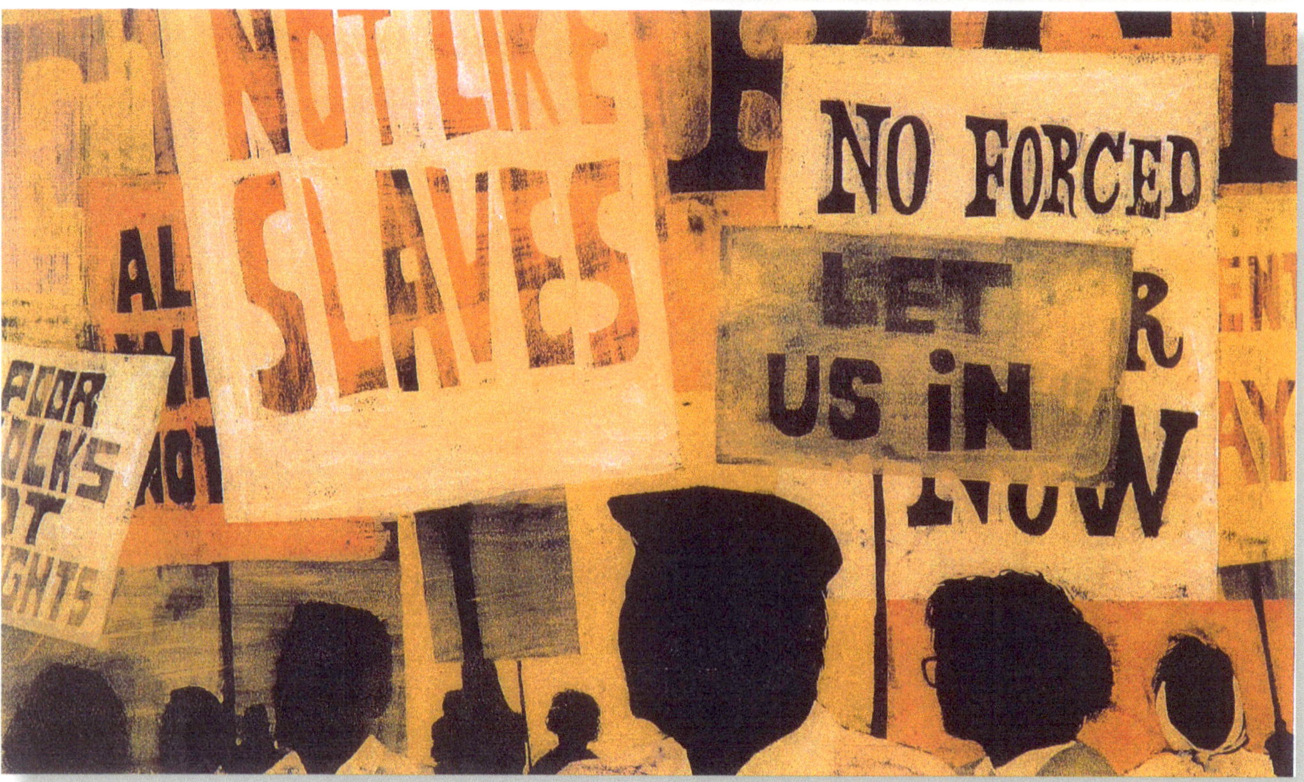
NOT LIKE
SLAVES
NO FORCED
LET
US IN
NOW

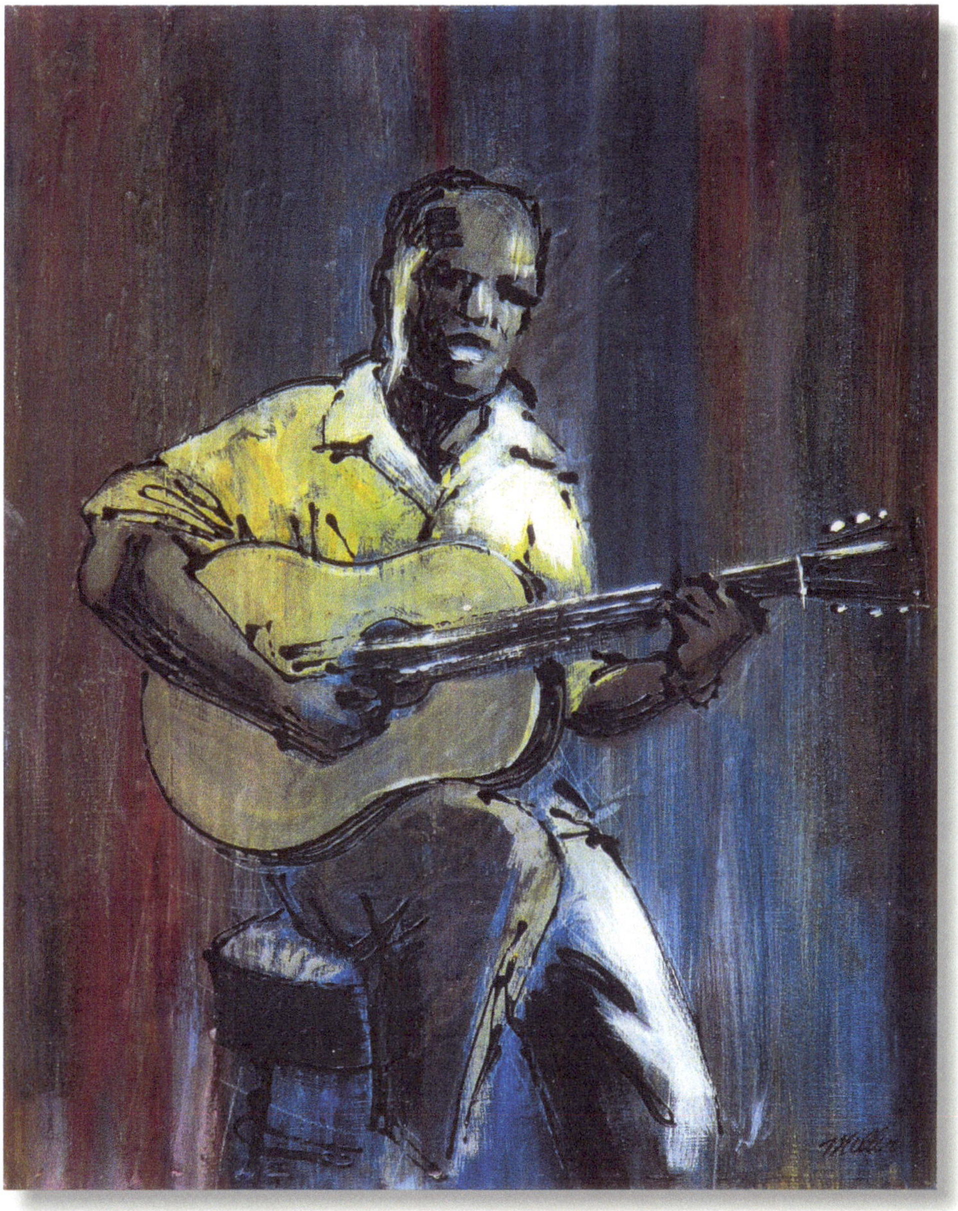

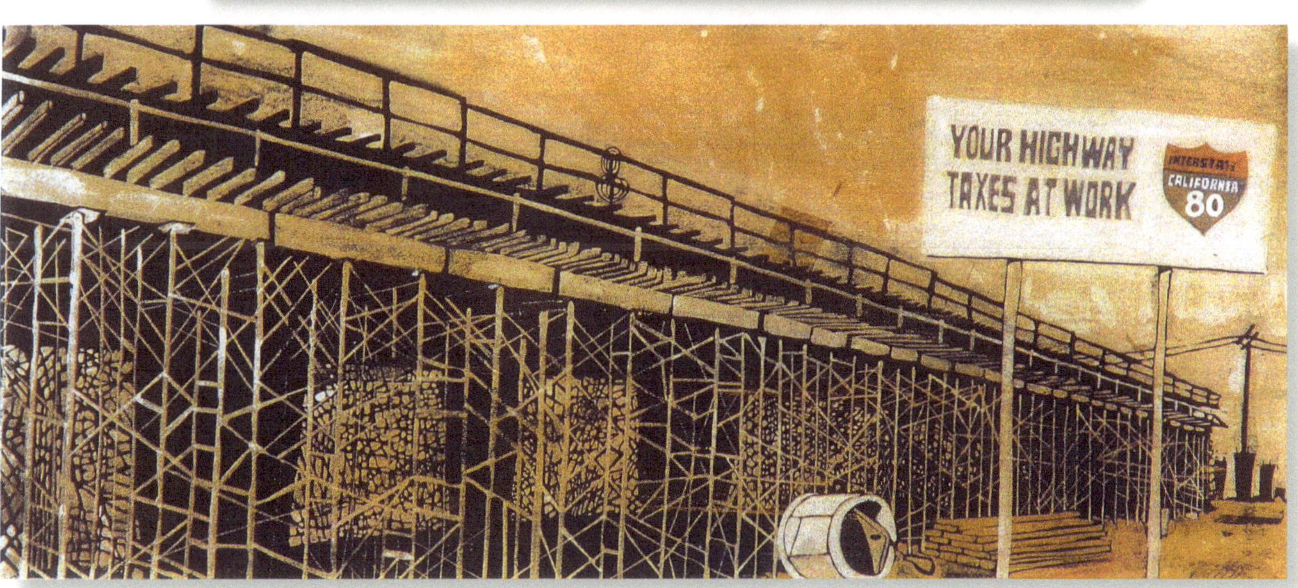
YOUR HIGHWAY
TAXES AT WORK
INTERSTATE
CALIFORNIA
80

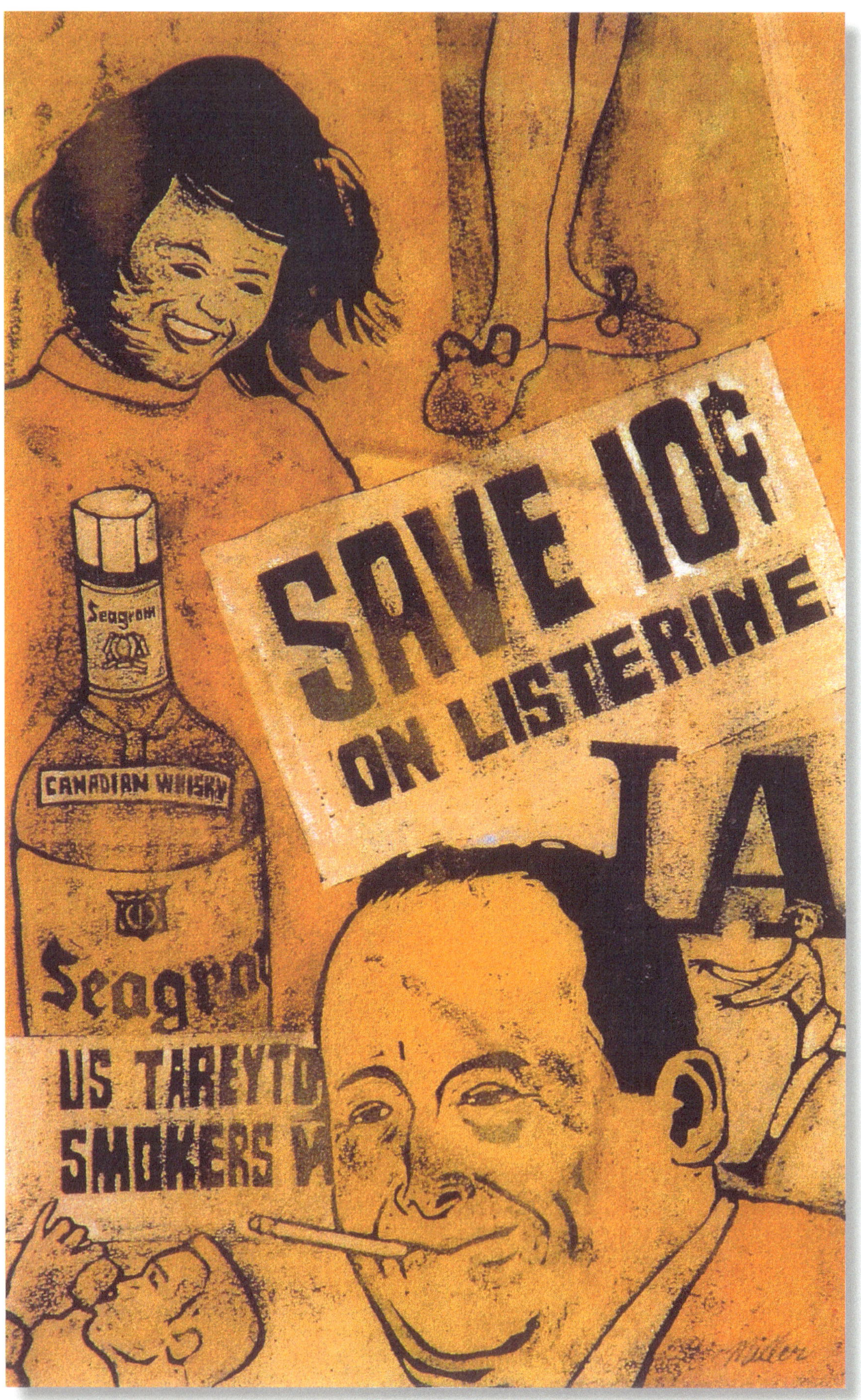
SAVE 10¢
ON LISTERINE
LA
Seagram
CANADIAN WHISKY
Seagra
US TAREYTO
SMOKERS W
Miller

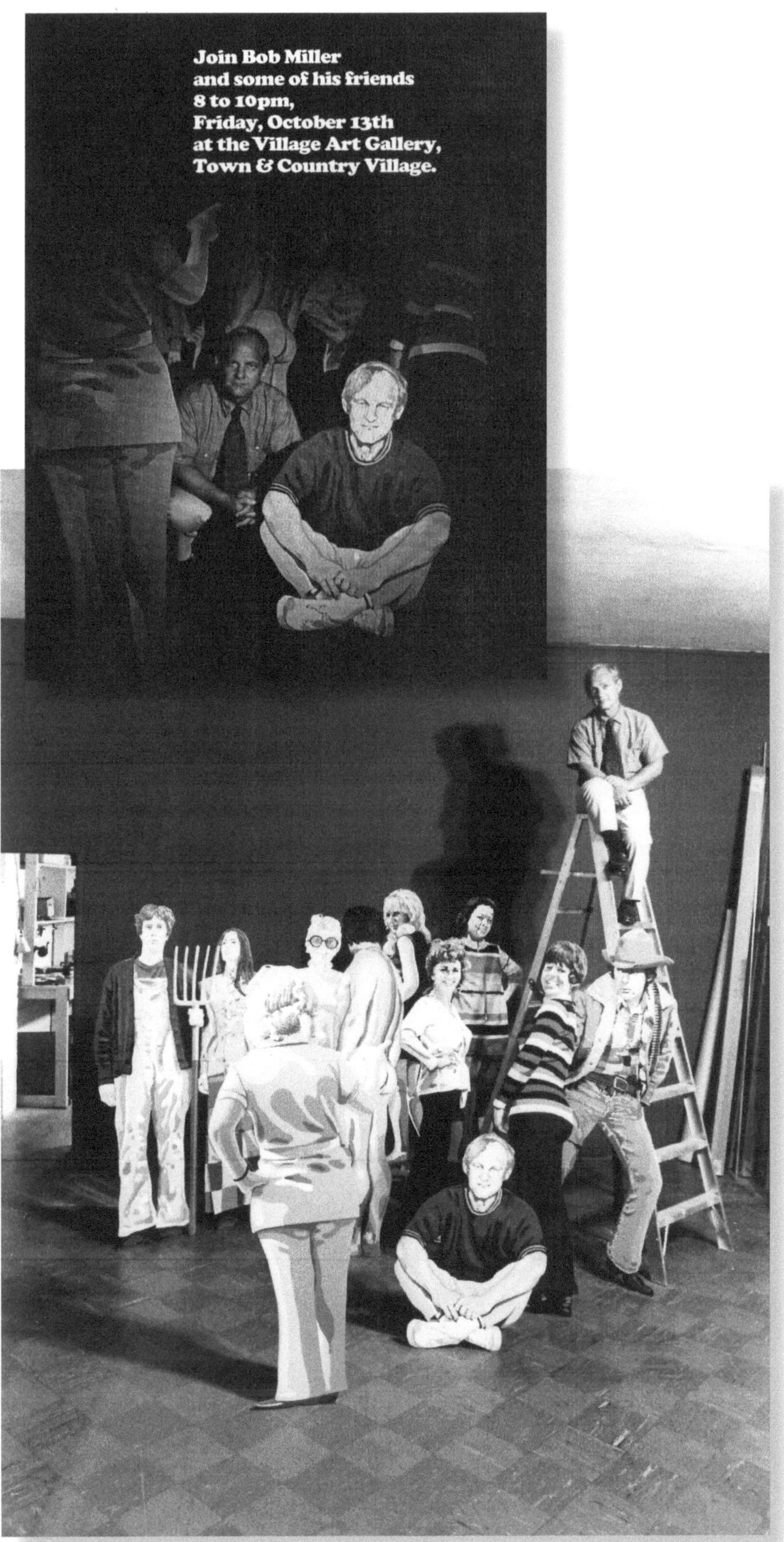

Cut-out paintings of friends I made for a show. That's Mike and Lindy Dunlavey at the far left in an "American Gothic" pose. I am cross legged in front and up on the ladder.

FROM MIKE DUNLAVEY

I've known Bob Miller a long, long time. When I was a kid--in the 50's--my favorite TV show was "Miss Patch" or something like that and I used to faithfully watch it.

My favorite part of the show was this guy, this artist called Uncle Bobby. He had this big pad and he would do a little scribble and then he'd turn it into something.

They'd have art contests. In fact, my dad, Edward--an accomplished watercolorist--used to enter the contests, too. He would sign his entry "Eddie" Dunlavey. I'm sure his were the first thrown out every time because you could tell they were done by a talented artist!

Anyway, one time, I was about 11, we had to draw beetles. I entered and won first prize! The TV show was in Stockton. My parents drove me down in our brand new, two tone green Plymouth Belvedere.

It turned out, another winner showed up and we flipped a coin--two out of three tosses--to see who would win first place. The other kid did. The highlight though, was I got to meet this artist character, my hero Uncle Bobby.

Years later, I had graduated from college and was having many one man art shows. One was at Town and Country Village. Bob Miller came to the show. I knew of him from his background at Channel 3 and the Art Directors and Artists Club. As he was talking about his background he mentioned the show on Channel 36.

"You're Uncle Bobby?!?!"

We have remained close friends ever since. He was my hero when I was a kid and he still is.

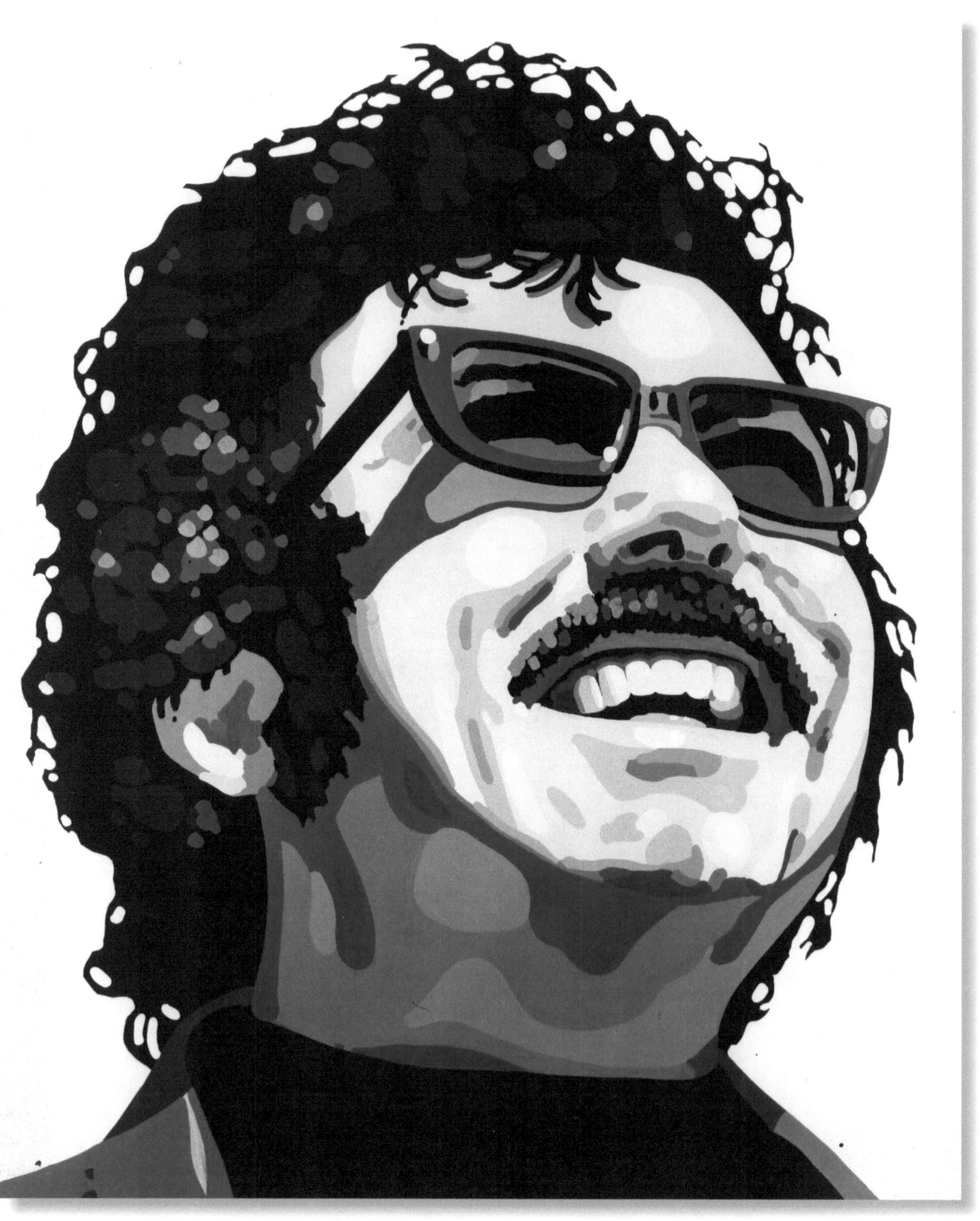

The next three images are large stylized portraits that were the rage in the 1970's.
This is Don Chandler. The following pages are Nancy Krier and Chuck Hillis. I made a lot of them.

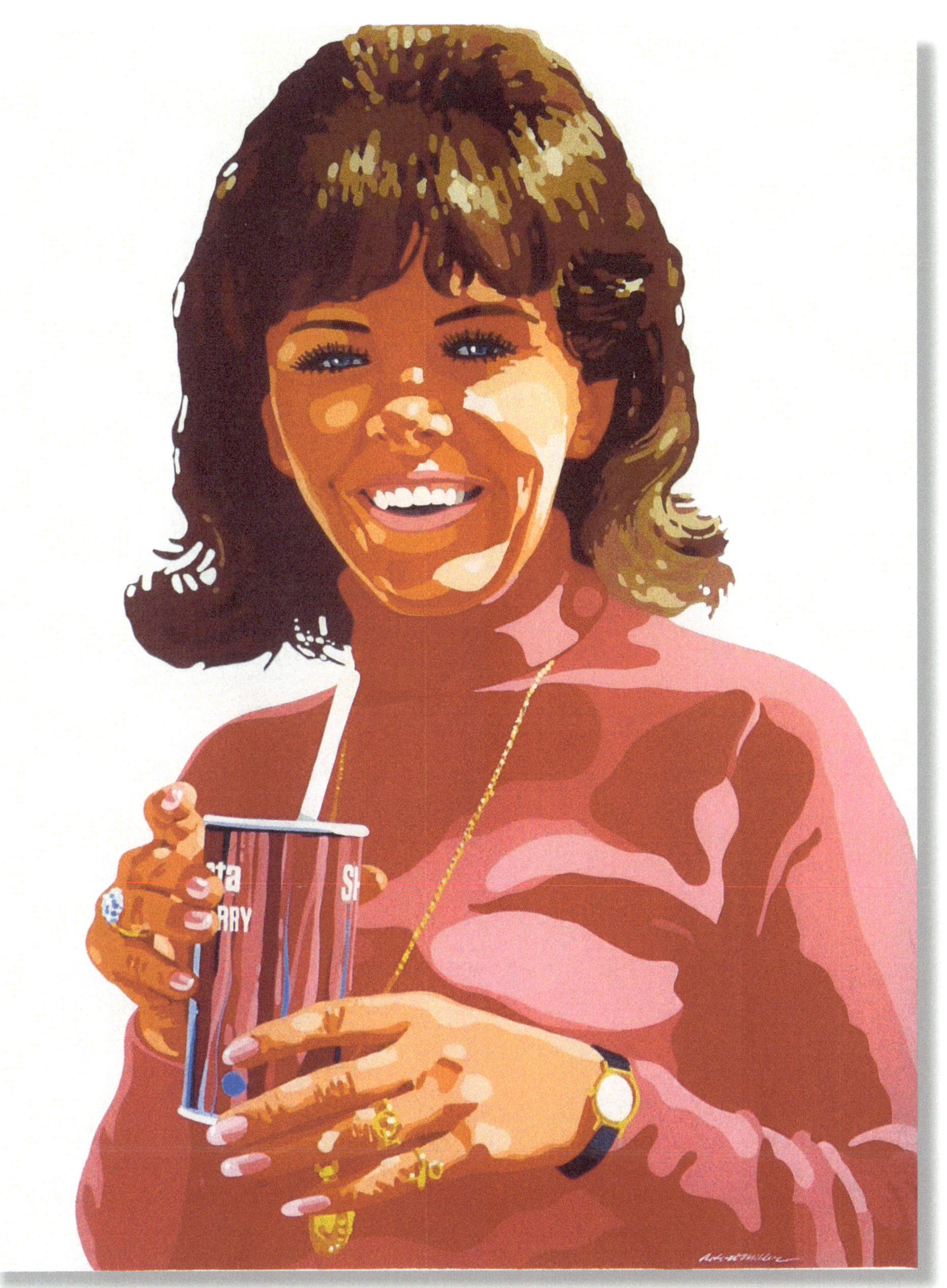

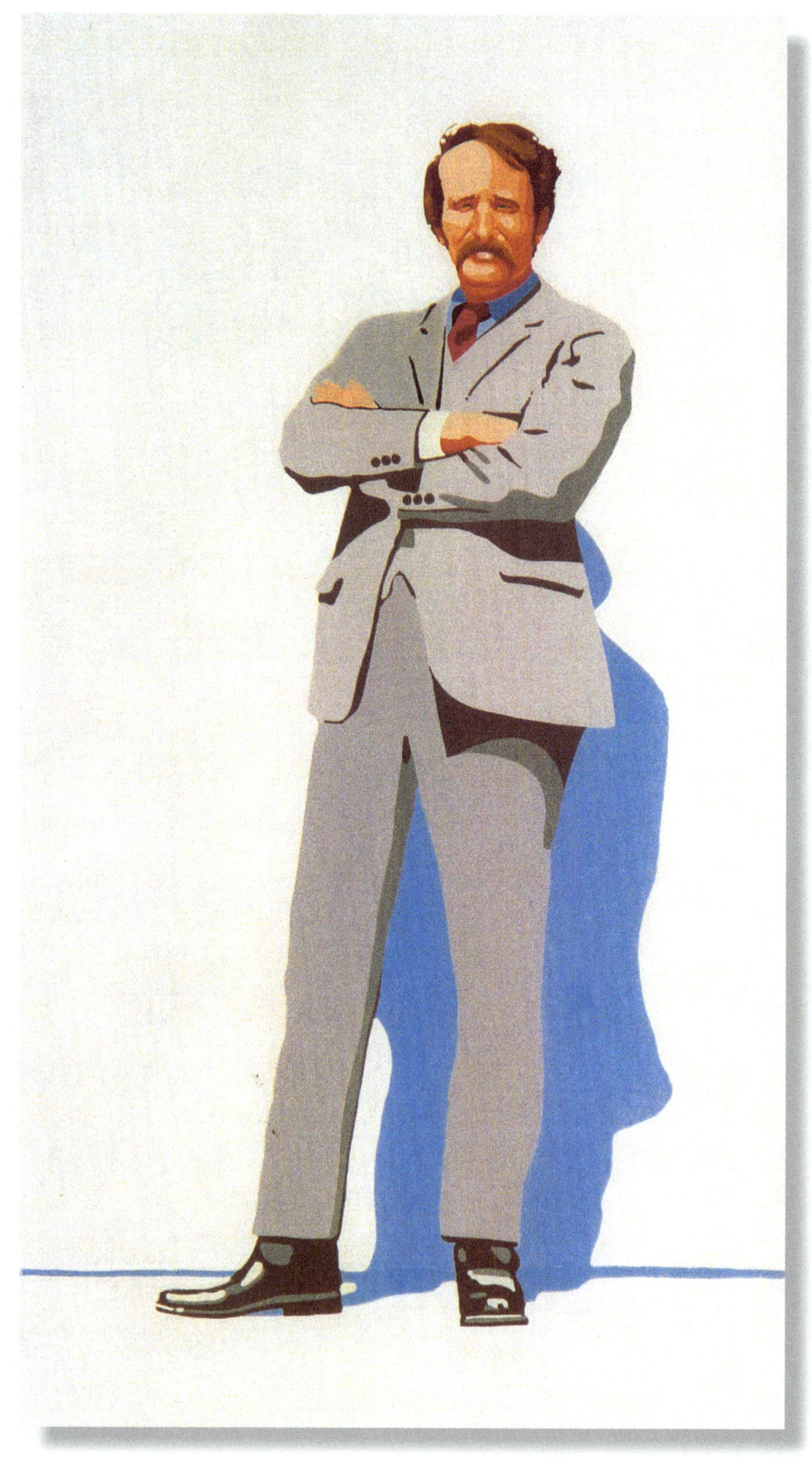

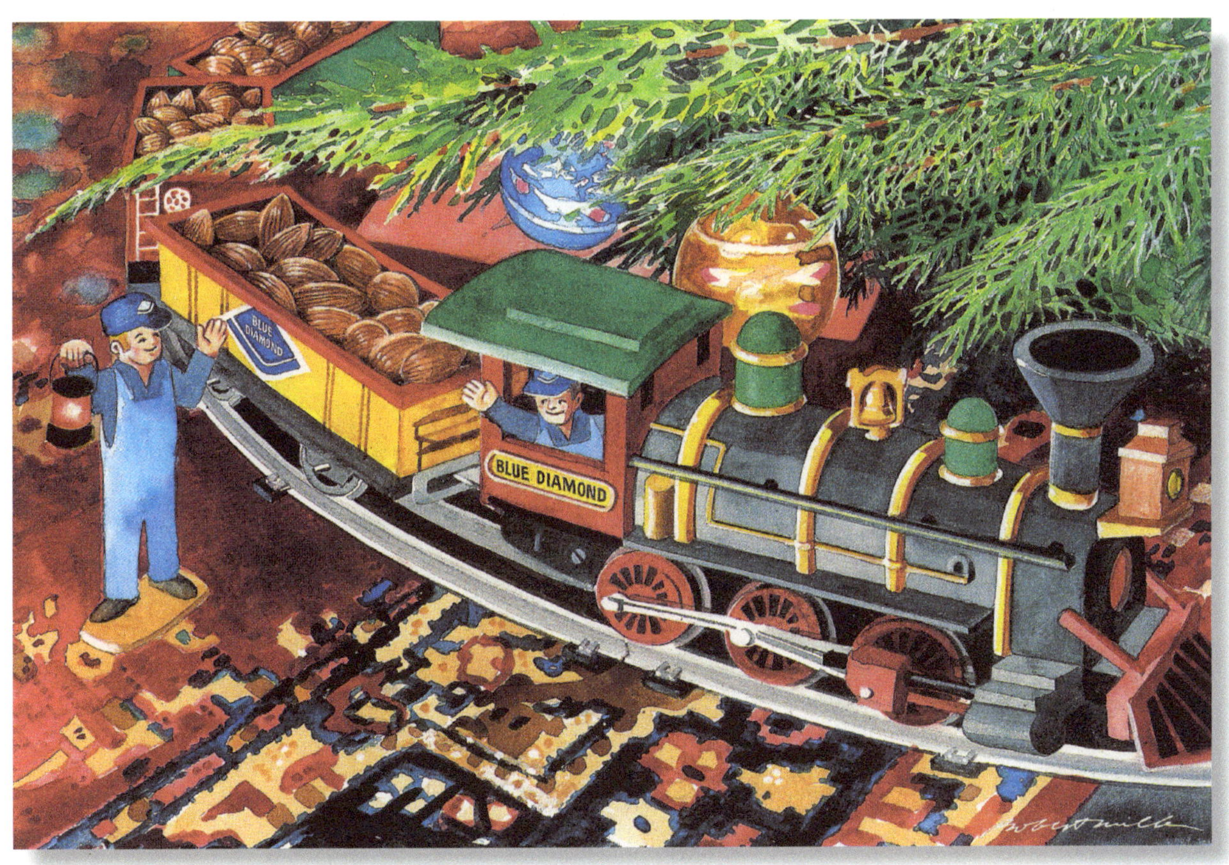
BLUE DIAMOND
BLUE DIAMOND

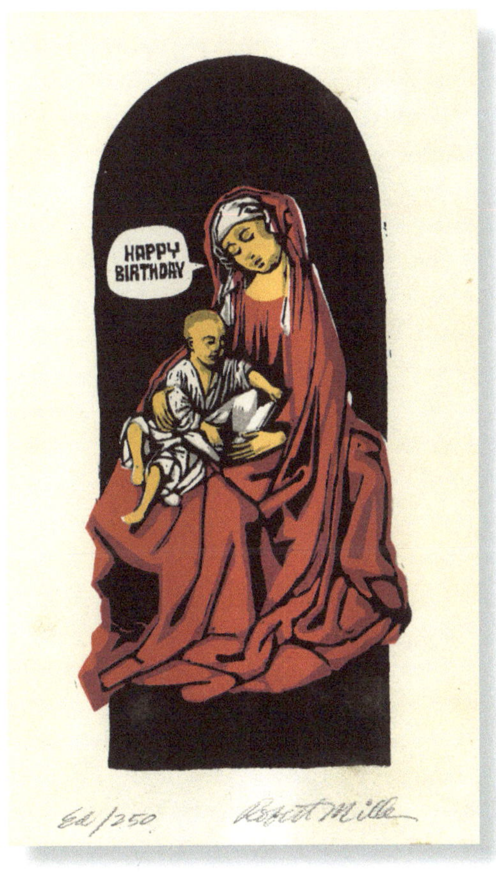
HAPPY BIRTHDAY
Ed/250

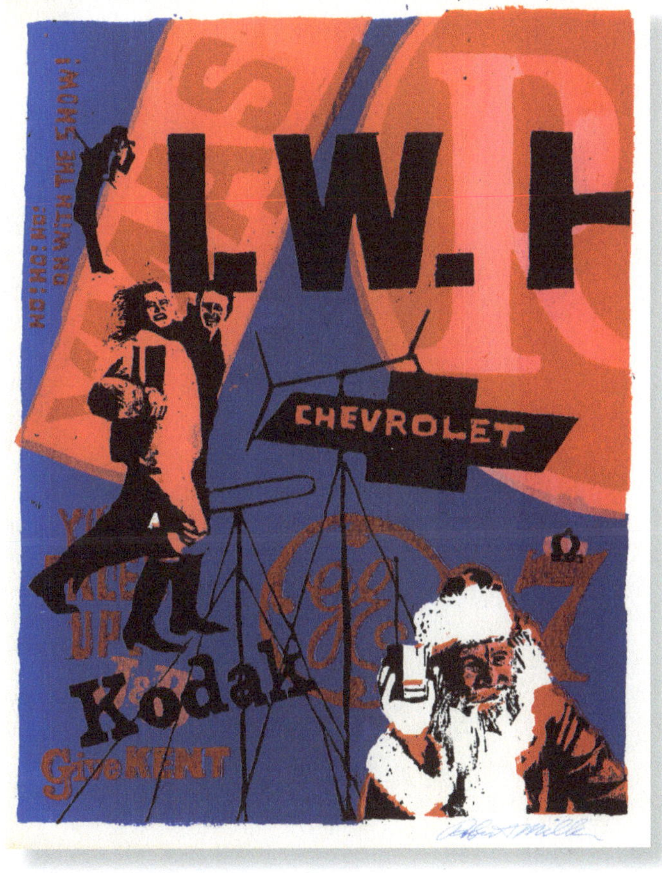
HO! HO! HO! ON WITH THE SNOW!
CHEVROLET
Kodak
Give KENT

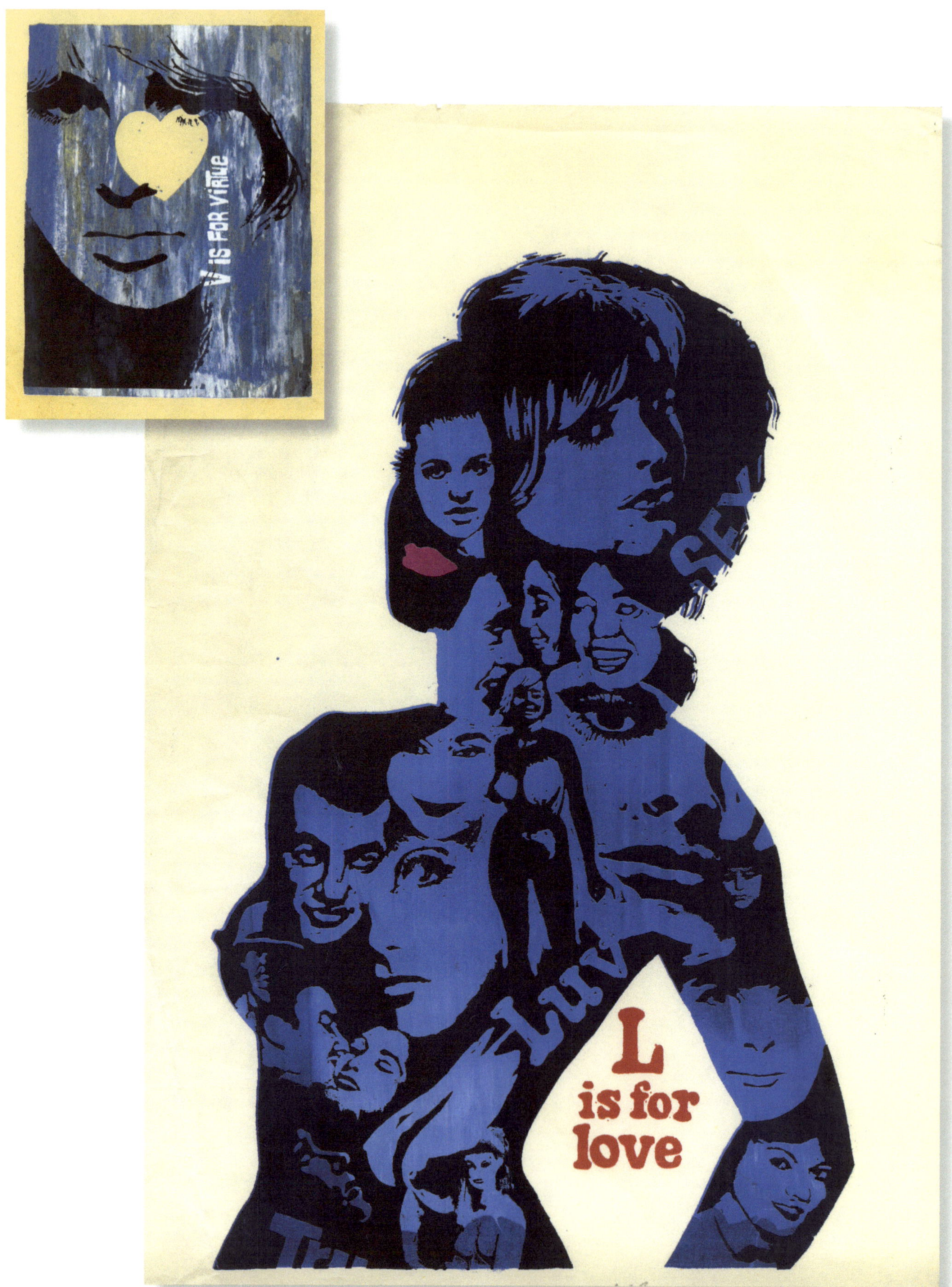
V is FOR VIRTUE
SEX
Luv
L
is for
love

Cary Bauer, director of the Village Allied Arts Center at Town & Country Village, is seen with an easel bearing "pop art" and a wealth of paintings in the background.

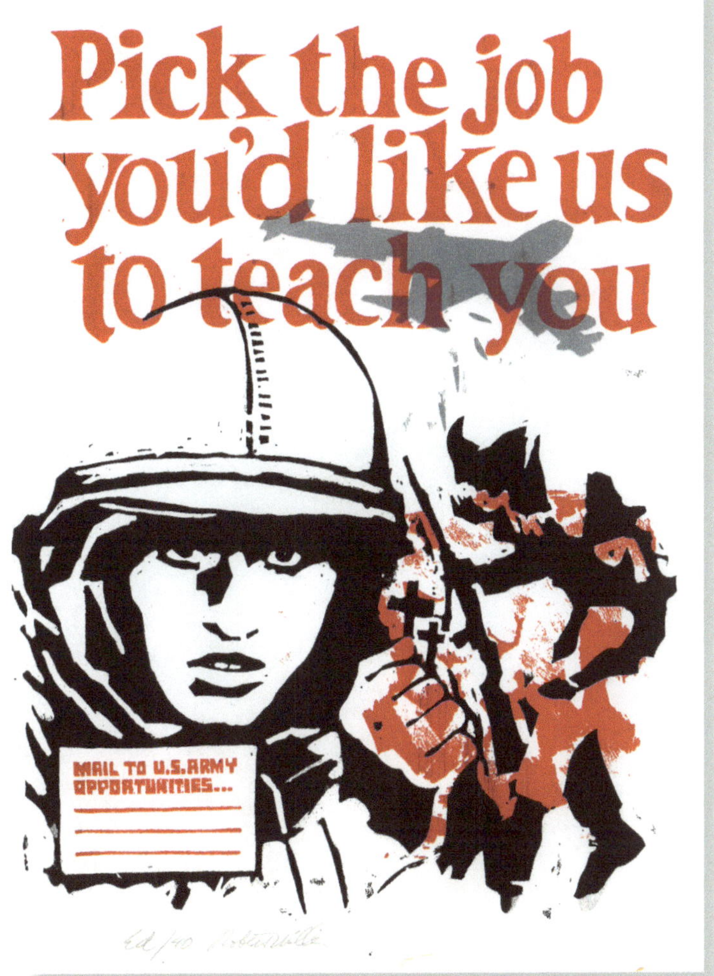

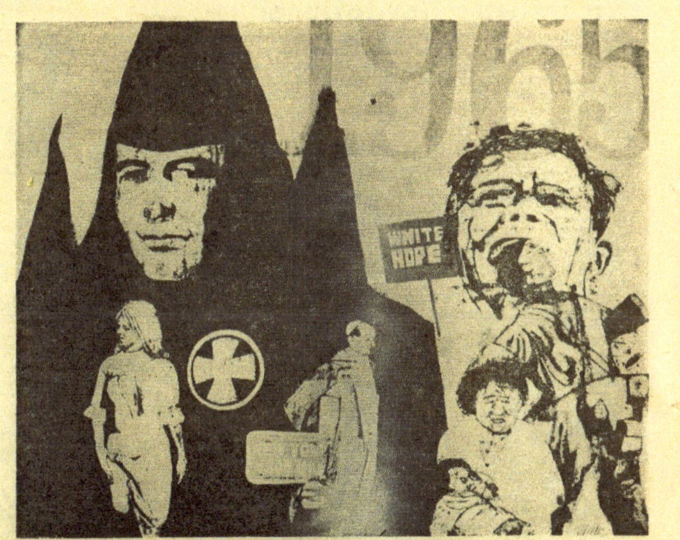

This Robert Miller print assembles a montage of faces from 1965. The caption is this unattributed quotation: "Anyway, now we can all look forward hopefully to what history will write on the fresh new calendar. Which is probably the one quality that's enabled the human race to endure in spite of itself: that hope for a better tomorrow that remains boundless no matter how often it's proven groundless."

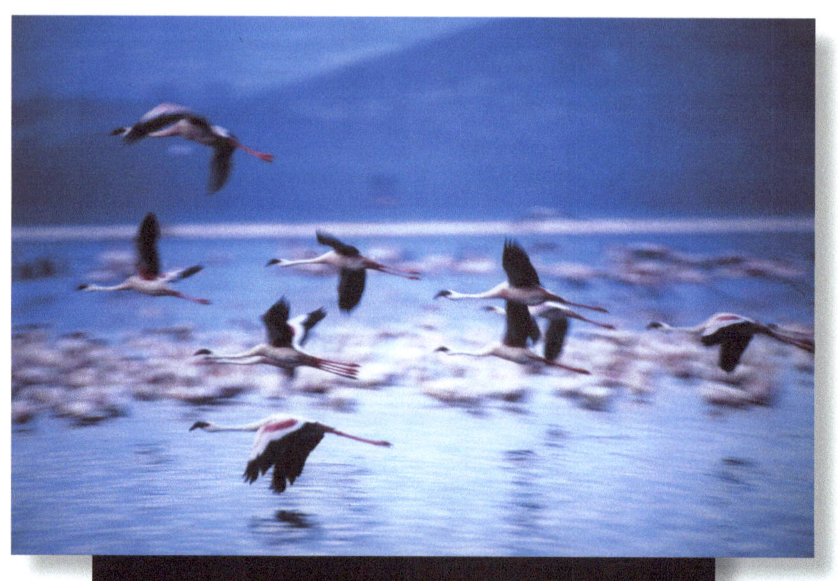

TRAVELS WITH ANITA

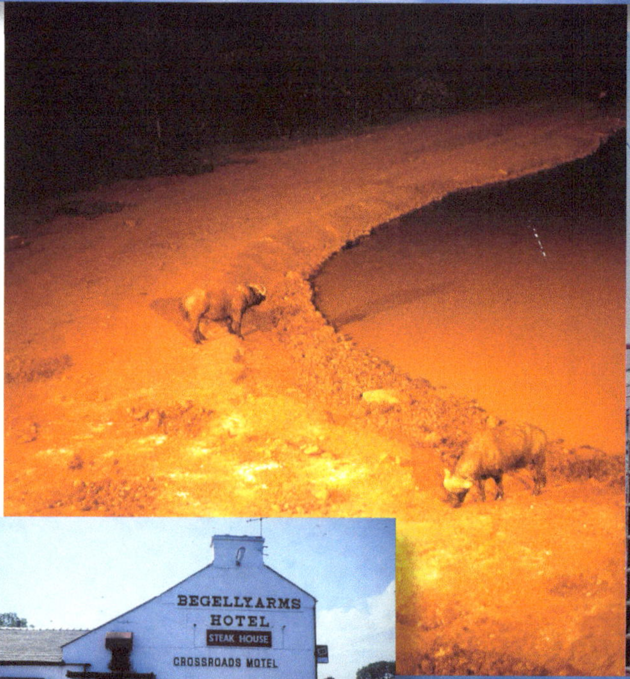

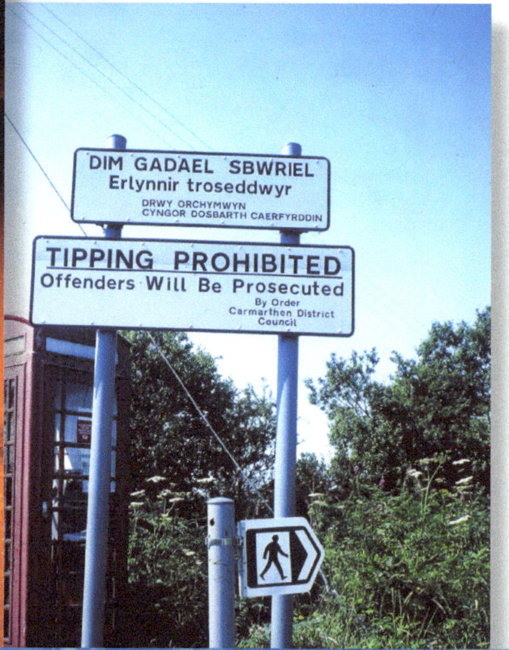

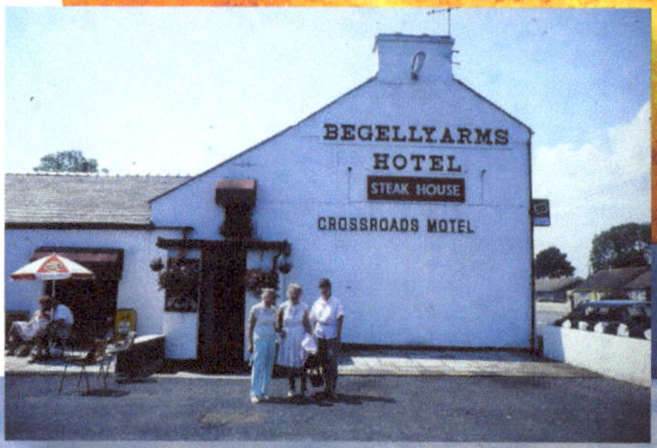

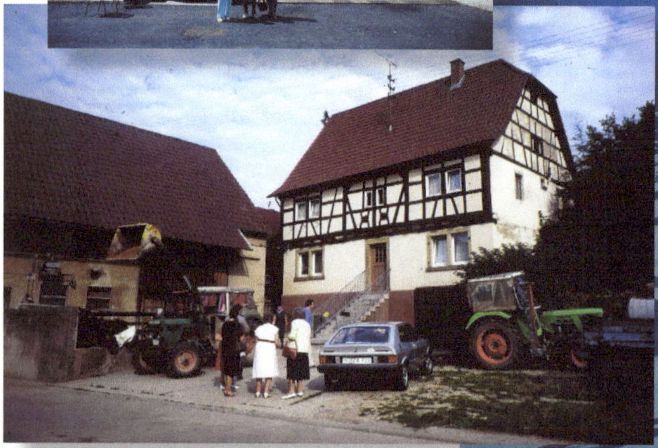

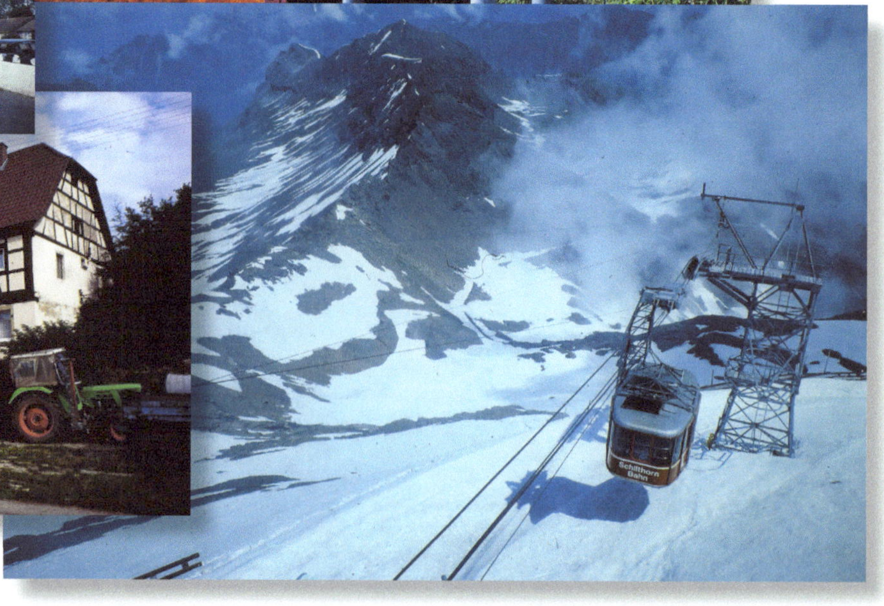

MEXICO 1964

Anita and I always had a desire to travel. In 1964, when we were in our thirties we decided to take our first foreign trip: Mexico. Dave Hume was an old friend and News Director at Channel 3. His wife Selma was a travel agent. Because we were travel novices we asked Selma to make all of our arrangements. We booked for a 12 day trip. In the 1960's one dressed to fly. Anita had on a nice dress and a hat and I wore my best blazer and a tie. On July 6th we flew from Sacramento Executive Airport to Los Angeles on a Douglas DC-6, then the most popular commercial airliner. We landed at L.A. International to catch our Mexicana Flight to Mexico City. We watched planes land and as our Mexicana plane pulled up from Mexico City I realized it was a British Comet. The Comet was the first popular commercial jet. It was sleek with its engines built into its wings. I was mildly concerned, though. Two Comets had recently blown up for no apparent reason. One was Queen Elizabeth's personal jet (she obviously was not on it). Another had fallen into the Mediterranean. Although they had flown thousands of hours safely I was still concerned. Several years later engineers determined it was the square windows in the fuselage. They had weak points in their corners and at high altitudes the windows were inclined to blow out, causing the plane to explode. They corrected the problem by installing round windows in all future models. I can't remember if our Comet had round or square windows. Nervous all the way, we had a fine flight to Mexico City.

We stayed at the Majestic Hotel on the Zocalo, the main square in the center of the city. We arrived just in time for a great meal with margaritas on the hotel's rooftop restaurant. We had a wonderful view of the square.

The next morning we had breakfast in bed. Our room overlooked the main cathedral: it could not have been more romantic. Mexico City was a whirlwind of sightseeing: the National Palace; Rivera frescoes; the Metropolitan Cathedral, followed by a visit to a glass factory, and a silver artisan's shop, and then a speeding trip to the pyramids. After lunch: the flower market; then Chaputedec Park; followed by the Castle of Maximillian and Carlotta; a tour through an area of beautiful homes and finally the Shrine of Guadalupe were all a whirl of color and lush images.

The next day we were driven to Curnevaca. We had lunch at the Vista Hermosa, a huge villa built by Cortez. We were reminded of the poverty that exists side-by-side with the very wealthy in Mexico. We walked around the walls and looked down on large camps of people in makeshift shacks made of discarded packing boxes or old scraps of corrugated metal.

Then we went on to Tasco, the Silver City of Mexico. What a beautiful city, nestled in a valley surrounded by mountains. It had cobblestone streets and architecture reminiscent of a time long gone, like stepping back in time. Our hotel was an old hacienda. Our room had an outside patio. From there in the evening we watched the "flying men". One stands on a platform in the center and plays the flute. Four others are spaced around with ropes tied around their legs. They are lying down each carrying a torch. With ropes tied to a pole, they flip up on their feet and begin spinning around, their feet not touching the ground. It was like magic with the torches flaming and the dancers defying gravity.

After the flying men performed there were flamenco dancers and fireworks. It started to rain and thunder and lightning. It was awesome! People with torches flying through the air, flamencos pounding away, fireworks exploding, the sky blowing up in supernatural colors. Wow! Every sense was overloading!

The next day we left Tasco to return to Mexico City. We had drinks that afternoon on top of the "Latin American Tower." At 25 stories it was the tallest structure in Mexico. Because Mexico City is built on an old lake bed the earth shifts now and then. The tower was built on an underground structure of caissons

"This was at a time when most people did not have credit cards. We travelled with traveller's checks. Because of the extended stay I was running out of funds. After I paid the taxi driver at the airport I had less than $20 left. I was beginning to panic! If there were no seats on the plane, I would have just $10 left."

which allowed the building to absorb the shocks of the unstable lake bed and remain upright. At 25 stories up it is a peculiar feeling for the building to adjust itself. And it wasn't the margaritas.

Later that day we met Paul and Helen Millar. Paul was a graphic designer and an old friend from Sacramento. He also had been to Mexico a number of times and had given us advice on what to see and where to stay. They took us to dinner at "La Cava," a great restaurant. For the first time in our lives we ate frog legs. They were wonderful.

Mexico City was a whirlwind of new sensory and intellectual experiences. At night we saw the Ballet Folklorico; the next day a bullfight and more Orozco murals. The Millars told us about murals that were in a nearby school but closed to the public. It was close by on a busy street. The entrance was a huge 12-foot high door. After a few moments it was opened by several lovely teenage girls. They were so impressed that we had come to see their murals that they took us on a guided tour. They spoke excellent English and knew a great deal about Orosco and his murals. I was as impressed by the students as I was by the murals. After fifty years has passed I wonder where they are those girls now? What kind of lives have they had? They took us to things we would never have seen without them: fantastic wood carvings depicting scenes from the Bible, paintings from the 16th and 17th centuries and giant tapestries. It was another case of sensory overkill.

The girls also gave us a tour of their art room and theater. What a great school. We stayed with them for almost an hour after our tour. We answered questions they had about us and the United States. They wanted to know about our children and about my art. When it was time to say goodbye they said, "Don't go, we'll take you to some nearby Aztec ruins." We went. After visiting the ruins they walked us back to our hotel. What a great heartwarming day. We will never forget them.

The next day we flew to Guadalajara, another beautiful, energetic city. We rented a horse drawn carriage for the day and toured the city at a slow, steady clip-clop, clip-clop pace. We had dinner at the "Copa Alleche" a restaurant recommended by Paul. The next morning we were off by plane to Puerta Vallarta. This was pre-Elizabeth Taylor and Richard Burton and the filming of the movie "The Night of the Iguana." We stayed at a nice hotel a short distance from town. We loved it. What a great little village. The roads from the main part of Mexico were so bad in those days that getting there by car was nearly impossible. The only practical access was by air or sea. We liked it so much we knew we would return.

Mazatlan was the next and last stop before heading home. Our first foreign vacation up to this time had been better than we ever could have imagined. Mazatlan proved to be different. We were booked at the Hotel Decima. What a dump! I was checking into our room at reception and Anita tapped me on the shoulder. She pointed at the swimming pool. It was full but covered in green slime. When we got to our room the drapes were closed. The room faced the beach and I wanted to see the ocean! I reached to open the drapes. There were no pulls or handles so grabbed them in my fingers, and fistfuls of fabric came off in my hands. According to our itinerary we were to stay at the Decima two nights. I decided one was enough.

I walked the mile or so to the Mexicana Airlines office in downtown Mazatlan. I wanted out the next day. The airline representative checked his lists and said, "I am sorry Mr. Miller. Not only are all flights tomorrow full, but we have no record of any return flight for you." He told me to check out of the Decima the next morning and take a cab to the airport. Maybe there would be a last minute cancellation. The next morning we went to the airport. The Comet jet landed (safely!) but there were no cancellations. Back to the awful Decima we went. We sunbathed the day away on the hotel's filthy beach. The next day we returned to the airport and again the same result. Back to the Decima, the filthy beach and another night in a room with wounded drapes. The third day was the same: out to the airport, no cancellation and back to the filthy hotel.

This was at a time, believe it or not, when most people did not have credit cards. We travelled with traveller's checks. Because of the extended stay I was running out of funds. The next morning after I paid the taxi driver at the airport I had less than $20 left. The hotel was $8 a day. The cab to the airport was about two bucks (this was 1964 remember!). I was beginning to panic! If there were no seats on the plane, I would have just $10 left.

We arrived at the airport about an hour before the plane was to land. No cancellations. We sat on our luggage and waited, anxiety ridden. I heard a woman crying nearby. She was talking to the Mexicana agent. "My baby is dying in Los Angeles! I must get home. He has just a few days to live!" The agent said, "You must talk to Mr. Miller. He has the last two seats on the plane." The woman came crying to me with her terrible tale. I told her I was sorry, but my mother had just kicked the bucket. A short time later as we were boarding she came up to me and said her kid was not really dying, but that she just "had to get out of this awful place!"

About eight hours later we were sitting in a friend's backyard enjoying a bar-b-que. It was hard to believe that earlier that same day we had been in Mexico's armpit, Mazatlan. It's hard to believe that dump is even part of that terrific country. And I still had ten dollars left!

MEXICO 1965

In 1965 I met Bill Cobbledick, whose family owned Cobbledick-Kibbe Glass. The company was significant in Sacramento's burgeoning home building business. Bill owned a home in Puerto Vallarta. We had fallen in love with the village on our visit the year before. Bill told us we could rent the house for $25 a day including a maid and houseboy.

I was still working for Channel 3 but was getting restless. Fred Wade, who had previously worked at KCRA now owned a very successful ad agency. He had some good Sacramento accounts: Crystal Creamery, KCRA TV and Radio, Rancho Murieta, Suburban Ford and more. I was doing freelance work for him. I mentioned Bill Cobbledick's house. He said, "Why don't we rent it for a couple of weeks?" I had vacation time coming up. I talked to Anita and she thought it was a great idea.

On April 19, 1965 we flew from Sacramento to Los Angeles; then onward to Mazatlan, where we were to catch our flight to Puerta Vallarta. There were only a few flights a week to Puerto Vallarta so we were obliged to stay in Mazatlan for several days. This time we stayed at the Hotel Playa: much nicer than the Decima! Even the beach was clean.

We rented a deep sea fishing boat. The weather was perfect: the water a deep turquiose; a clear blue sky and a slight breeze. We trolled for several hours before a marlin hit Betty Wade's line. It put up a great fight but Betty finally reeled it in. He weighed about 50 pounds. We celebrated with a cold beer. About 15 minutes later Anita

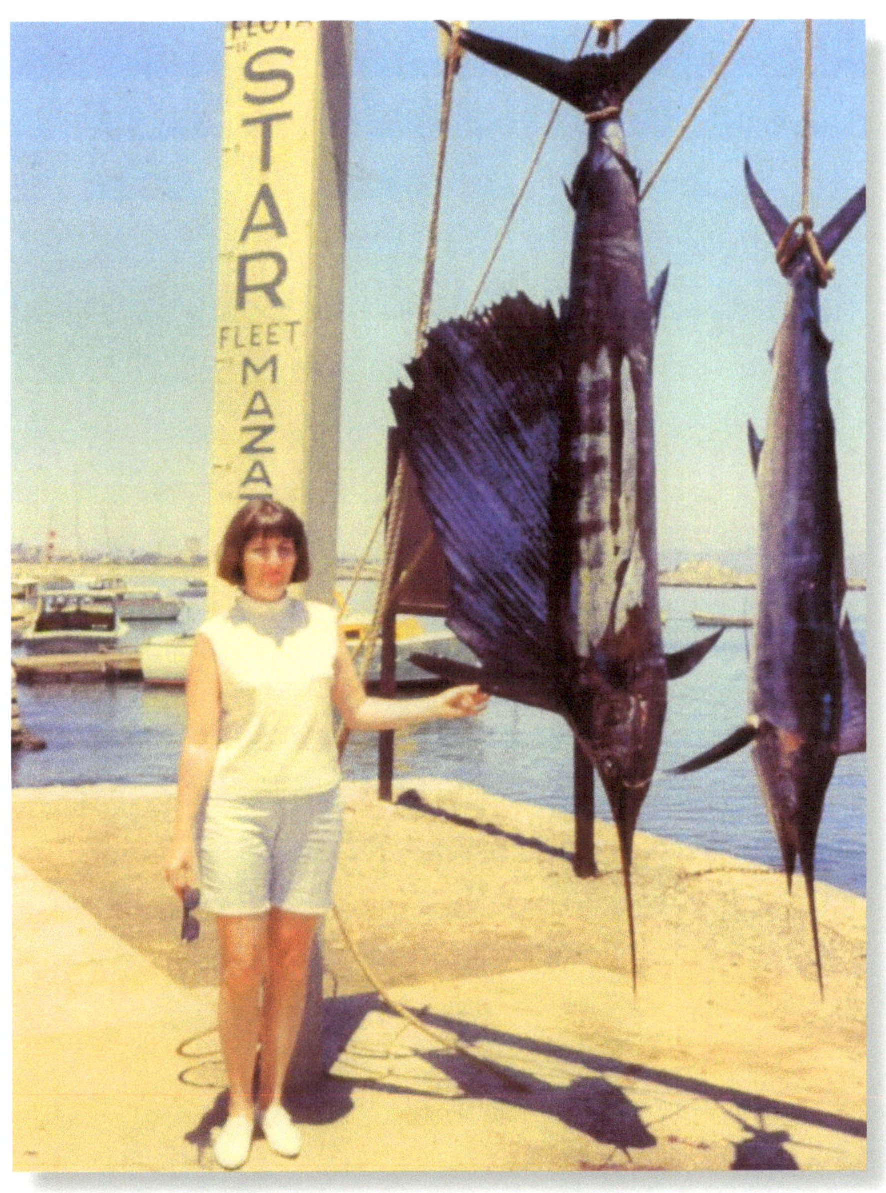

"...Anita started fighting with her marlin. It was huge. She could hardly reel him in she was so exhausted. Hers weighed 120 punds! What a great day!"

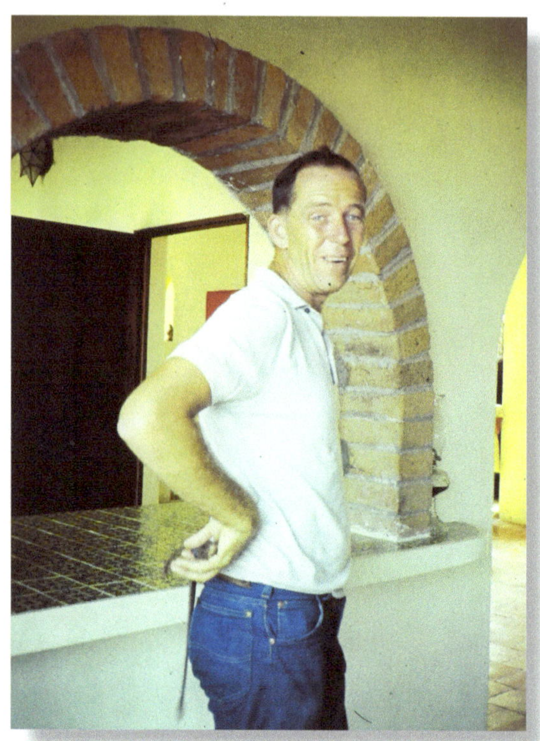

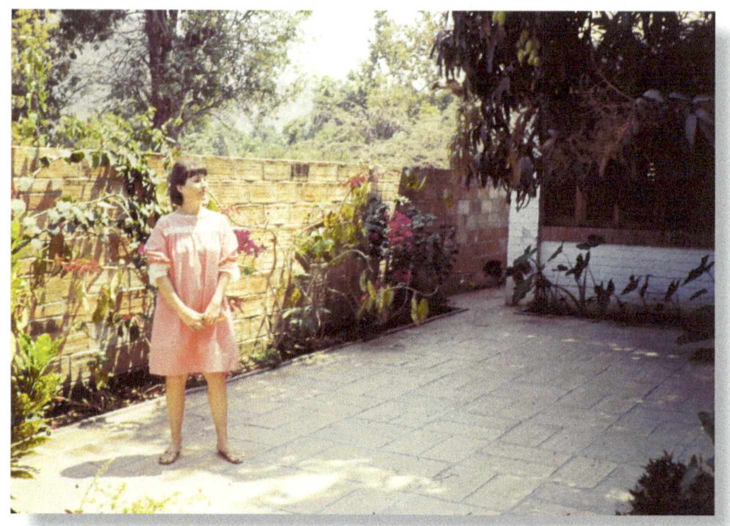

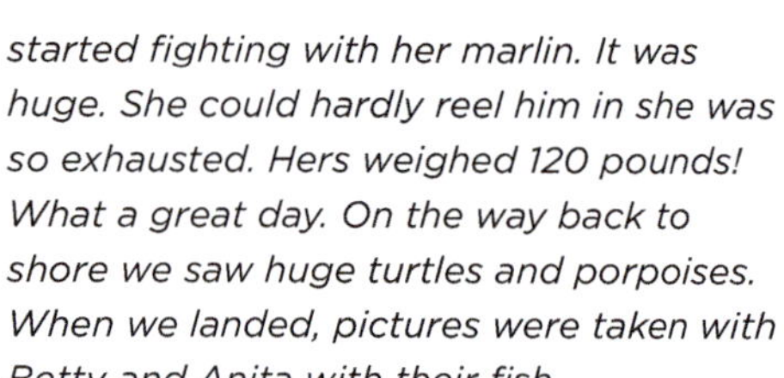

started fighting with her marlin. It was huge. She could hardly reel him in she was so exhausted. Hers weighed 120 pounds! What a great day. On the way back to shore we saw huge turtles and porpoises. When we landed, pictures were taken with Betty and Anita with their fish.

That same day we flew to Puerto Vallarta. We were met by Bill Cobbledick. He took us to his house. Wow! It was way nicer than we had imagined. It was named "Casa de las Arbales," House of The Flowers. It was walled. Inside the walls was a house of about 2,500 square feet, surrounded by beautifully landscaped flowers everywhere, shaded by avocado trees that dropped their fruit on the red tile of the garden. The tile ran from the garden throughout the entire home. Bill introduced us to Eddie the houseboy and Rosa the maid. They were fantastic and never ever disappointed us.

I went to the carpenter's shop and picked up pieces of discarded masonite, then to the paint store. I bought small cans of water based paint in the primary colors--yellow, blue and red--plus green, white and black. Then I went to the grocery store and bought a plastic squeeze bottle of ketchup. I emptied the squeeze bottle and filled it with black paint. I had brought brushes

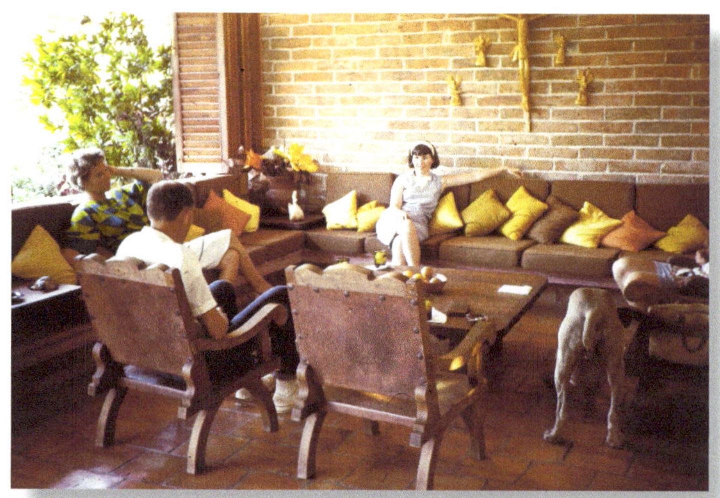

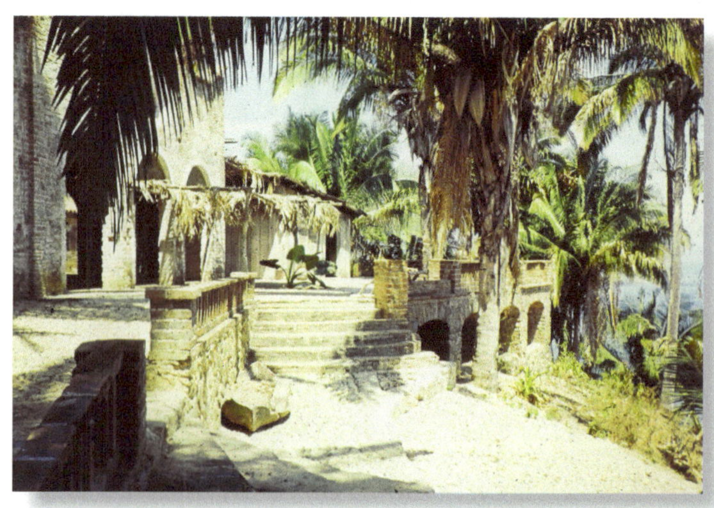

Bill Cobbledick's house in Mexico, "Casa de las Arbales," was way nicer than we imagined! And it came with a houseboy and maid!

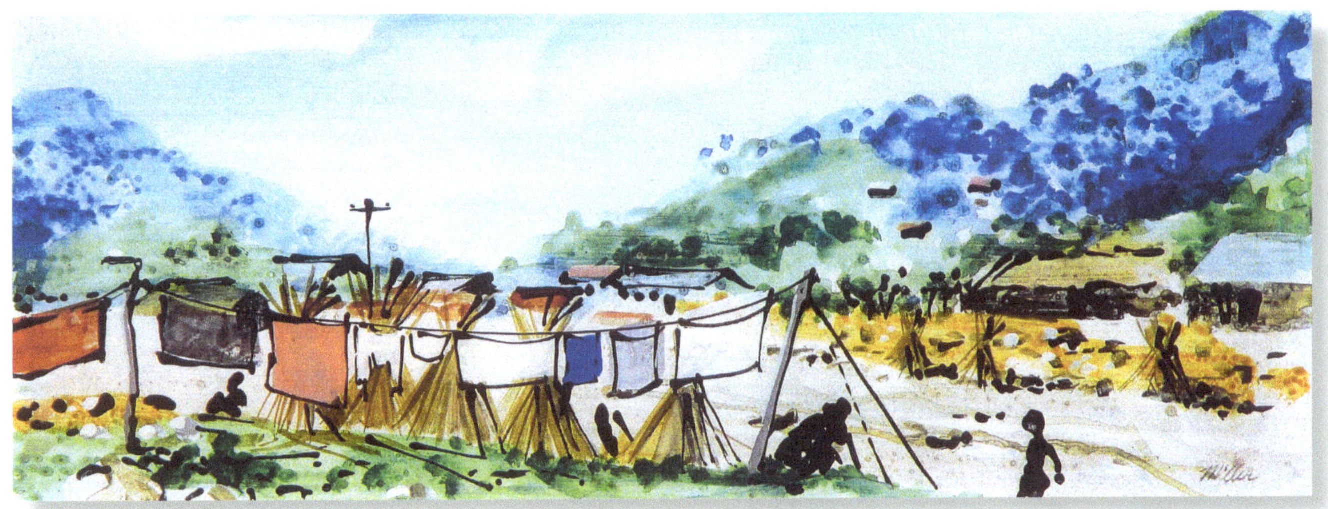

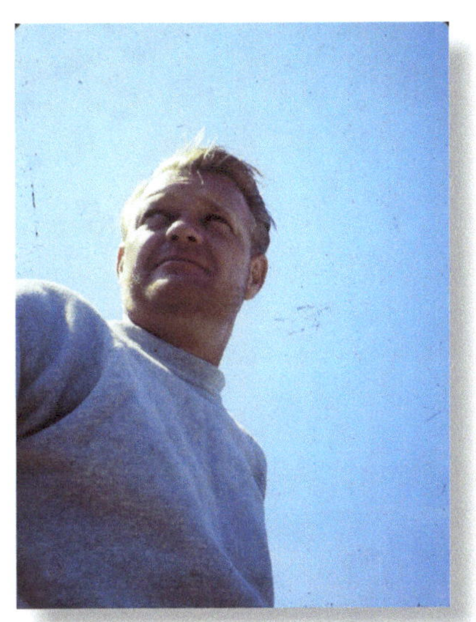

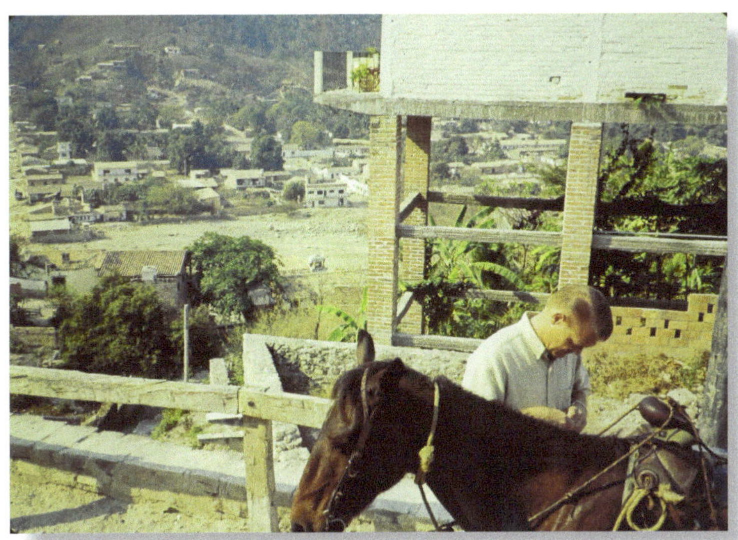

with me from Sacramento. I painted the masonite white. Puerto Vallarta was full of subjects to paint. I still have a few of the originals I created on the trip although most were sold when I returned home to Sacramento. I would roughly apply color to the white masonite, then with the ketchup bottle squeeze out the black line that brought the subject together. The technique made for very loose but charming paintings. They were more like painted sketches that well represented Puerto Vallarta. It's a technique I have not used since then and should try it again.

The four of us rented horses and meandered around the area. After several hours of sightseeing on horseback, Anita and Betty decided to go shopping. Fred and I went back to the stable thinking we might ride to Mismaloya, where they had filmed "The Night of the Iguana." It was about a five mile ride. We headed south at a very pleasant trot. We felt like real cowboys. About two miles out of Puerta Vallarta Fred's horse suddenly took off at an uncontrollable gallop toward the beach. My horse hesitated for a few moments and then flew off after him. I had no control over the horse. As we arrived at the edge of the beach my horse stopped. Fred's whinnied and took off again at a gallop along the edge of the surf. He traveled about a quarter mile, turned and came galloping back towards us. He whinnied again as he galloped past us, turned and repeated the circuit. My horse stood still and would not move. Finally after Fred's horse had made three or four laps he whinnied at my horse again and they roared back to town galloping as fast as they could go. By now Fred and I were riding side by side. Nothing we could do could dissuade our steeds. By now the galloping seemed normal. We were at full speed talking about what fun we were having! "What a great place this is!" "I wonder what the girls are doing?"

We arrived at the stable after about two hours of whinnying and galloping. We had rented the horses for four hours. We told the stable owner since we had only ridden for two hours we should get some of our money back. He told us if we didn't know how to ride that was

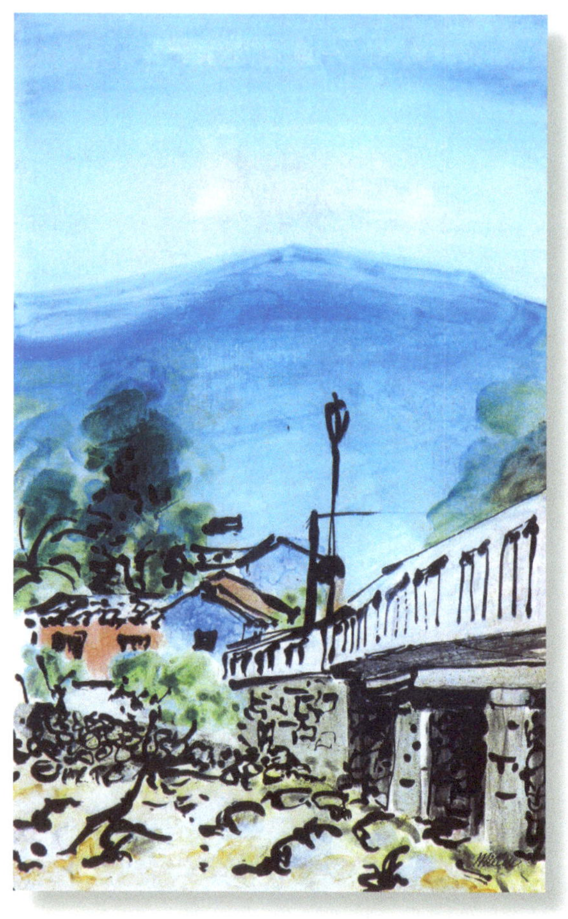

" I reached up to pull myself up and into the boat but couldn't do it. The young Dutch girl clamored into the vessel and pulled me out of the water onto the deck.
I was exhausted. Any ideas of romance had faded about halfway through the swim.
I felt lucky to be alive!"

our problem! Boy those horses really liked their stable.

Several days later we thought it might be fun do do some more horseback riding. Anita asked Eddie the houseboy if he would please go to the stable and rent "quatro caballeros." Eddie was confused and very hesitant. Anita said, "Eddie, I would like you to rent four caballeros." She was so persuasive Eddie was ready to go to the corner bar and see what he could rustle up for this peculiar lady. Finally Fred took Eddie aside and said she meant "caballos!" Eddie was so relieved.

The Oceano Hotel became a place we enjoyed. It had good food and a jumping musical group. The leader of the group introduced himself to us. His name was Dino Verduzzco. He became attached to us. Later he came to our house for drinks. By this time we had met two airline stewardesses from Holland. We all started to hang out together. It was fun. Dino told us stories of his life. We were not sure how many were true. He had been a helicopter pilot in Vietnam. He told us that he had returned to his home in Oklahoma on leave from Vietnam and wanted to surprise his wife. He very quietly entered their home only to discover her in bed with another man. She didn't see him. He quietly left and she had no idea he had ever been there. After the service he came to Puerto Vallarta to start his band. He said he

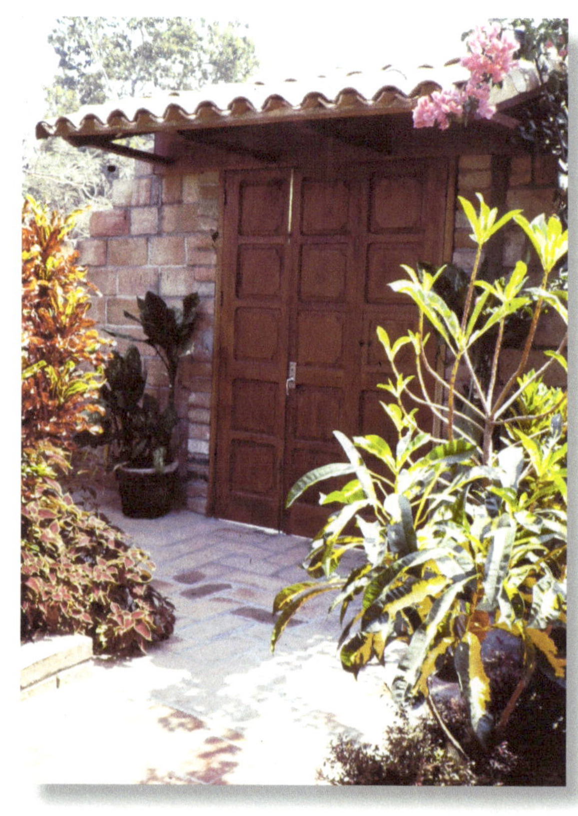

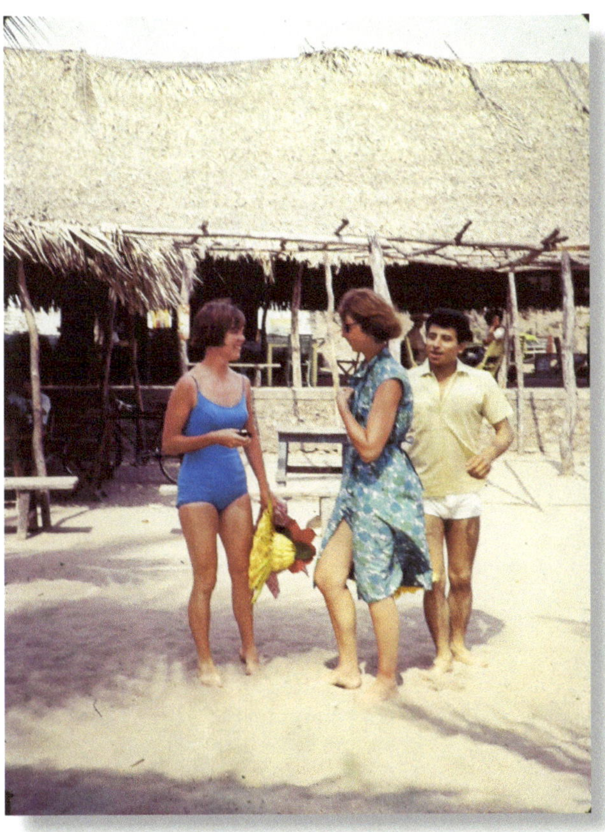

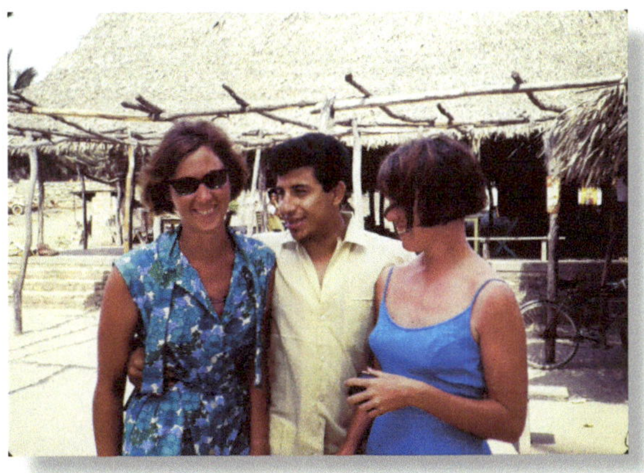

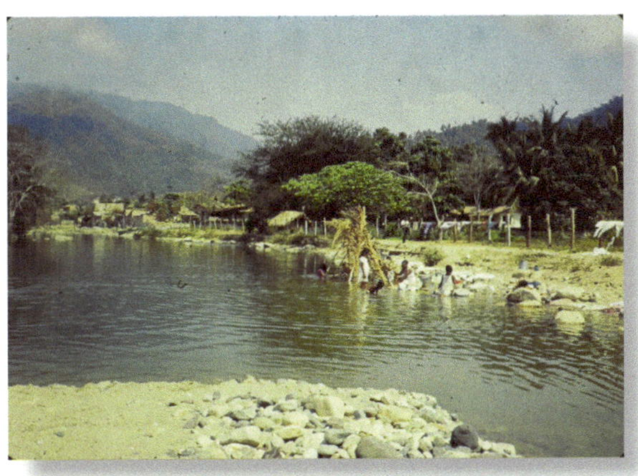

missed his famly. He claimed his father was a part of the Italian Resistance during World War Two. His father was so highly regarded by the U.S. military for his bravery that they re-settled him, with a pension, in Guadalajara. I never asked why there and not a city in the U.S.

Even though we were not sure of the truth of Dino's stories we had a lot of fun with him. Anita's birthday was on April 27th. Dino and the airline stewardesses brought a cake, especially made for Anita by a local bakery. She had a great birthday celebration. Several days later we were all sunbathing on the beach. Suddenly Dino stood up and said, "My God! Here comes my wife and kids." That was the last we saw of Dino.

Later in the afternoon of the same day I was sunning on a beach towel between Anita and one of the Dutch girls. Anita was asleep. I was awake and looking at the boats anchored about a hundred yards off the beach. The Dutch girl next to me was awake. She was about 23 or 24 years old. I was 34. "Why don't we swim out to the boats?" she said. It really seemed like a good idea to me. We started to swim. While we swam she asked me questions like, "Is the water in California as warm as this?"

"Do you have a boat?"

"Have you ever met John Wayne?"

I answered as best as I could but I discovered I was not in very good shape. My arms were getting heavier and every time I answered one of her questions I took on water. I kept looking up towards the boats, but they seemed further and further away. We finally made it to a power launch about twenty feet or so long. The deck was no more than 24 to 30 inches above the water. I reached up to pull myself up and into the boat but couldn't do it. The young Dutch girl clamored into the vessel and pulled me out of the water onto the deck. I was exhausted. Any ideas of romance had faded about halfway through the swim. I felt lucky to be alive!

She continued to talk and ask questions but I was too exhausted to respond. I kept looking toward the beach, wondering how I was going to make it back. Finally after a half hour or so of rest we slipped back into the warm water. Fortunately the action of the waves gently nudged us toward the beach. I was even able to answer most of her questions.

It was a great vacation. After the two weeks I bundled up about twenty paintings and carried them on the plane back to Sacramento.

About this time I went to Jon Kelly asking for a raise. I told him if he would pay me $1000 a month I would never again ask him for another raise. He, thank God, turned me down. I got an offer from a TV station in Kansas City...it was then that Fred Wade persuaded me to come work with him....and I was glad I did!

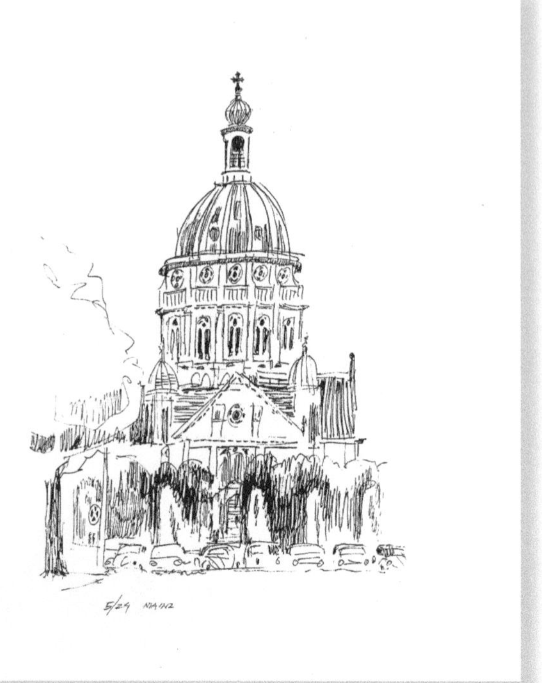
5/24 MAINZ

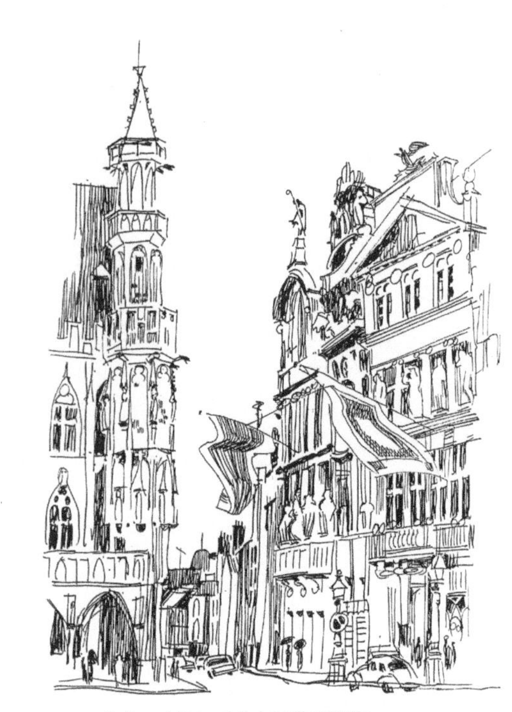
5/28/71 LA GRAND PLACE DE BRUXELLES

EUROPE 1971

In the Spring of 1971 we took our first tour of Europe. I found a tour company called Branden. They advertised 18-day tours of Europe for about $600, including hotels and meals. Even by the standards of the day it was a great price. It included England, France, Switzerland, Germany, Holland and Belgium on its itinerary.

We found a cheap charter flight out of Oakland. We landed in London on May 3, 1971. Our hotel was in Hampstead. It was wonderful. All the new smells, and for the most part everyone spoke our language. Occasionally in a pub we would need an interpreter when the Cockney accents were too much for our Sacramento ears. We did things one does when new to a country. We rode the tube, took a ride on a double-decker bus and went to as many museums as we possibly could.

We met Mike and Lindy Dunlavey at Victoria Station. They were on a round-the-world trip. Mike had inherited a small amount of money. He said "Before we do anything responsible with the money we want to take a trip around the world." So they did. They were coming west from Asia to Europe. We had planned to meet them before we left Sacramento. Mike and Lindy were just starting their creative careers. They ultimately became the premier design studio in Sacramento. They were not only talented and creative, they had great business sense. We spent the day with them and went to Stonehenge and Salisbury.

The next day we said goodbye to them and took the ferry from Dover to Calais. A bus took us to Paris. It was an artist's paradise. We were there for four days. We walked and saw the sights... and I drew almost twenty drawings in those four days. The delights of Paris have been described so well by others I may sound corny--I have too limited a vocabulary--but the Woody Allen movie "Midnight in Paris" says it all for me.

From Paris we moved on to Engleberg in Switzerland, then to Lucerne. We stayed in wonderful old hotels in the center of the cities we visited. A first class Globus tour became attached to our tour. It turned out their tour did not have enough people to qualify for a full tour. They paid much more than we did and the only difference in the quality of the tour were the hotel accomodations. They stayed in fancy high rise hotels at the edge of the cities and had to get transportation to get to the really interesting parts of the cities. We stayed at the cheaper, more colorful hotels in the heart of the action. They were pissed and

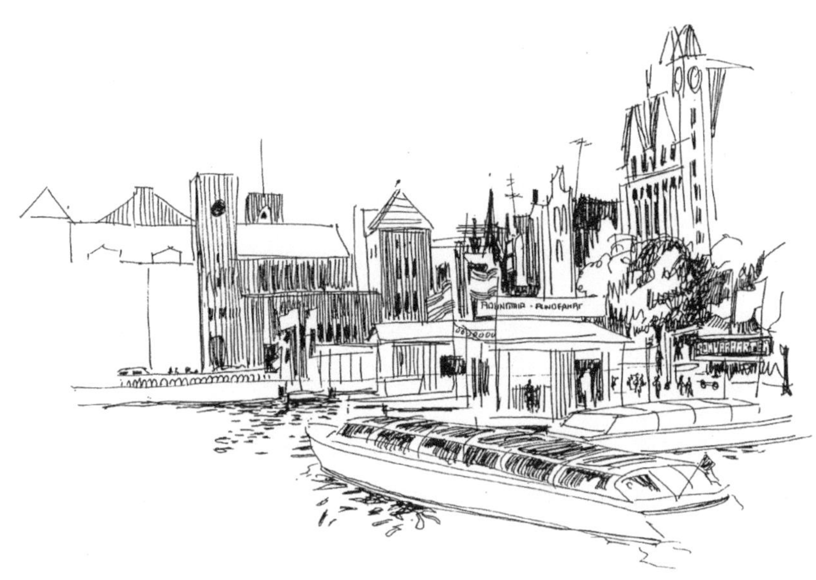

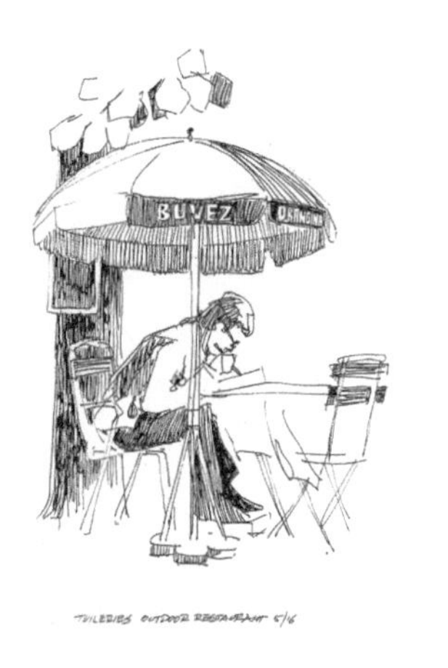

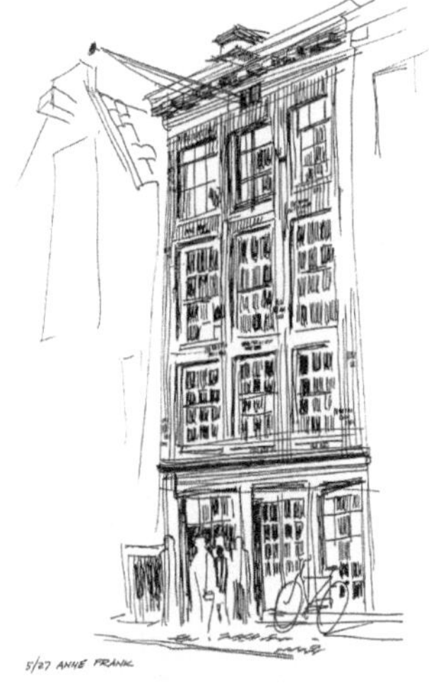

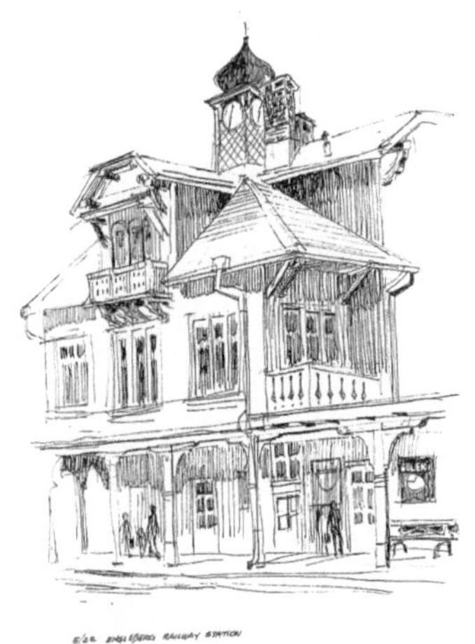

it created mild friction throughout the trip.

From Switzerland we went to Mainz, Germany, then to Amsterdam and Belgium. From Belgium we returned to Oakland. It was a great tour and gave us a great survey of what we would like to see again, but we vowed not to take tours in the future.

We like travelling on our own. If you see something interesting you can stop and explore. Many of the things we are intersted in are of little interest to others. We have taken one tour since then, but that was to the old Soviet Union. Once we got there we discovered we coud have done it on our own.

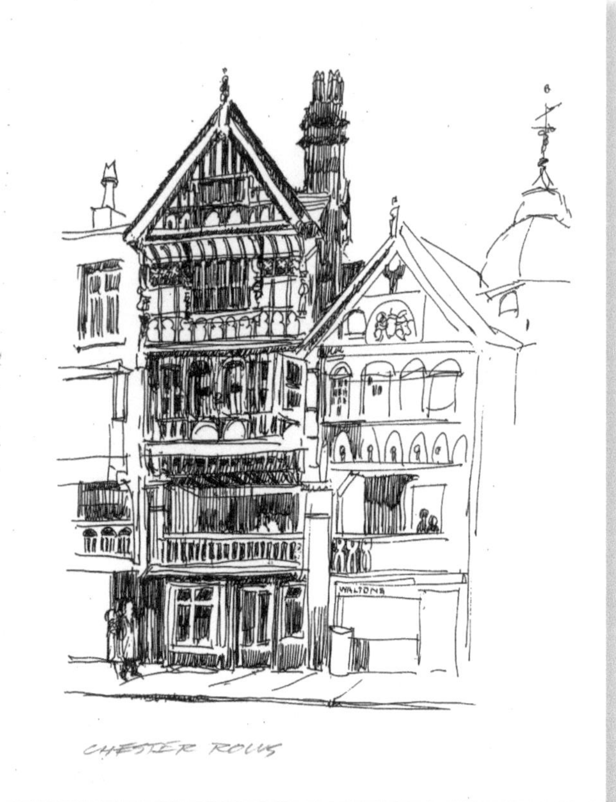

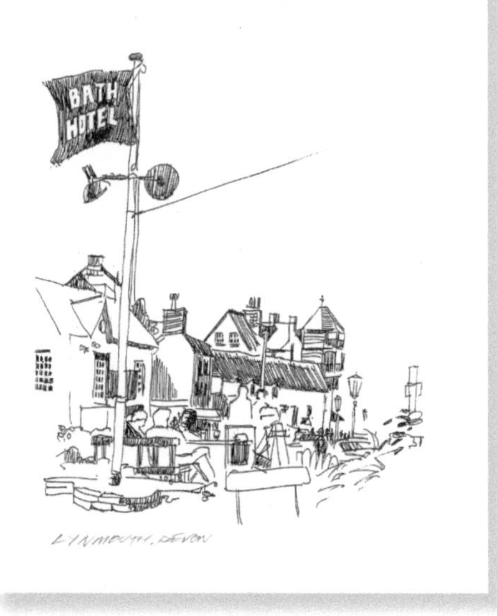

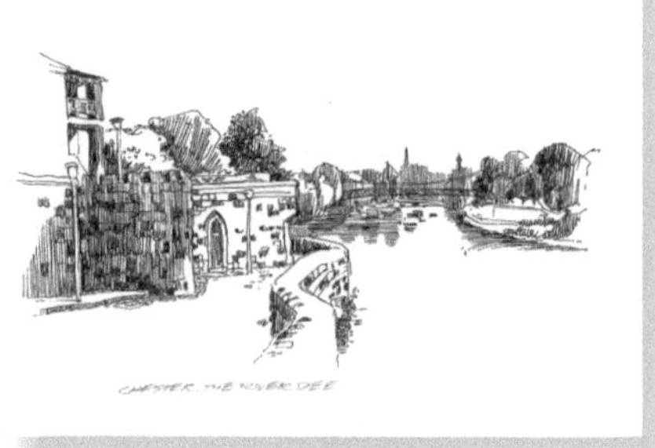

ENGLAND 1973

We returned to England in 1973 armed with month-long rail passes. We had no specific plans, just a brief outline of what we would like to do. We stayed at the John Douglas Hotel in London's Earl Court. Earl Court was a polygot area with good, cheap restaurants and an interesting mixture of nationalities and races. It was called Roo Valley by some because so many Australians live there.

From London we went to Lynton, which is about 100 miles to the west on the coast. It's a lovely setting and was recommended by the Dunlaveys who had stayed there the year before. They also recommended we stay at Mrs. Creasey's Bed and Breakfast. What a charming place. Mrs. Creasey welcomed us. What a nice lady! We stayed for several days. She even made lunches for us to take on our various jaunts.

Lynton and its twin town Lynmouth are on the north Devon coast. It's as beautiful as any place I have ever been. Soft rolling moors cascading into the ocean cover high rugged cliffs. Trails wound through the woods along meandering streams, punctuated by waterfalls, all ending at a picture perfect harbor. From Lynmouth we traveled to Chester. Chester is a walled city of about 120,000 people. It was founded by the Romans. We walked the walls: it's about a two mile walk all around the city. It was famous then for its shoe manufacturing. I'm not sure if that's still true considering how much manufacturing has moved to the far east. But then there was shoe store after shoe store located in the Chester Rows. The Rows were built in the mid 19th century. They are a mixture of shops and residences. The architecture is unique, with strong contrasts of dark beams with what looks like light stucco. The River Dee meanders through the town. A very pleasant place to visit.

And then we went on to Conway in Wales: great old castle ruins, a delight to draw.... and the Welsh countryside with its rolling moors was a beautiful sight from our train windows.

Bowness, on Britain's largest lake,

Windemere, was our next stop. Full board at Mrs. Merritt's "Hazeldine" was $12. That included room, breakfast, lunch and dinner...and if we were hiking Mrs. Merritt would pack our lunch! Bed and breakfasts are great!

Large steamers sail up and down the lake. It was a great way to see the little villages along its shores. We were told Britain's largest waterfall was just a short distance from Bowness. It turns out that it was not the largest, as local pride got in the way of the truth. It was called the "Skelwith Force." We took a bus ride with a class of school children to the parking lot of the force. The walk to the falls was about half a mile. When we got there it was truly lovely: about a fifty foot drop, lovely but not impressive.

One of the school children said that he had been to Yosemite in California and they had one that fell over a thousand feet. His classmates all said, "He's lying... " He turned to me to varify his claim. I said it was true and had seen Yosemite Falls many times. I'm not sure if they believed me!

When it was time to leave Bowness we went to the train station with our train passes in hand. The waiting room was closed so we walked around it to the track. This was the last stop on the line so there should have been a train. No train. We were not sure what to do. Soon there was a loud honking from the parking lot. We walked around to find a huge double decker red bus waiting for us. The driver said "I'm your train today." We were the only passengers for about thirty miles. We sat upstairs to see the sights. The bus took us to Wilmcote where the trains run on Sunday.

From Wilmcote we caught a train to Edinburgh. What a beautiful city. We arrived late, checking into a bed and breakfast. We walked the streets trying to find a place open to eat. Edinburgh closes early. We finally found, believe it or not, a McDonald's next to a rather nice looking restaurant. The restaurant had few diners, as it was late; but it had linen table cloths and nice looking place settings, and on the window in gold leaf and lovely script it said "Cafe." What a find! We were seated by a maitre'd and waited on by a nice waitress

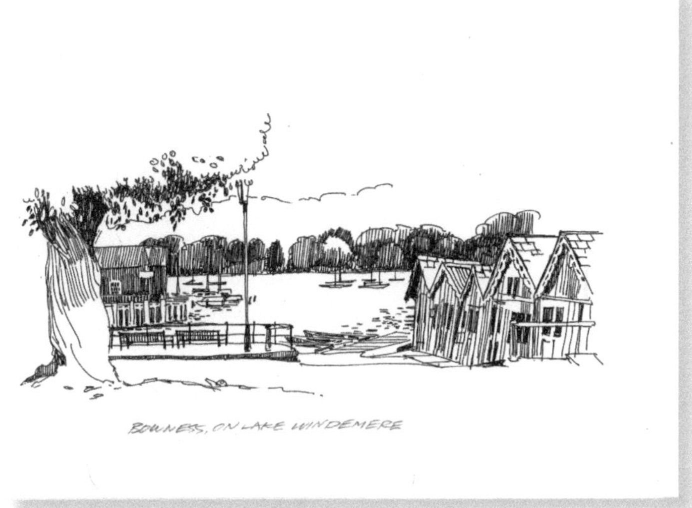

BOWNESS, ON LAKE WINDEMERE

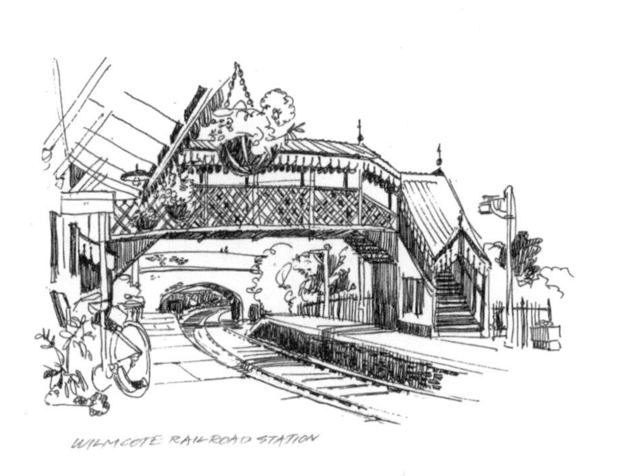

WILMCOTE RAILROAD STATION

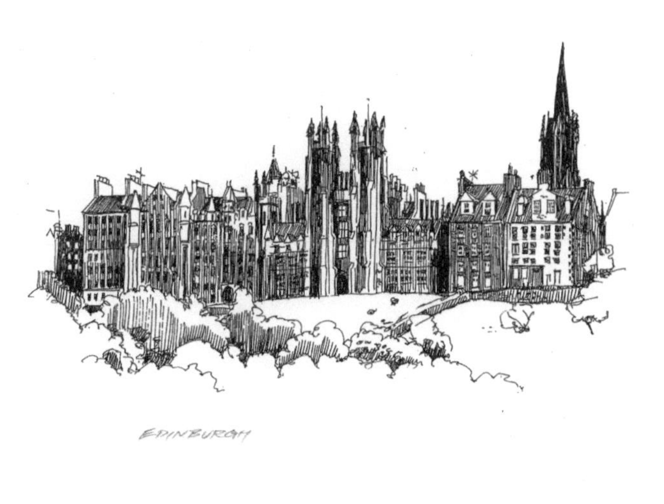

EDINBURGH

with a Scottish accent we could barely understand. The menus were very stylish. There was steak on the menu. We had not had any for awhile so we ordered a steak dinner and a highball for both of us. The highball was great. The salad was a little wilted. The steaks arrived: I'm sure the soles of my loafers would have been more tender. The potatoes were under done and the peas were canned. When we decided to have apple pie for dessert the waitress warned "It's not like yours in America." She was right. It was moldy! We could not eat it. Finally, after coffee (the coffee was by far the best part of the meal) we looked for our waitress. She was nowhere to be found. I finally managed to find a different waitress hoping to get our bill. She told me "Oh, I'll have to get your waitress. She's on her break eating at McDonald's next door!"

Later in our stay Anita said, "Why don't we try some haggis?" Haggis is the national dish of Scotland. It is made of things I don't ordinarily eat but we were in Scotland! I am told the recipe goes something like this: heart, liver, offal and lungs minced with onions, suet, spices, salt and pepper. The minced pulp is encased in a sheep's stomach and simmered for three or four hours. I have been told that some haggis instead of being cooked for a long time is allowed to ferment in the stomach and then cooked briefly. We figured we had not heard of a recent outbreak of haggis fever so we tried it at a restaurant recommended by the proprietor of our bed and breakfast. We liked it. If we had not known what was in it we probably would have liked it better. It was a very strong, spicy, meaty flavor, but good.

From Edinburgh we took the "Flying Scotsman" back to London. It's a great overnight train with sleeping compartments. Shortly after leaving Scotland we went to bed. By 5:30 A.M. the train arrived in London, but very thoughtfully, for those who wanted to sleep in, the conductors didn't wake you until 7. We slept in.

We spent the next few days in London. We did all the things one does while visiting London: Buckingham Palace; the Tower of London; Westminster Abbey; Parliament; Big Ben and most important, we visited with Emma Wilcox.

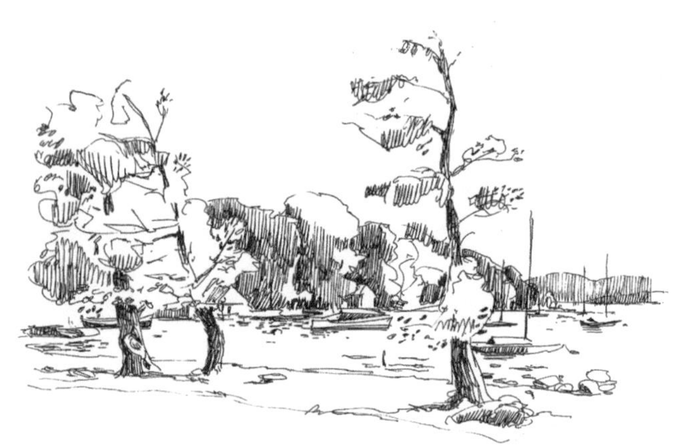

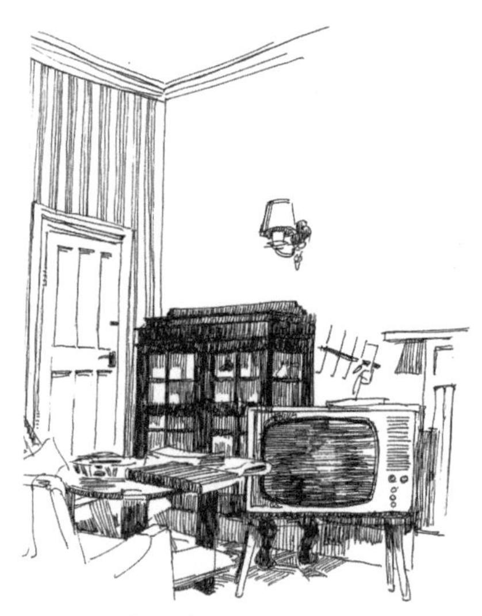

MRS. MERRITT'S LOUNGE, WINDEMERE

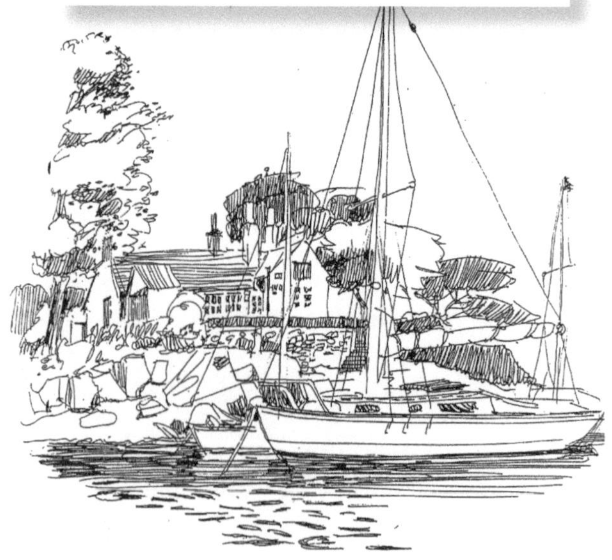

FIRTH OF FORTH

We met Emma on the way to Lynton. Shortly after we got on our train at London's Charing Cross station we were joined in our compartment by a young English lady. She introduced herself and we exchanged pleasantries. She was an interior designer. She lived in Esher, a suburb of London near Hampton Court and the Thames. She was on her way to Exeter, where her family was originally from. She got off the train before we arrived at our destination, but before leaving she gave us her card and invited us to tea and to meet her mother.

We continued on our trip around the UK, and we never forgot Emma...so when we returned to London we called her. She was surprised but she asked us to come on an afternoon a few days away and gave us instructions on what train to take. The tea was at her mother's house in Hampton. It was a lovely small two story flat. Many years before it had been servants' quarters for those that worked at Hampton Court Palace. Her mother, Isabel Wilcox, was very uncertain about us. Who were these Americans Emma had invited into her house? At first her attitude was very stand-offish. It seemed she could not wait to serve the tea and get us out of her house. As time passed we found we had things in common. Her husband, Emma's father, had been the organist at the Exeter cathedral. Anita's love of music and opera was an ice breaker. Before long we were in an animated conversation on a variety of different subjects: the Royal family; American politics; books; movies; and more places to visit near London.

It wasn't long before whiskey was substituted for tea. We were having a wonderful time. Hours passed. Emma said, "I have a date and must leave, but please stay. Mother will take you to the train."

We must have talked for another hour or more. It started to rain. Very hard. Finally it was time to go as the last train to London was to leave shortly. We went outside to Isabel's car. It was a Triumph convertible! The top was down. It was full of water as if it had been a bathtub. When we opened the doors, water poured out! The car started okay. We got the top up and drove off in the soggy car to the station. We made the last train to London.

Thus began a friendship that has lasted to this day. Emma was in her late twenties when we met. She is now close to seventy. Isabel died in her nineties. Our first meeting was only the beginning of our friendship. Emma invited us to stay with her at her home in Esher every time we have gone to England. Her hospitality has been warm, wonderful and enfolding. She has become part of our family. Our daughter Meredith named her daughter Emma. She also from time to time has offered a haven to our children when they visited England. Our son Dan went to Burrlyfield Art School in High Wycombe about 100 miles from London. He was a frequent visitor at Emma's and Isabel's. She was hostess to Mike and Van on their backpacking hikes through England and Europe. Van later went to school in Paris at the Sorbonne and on vacations would visit. She never seemed to tire of the Miller family. It would be interesting to hear their conversations after the Millers left.

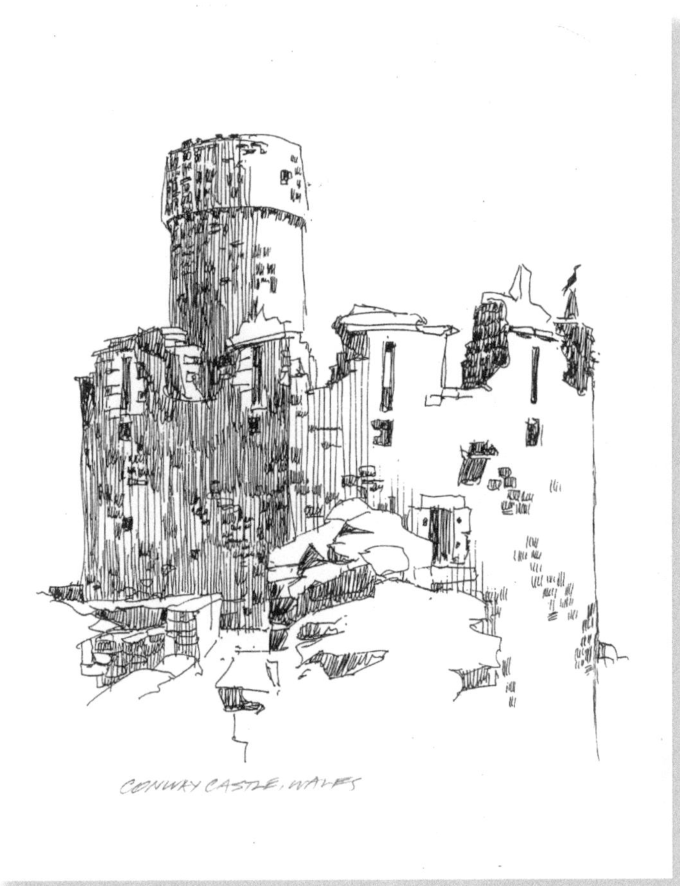

In the 1980's I sent airfare to Emma to come visit us in Sacramento. She came with George Neale, then her boyfriend, now her husband. George is an artist like me. His birthday is March 27, 1931, mine is March 28 of the same year. We have a lot in common. We took them all over California: Yosemite; we visited my sister in Bakersfield; San Diego; the delights of Los Angeles; and then up the coast on Highway One. We visited Hearst Castle, Monterey and Carmel, San Francisco and Napa (Napa was more affordable then!). We have not been to England since 2000, but we are in constant contact with Emma and George and their adventures.

You never know who you might meet on a train.

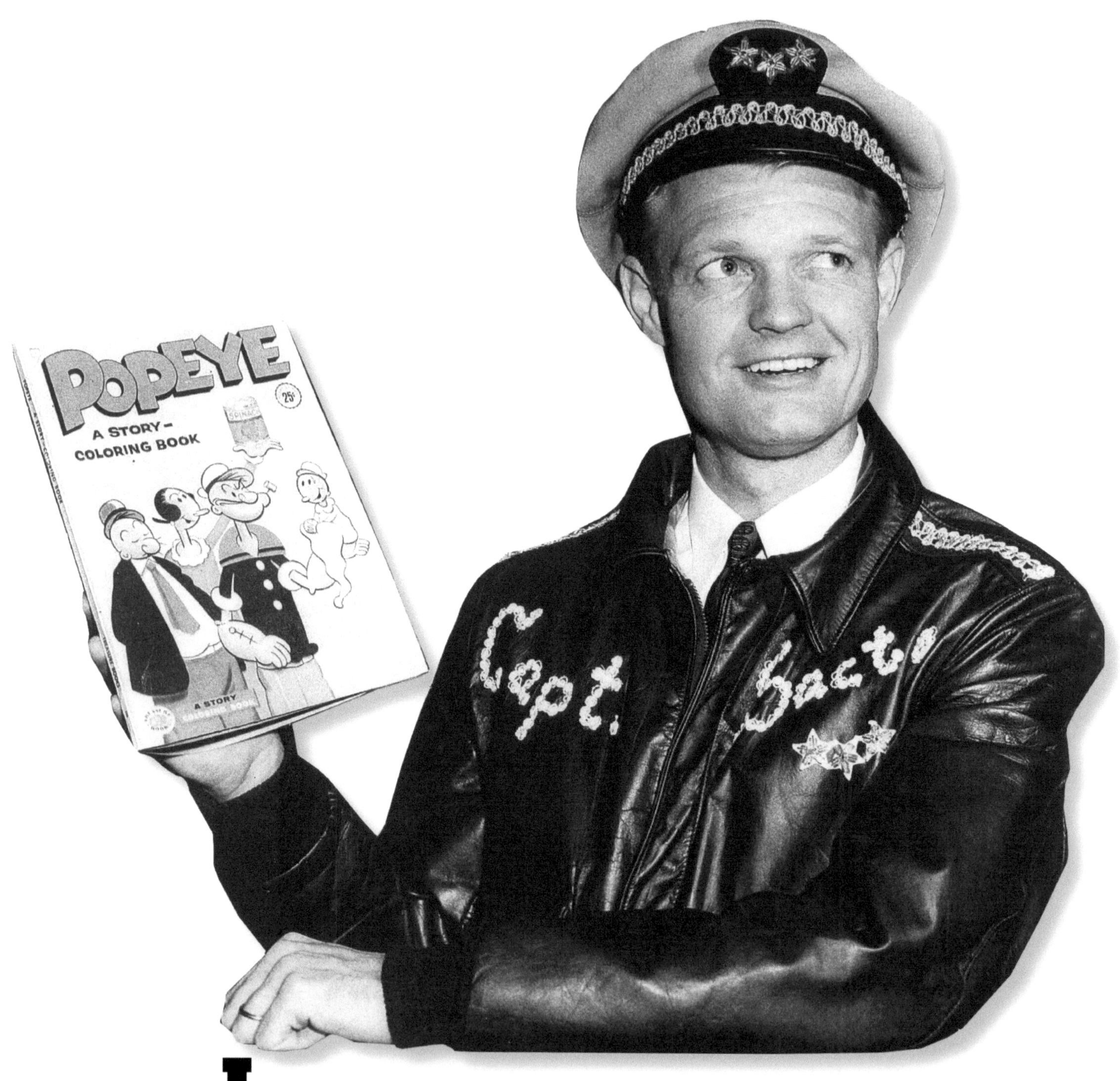

I stayed at KCRA for another seven years. I was offered a job at the ABC affiliate in Kansas City at a somewhat higher salary. It was very appealing but in the meantime I had been doing freelance work for Fred Wade. Fred owned Wade Advertising and previous to that he had worked at Channel 3. He was the first Captain Sacto, before Harry Martin.

Fred was very creative and an excellent businessman, two talents that frequently don't go together. When he heard I was interested in the Kansas City job he said, "Come work for me." I accepted. Don Chandler became the new art director at KCRA. Don was my talented assistant and made an excellent art director.

"Fred's accounts were like a 'Who's Who' of Sacramento advertisers: Crystal Creamery, KCRA Radio and TV, Rancho Murieta, River City Bank..."

Fred's accounts were like a "Who's Who" of Sacramento advertisers: Crystal Creamery; KCRA Radio and TV; Rancho Murieta; River City Bank; Don Burton Shoes; Potter, Taylor Scurfield; MadeRite Sausage; and many more I can't remember.

Our first office was in an apartment behind the Sacramento Inn. I've forgotten the name. It was next to the Jayrob Theater. Jayrob was a very popular innovative group of players organized by Justis Wyman and his son Rob. We were in the center of social energy. Nearby was the Arden Fair Shopping Center and a group of movie theaters.

Pete Higgins was our sales rep and marketing guy. He was good, smart, perky and a good dresser; very contemporary. One afternoon Pete and I got into Fred's supply of Tanqueray gin. We managed to diminsh most of a bottle. We went to the liquor store and bought a very cheap bottle of gin to refill the Tanqueray.

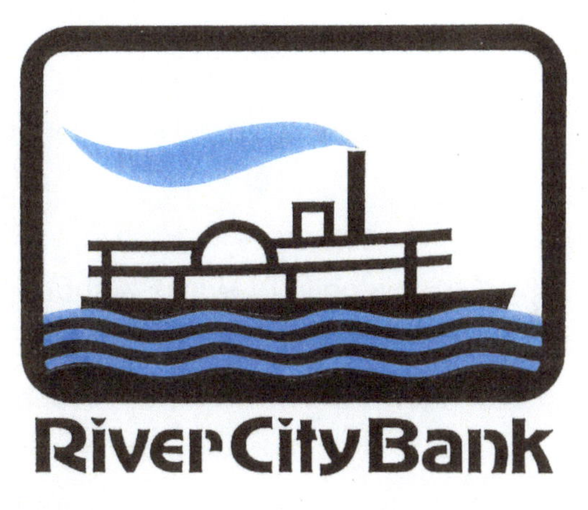

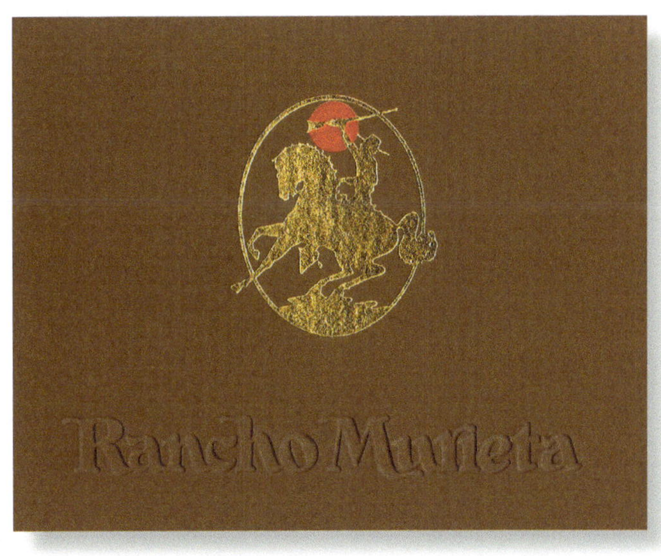

Don Burton, a client who owned Don Burton Shoes stopped by three or four days a week to have a relaxing drink with Fred. This day he came in looking glum. It had not been a good day. He went to the kitchen where my art department was and took out the bottle of gin. He poured a generous glass, and sat back trying to forget the problems of the day. He took a gulp of the gin. He looked at the gin, looked at me and said, "Bobby, it's been such a crappy day, even the gin tastes bad."

I worked for Fred until 1977. It was a great ride. Fred gave me a great amount of freedom. I think we did the best, most innovative and compelling advertising and promotion in the Sacramento area at that time. In 1977, Fred encouraged me to open my own art service. I did art and design for all his accounts as well as any new accounts I would acquire (as long as my new accounts did not compete with Fred's).

Fred set me up in business. Although he was paying me well, he felt I could do better financially if I were on my own. Fred was an entrepreneur and wanted to pass that spirit of adventure in business on to me. I have not had a job since. From 1977 until now, I have been self employed...and glad of it!

I have always been grateful to Fred. He was my best friend and a superb mentor.

Fred was also a concerned citizen. He was a Republican (I was a Democrat). We handled a number of Republican campaigns. Most were moderate enough so I was able to soothe my more liberal conscience (Well I did have children in college!). However, when the agency worked on the campaign of Max Rafferty, who I considered a right wing nut, I refused. He won his campaign for Superintendent of Public Education for California and made a mess of his job. Later he left and took the

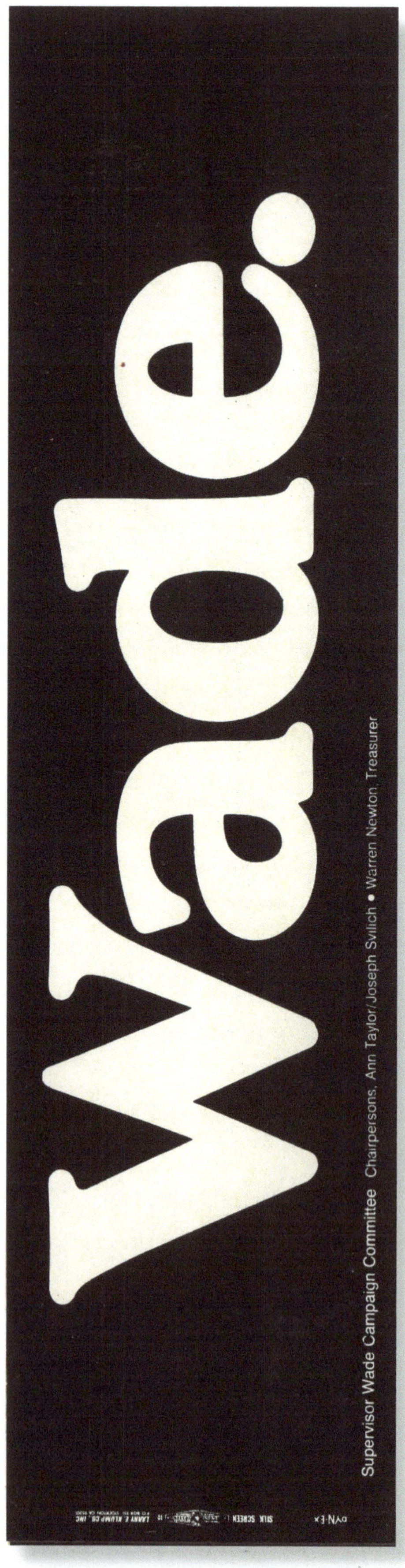

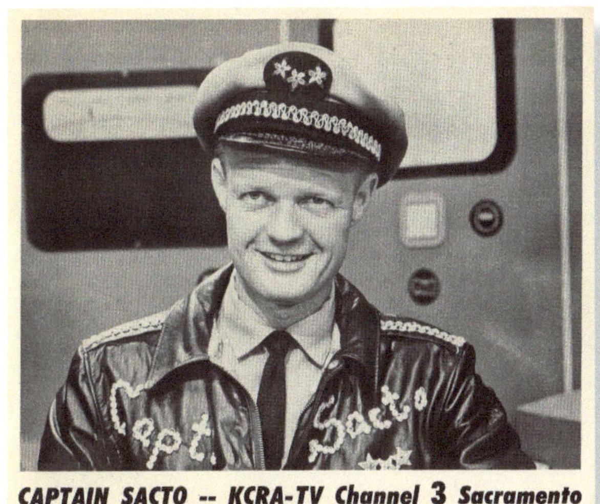

CAPTAIN SACTO -- KCRA-TV Channel 3 Sacramento

same position in Alabama. It was said when he left California he raised the state's IQ and when he arrived in Alabama he lowered theirs even more.

In 1975 Fred was appointed Sacramento County Supervisor by Governor Reagan. He was a good Supervisor and did a fine job for his constituents. Pat Melarkey, a much more liberal politician, served with him and still speaks highly of him.

We all have weaknesses (I'll talk more about mine later). Fred's was alcohol. Although he never neglected his accounts, personal relationships could suffer. I can remember working late nights with Fred. I would hear pebbles hitting the window from below. It would be Dick Hubbard of Hubbard Moving and Storage (one of our accounts). Dick would say, "Can little Fred come out and play?" I would get Fred and tell him Dick was at the window. Fred might say to Dick, "I'll be right down," or "Just one." Sometimes he would be gone for just an hour or so, but occasionally he would be gone for a day or more. Usually I didn't know where he was. Bette, his wife would call and all I could tell her was he was out with Dick. She presumed I was hiding his real whereabouts but usually I really didn't know. Sometimes he would call from Las Vegas or Los Angeles. He and Dick would drink a lot and then hop on a plane just for fun. In those days you could get on a PSA jet (with no security), and pay your $25 round trip ticket on the plane. What an airline!

In the spring of 1981 after he retired from the Board of Supervisors he came to my home studio. We spent several hours talking about our future together. He was full of energy and optimism about the new accounts we might acquire now that he was off the board and could put all of his energy back into the business. I was really pumped up. The next day he was dead. Apparently after he left me he went to several bars in Old Sacramento. I don't know for sure what his movements were. He drove home, a little over 10 miles, drove his car into the garage and let the door close behind him. His radio was on and so was the engine of his Thunderbird. Some have called it a suicide. I don't think so. He was too enthusiastic and optimistic the night before. I think it was alcohol. I think he sat in his car, drunk, tired and sleepy, listening to music on the radio and forgot to turn the engine off and slept his last sleep.

He was in his early fifties. He had done so much with his life up to then. Who knows what he might have accomplished if he had lived.

I think about him every day.

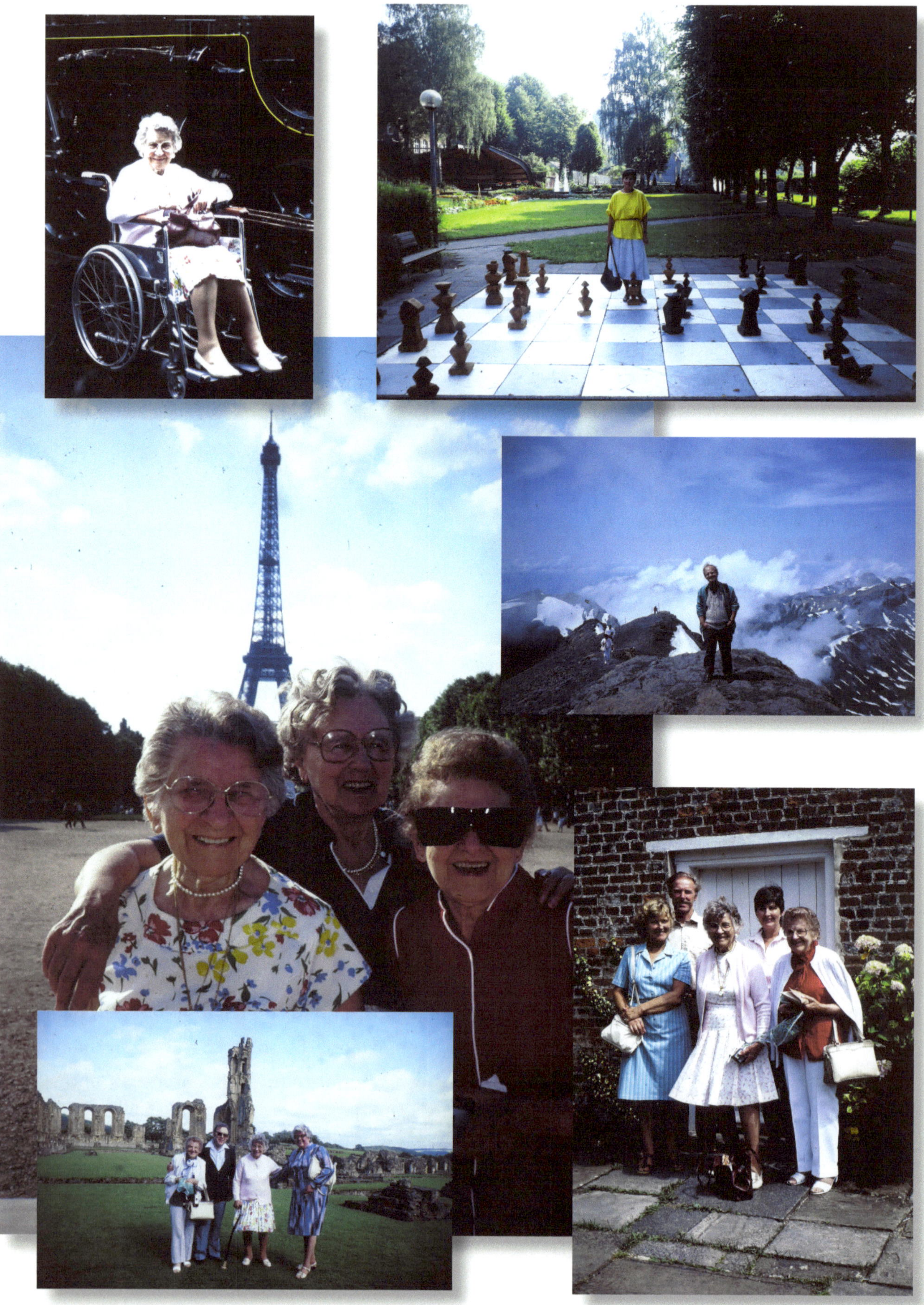

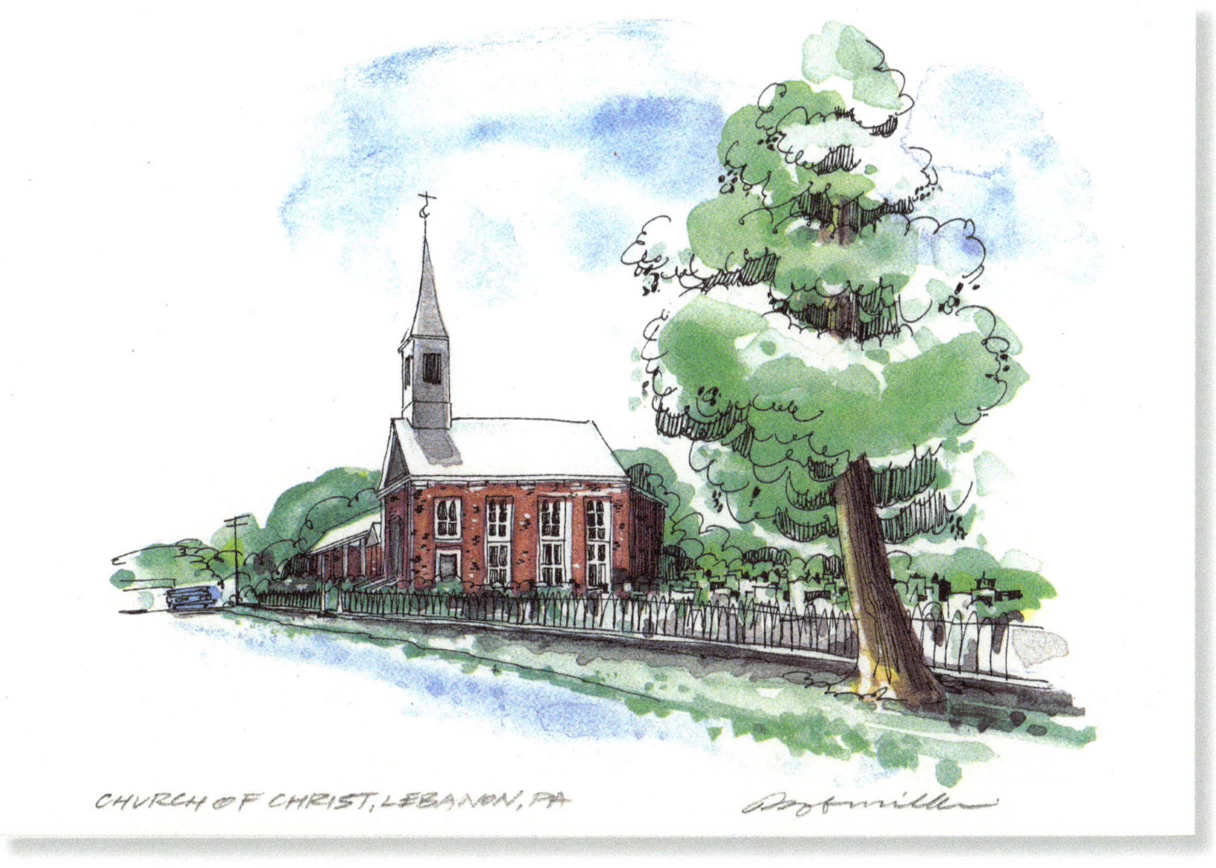

ANCESTRAL JOURNEY 1985

In the summer of 1985 Anita and I took my Aunt Emily Morse and my mother, Mae Miller on a trip to Europe. Emily was my mother's sister. Emily lived in Montclair, New Jersey. My mother and Anita and I flew to Newark, rented a car, picked up Emily and drove to Meyerstown, Pennsylvania for a Swope family reunion. Swope was my mother's maiden name. Every year the family held a reunion in Meyerstown. For me, having been raised on the west coast, it was interesting, almost foreign, to meet people to whom I was distantly related; many who looked much like me, who still spoke German or spoke with strong German accents.

The counties of Lebanon and Lancaster were settled by German immigrants beginning in the late 17th century. The primary language was German until the late 1940's. It was known as Pennsylvania Dutch but it was not Dutch, but a mispronounciation of "Deutsch."

The original family name was Schwob but the English colonials pronounced it Swope. One can tell the difference in immigration dates by the spelling of the name. If one immigrated to the English colonies the name was Anglicized to Swope. If immigration occurred after the Revolutionary War the name kept its original German spelling Schwob. At the request of the Swope family committee I was commissioned to paint a picture of the St. Jacobs United Church of Christ, located in Lebanon. One of our ancestors, Jacob Schwob, was a member of the church in the 1750's. Jacob was originally from Bennwil, Baseland, Switzerland. The church was built by Schwobs who were from Switzerland. In the 18th century national borders between Switzerland and Germany had not been established so it was not uncommon for Schwobs to live in what we now call Germany and Switzerland, but in those days it was all the same.

I painted a big watercolor of the church. It was to be a gift to the town of Bennwil. I shipped the painting to the town in advance of our planned visit. I also made 100 small notecards, with envelopes, of the art for the town to sell in the gift shop.

After the Swope reunion we flew from Kennedy Airport in New York to Heathrow in London. We rented

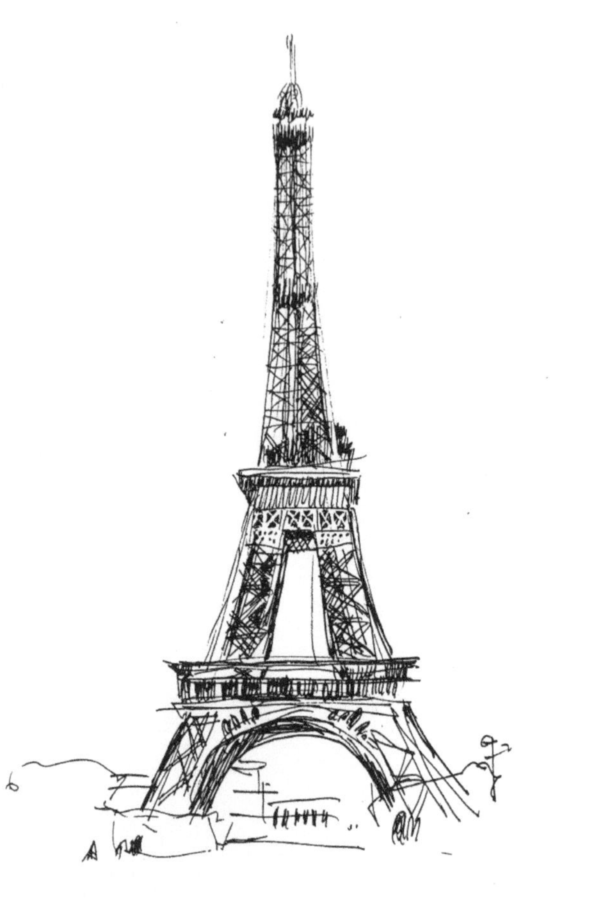

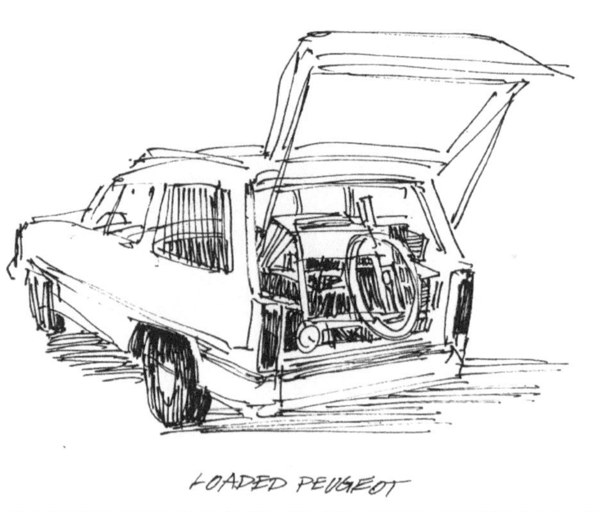

LOADED PEUGEOT

a car and visited our friends Emma and Isabel Wilcock in Esher. Before leaving for the continent we took Emily and my mother on the quick tour of London. We saw Buckingham Palace, Big Ben, Windsor Castle and London Bridge. After a few days in London we left Victoria Station for Folkestone. We invited Isabel to come with us. We now had three women over 85 in our group.

As there would be a lot of walking, to accomodate my mother we rented a light wheelchair in London. I was also concerned about the distance between the train station in Folkestone and the ferry to Bologne, France. It was probably a little more than 200 yards, a long walk for someone 89 years old. I didn't need to worry. As we got off the train the railroad guards spotted Mom's wheelchair and pushed her to the boat. We were the first ones on the boat. When we arrived in Bologne the French guards saw the chair, quickly took us off the ferry and rolled us to the waiting train. We were the first on the train. The train took us to Gard du Nord station in the center of Paris. Guards rolled the chair off the train and to the car rental office. I was beginning to like that wheelchair!

We rented a big Peugeot station wagon. It had three rows of seats. Plenty of room for our luggage and the wheelchair... and Isabel could sit in the third row of seats and smoke (with the back window down) and not bother anybody else.

We stayed several days in Paris, saw most of the obligatory sights and visited the Louvre. There was a slow moving line waiting to see the Mona Lisa. The guards saw the chair and pushed mother--and the rest of her party--to the front of the line.

After the Mona Lisa we took the Bateaux Mouches, a dinner boat on the Seine that takes you through the heart of Paris. You dine as you leisurely enjoy the sights.... and of course the wheelchair got us on and off first.

After Paris we drove toward Stasbourg, about 300 miles on great highways with no billboards through beautiful rolling green countryside. We stopped in Reims for lunch and visited its beautiful cathedral. Not far away was the battlefield of Verdun and the wreckage of the Maginot Line. Emily's husband Wilbert had fought in the first World War in battles in the Argonne Forest. The killing in this area of France was on a monumental scale. Cemeteries ran as far as the eye could see.

We stayed the night in the Holiday Inn at Strassbourg. The next morning we crossed into Germany. On the autobahns there were no speed limits. The Peugeot easily did 100 miles per hour, even fully loaded. On the autobahn, 100 is like 60 in California. We traveled in the slow lane and were passed by cars that were going in excess of 150 miles per hour.

We arrived in Heidelberg along the Neckar River and made our headquarters at a hotel located on the side of a mountain overlooking the city. Heidelberg was close to our ancestral villages of Sinsheim and Duhren. Jost Schwab, a distant grandfather, was born in Sinsheim in 1656. In 1720 he emigrated to America. His wife Katherine was a Wolfhard. We met with our distant relatives, the current Wolfhards. They were very hospitable. Aunt Emily had written them to let them know we were coming.

We met the pastor of the Duhren church (I can't remember if he was related or not!). He took us to the church's graveyard which was remarkably large considering the size of the village. He told us how the Americans bombed Duhren during World War Two, explaining it had no military value. The church was destroyed and the little village was seriously damaged. The church was significant in our genealogy having been the place where our ancestors were christened and later attended services. The pastor was bitter about what the Americans had done to his church and his town--and let us know his feelings. At the time I was mildly offended by his attitude--after all, he lived in Germany at the time of Hitler. War is a terrible thing though, and there are probably more innocent bystanders killed than actual fighting participants.

Although my mother and aunt had never been to Germany, since their first language was German they were able to communicate. Since Pennsylvania Dutch had taken its own course since leaving the old country in the 17th century, it was considered "low German." Nevertheless it could be understood so we got along well

"As there would be a lot of walking, to accomodate my mother we rented a light wheelchair in London. As we got off the train the rail-road guards spotted Mom's wheelchair and pushed her to the boat. We were the first ones on the boat. When we arrived in Bologne the French guards saw the chair, quickly took us off the ferry and rolled her to the waiting train. The train took us to the Gard de Nord station where guards rolled the chair off the train and to the car rental office. I was beginning to like that wheelchair!"

even though Anita and I could barely speak or understand anything outside of "auf wider sehen."

We spent several more days in the Heidelberg area visiting distant relatives then moved on to Rudesheim on the Rhine river. Anita and I had stayed at a hunting lodge called "Jagdshloss Neiderwald," meaning Castle Lodge in the Forest. It overlooked the Rhine with a beautiful, panoramic view. We were told this was a favorite place for Luftwaffe chief Air Marshal Hermann Goering to relax and play. That night we had a great meal of venison and Germanic delicacies and then a great night's sleep in a huge, comfortable, studded brass bed.

Rudesheim is in the middle of Germany's wine country. Vineyards climb up and down the steep hillsides. It's amazing that they can be tended. We took a cable car ride which provided a great view of the vineyards and the river. Helicopters were flying around spraying the vines. After the cable car ride we boarded an excursion boat for a leisurely tour up and down the Rhine. We passed castles, which are now primarily used as youth hostels and the Mouse Tower. According to legend the cruel Bishop Hatto of Bingen, infamous for his burning of peasants, was attacked by mice to avenge his bad behavior. He took refuge in the tower but was devoured by the rampaging rodents. Today it serves as a signal tower for ships passing through the narrows of the Bingerloch. I am sure there are still a few mice taking their well earned leisure around the tower.

After another night's sleep in Goering's favorite lodge we drove to Rothenburg, well known as a place to shop for Christmas decorations and goodies. Anita did some shopping and mother, Emily and Isabel went to a beauty parlor to have their hair done. Boy, did they look good! Rothenburg is near the Black Forest so there are many items made of wood for sale, such as toys, musical instruments and cookoo clocks. It was really a magical place. I can imagine me as a twelve year old in Rothenburg: it would have seemed like heaven!

Our drive from Rothenburg to our next destination, Alpirsbach in Schwabia took

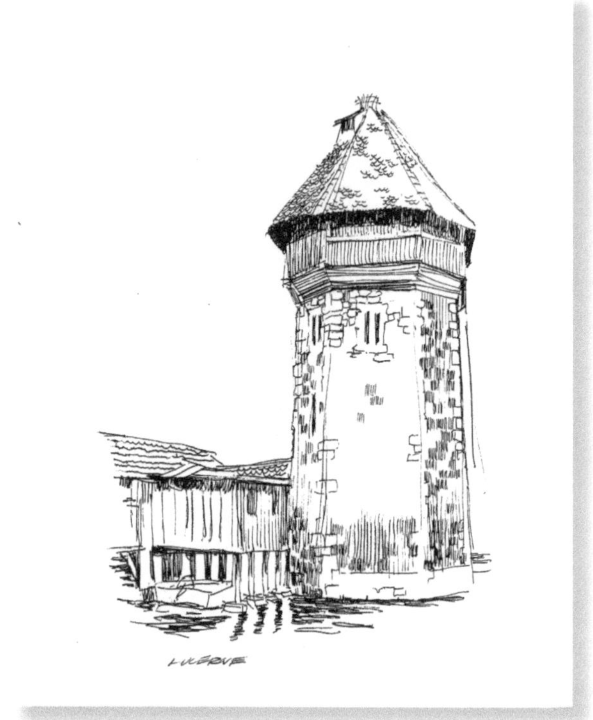

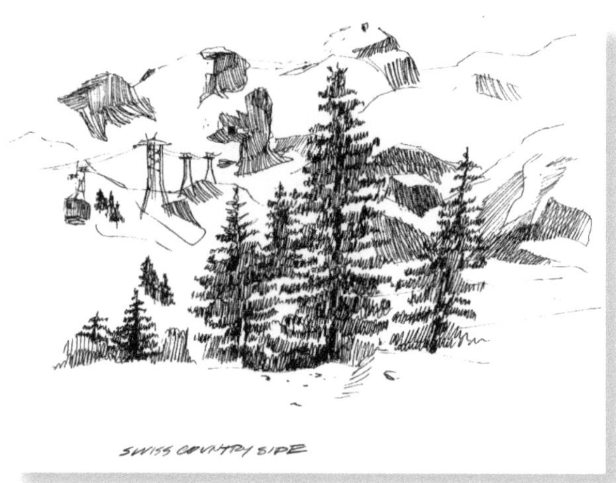

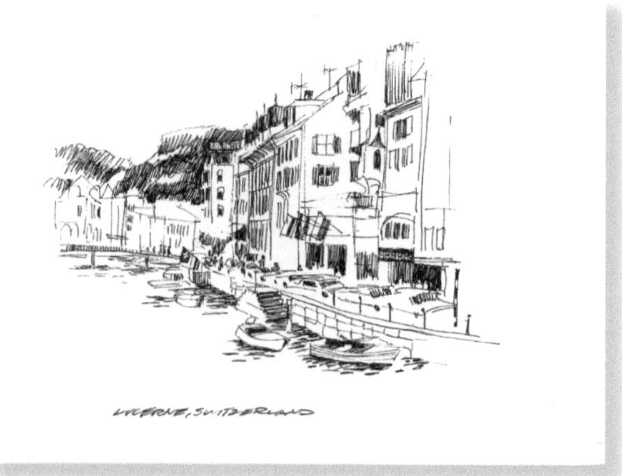

us through the dark firs of the Black Forest. We came to Alpirsbach to visit places our distant Schwab and Wolfhard relatives had lived and worshipped in. It was a brief but action-packed visit. The same day we moved on to Bennwil, near Basel, in Switzerland. It was a small village of about 400 people, but very well ordered. They were expecting us and I thought that the watercolor I had sent from New Jersey would have arrived but it hadn't. The note cards (with the image of the painting) had arrived, so they knew what the painting looked like. The city council gave a very nice lunch in our honor. They were very generous with their hospitality. On that day we met Elizabeth Schaublin, who became our interpretor. She was about our age and ultimately became a lifelong friend.

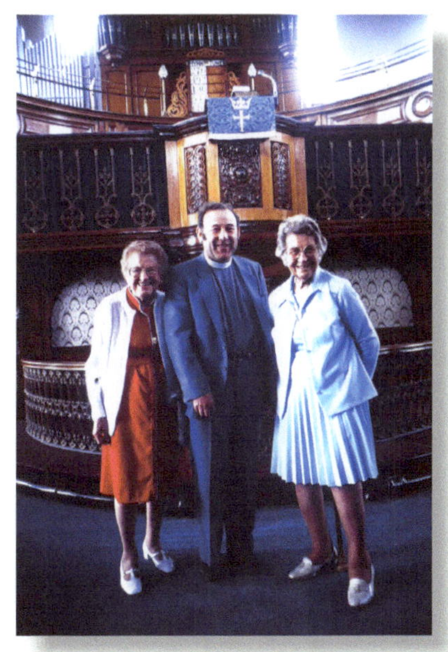

After lunch we were taken on a tour of the town. The tour included a vist to the town's bomb shelter. The shelter was buried deep inside a mountain next to the town. It had beds, kitchens and recreation facilities that could accomodate the whole town. It even had a basketball court! I was told every town in Switzerland had a bomb shelter. When I commented on the shelter they were surprised to hear we did not have the same. "You mean you invented the atomic bomb and you have no shelters?" I had no response except to admire the Swiss trait of preparedness.

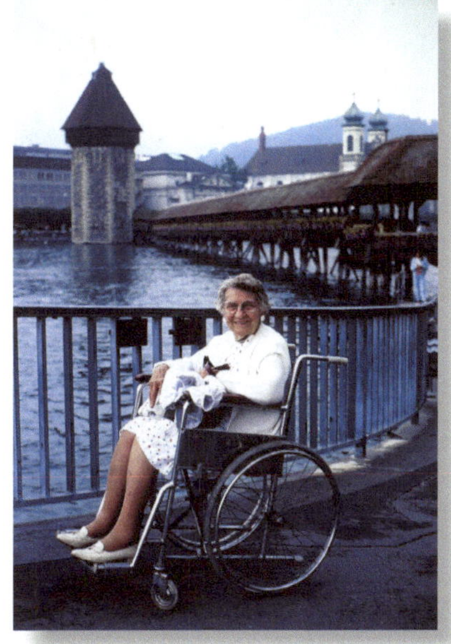

The next day was Sunday. For services we went to the small Bennwil church. What I had not known is that the pastors of the churches are state employees. Because Bennwil's congregation is small, a rural pastor will serve several churches. Our pastor served three. We sat in our pews. The pulpit was empty for about ten minutes, then a Volkswagen drove up. The pastor, with his robes flying, walked swiftly into the church and, with his head down, delivered a ten to twelve minute sermon in clipped German, slammed the Bible shut, walked quickly back to the Volkswagen, burned gravel and sped off to the next church down the road . Thank God for the separation of church and state.

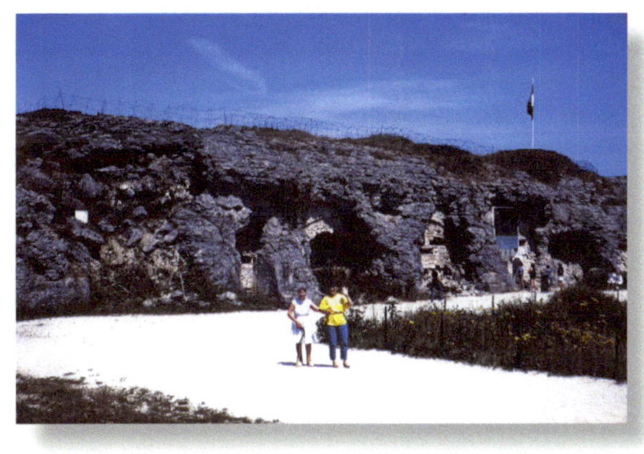

After a most enjoyable visit in our hometown of Bennwil we drove on to the Swiss Alps. Our goal was the Schilthorn, a mountain ten thousand feet high with a round revolving restaurant on the top

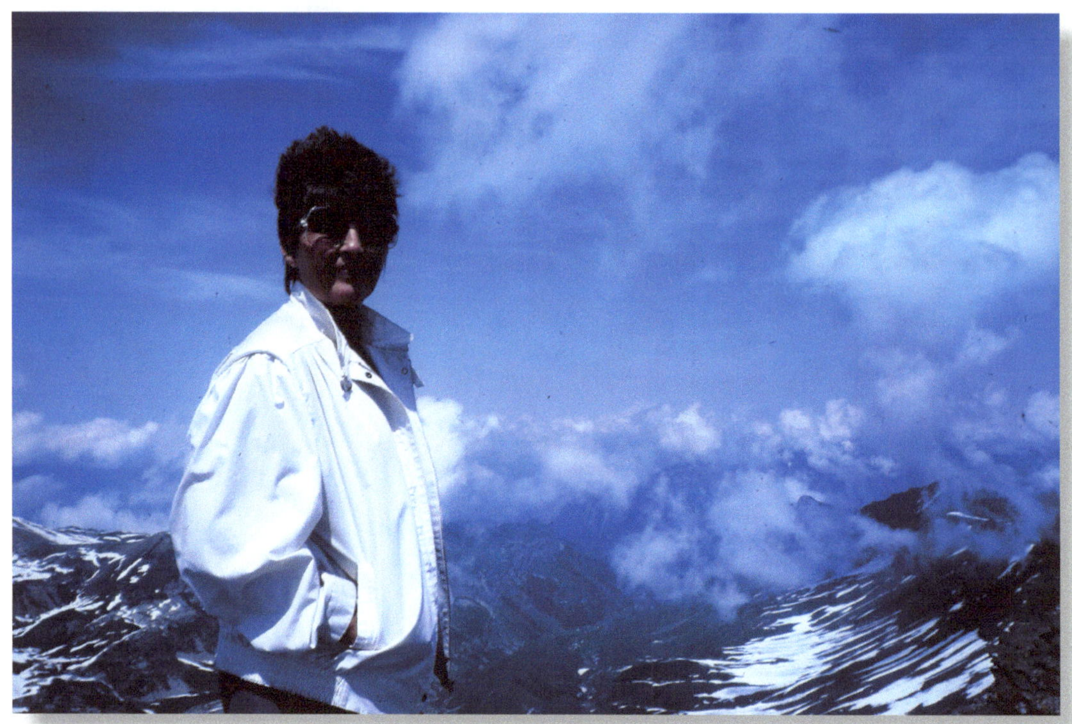

(I believe it may have had a part in a James Bond movie). We drove to Jung Frau station and parked our car for the night and took the cable car to Murren. Murren is a small village about halfway up the mountain with no automobiles. From Murren we changed cable cars to go to Shilthorn for lunch. From the restaurant you could see Italy, France, Austria and Germany all at once!

From the parking lot at the base of Jung Frau we drove to Lake Lucerne. We found the beautifully situated Hotel Vietnauerhof. The hotel overlooked the lake opposite the city of Lucerne. Every hour or so a ferry, in its route around the lake, would make a stop in front of the hotel and pick up passengers travelling to Lucerne or other lakeside destinations. We took the boat into Lucerne. What a beautiful ride. What a wonderful city. The three girls shopped for watches and jewelry--after all, we were in Switzerland! In the evening we took the boat back to our lakeside hotel.

The next day, from Lucerne we drove across France back to Paris. We returned the Peugeot wagon. What a great car it had been. Perfect for our trip. From Paris we took the train to Bologne, the ferry to Folkestone, and another train to London.

We rested a few days in London, then rented another station wagon and drove through the beautiful countryside to the city of York. I wanted to see the railroad museum there. I am told our railroad museum and the York museum tie for being the best of their kind in the world. It was no disappointment. What a museum. And the wheelchair came in handy again!

Emily's husband Wilbert had died several years before our trip, but had been born in Tenby, Wales. We drove to Tenby to visit his birthplace. It was an apartment above a pub. When I explained to the pub owner who we were and why we were interested in seeing the apartment he said, "No fucking way. It's occupied." He was unimpressed we had come 3,000 miles to see my uncle's birthplace. I did get a picture of the outside of the building. We stayed overnight in Tenby but not at the pub!

After a few more days of sightseeing in Wales and England we flew back to New Jersey, then on to California with my mother.

I think we were gone about a month. The trip was like going back in time. Being with the three eighty year old women was one of our most gratifying experiences. We usually like to travel alone; just the two of us, Anita and me; but these old ladies were so interested in everything there was no time to be bored. I will never forget it--and I highly recommend renting a wheelchair!

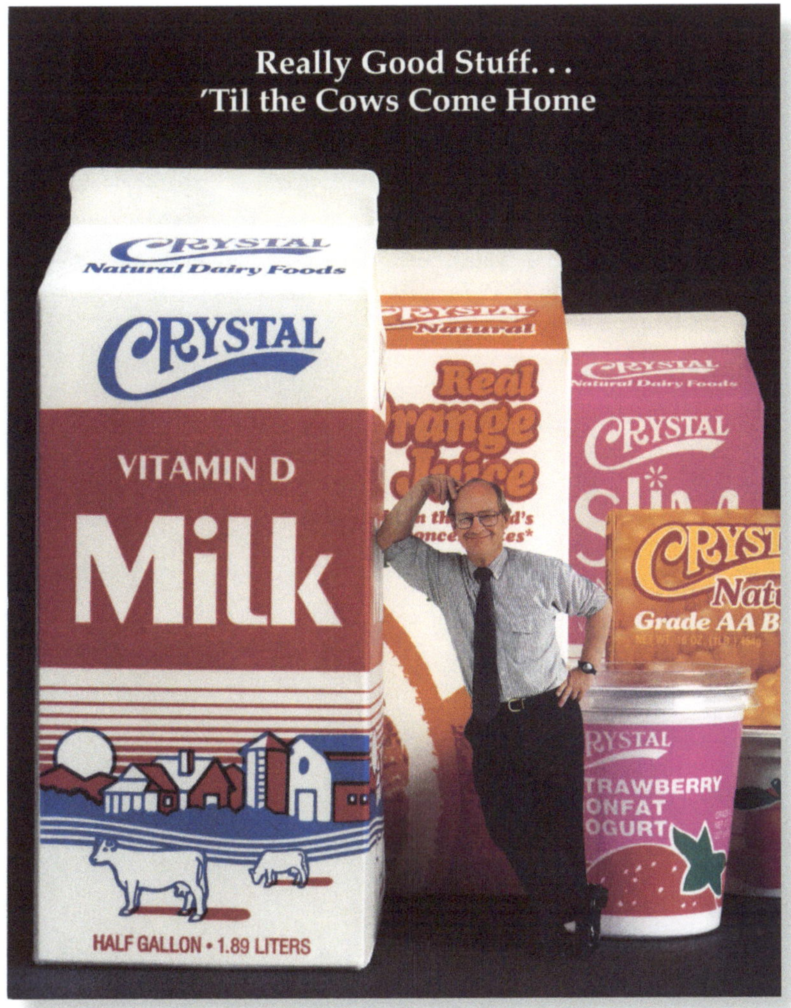

I decided to call my new business "Bob Miller's Art Department" because at Channel 3 we always answered the phone with a sharp, "Art Department!" We thought it really sounded professional.

Gale Okumura came along with me from Fred's and became my art director. She was even shorter than me but was she a bundle of energy and talent. I'll never forget my first meeting with Gale. She made an appointment by phone. She arrived at exactly the appointed time. Her presentation was an example of how a young artist, looking for a job, should present one's self. She was wearing a black blazer, white slacks, and high heels. She really looked like a seasoned professional. She said to me, "I would really like to work with you." Her portfolio was terrific: professional quality work presented with style and confidence. We worked together for almost twenty years and Gale never disappointed me. Finally, in the 1990's she left me to open her own business. She is still designing and, in addition is teaching at the University of California at Davis. I admire Gale. She is the real thing: talented, dependable and full of energy. She might be small in stature, but when she enters a room she fills it with her bright, confident personality. I miss our time together.

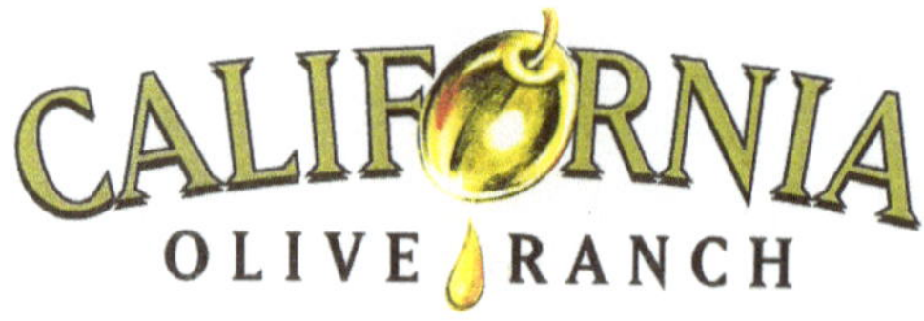
CALIFORNIA
OLIVE RANCH

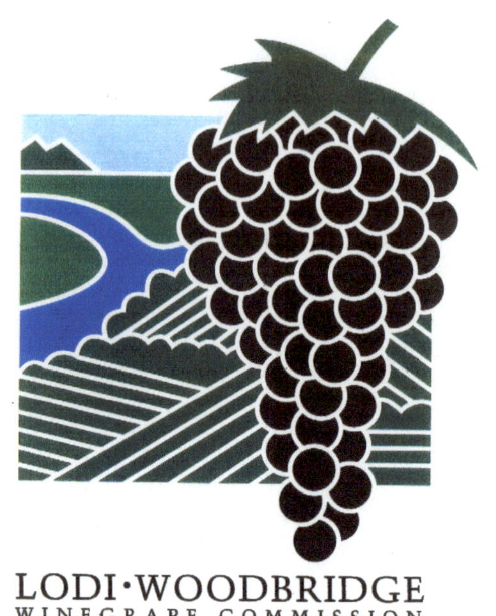
LODI·WOODBRIDGE
WINEGRAPE COMMISSION

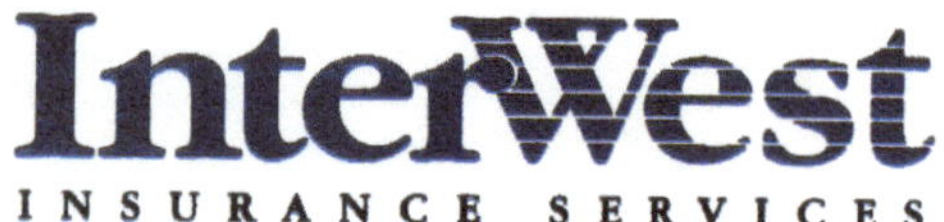
InterWest
INSURANCE SERVICES

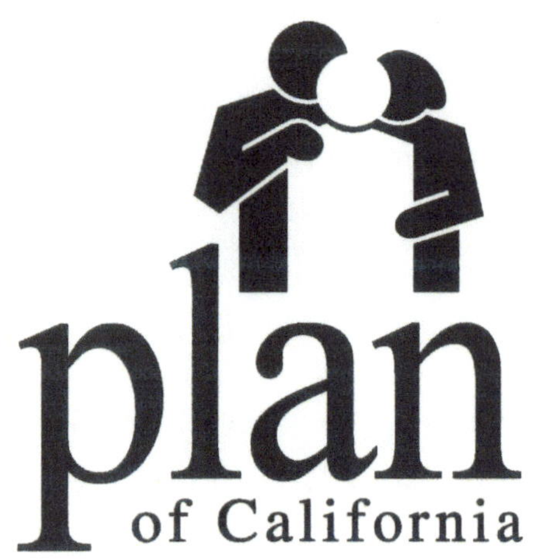
plan
of California

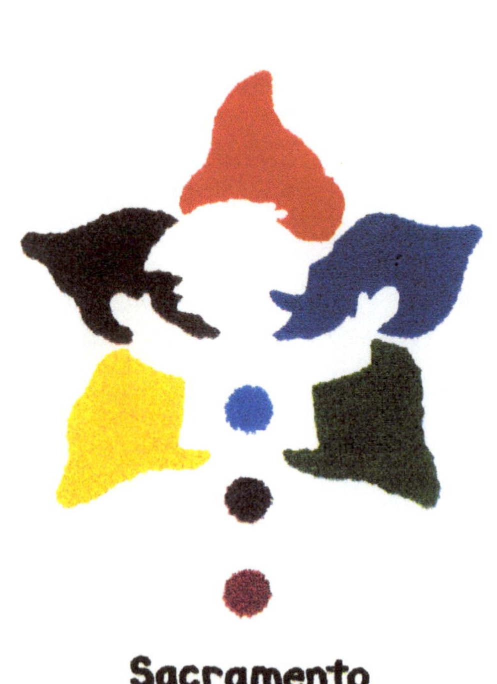
Sacramento
Children's
Festival

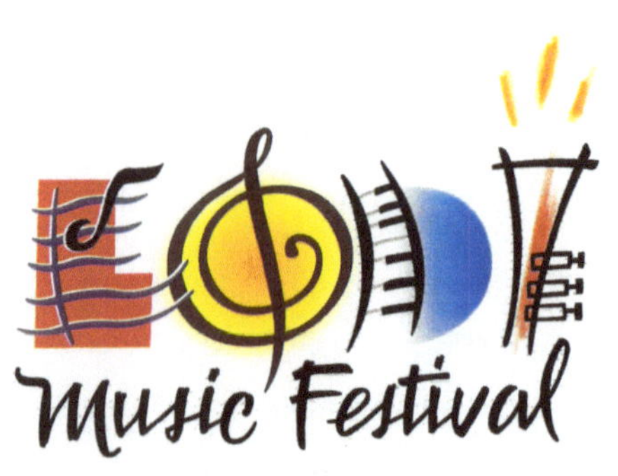
Music Festival

BOB MILLER · 1990 Sacramento Advertising Club's Ad Person of the Year.

Put Bob's creativity to work for you.

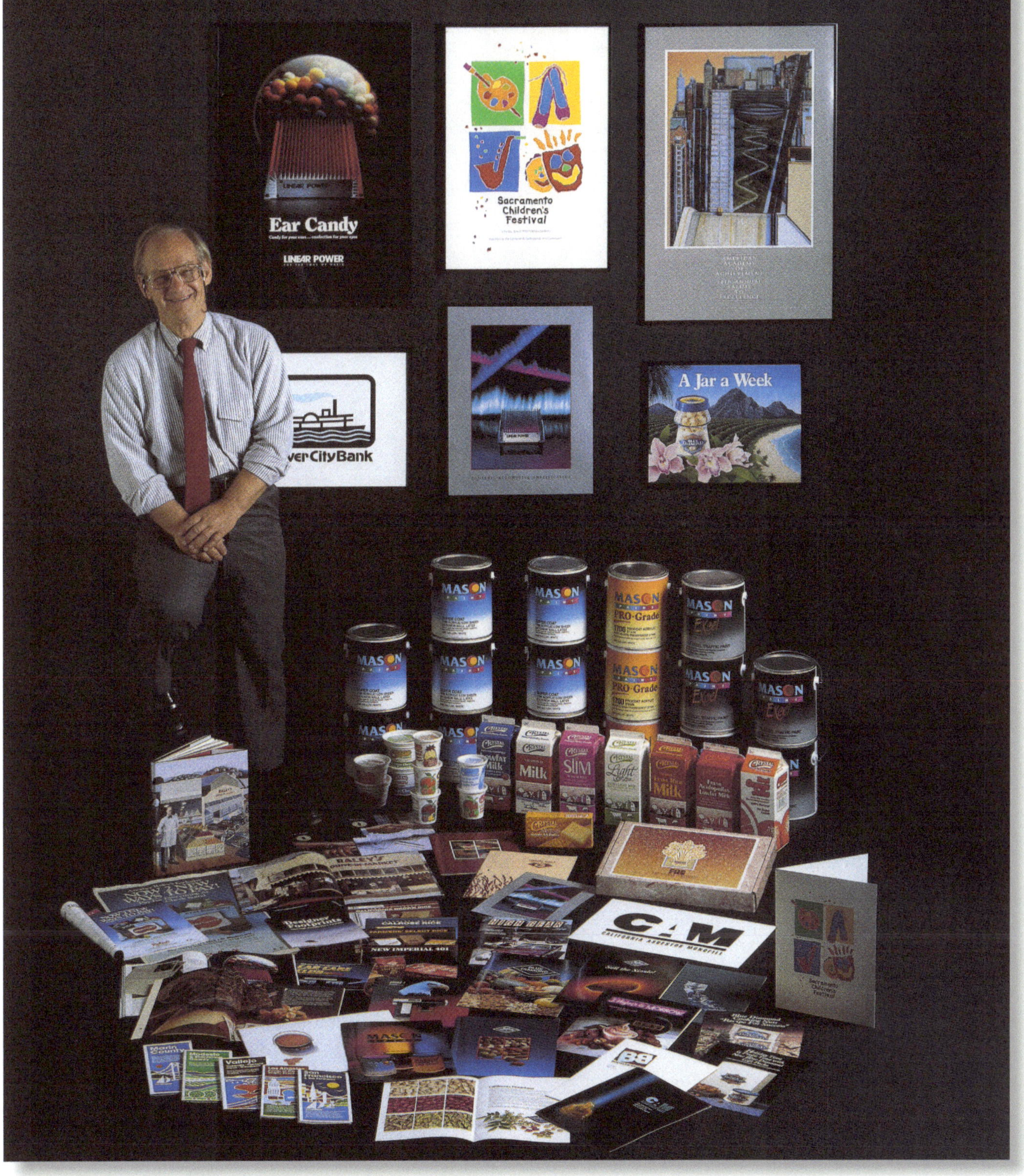

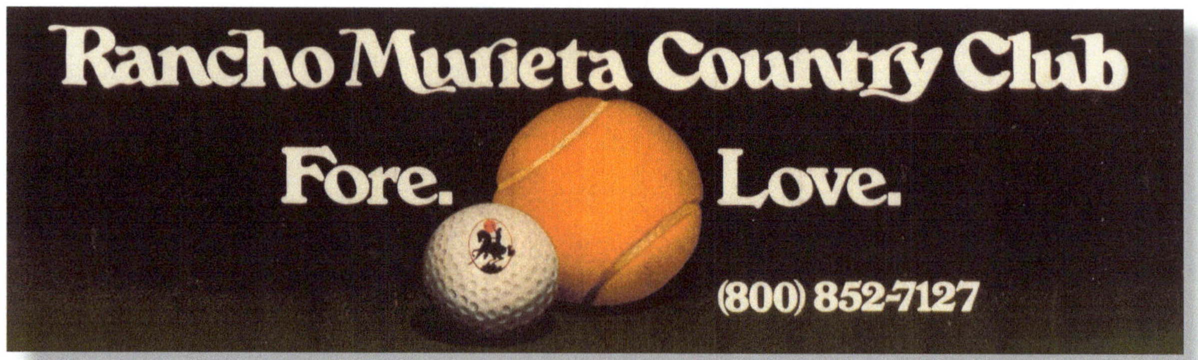

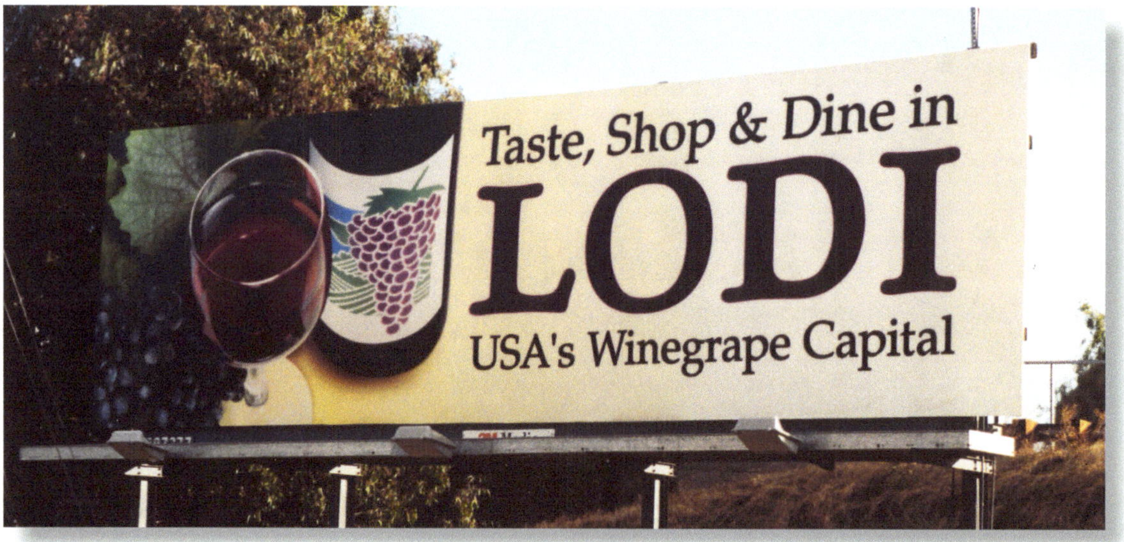

Sally Flannery became my office manager. She too worked with me at Wade. She was Nancy Krier's assistant. Nancy was Fred's private secretary. Sally kept me in line, seeing to it that I made my appointments and helping make sure that jobs were flowing through the studio in a timely fashion. We even made sales calls together. Sally projected a friendly confidence that I felt gave more depth to our little company in the eye of a professional client.

We were responsible for the art and design of all the Wade accounts I inherited from Fred, and in addition, we acquired Rancho Murieta and the Lodi Grape Commission. Chris McGlasson worked with me as a freelance creative person. Chris was great with concepts and imaginative themes. Her work for Rancho Murieta is still remembered. "Fore Love" was the original theme for a series of ads that included other headlines such as "Fore Fun," "Fore Brunch," and "Fore Business." Although we toyed with "Fore Play" it was never used.

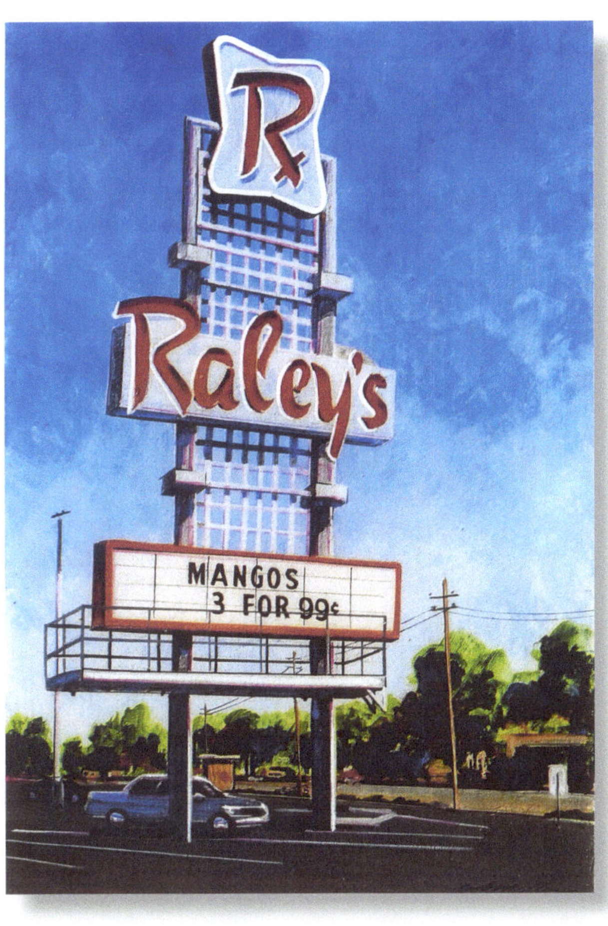

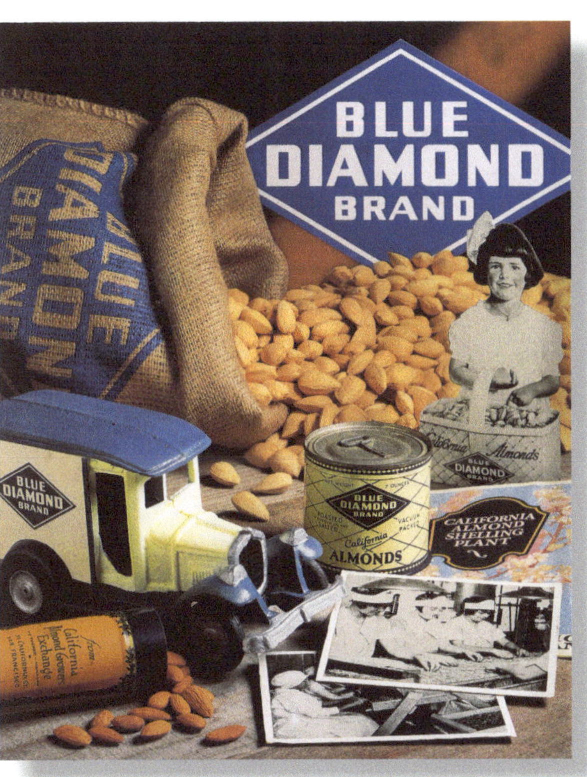

FROM CHRIS McGLASSON

I was hidden away at KCTC Radio voicing and writing commercials when I met Bob--at the time when people were actually listening to, reading and watching our ads. Perhaps he was at Wade Advertising or in his own business -- seems like he was always doing business somewhere in downtown Sacramento -- always moving around from one office to another -- downscaling -- upscaling -- all alone -- with partners and without -- but always the same Bob.

Bob seems to make magic wherever he goes -- and wherever I go. He created the world's best supermarket campaign for Raley's Bel Air Fresh Markets using just one illustrated or photographic depiction of a tomato, carrot, ear of corn, head of lettuce or side of beef. I loved those ads -- even before I started to work at Raley's -- simple, dramatic and yummy in all graphic aspects. It was the best of newspaper advertising created by my buddy Bob.

Then there was Rancho Murieta, a 3500-acre resort community in the foothills. Bob was the mastermind of our award-winning marketing campaigns -- most of his graphic ad creations won local, regional and national awards in the 60's, 70's, 80's, and 90's -- and the print ads in local publications were so sophisticated and memorable that they helped increase home and lot sales by over 60% in one year! We developed the popular, "Rancho Murieta. Fore. Love." concept using a close-up of a golf and tennis ball -- two hallmarks of Rancho Murieta's amenities.

After his stint at Wade Advertising, he moved to an office on 19th Street. I moved in with him as well and we had a glorious time creating ads for our list of prosperous and quite dubious clients. One of the most memorable clients was a gasoline saver introduced to consumers during our worst gas hike. The product was called LIFT (because your car will get a little lift?) and Bob developed one of his "right-on-target" logos. We trusted this guy since he came from a well known local family. Little did we know that he was the family's black sheep and subsequently never paid our invoices. Lots of promises -- but no money for all the time, effort and expense we put in to this bogus product.

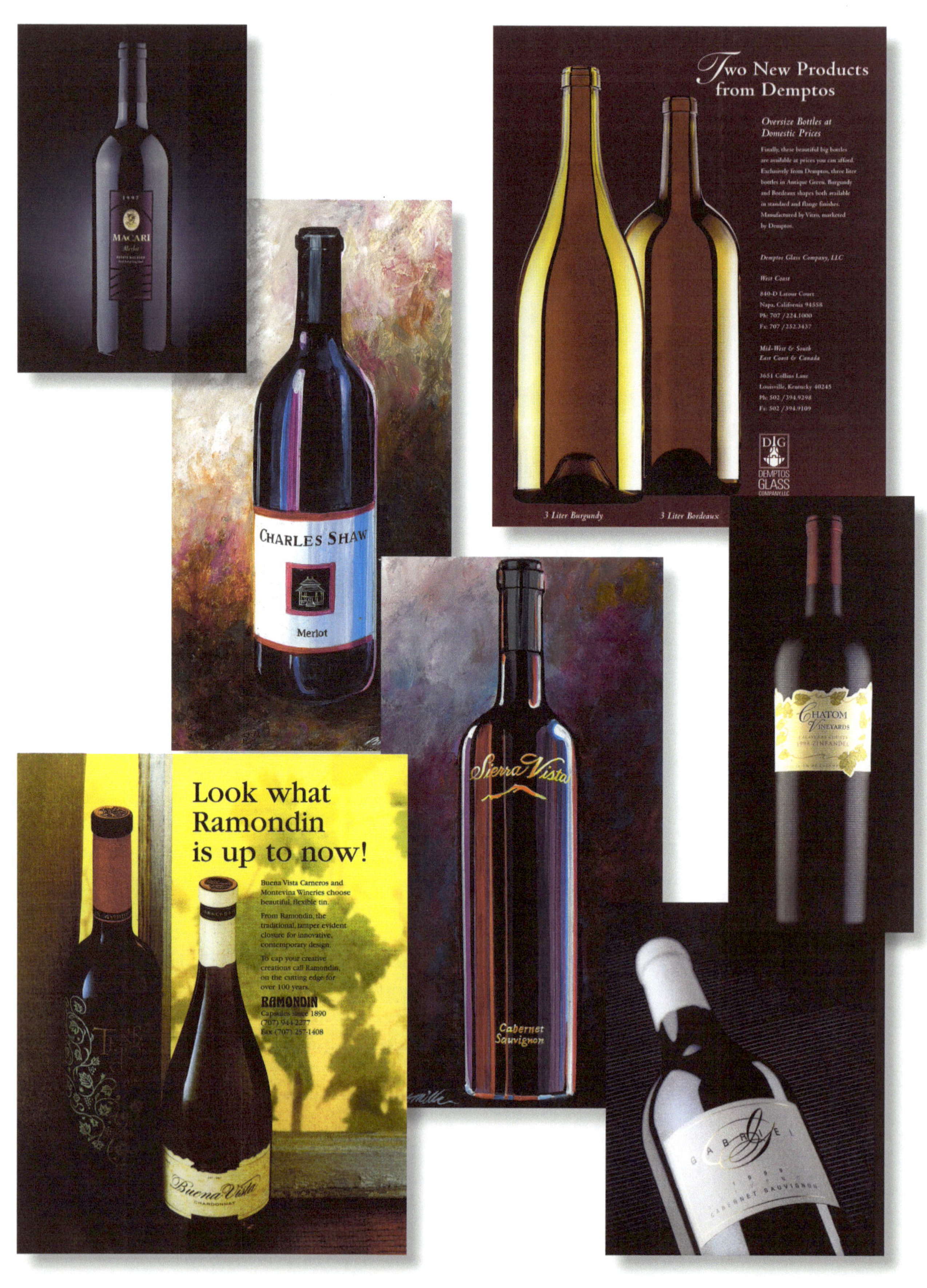
MACARI
CHARLES SHAW
Merlot
Two New Products from Demptos
Oversize Bottles at Domestic Prices
Finally, these beautiful big bottles are available at prices you can afford. Exclusively from Demptos, three liter bottles in Antique Green. Burgundy and Bordeaux shapes both available in standard and flange finishes. Manufactured by Vitro, marketed by Demptos.
Demptos Glass Company, LLC
West Coast
840-D Latour Court
Napa, California 94558
Ph: 707 / 224.1000
Fx: 707 / 252.3437
Mid-West & South
East Coast & Canada
3651 Collins Lane
Louisville, Kentucky 40245
Ph: 502 / 394.9298
Fx: 502 / 394.9109
DIG
DEMPTOS GLASS COMPANY, LLC
3 Liter Burgundy
3 Liter Bordeaux
Sierra Vista
Cabernet Sauvignon
CHATOM VINEYARDS
Look what Ramondin is up to now!
Buena Vista Carneros and Montevina Wineries choose beautiful, flexible tin.
From Ramondin, the traditional, tamper evident closure for innovative, contemporary design.
To cap your creative creations call Ramondin, on the cutting edge for over 100 years.
RAMONDIN
Capsules since 1890
(707) 944-2277
Fax (707) 257-1408
Buena Vista
CHARDONNAY
GABRIEL
CABERNET SAUVIGNON

It was about this time I changed the name of the studio to "Bob Miller Design." I thought it sounded even more professional than Bob Miller's Art Department!

In the late 1980's Mary Jo Corcoran joined our little group. She soon became a star. She did sales. I always had a hard time selling but Mary Jo had an engaging manner over the telephone. I don't know how she did it. She made cold calls, the kind of calls that I, after hearing a sentence or two, hang up on. Somehow she managed to get to and engage the prospective new client.

She started making phone calls to wineries and wine related businesses in Napa and Sonoma counties. We got appointments like crazy. Mary Jo and I were in the wine country two or three times a week. New accounts were pouring in.

I was producing a brochure and some wine labels for a winery located in the Dunnigan Hills near Zamora. The winery owner came to our office for a meeting about some new projects. During the course of the meeting he said, "Excuse me. I need to get something out of my car." I could see him through our office window. He walked to his car, got in and drove away. I have not seen him since.

Over a period of about five years we developed a relationship with over forty wine related accounts. Not just wineries, but capsule manfacturers, bottle makers, label printers and magazines. We had as many as ten people on staff.

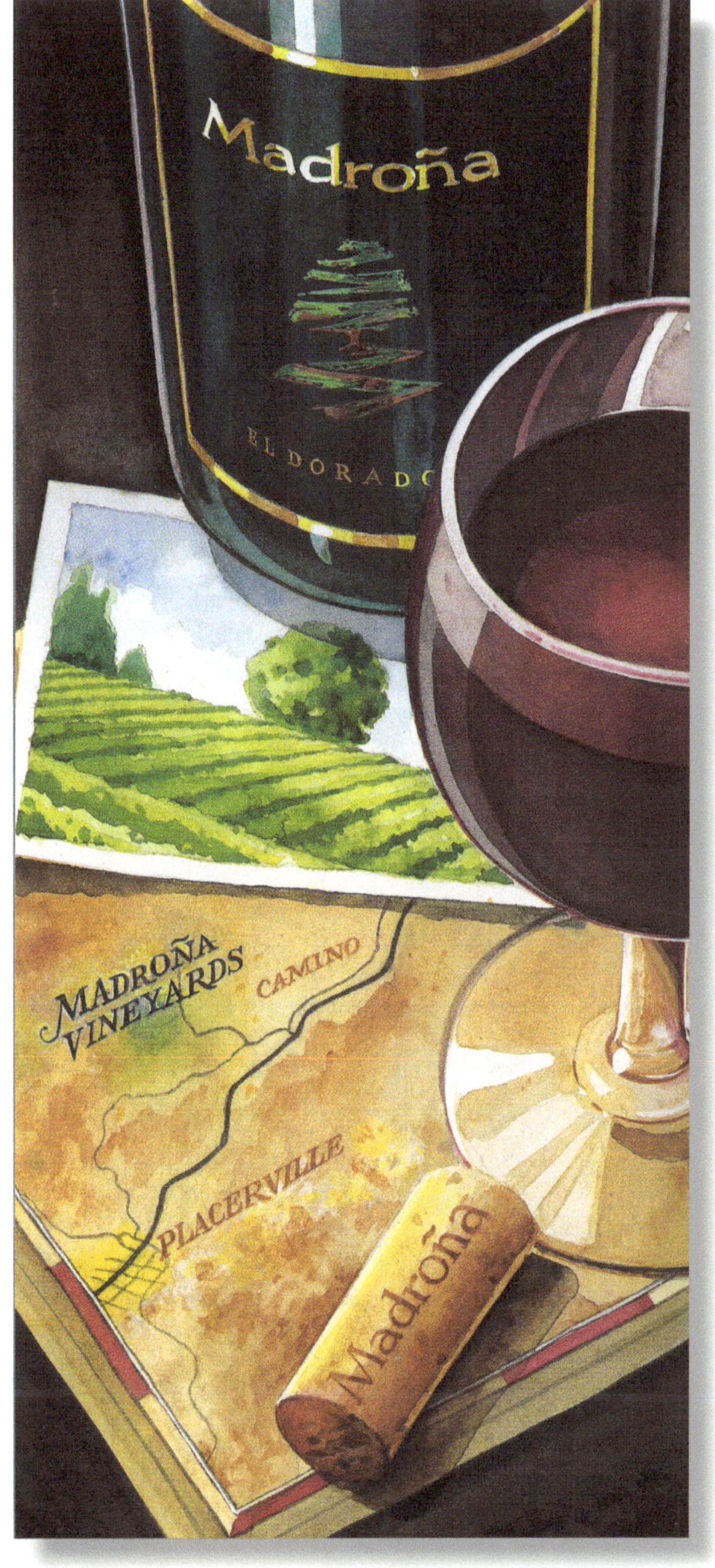

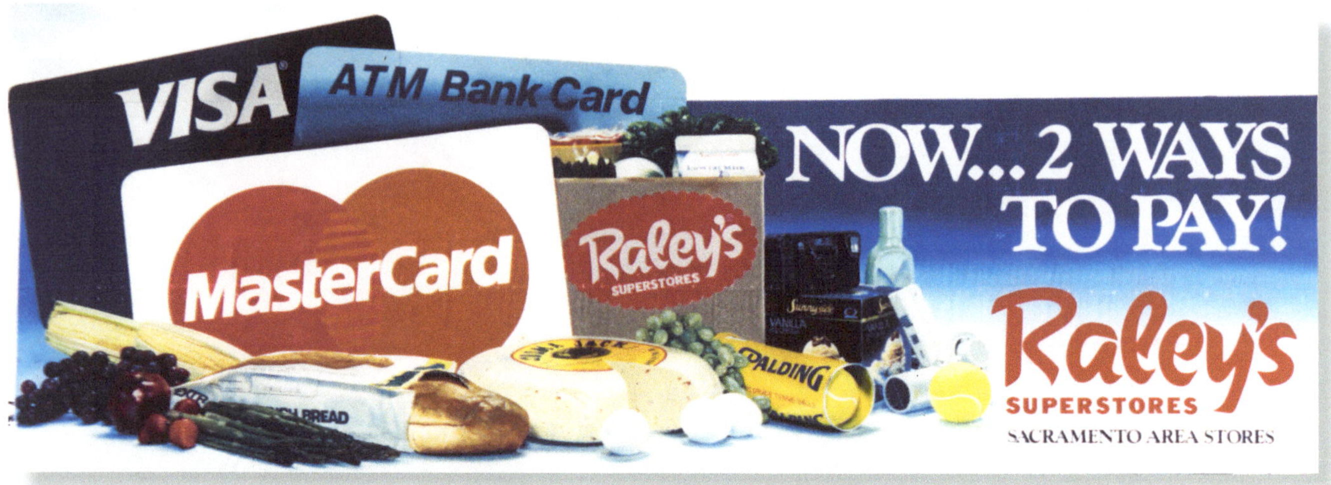

Considering all the work we did for them, this is all I could find of Raley's work in my files.

At the same time, we acquired Raley's as an account. Raley's newspaper ads needed an overhaul. We opened them up, gave the featured items more prominence and drama. Raley's developed their own huge and capable art and photo department. Ultimately they took over the design and production of all of their ads.

To this day, almost 20 years after our re-designing, the ads look similar to our layouts. We also designed and produced a book, The History of Raley's. In the book is the last official photograph of Tom Raley, shot by my friend Ron Busselen.

Gale Okumura had recently left to start her own company and teach design and marketing at University California, Davis. She was replaced by other talented designers : Lisa Pujal and Stacey Gibbs.

It was a great ride. Boy did I have fun. Probably too much! I did a lot of long lunches with a few glasses of wine here and there. I did not pay a lot of attention to the business end of the business. Although we were very busy we were not efficient and therefore not very profitable.

Anita was on the board of the local Kidney Foundation. They did a lot of fundraising. Their foundation's director resigned and needed to be replaced. Anita thought, "Fundraiser? Who better than Mary Jo Corcoran?" She offered Mary Jo the job at a somewhat higher salary than I could afford to pay and Mary Jo took her up on the offer! I really missed her great personality and remarkable ability to bring in clients. What a woman!

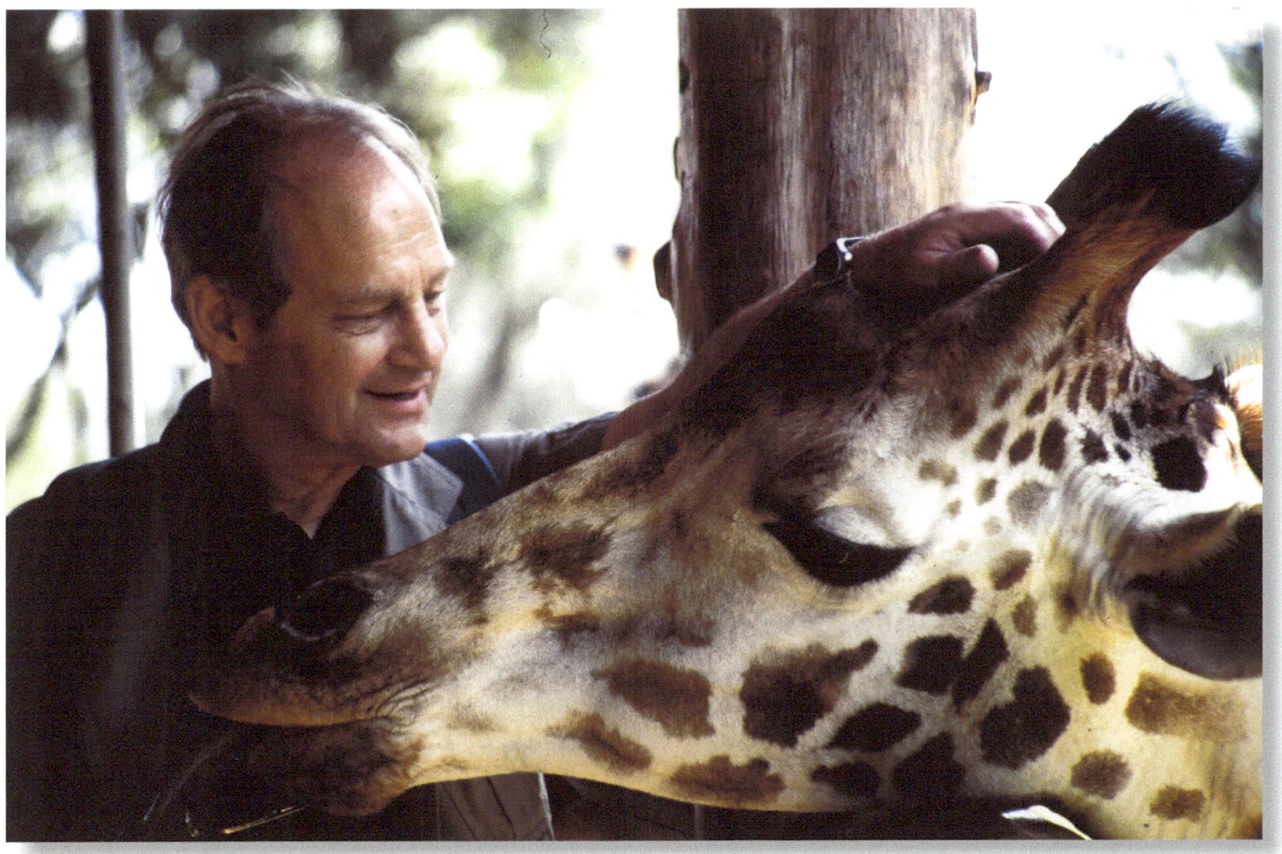

KENYA 1988

Africa was a continent Anita and I had always wanted to visit and Kenya seemed to be the most stable of the countries in the area we wanted to visit. It had large animal parks and relatively safe cities and a stable government.

At first we worked with a travel agent, knowing little about how to make arrangements on our own. However, she booked us into the Stanley Hotel in Nairobi at $200 a night. Wow! I thought where the average salary is $5 a day this seemed a bit much! My friend Olive Horrell, a very seasoned traveler, loaned us a magazine published in Kenya. In it were ads for various hotels. One looked particularly interesting. It was called The Fairview. It was located on the outskirts of Nairobi. It was advertised at $36 a day including all meals. I called the hotel directly from Sacramento and made reservations.

Because I had been having pancreas attacks before we left we were reluctant to make solid plans before we arrived. In other words, no pre-arranged tours. Our round-trip flight, via Pan American, from San Francisco, cost $2,900.

Our first stop was London, where we spent time with our good friends Emma, Isabel and George. It turned out our next door neighbors, Clair and Nelson Waters, were also in London. We all had dinner together at Emma's. What a great time we had.

The next day we flew from Heathrow to Frankfurt, then on to Nairobi. The Fairview was wonderful with beautiful gardens and lots of big trees. The next morning we woke to the sounds of birds singing in the Jacarranda trees. After breakfast we toured Nairobi, visiting the city market, the snake park and the giraffe park. Then we saw native dancers in wonderful ceremonial performances.

To make arrangements to go to the game parks we went to a local travel service. It was a small office run by a very friendly black woman. There were many agencies like hers. We didn't know one from another so we chose hers. We made arrangements to go with her to Amboseli, a major game park about a hundred miles away. The next day Isaac, our driver arrived at our hotel in his Toyota station wagon to take us to the park. On the way we passed many Masai walking along the road. They are very tall and lean and dress traditionally. We were told not to take pictures of them. They believed their souls were being taken when photographed. About fifty miles from Nairobi we stopped at a little country store to get some refreshments. There were many Masai near the store. Anita took a polariod of me in front of the store. One of the Masai saw the instant picture and asked Anita to take a picture of him. She did. He showed it to his friends. Pretty soon Masai warriors were coming from all directions to have their picture taken. Anita used up all of her film. She must have shot up to fifty pictures of these tall, beautiful people. They gathered like schoolboys having their pictures taken for their yearbook. So much for losing your soul.

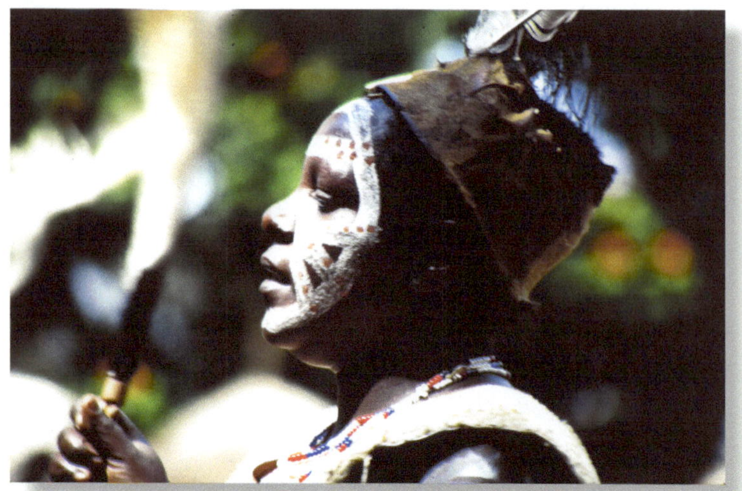

We arrived at Amboseli's beautiful lodge in the middle of the afternoon. We took a short nap, then Isaac picked us up for a tour around the game park. The geography reminded me a little of the foothills in the El Dorado Hills area. We saw elephants, giraffes, gazelles, wildebeest, zebra and buffalo. What a remarkable treat. And we had only been there a few hours. The next day in the early morning light we saw more animals: baboons, hyenas and huge storks. At the end of the day we returned with Isaac.

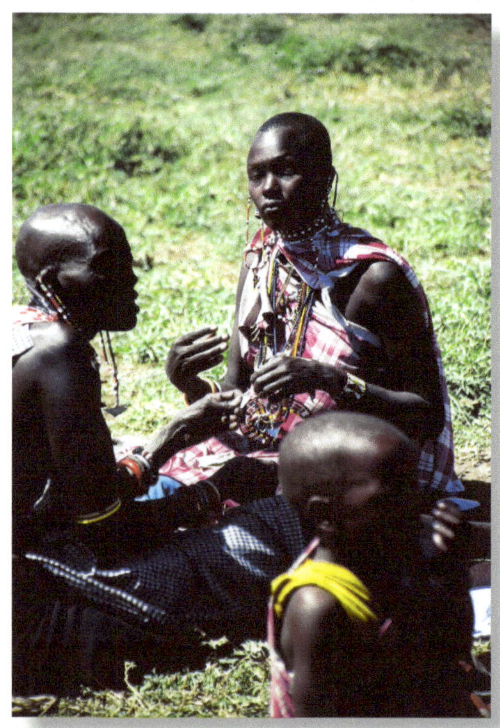

That night we went to a restaurant called "Carnivore." Anita is an animal lover if there ever was one. I have often said if I could come back in another life I would want to come back as a dog in Anita's household. Anyway, my wife the animal lover, showed a side I had not seen before: she ordered a main course of giraffe. I had water buffalo. She said hers was better than mine.

The next day Isaac drove us to Lake Nakuru. We drove through the beautiful Kenyan highlands, lush with tea and coffee plantations and then down to the Rift Valley. In the Rift Valley is Lake Nakuru. It is salt water. In the valley are many flats mined for their salt. Lake Nakuru is covered in pink flamingos. From a distance the water looks pink. As one gets closer to the flamingos they move, keeping a distance from you. It was like having control of a giant paint bucket. When the flamingos would fly off it was like hearing a jet engine and their wings flashed not only with pink, but also black. It was a once-in-a-lifetime experience.

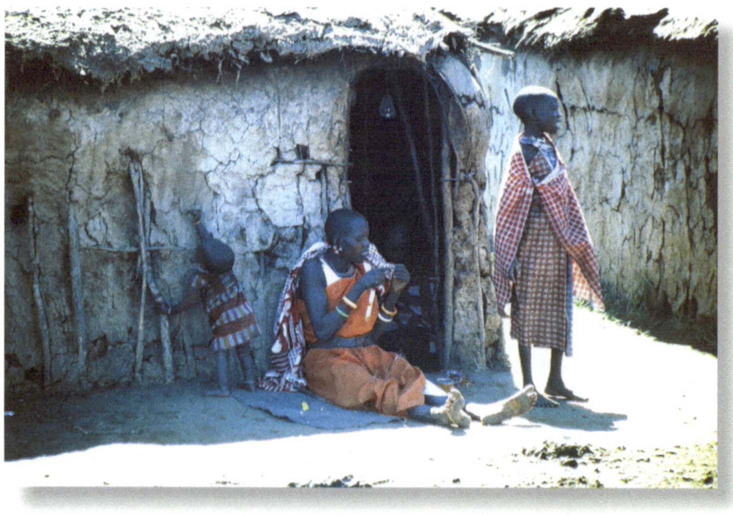

The following day Isaac took us to a country club to rest. It had a pool and some nice shaded areas to relax. Suddenly, I heard a scream from Anita! I sat bolt upright and saw a huge snake moving as fast as it could

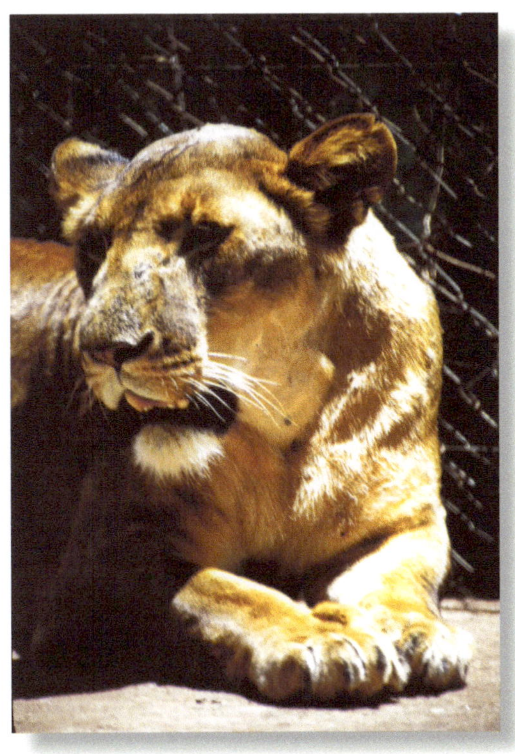

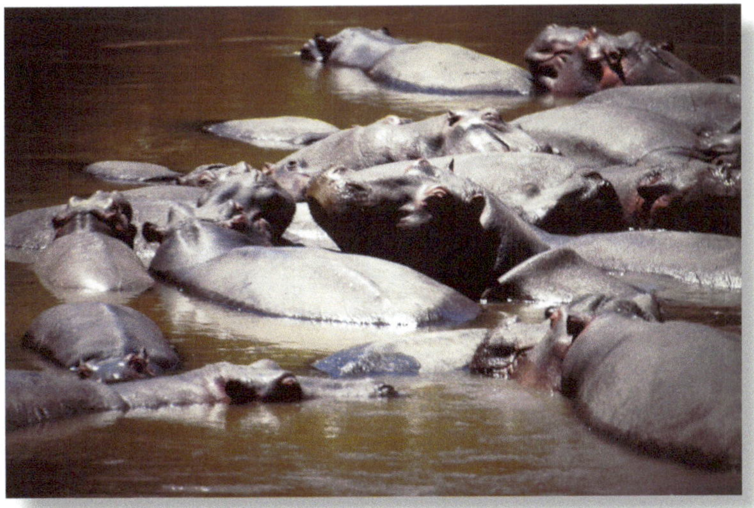

away from Anita. The snake had apparently lost its grip and fell out of a tree on to the sleeping Anita. Both were frightened nearly to death! About that time Isaac arrived. He was deathly afraid of snakes. He threw us in to the station wagon and drove as fast as he could back to Nairobi.

Our next stay was at Treetops, a small hotel actually built into the tree tops; a giant tree house. It was here that Princess Elizabeth was staying when she was informed her father had died and that she was the Queen of England. Our room was over a water hole where the animals came to drink. It was dimly illuminated so we could see them. All during our stay elephants, hyena, buffalo and warthogs came to the water hole.

From Treetops we traveled to Meru, in the center of Kenya. That night at Meru, lions roared until morning. The next day we saw many lions, both male and female laying around like couch potatoes. They apparently roared themselves into a daytime torpor. Later in the day we spotted some rhinos being guarded by armed rangers. The rhino population is dwindling because thieves kill them for their horns, a reputed aphrodisiac, and leave the rest to rot. What an awful business. The guards were wonderful. They

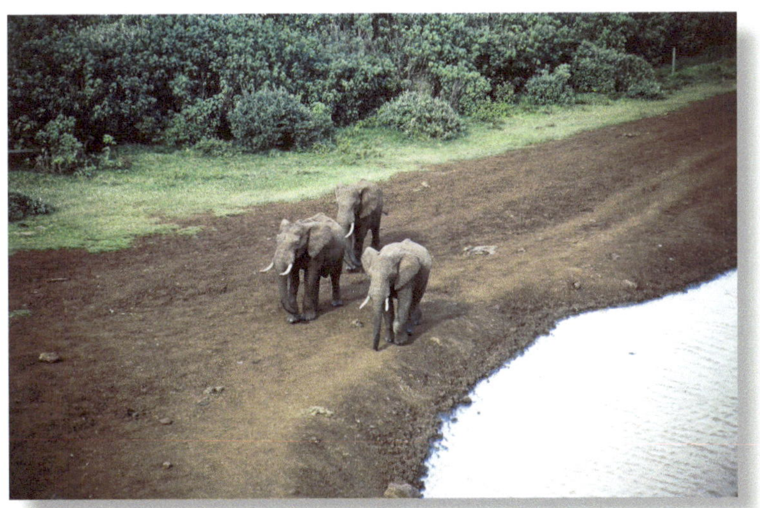

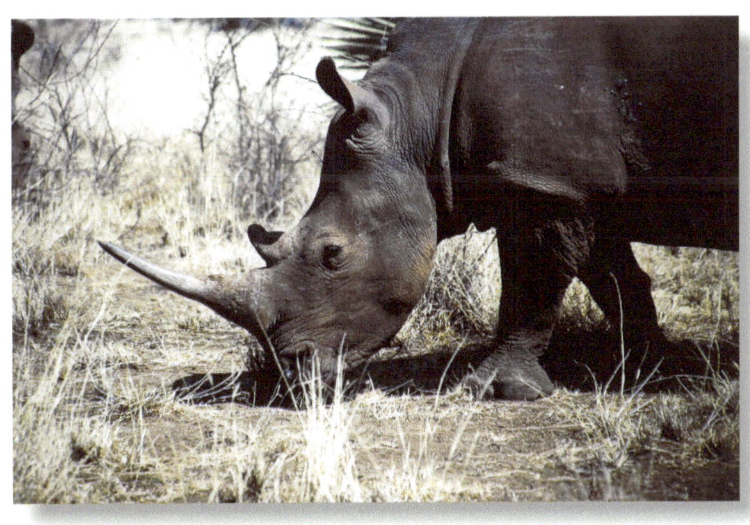

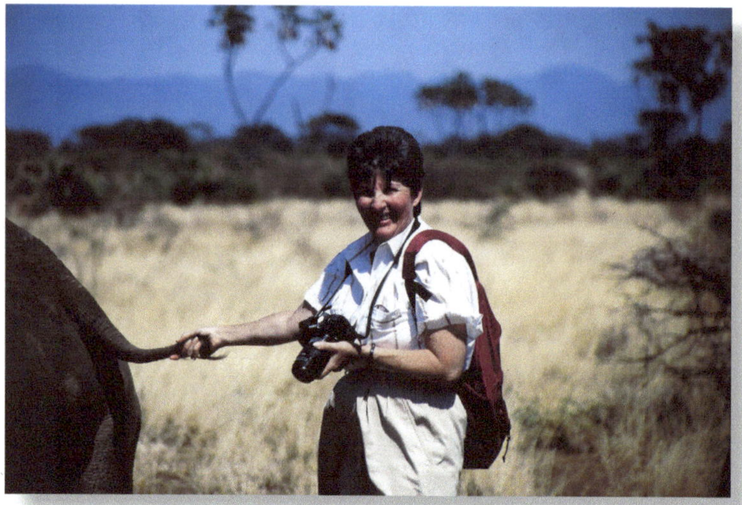

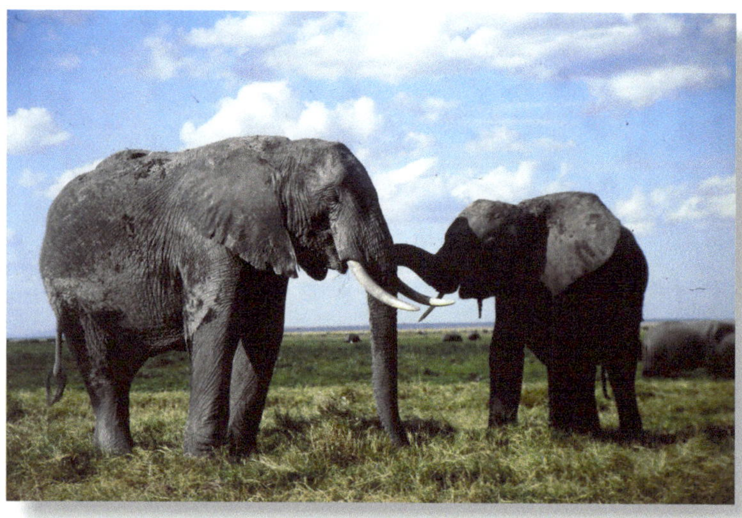

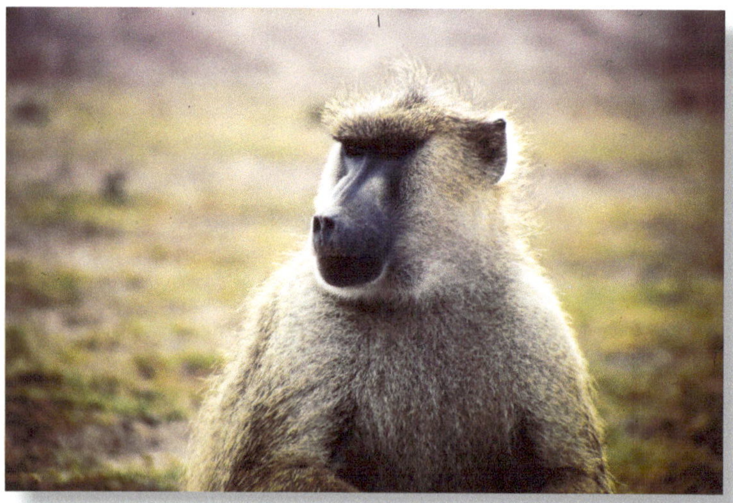

encouraged both of us to touch and pet the huge beasts. We later learned that not long after we left the rangers were killed and the rhino slaughtered.

That night we met with Bishop Kanake and his wife Jennifer. My brother Bill had arranged the meeting. Bill met him when the Bishop was studying on an exchange program in Southern California. He was the Bishop for that area of Kenya and they also ran a school. They are both very energetic and I was impressed by their dedication.

Our last game park was Masai Mara, near the Tanzanian border. We stayed at Cotter's Camp. Instead of a lodge, we stayed in small bamboo huts. The next morning with a guard armed with a bow and arrow we walked with wild animals: elephants, giraffes, gazelles and impalas. There were probably more that we didn't see. Later near the Mara Sapa Lodge at the Mara River we saw enormous hippos. They hardly stirred. They were not impressed by our presence.

One of our most interesting experiences was our visit to a Masai village. Their huts were made with bark, sticks and dried cow dung. Surprisingly, although there was a cow odor the smell was not unpleasant. They showed us inside their homes. The cow dung was also used as a floor covering. These people hold on to their old ways. It will be interesting to see how long that can last.

Our last night in Nairobi we ate at the Norfolk Hotel. It was an elegant meal. The next morning we went to the airport to catch our huge PanAm 747 back to London. We checked in and waited for our plane to arrive. And waited....and waited. Finally after many hours and with no explanation an airline representative told us a bus was waiting to take us to the Norfolk Hotel. We spent a very nice evening as guest of Pan Am. The next day when they returned us to the airport, our 747 was waiting.

We arrived at London with Emma and Isabel waiting for us at the airport. What a great adventure! One of our best!

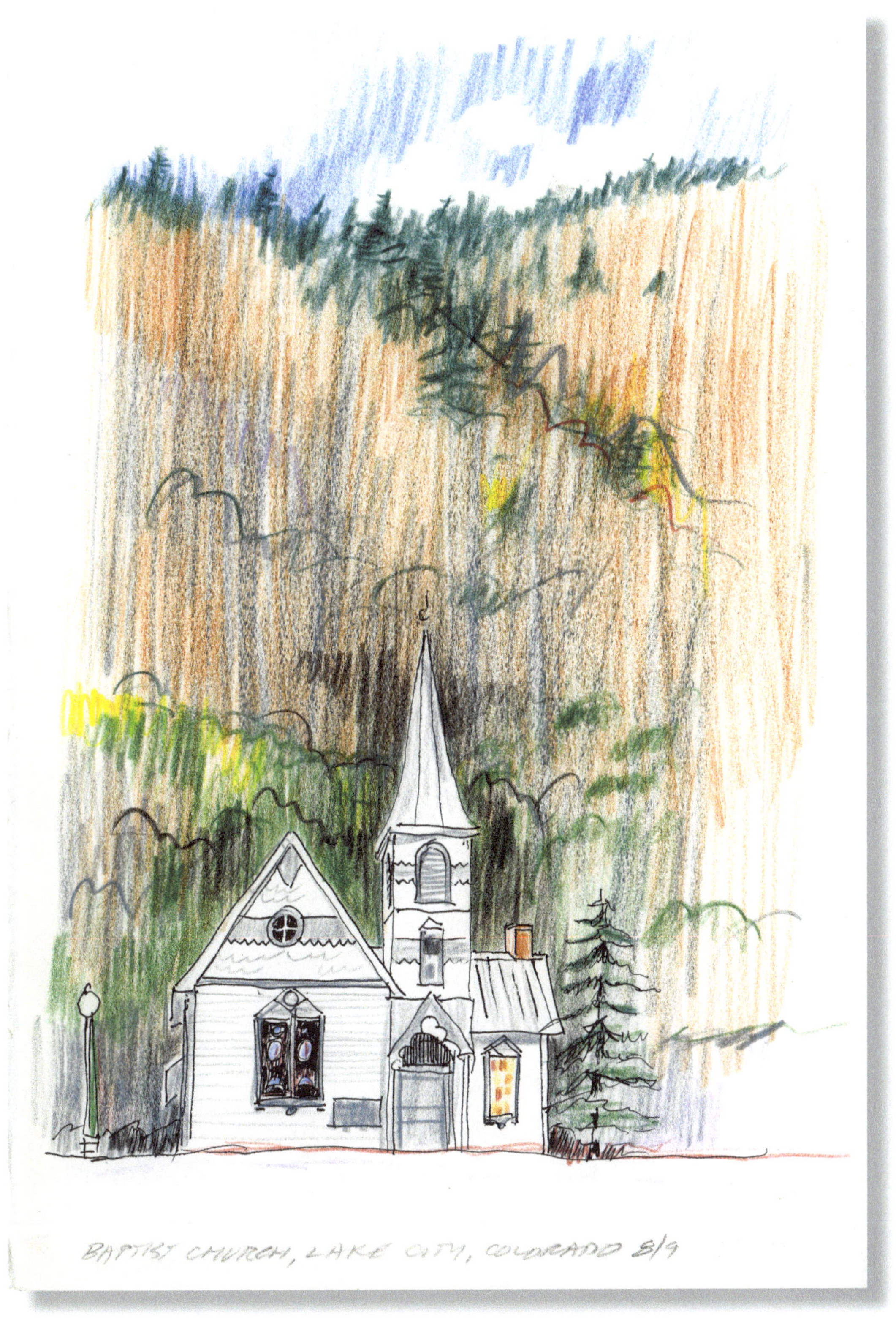

" Sketches from vacations in 1992."

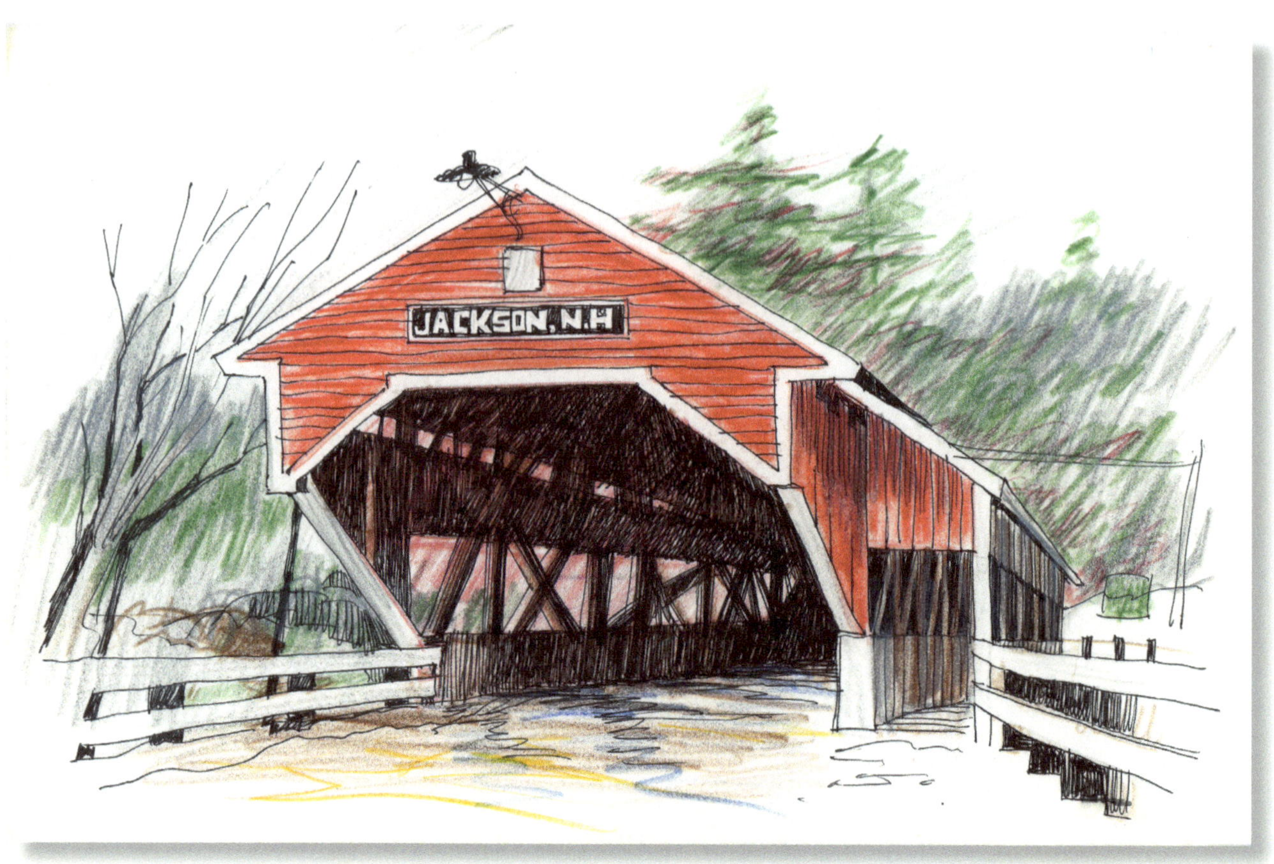
JACKSON, N.H

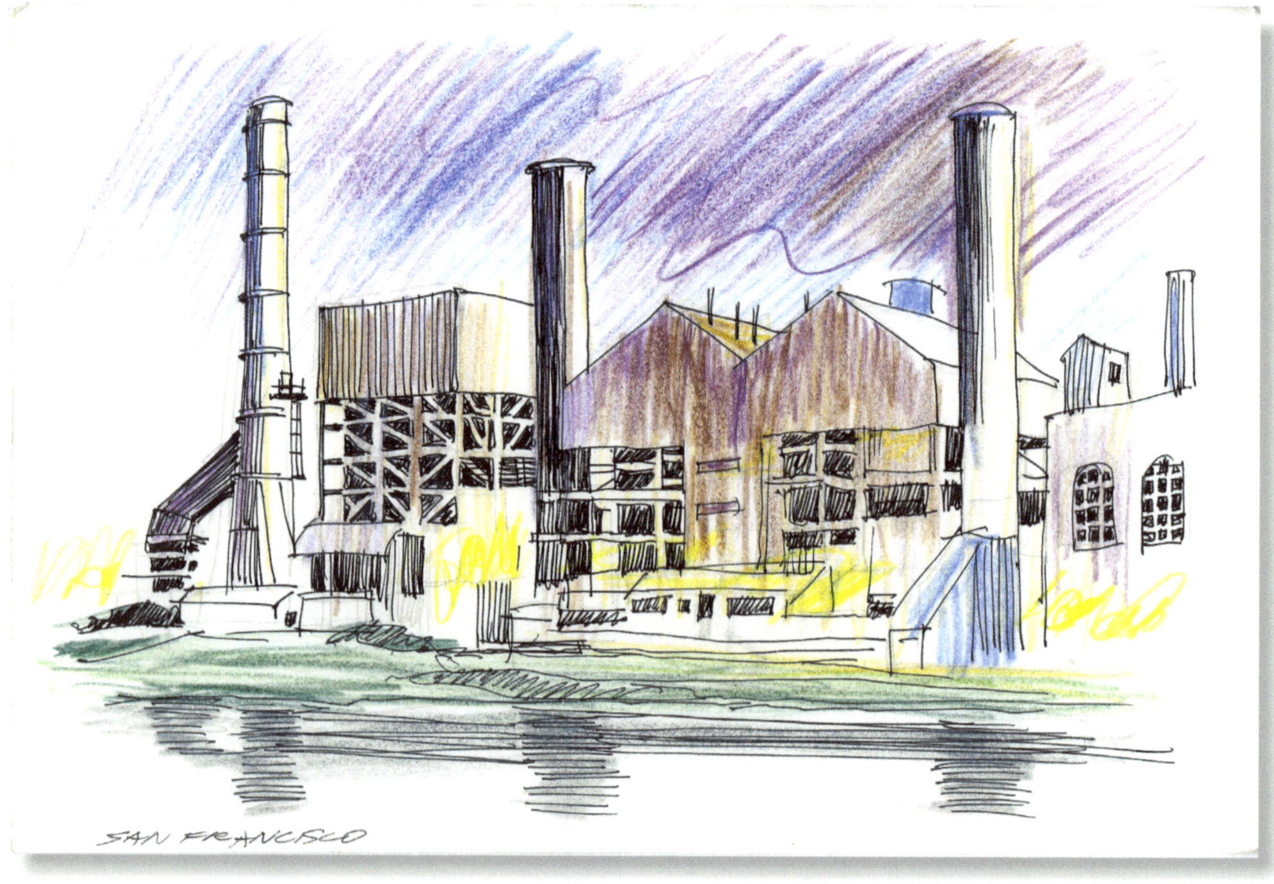
SAN FRANCISCO

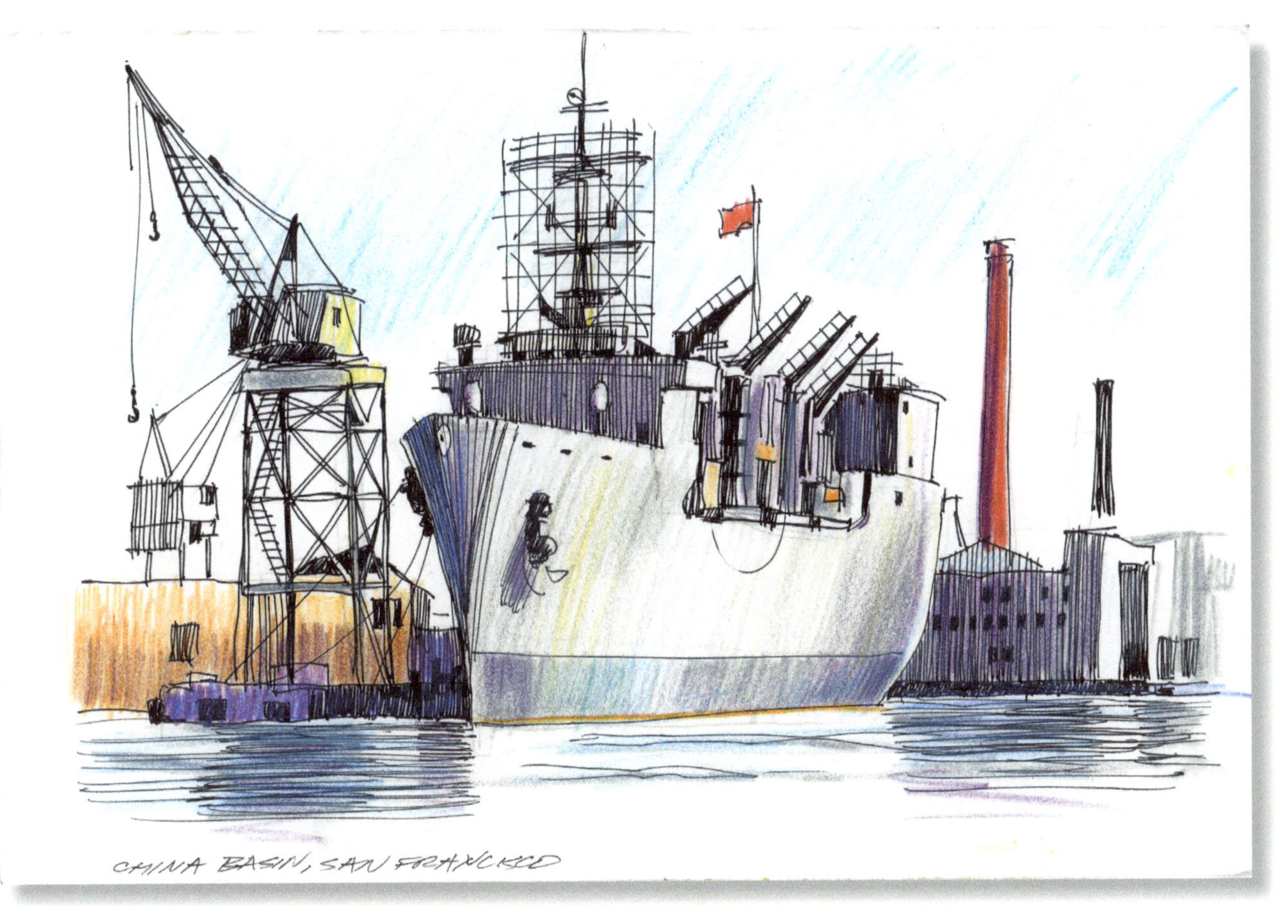
CHINA BASIN, SAN FRANCISCO

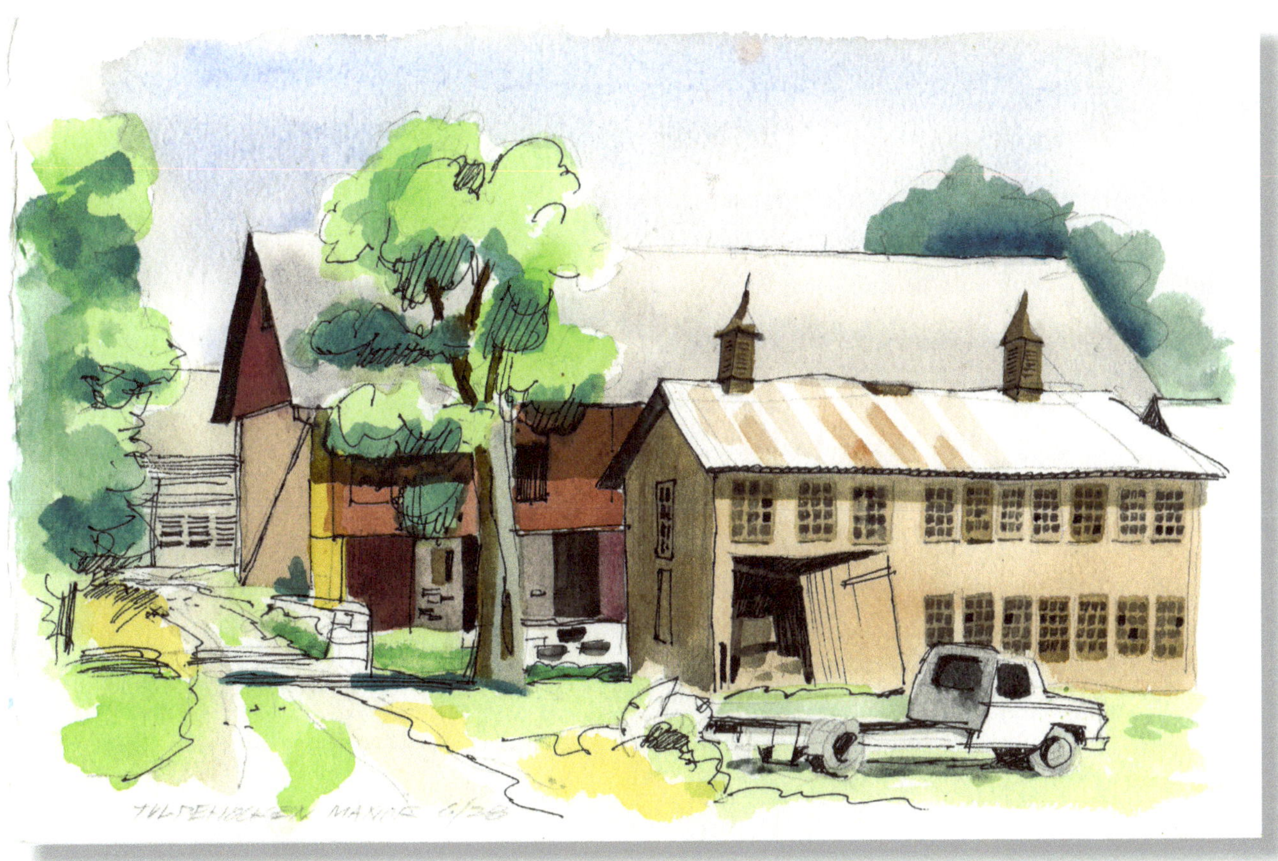

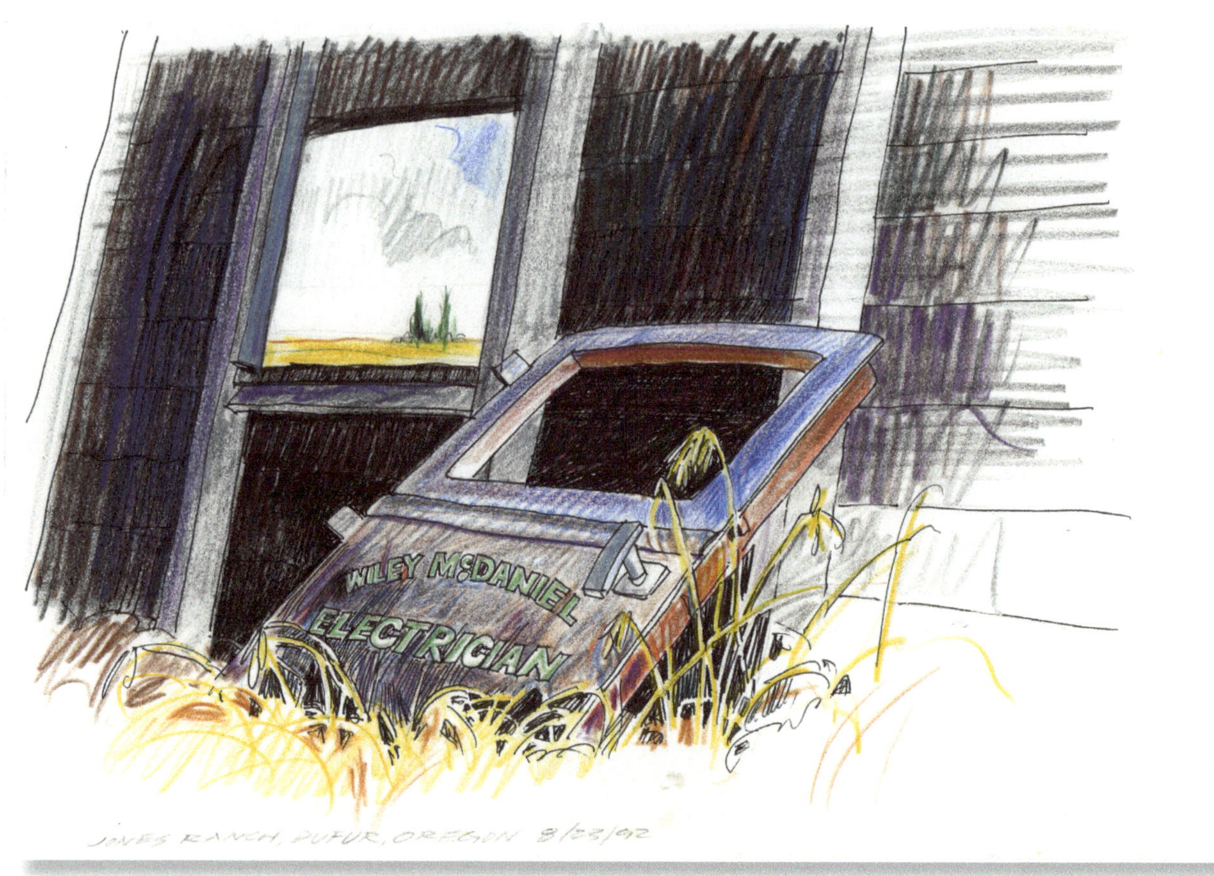
WILEY McDANIEL
ELECTRICIAN
JONES RANCH, DUFUR, OREGON 8/23/92

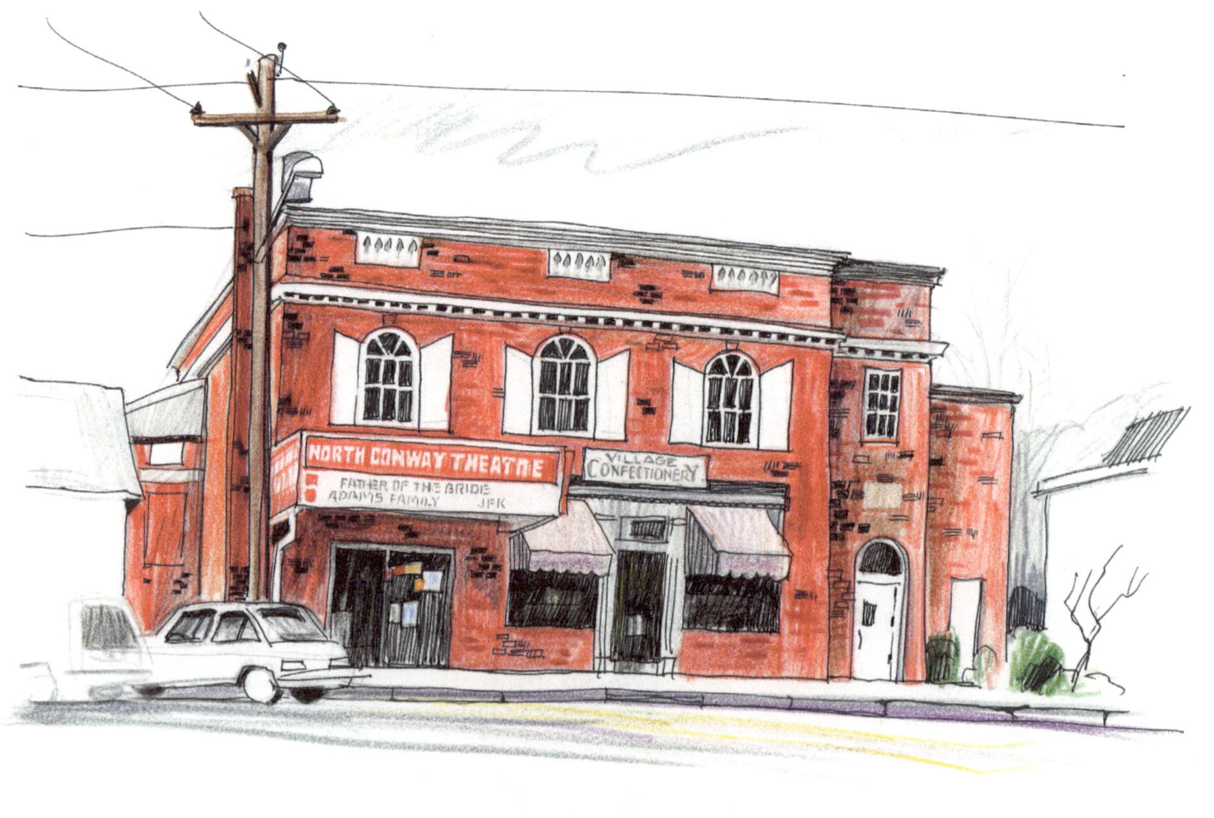
NORTH CONWAY THEATRE
FATHER OF THE BRIDE
ADAMS FAMILY JFK
VILLAGE CONFECTIONERY
NORTH CONWAY

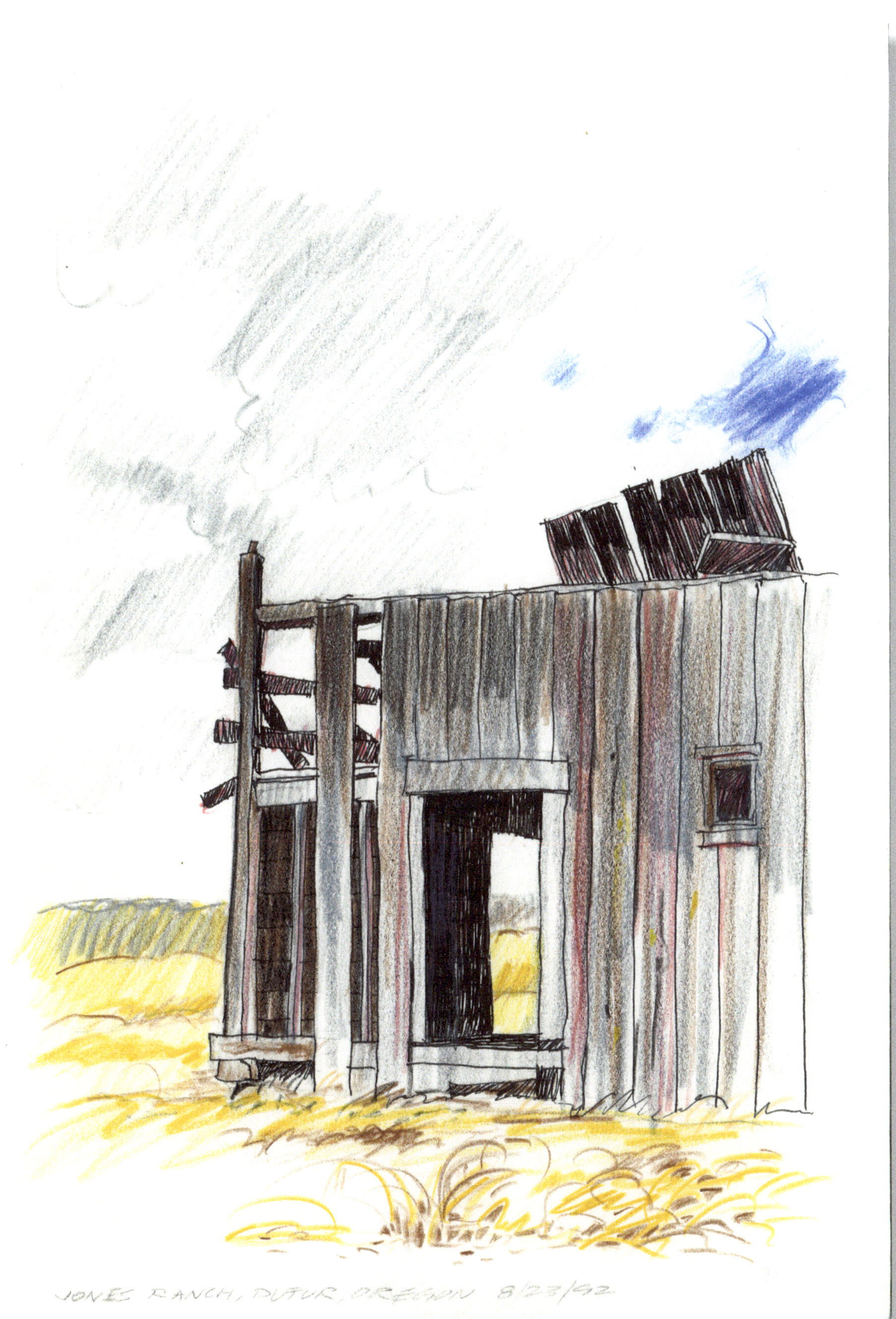
JONES RANCH, DUFUR, OREGON 8/23/92

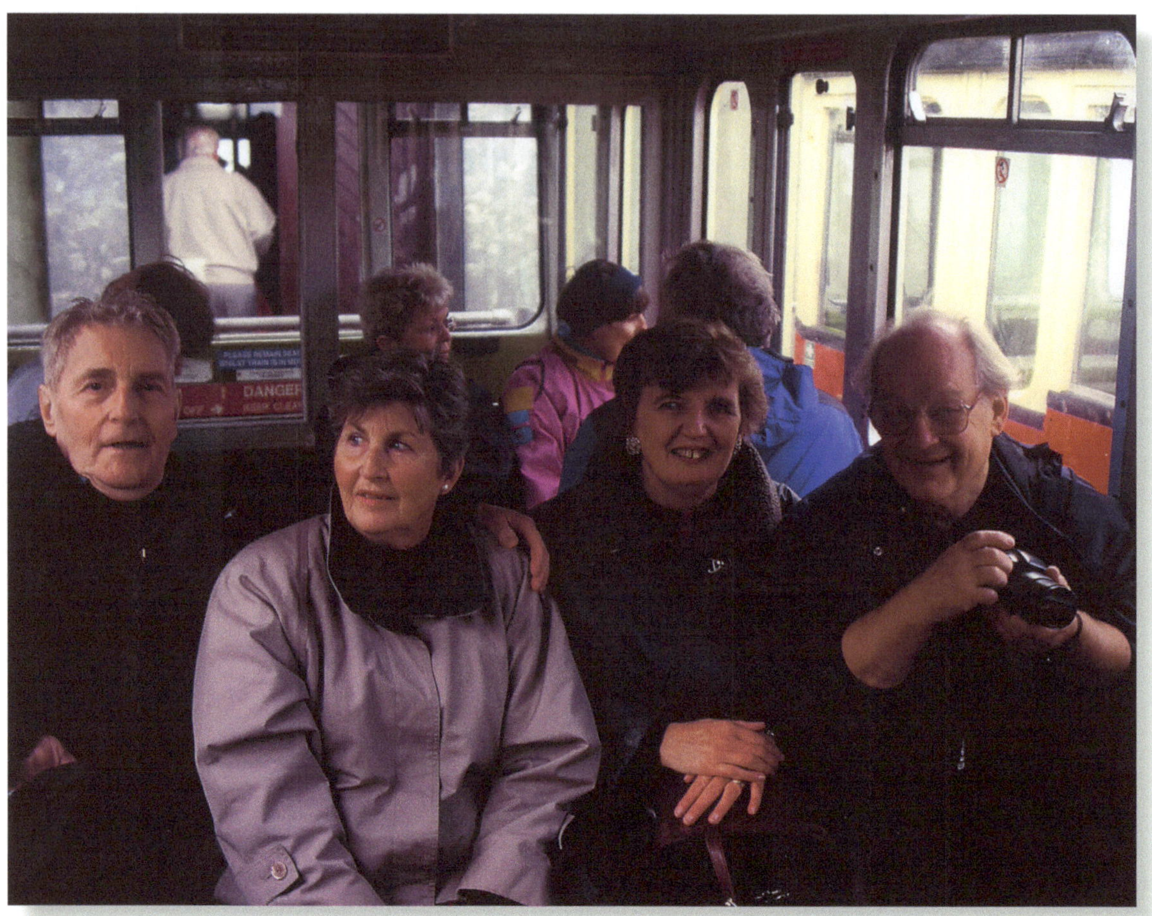

RUSSIA 1998

In 1998 Anita and I decided to visit the USSR. We were curious about this colossus that seemed to be our mortal enemy. Intourist, the Russian agency responsible for all travel in the USSR, ran ads in the San Francisco Chronicle for very inexpensive tours: 18 days for less than $600. This included round trip airfare to and from Russia, and all hotels and food. It seemed too good to pass up. It was cheap! We made all of our arrangements. It was not as difficult as we thought it might be. It was all done through Intourist.

We flew from San Francisco to London and stayed a few days with Emma. Our Aeroflot flight to Moscow was scheduled to leave from Gatwick airport. We watched as our Illushyin jet landed. People got off, but the crew just stretched their legs on the tarmac below the aircraft. It turned out Aeroflot--and the Soviet authorities--would not allow their crews to enter the terminal at Gatwick, fearful of defection.

Our flight to Moscow was comfortable. Stewardesses served us tea and cakes from a rolling samovar. We arrived at the Moscow airport late at night. We were the only incoming flight. I had brought Time and Newsweek magazines from London to read on the flight. They were confiscated by sour looking custom agents. They took hard looks at my sketchbook but to my relief, returned it to me.

Our hotel was the Cosmo, an Intourist hotel. It was very large and very well maintained. On checking in we were required to hand over our passports to the front desk. This made us feel uncomfortable. It seemed to be a ritual at all the hotels--and was never a problem. Each floor of the hotel had a dour looking lady who ran a concession of snacks and reading material. The rooms were generous in size. After getting settled in I turned on the television. It took about a minute to warm up.

Our tour gave us several days to see the sights in Moscow. From Moscow we were to fly to Baku in Azerbaijan (all then part of the Soviet Union). From Baku we were to go by bus to Tsiblisi, in Georgia. Then to Yeravan in Armenia and from there we were to fly to

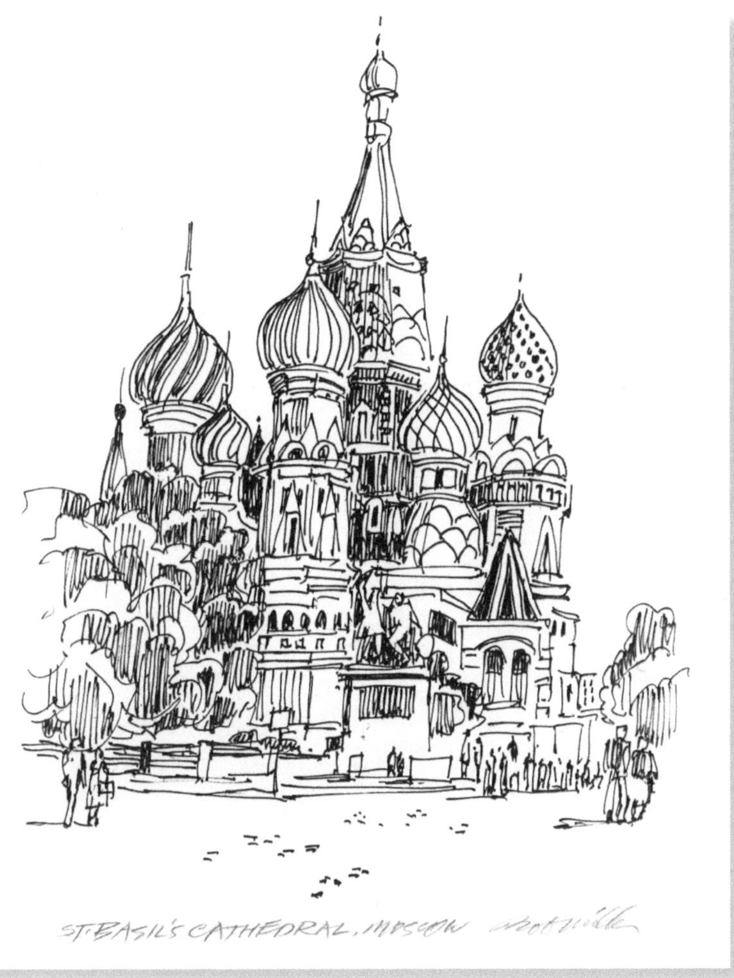

"...Although Moscow was a metropolis of over six million people it had the look of an overgrown small city."

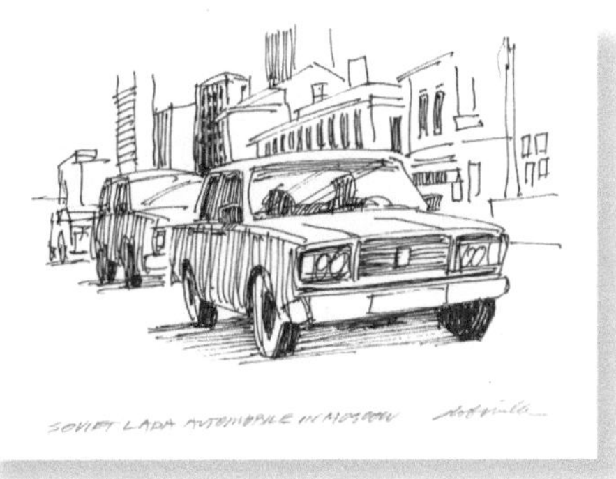

Leningrad.

When we woke up our first day in Moscow we could see a large park outside the window. I think it was Gorky Park, but I'm not sure. Nearby was a huge exhibition building where they were showing off Soviet-made products. We decided to take a look-- after a hearty breakfast of eggs, toast and brown stuff. Yes, brown stuff. It was good, had an apple-like flavor. Everyone on our tour thought it was good but none could pin down the flavor.

We walked to the exposition hall. On display was the spacecraft from Yuri Gagarin's pioneering trip around the earth. It looked as if it had been put together at a madhouse Lego factory, with lots of masking tape. I would not have ridden to Raley's market in it. There were lots of consumer goods on display, too: washing machines, right out of the 1930's; TVs like the one in our hotel room; refrigerators right out of a Betty Furness endorsement from the 50's... and the Lada car, a Russian-built version of a cheap 1970's Fiat. The Lada was everywhere on the streets of Moscow. I don't mean the streets were crowded, but the primary automobile was the Lada.

The big department store in Moscow was GUM. I broke the strap for my camera so we went to the camera department at GUM to get a replacement. The window displays outside the store were very stylish, but when we went inside the store , it was all a front. There were very few products for sale. At the camera department there were no straps and very few cameras. I was told to go to the shoe department and buy a shoelace.... which I did.

I waited in line at the shoelace counter and picked out a shoelace and received a receipt. Then I stood in a line to pay for it. The line was very slow. I peeked around to the front of the line. The cashier (I kid you not!) was doing her nails! I was amazed. Everyone was so patient. After finally paying for my shoelaces I waited in another line to pick them up. The whole transaction took about an hour.

Although Moscow was a metropolis of over six million it had the look of an overgrown small city. There were some large, Soviet-style buildings and some great cathedrals but it had almost no signs, no neon. It lacked the enormous energy generated by western cities. It was gray.

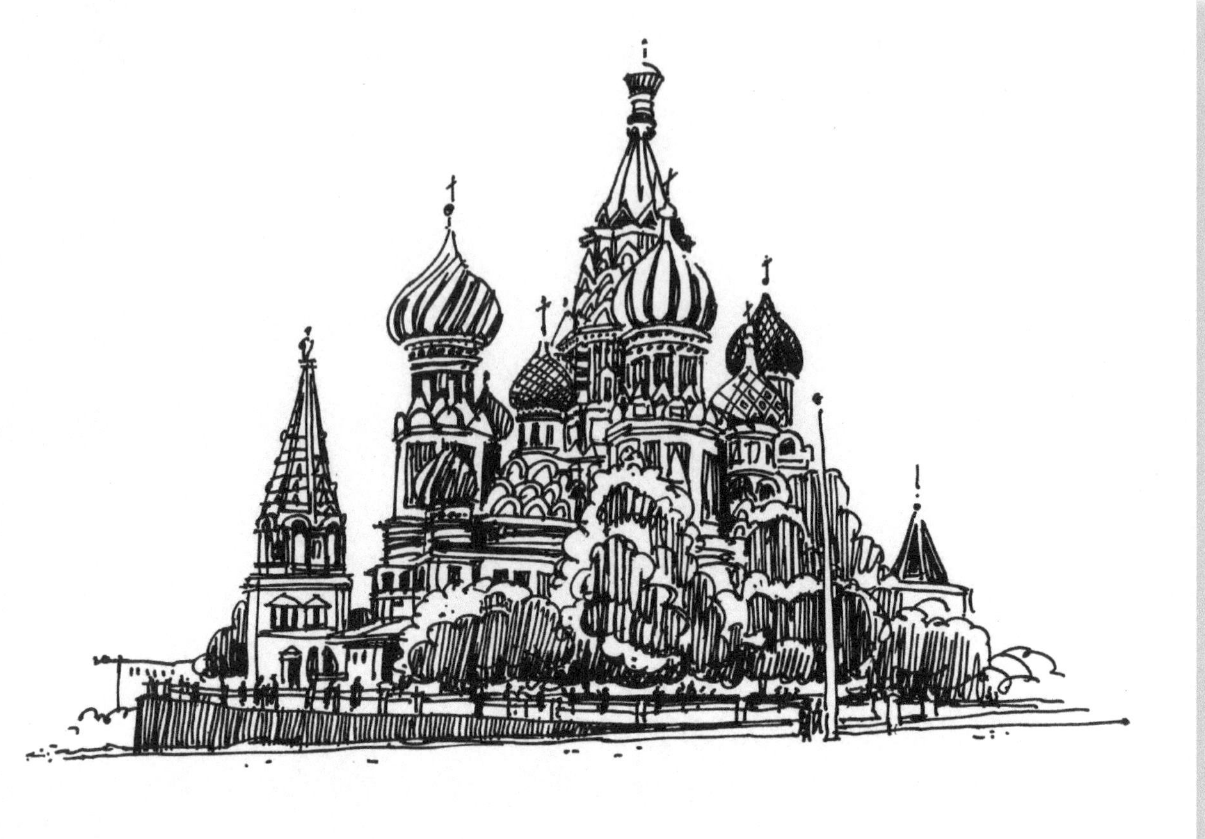

Our tour group was small, just about ten of us. We were the only Americans. The remainder were from England, Australia and New Zealand. Our Russian guide was Svetlana. She was middle aged. She reminded us of a Sunday school teacher but her religion was Communism! She was very tolerant of us and our questions, and as our tour continued we became good friends.

One of the most impressive things about Moscow was its subway system. Svetlana proudly showed us how to use it. The subway was clean, shiny and worked very well. We managed to use it on our own. Although the Cyrllic alphabet sometimes got us lost, fellow passengers were very friendly and helpful. This was something we found throughout our stay in Russia. I don't recall an incident when we were not treated well.

After visiting the sights of Moscow, we took a walk through Red Square and The Kremlin at almost midnight. It was summer and the square was still illuminated by the fading light of the sun that had just set.

We flew from Moscow to Baku in Azerbaijan. Our big jet landed at Baku's airport, about ten miles from the city. The runway was like a county road. The jet landed and stopped at the very end of the runway. As we turned around to get to the terminal a dog came out of the desert and barked at our tires until we stopped. The terminal was an apartment house with laundry hanging over its balconies. The reception area was the lounge for the apartment building. We were picked up by a bus to take us to Baku.

The drive took us through the ugliest landscape we had ever seen. Baku is an oil producing area. Oil derricks were everywhere. Some had toppled over into ugly pools. Rusting trucks had been driven onto soggy paths, got stuck, and were deserted. After driving through the despoiled picture out of hell, we arrived in Baku.

Amazingly enough, the city was beautiful. It is situated on the Caspian Sea, and has a very Mediteranean feel. We stayed at a high rise hotel, probably ten or twelve stories high. We were on the third or fourth floor. Thank goodness we were not on a higher floor because the elevators didn't work!

At breakfast we met a British tour group. They complained to us that we were not liked by the Russians and found Azerbaijan to be unfriendly.

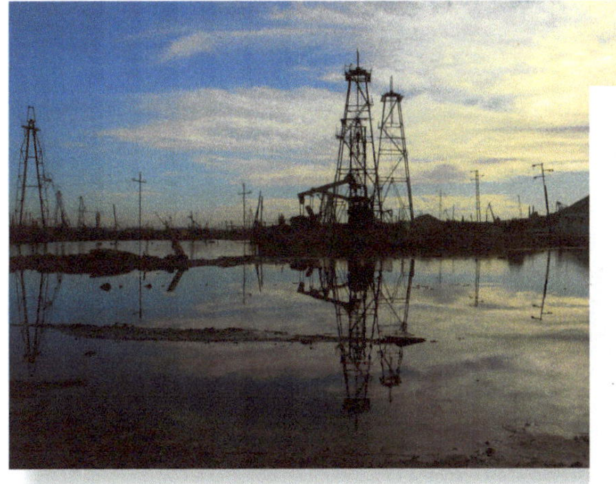

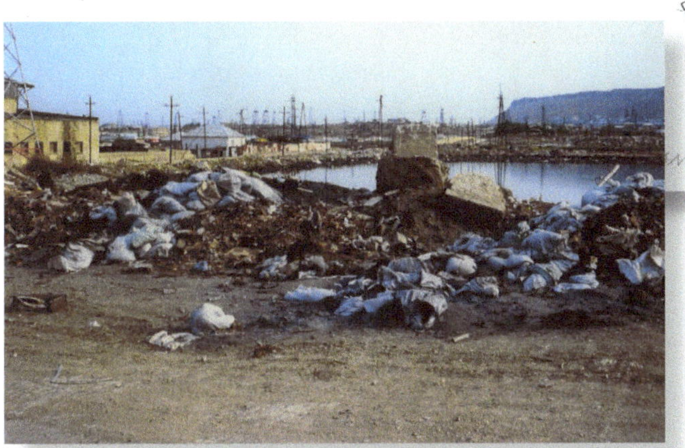

That evening we met them again at the restaurant for dinner. The British tourists were there. We learned later they were from the same village in England. By the time we arrived, most were very drunk. There were about twenty of them. By any standard they were behaving badly. Swear words, insults and bawdy songs were flying through the room as well as beer cans. The poor waiters just stood by and accepted the bad behavior as if it was a daily occurrence... and maybe it was. Anyway, it occurred to me why we were not liked in Baku. We managed to separate ourselves from the raucus behavior but it was a very uncomfortable evening.

From Baku we went by bus to Tiblisi, the capital of Georgia. The main highway, the equivalent of our I-5, was a gravel road. As we got closer to Georgia the road got better and the scenery changed. Vineyards and orchards began to appear. Then the suburbs of the city began to appear: neat cottages, small businesses and churches, and lots of trees. Big trees that created shady boulevards.

Tiblisi was beautiful. Many outdoor wine bars and cafes. Although it was part of the Soviet Union it was if they paid no attention to Moscow. Even our hotel was nice. The city had a very Italian atmosphere: parks with concerts and energetic people going about their business, ignoring Communism. We were in Tiblisi for several days, sitting in outdoor cafes, drinking wine and people watching. I even got a little sketching done. We hated to leave but so soon our little tour was on its way to Yeravan in Armenia. The paved Tiblisi highway again turned into a gravel road as we approached our destination.

There had been a severe earthquake several years before we arrived. Much of the city had not been repaired. Intourist, in all of its wisdom, placed our hotel in a part of the city that had not been rebuilt. Our hotel was about seven stories high, very modern, but it was surrounded by rubble. From our room, high above the ruined landscape we could see a community water faucet not far from the hotel. In the morning families would come out from the piles of wreckage and wash themselves. Men would shave, then walk to a bus, or get in their Ladas and go to work.

I was drawing on an embankment near the hotel. Soon I was joined by a teenager who asked if he could practice his English with me. He spoke pretty good English. His last name was Malkasian. He wanted to know more about our family. He was curious about everything American. Finally he asked if I would like to come home with him. We walked about a hundred yards or so from the hotel. He guided me through a

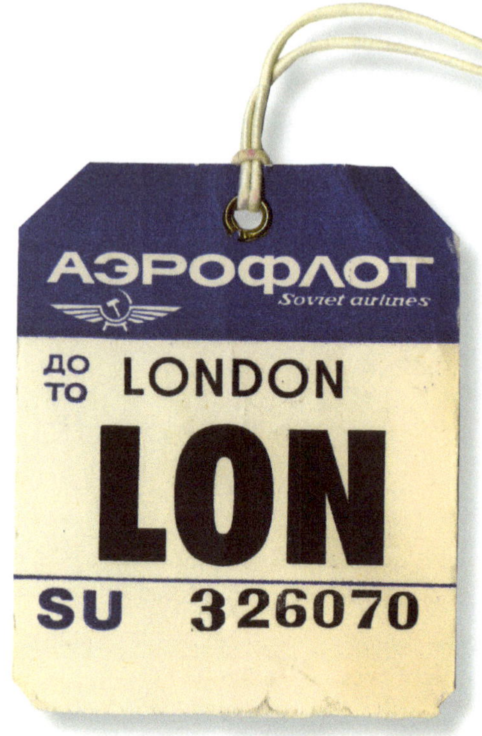

cobbled-together arch his father had created from the masonry in the rubble. Inside the home made arch was a patio-like area with an outdoor bathtub and a picnic table. It was about fifty feet square and shaded by olive trees. What an inviting and comfortable place to be. Then he took me into his home which they had put together from the wreckage around them. In his room he had a picture of Muhammad Ali on the wall. He was just like many teenagers, he just happened to live in Armenia.

He wanted to meet Anita and invited us to meet his family that evening. We spent a wonderful time with them. The whole neighborhood came to meet us. Later in the evening a policeman came in. I was really concerned. We were not supposed to be there. It turned out the policeman simply wanted to meet us. We hated to leave Yeravan. We stayed in contact with the Malkasians. They were fortunate enough to be able to migrate. Now they live in Los Angeles.

Had I not been sketching, this would have never happened!

After several days of being entertained by the Malkasians we flew from Yeravan to Leningrad. The flight was interesting, mostly Russians. It was like a local bus. Many of the passengers used cardboards boxes for luggage.

Leningrad was beautiful. It was called the Venice of the north. It too seemed untouched by Communism. It had large, beautiful squares and majestic opera houses. It is home to The Hermitage, a museum full of art created by the world's most renowned and respected artists. Nearby, up the Gulf of Finland was Petrovert, a castle from the days of the Czars. It was beautifully maintained: vast gardens, shimmering pools and a palace fit for royalty in its highest form. We were amazed that the Communists had been such good custodians.

Our tour group was then taken on a picnic in the country. I remember a farmlike setting with a very large picnic table. Near one end of the table, tied to a stump, was a bear cub. He seemed happy to see us and was very playful during our visit. In the middle of the table was a very large roast of beef which from a distance looked over done and burned. When I sat at the table to be served, my elbow banged its edge. What I thought was a crust was actually a swarm of flies that had settled on our meat! Our server didn't seem to notice and no one said anything. The roast was carved and we ate it. A few of us did get sick but no one ended up in the hospital. Russian standards of hygiene were not high. Frequently when we visited delicatessans to buy sandwiches we saw wax paper covering the meats and cheeses to protect them from the flies; however, the flies always managed to get between the delicacies and the wax paper.

We flew from Leningrad back to London. When we left Leningrad we were the only flight. When we landed in London, the airport was teeming with activity. There were airplanes everywhere, taxiing, taking off, landing. We watched the Russian passengers looking out our windows in amazement.

Although our glimpse inside the Soviet Union was filled with all kinds of questions about its viability we had no idea it was coming to an end. It was truly a closed society. The few English newspapers we were able to find during our stay were filled with lies about the west. It was the kind of society that, now with the Internet, could not exist.

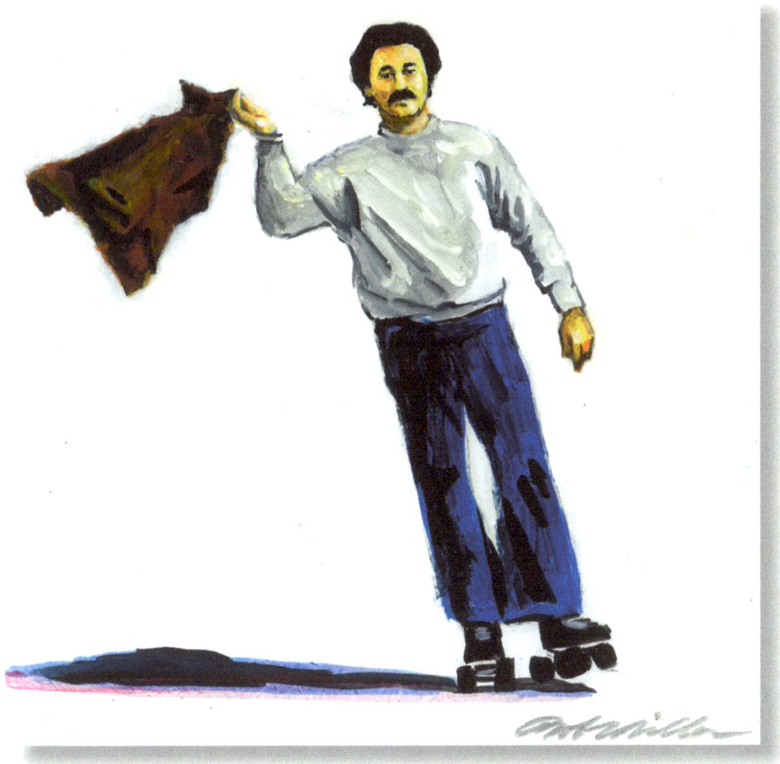

A portrait I made of Bob Rakela during his roller skating days.

At the beginning of the new century things began to slow down. Business flagged. I had to let Sally Flannery go. She had been my right hand for over twenty years. It was sad.

And then one morning just as Anita and I were to leave for Charlotte, North Carolina for our son Van's wedding, Lisa Pujal and Stacey Gibbs--now my whole staff--appeared at my door. I could sense something calamitous was about to happen. Lisa spoke first. "Bob, we hate to tell you this, but today is our last day. Remember that long lunch we took yesterday? Well, we were invited to interview at a brand new, hot agency in Fair Oaks. They have a huge campaign and they want us to start Monday--and the pay and the benefits are really good. We know this will be a hardship but we must think of our futures."

I was staggered. We were not super busy, but we had projects and no one would be in the studio for two whole weeks. So I said "Sure, what the hell! Worse things could have happened. " But I couldn't think of any at the time!

So I called Bob Rakela. I explained my dilemma. I asked if he would watch over my business while we were gone.

"Hell yes!" Bob said. "We'll take care of you. It could have been worse. It could have been the Board of Equalization!" So good old Bob did it. As a matter of fact I liked the arrangement so much I moved my business in with his. He had a great staff.

We had a wonderful time in Charlotte and Anita and I met our super new daughter-in-law Katherine. I must admit while I was gone I had some anxiety about my new arrangement but Bob and his staff were great custodians of my meager list of customers.

A word about Bob Rakela: Bob is about ten years younger than I am. I first met him when he showed me his portfolio. I was one of the older designers he was looking to knock off. I was working for Fred at the time. I was very impressed by his portfolio, and I thought, "Oh poop! Here comes some real competition!" When I first came to town that's what I wanted to do, knock off the old fart commercial artists. I thought they were staid and unimaginative. Now I was the old fart.

Bob worked for the Pettit Brothers, an up-and-coming agency but it wasn't long until he was in business for himself. I admired his talent as well as his business sense. Bob was my landlord for about five years. My studio was in a mezzanine above his studio. I still had some of the wine accounts Mary Jo had acquired. In fact, it was a pretty good list. I designed labels, brochures and point-of-sale materials for 40 firms.

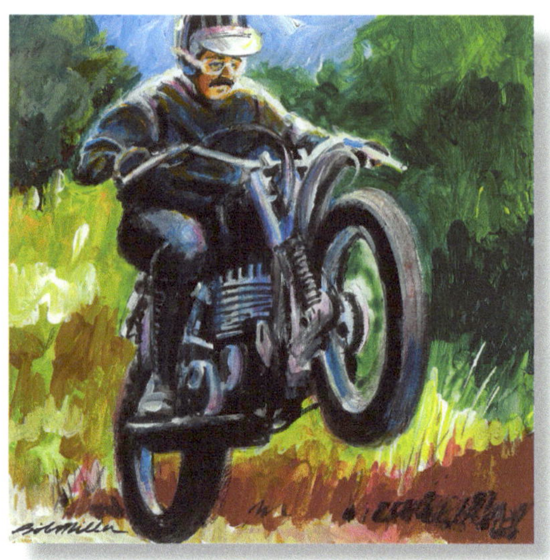

FROM BRUCE MARWICK

I met Bob when he was downsizing his business and he rented space from Bob Rakela, where I was Art Director.

The Rakela Building had a loft, at least 1,500 square feet that was divided into two offices. Bob Miller had one side and I had the other. For eight years, when it was shoot-the-breeze time, he was close, and I became charmed, liked so many other people, by Bob.

He is gregarious, gracious, well read. He's a bit of a--puck. Even though he's not that tall he has a lot of stature. The way he blows into a room, with that really positive energy, is like a mischievous sprite.

The main thing is that Bob Miller is young of spirit. Bob is an artist, will always be an artist, and he's gonna go out of this world cutting or painting designs on the commercial or fine art side.

By the time Bob joined us at Rakela, the Macintosh had revolutionized the design process. We would take a design, do a computer mock up, print it and present that to the client.

What captivated me about Bob Miller was how he did his presentations for clientele. He would take his design, pull out his paints; he would hand-letter lettering whether serif or san serif, Times Roman or Helvetica; he would do his own illustrations and put the illustration in so the mockups became these beautiful little art pieces. I hadn't seen anybody do that in 10 years.

It was good work, but by about 2003 or 2004 I became more and more interested in pursuing my painting to make a living. Some of my accounts were leaving, some from my neglect, others because of changes in their staff. I was approaching 80. I would call on a long term account and be introduced to their new advertising manager. That person may have recently graduated from college and was usually around 23 or 24. I could sense that soon a young graphic designer would be taking my place. I understood. I tried to knock off the old guys when I was a young commercial artist. I understood, but I didn't like it.

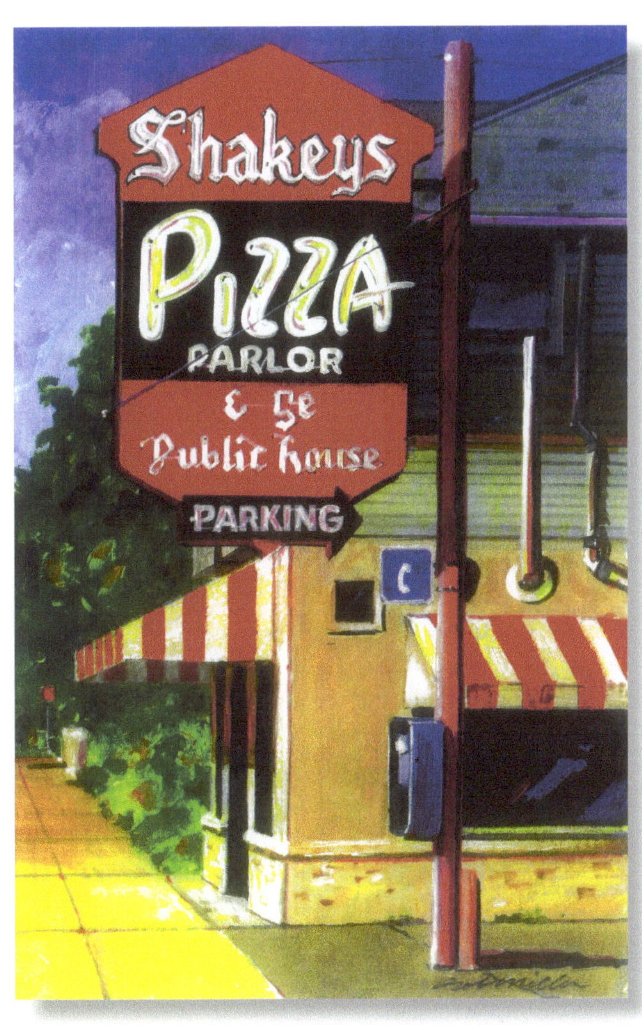

I didn't plan well for my retirement. We spent large amounts of money on travel that others would have put into a retirement fund. Although at 85 I still have to bring in additional income each month, I would not trade the travelling we have done for a more secure future.

We made two trips to Mexico; nine trips to Europe; plus journeys to Kenya and the old Soviet Union. The travelling we do now is within the United States. We have sons who live in Charlotte, N.C., New York City, and Portland, Oregon. Visiting them each year is all the travelling we can afford. And frankly, we really enjoy visiting with our children.

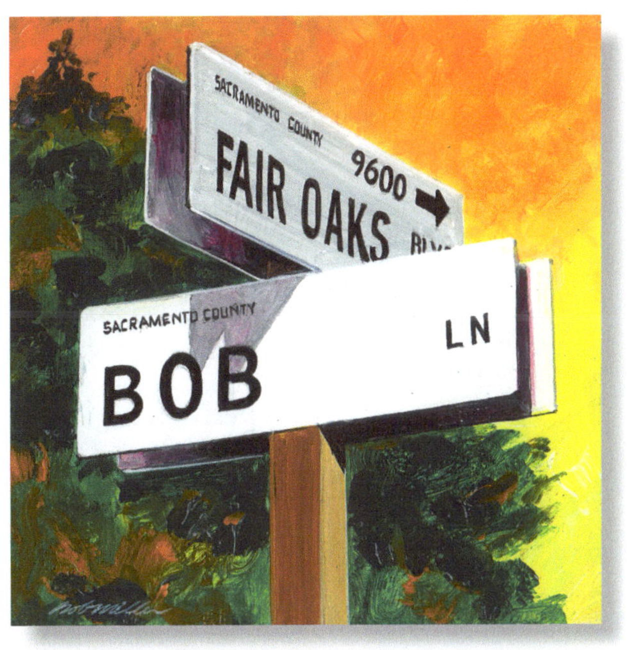

I started off selling my pictures at galleries. The Twentieth Street Gallery between I and J Streets was very energetic and promotion minded. It was owned by Jim and Joanne Ferry. Annually they would have an event called 50/50 or sometimes

20/20. They would pass out masonite panels that were 6"or 8" square. The challenge to the artist was to create 50 pieces of art in 50 days (or 20 in 20). The first time I was involved I chose oranges as my theme. It was a great success. We sold them for $100 each and I sold over half of mine.

The challenge for the next show was to paint 180 pictures in as many days. I did a variety of subjects in a variety of sizes. Jim and Joanne promoted it well. The opening was well attended and I sold about half the pictures in the month the show was up. They also were able to secure me commissions and calendar illustration. I miss the gallery: not just the sales, but I think it was a loss to the Sacramento art scene. They showed energy, enthusiam and professionalism unmatched in any area.

Over the past decade, I have become known as a painter of Sacramento icons. Name a place that is visually conspicuous and I have probably painted it or soon will.

I seldom show at galleries anymore. I find I can sell my pictures pretty well on my own. I am developing a network of people who like my work, so most sales are by word of mouth. I make an effort to make my work visible to the public. For example, 33rd Street Bistro has a banquet room in use for breakfast, lunch and dinner meetings almost every day. So each day you have a new set of prospective buyers. It has been a very good venue for me. I try to show there every year.

I am always working.

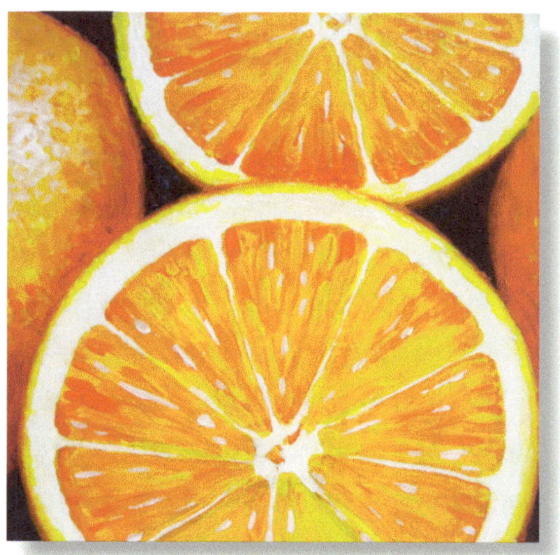

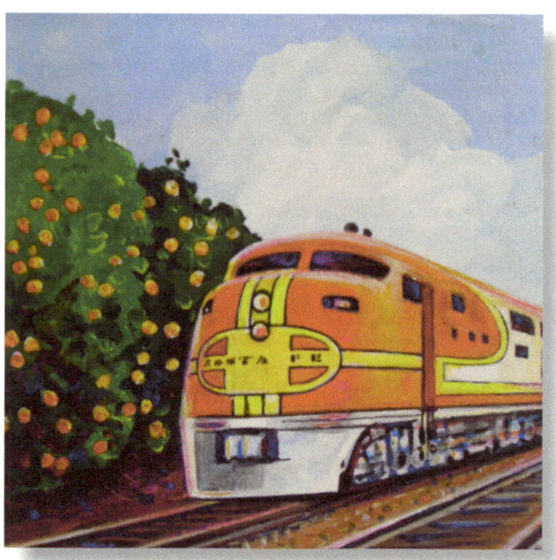

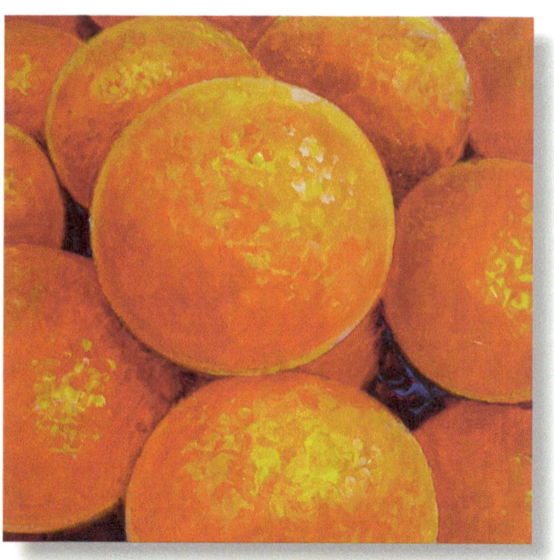

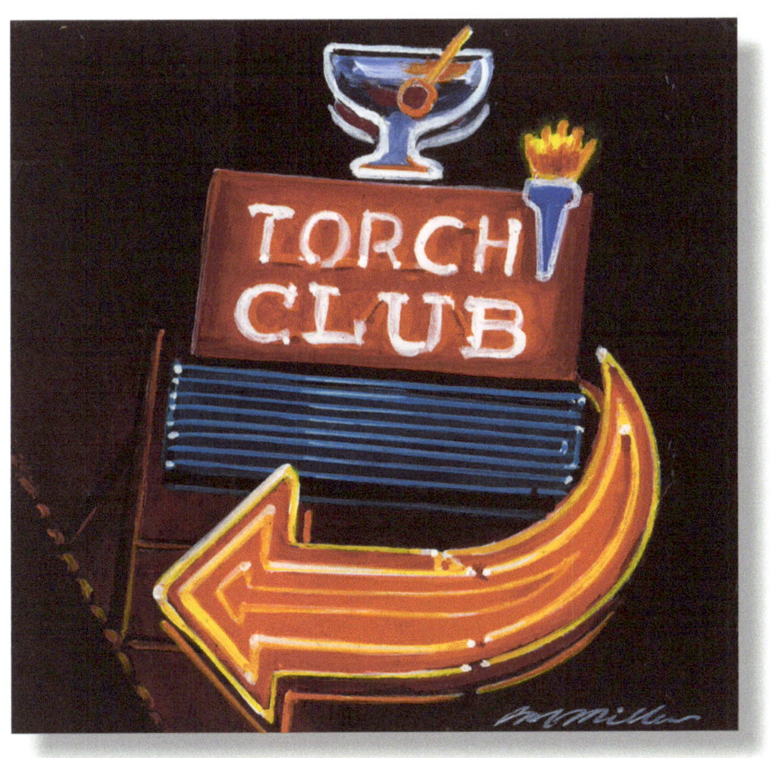

"...Over the past decade, I have become known as a painter of Sacramento icons. Name a place that is visually conspicuous and I have probably painted it. Or soon will."

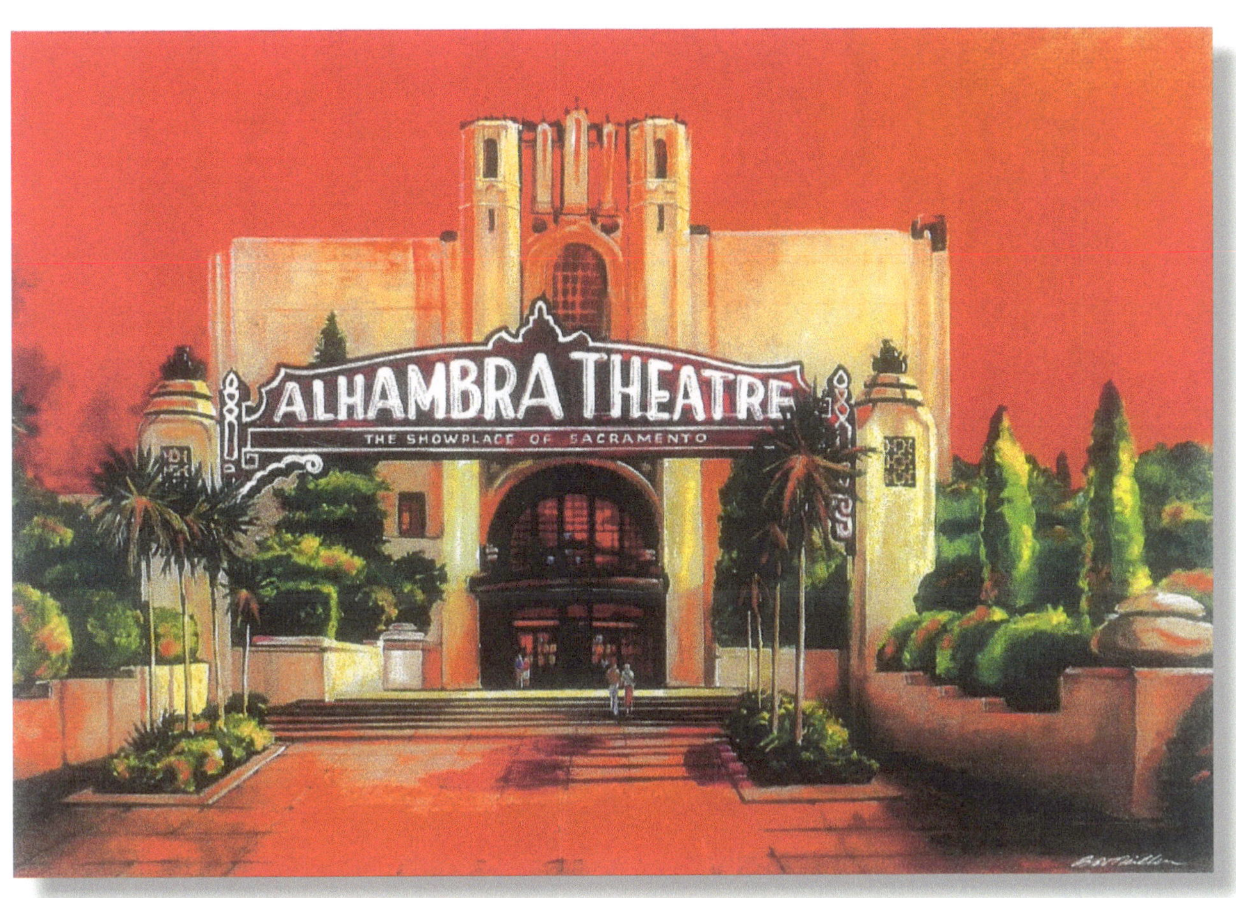

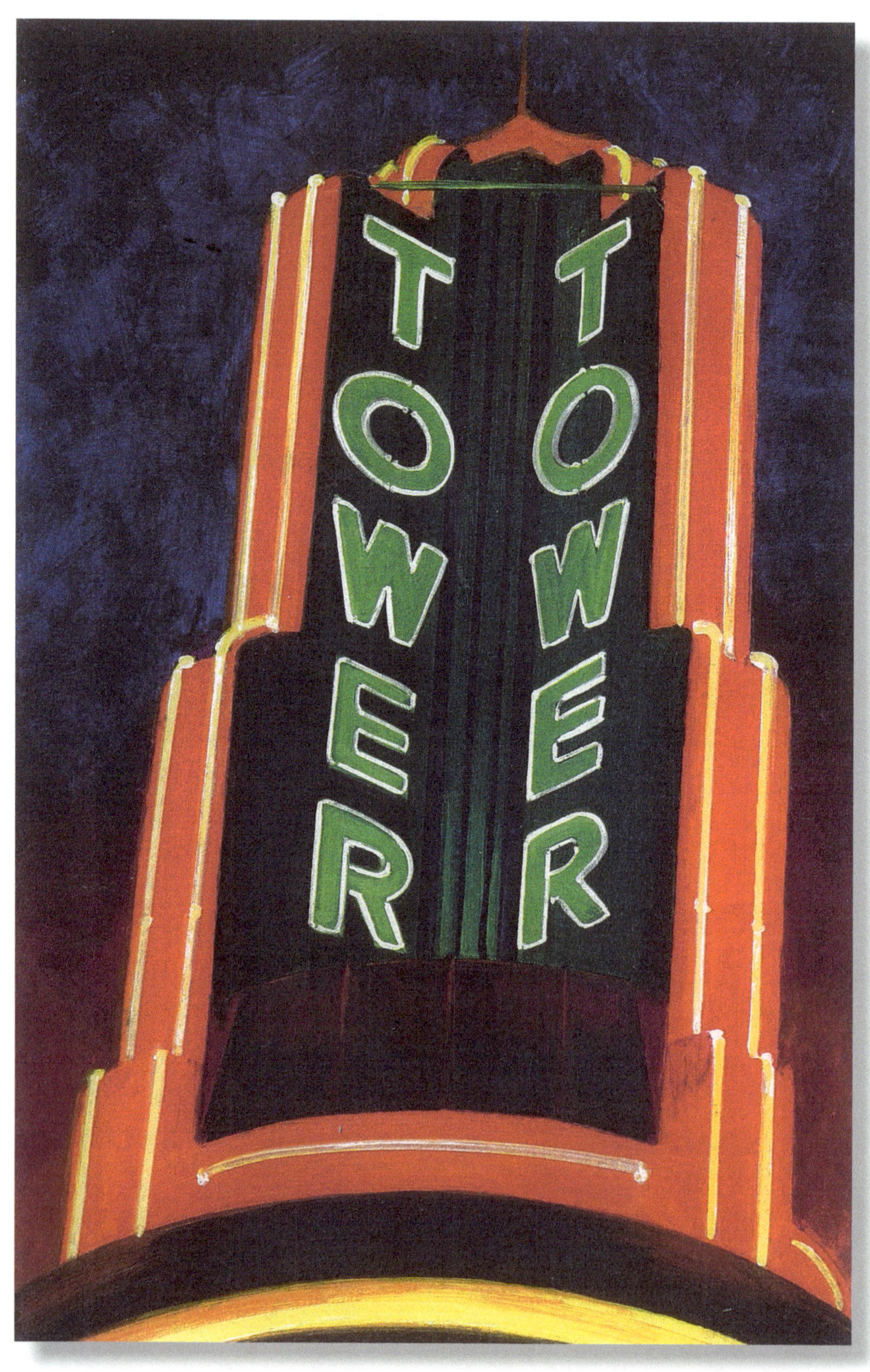
TOWER
TOWER

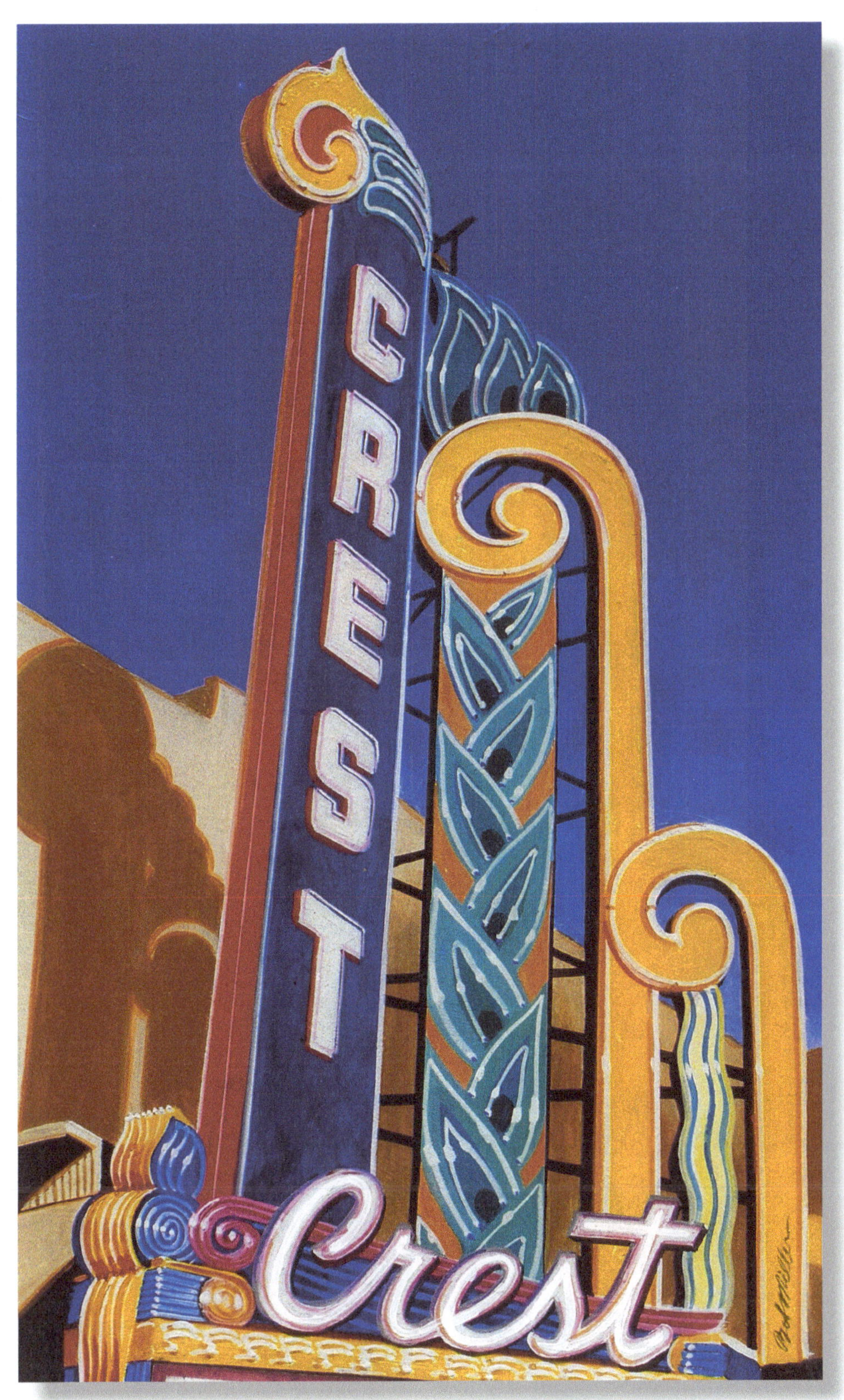
CREST
Crest

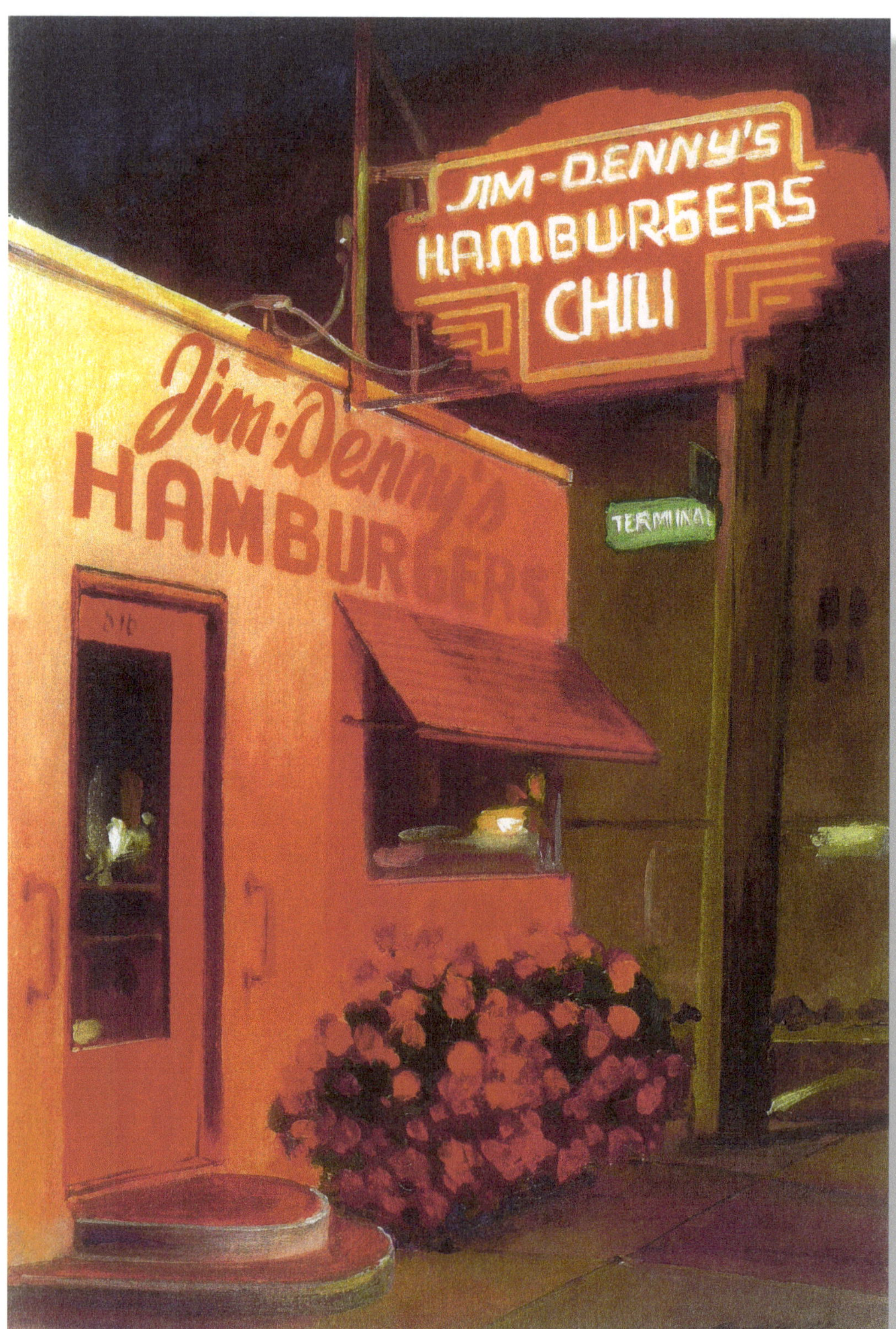
JIM-DENNY'S
HAMBURGERS
CHILI
Jim-Denny's
HAMBURGERS
TERMINAL

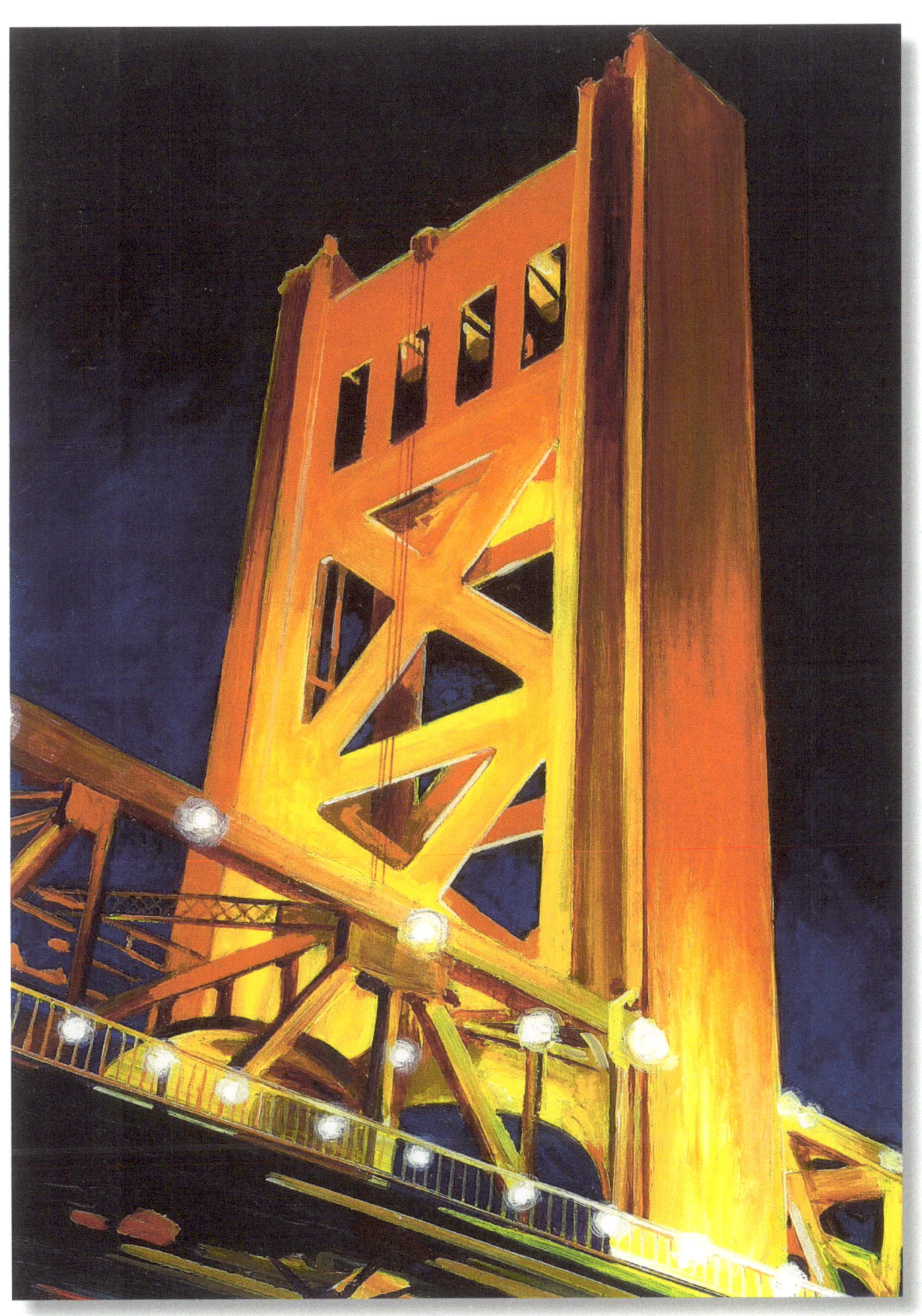

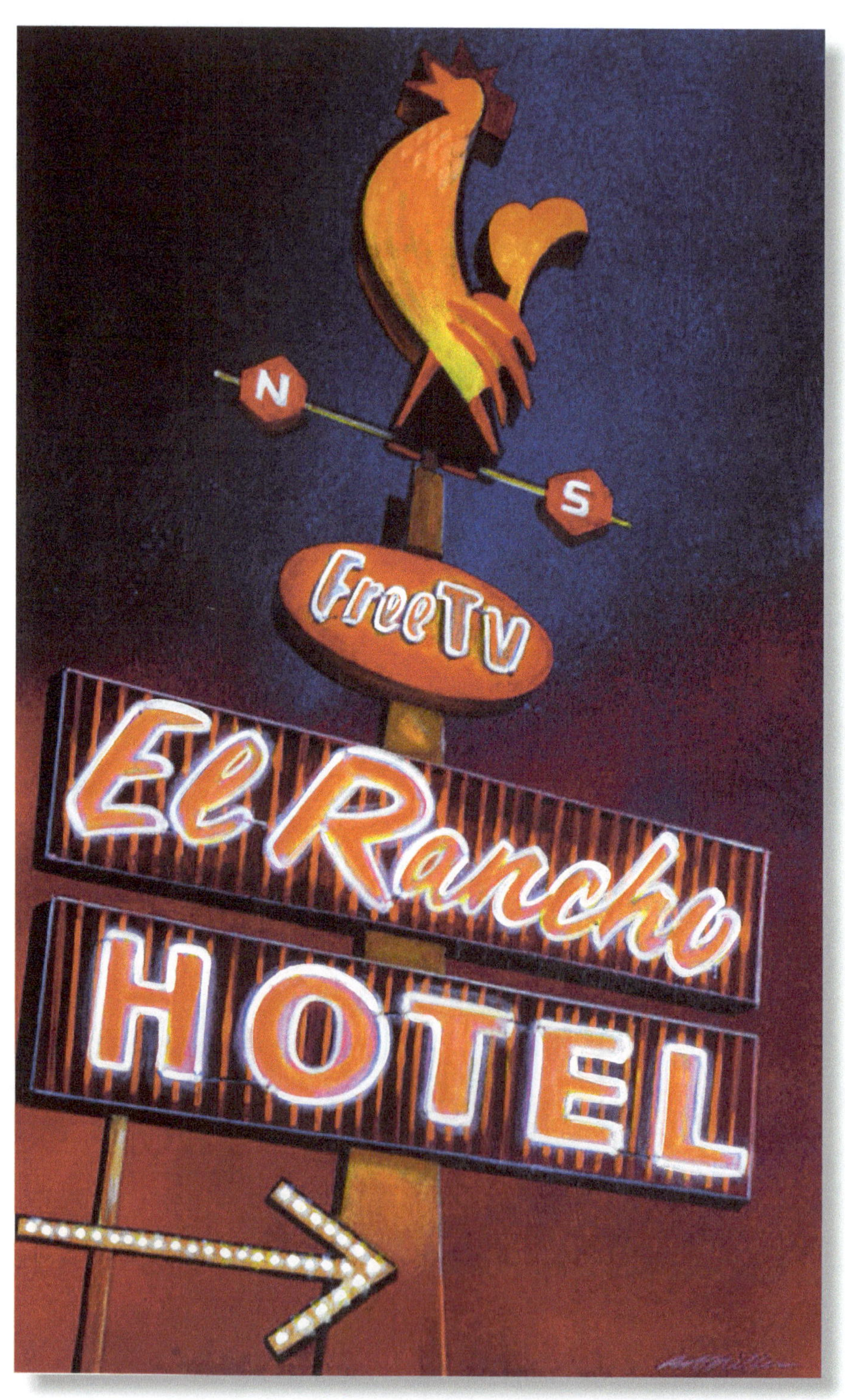

N
S
Free TV
El Rancho
HOTEL

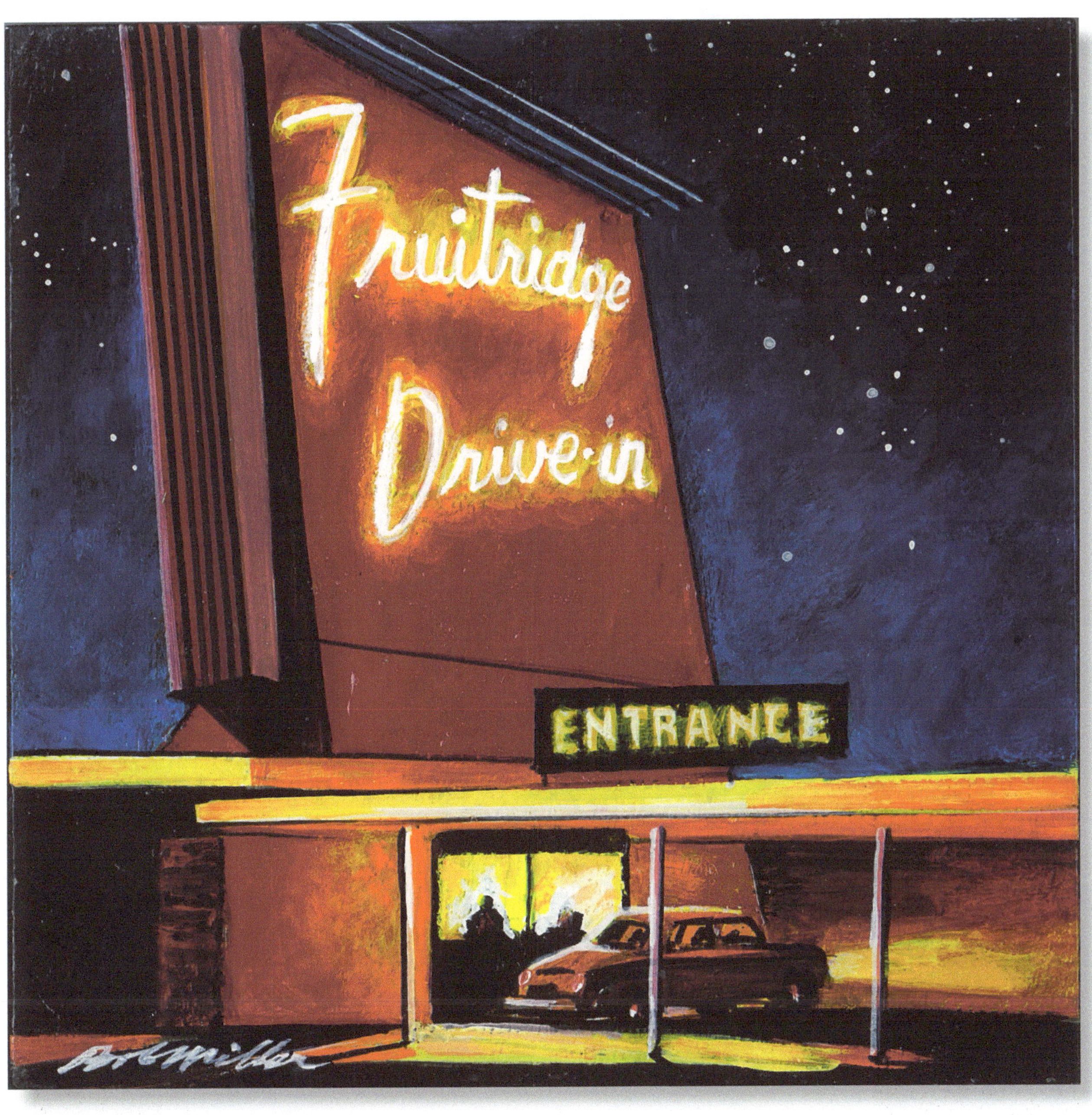
Fruitridge
Drive-in
ENTRANCE

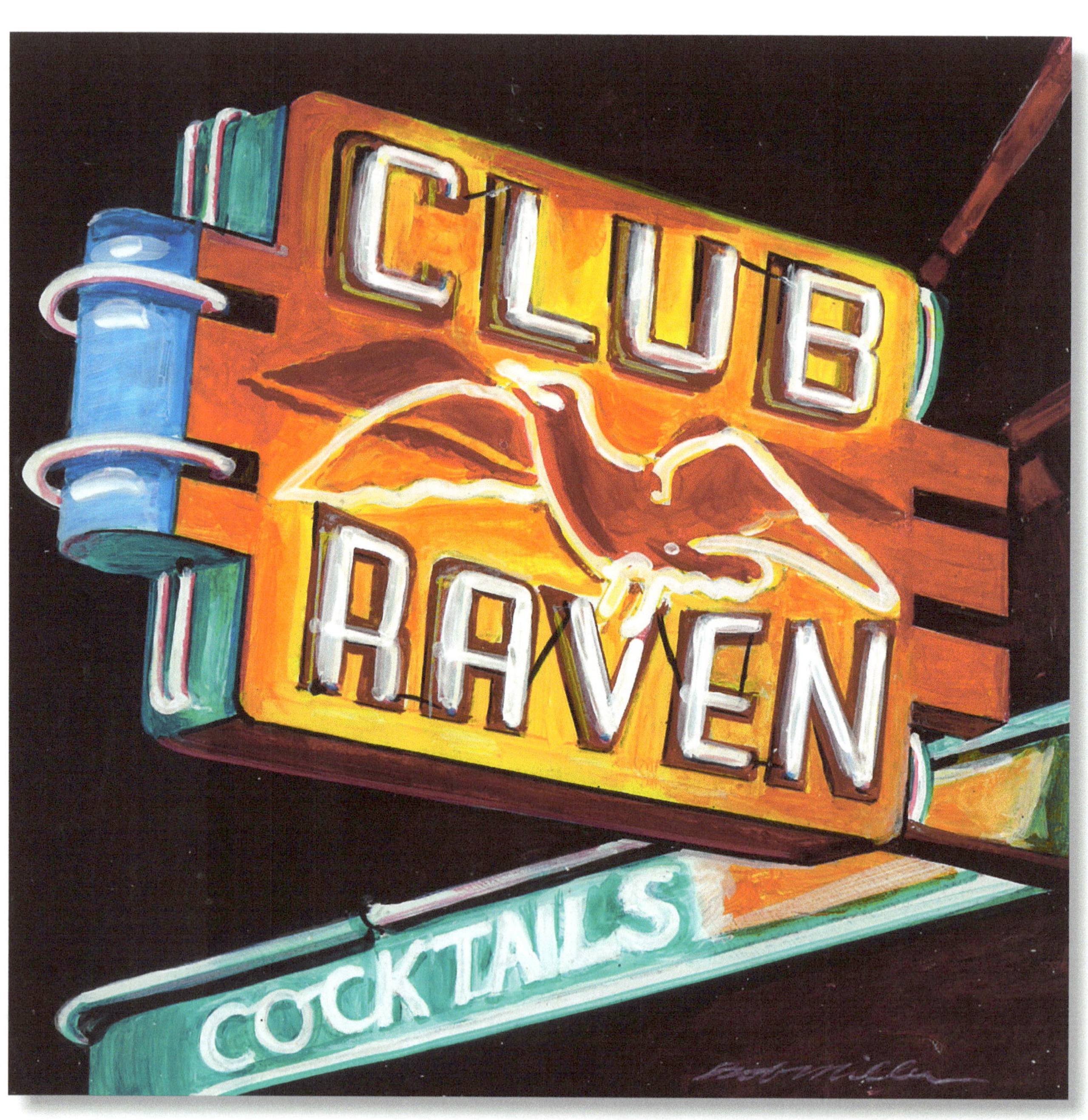
CLUB
RAVEN
COCKTAILS

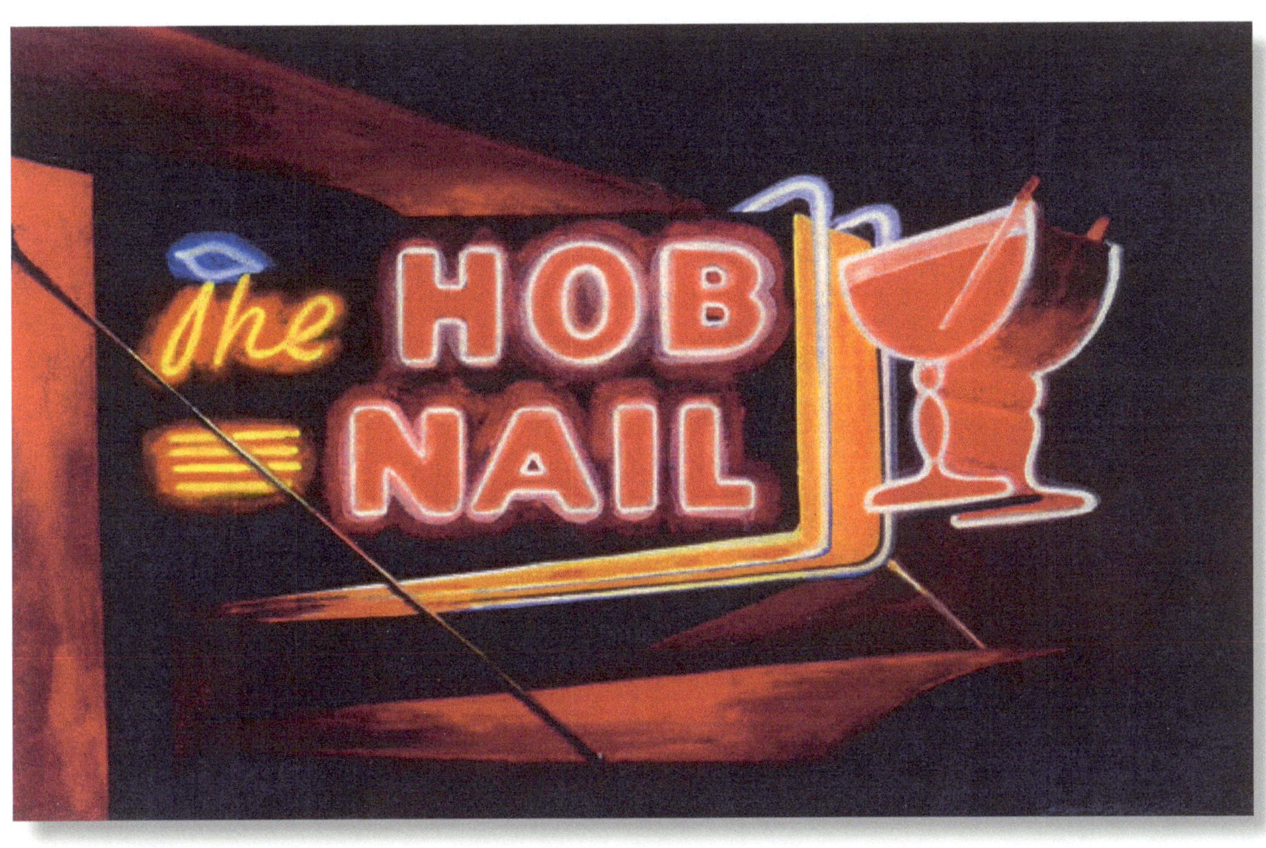
The
HOB
NAIL

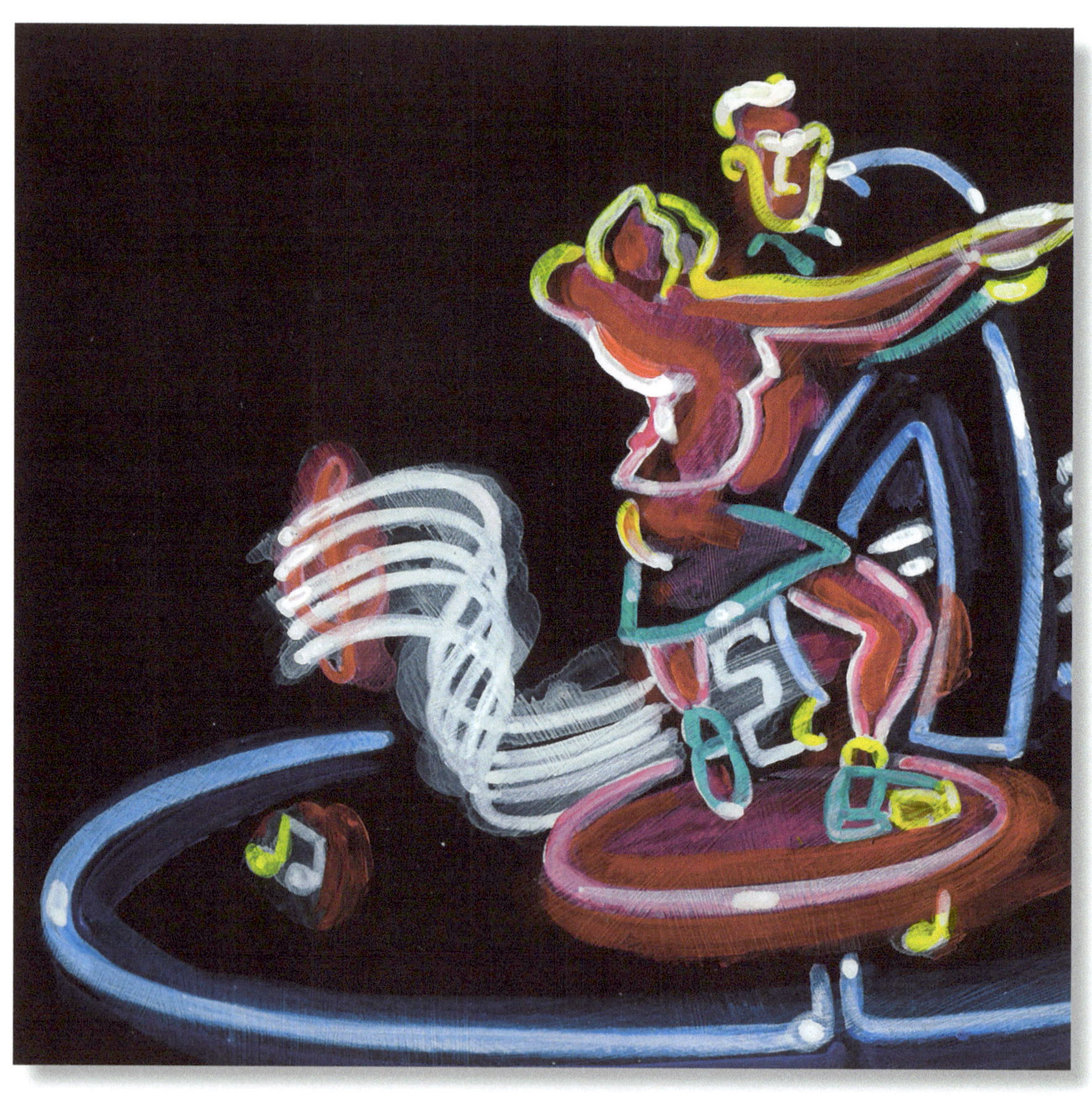

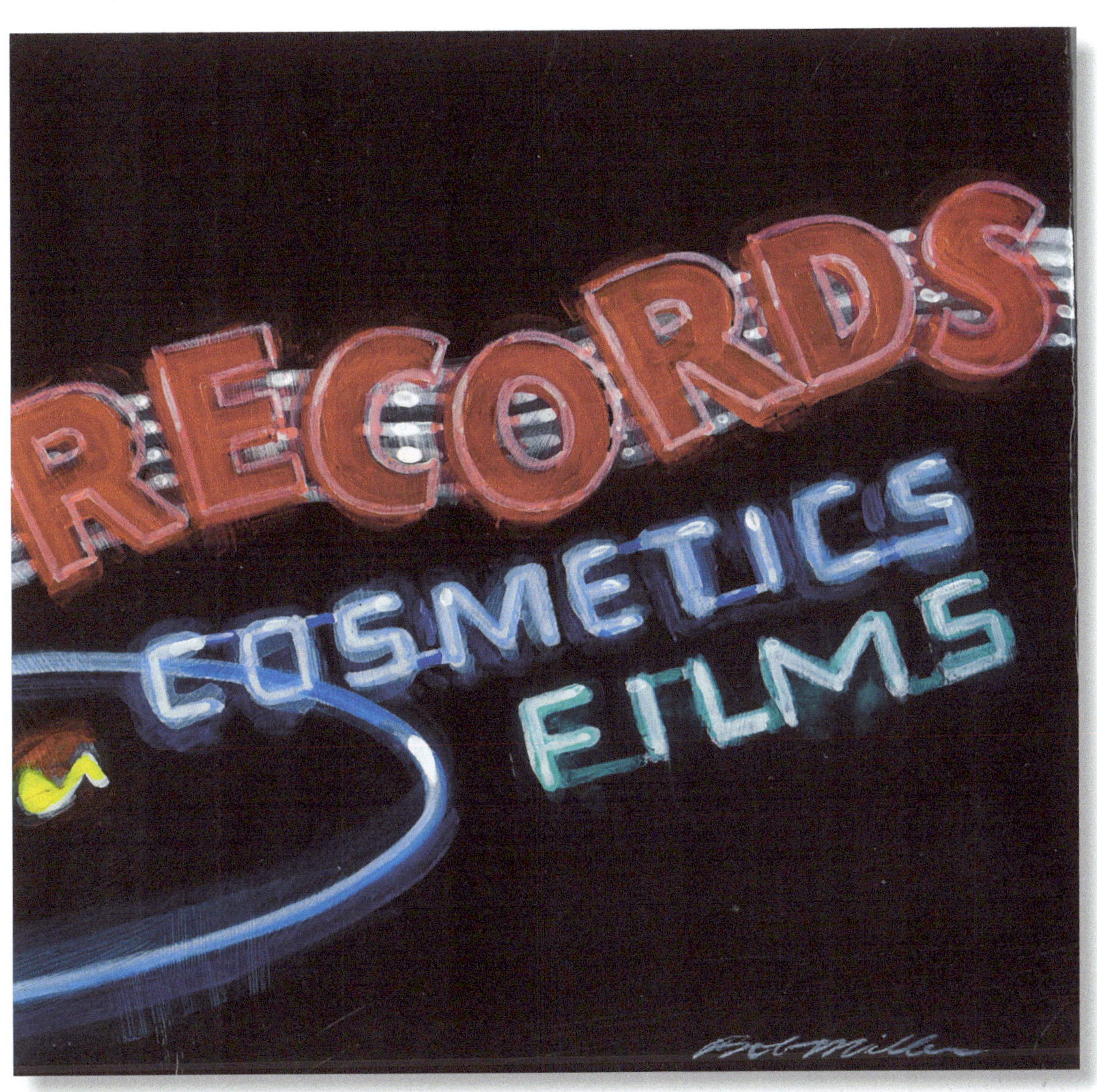
RECORDS
COSMETICS
FILMS

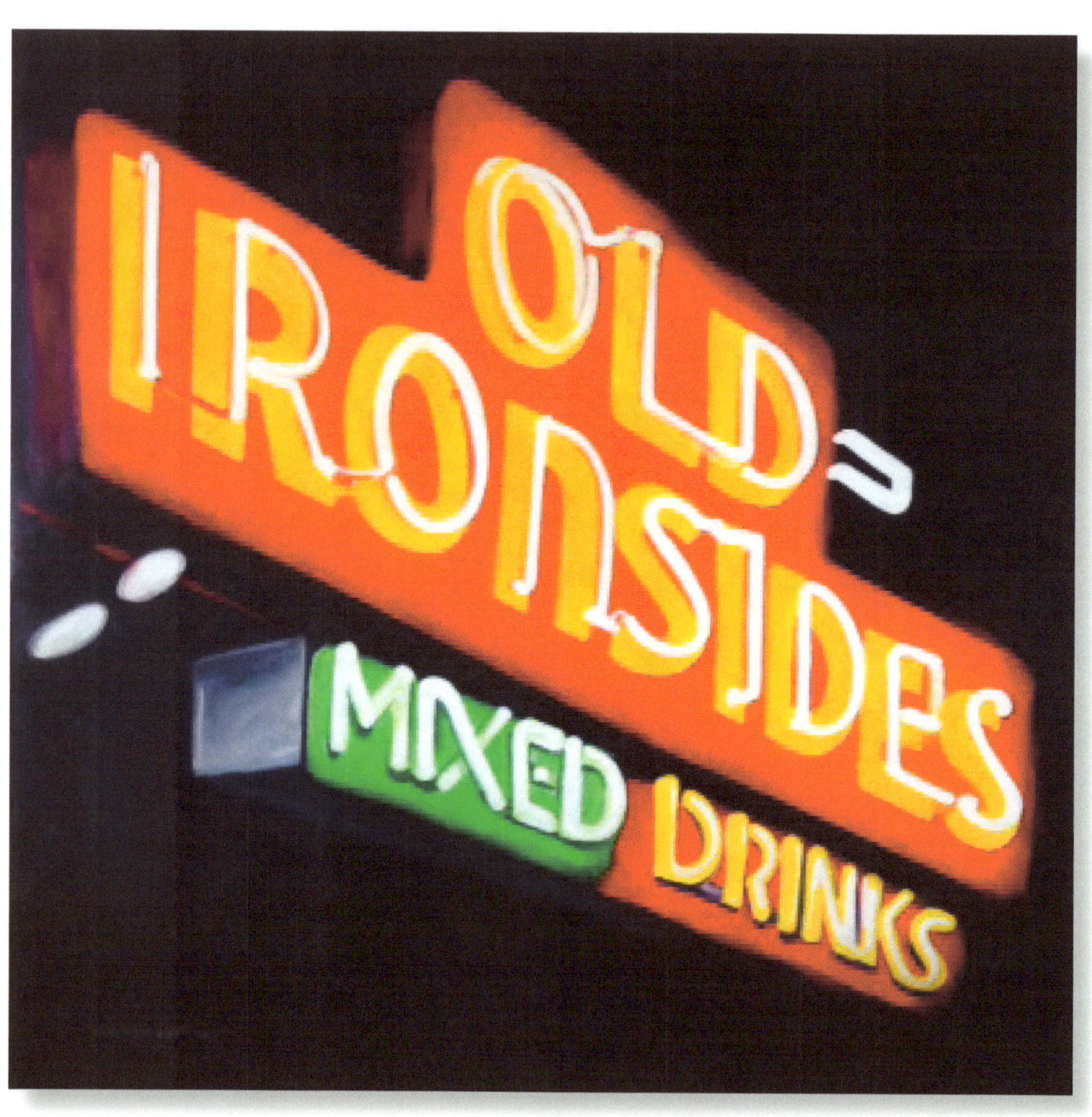
OLD
IRONSIDES
MIXED
DRINKS

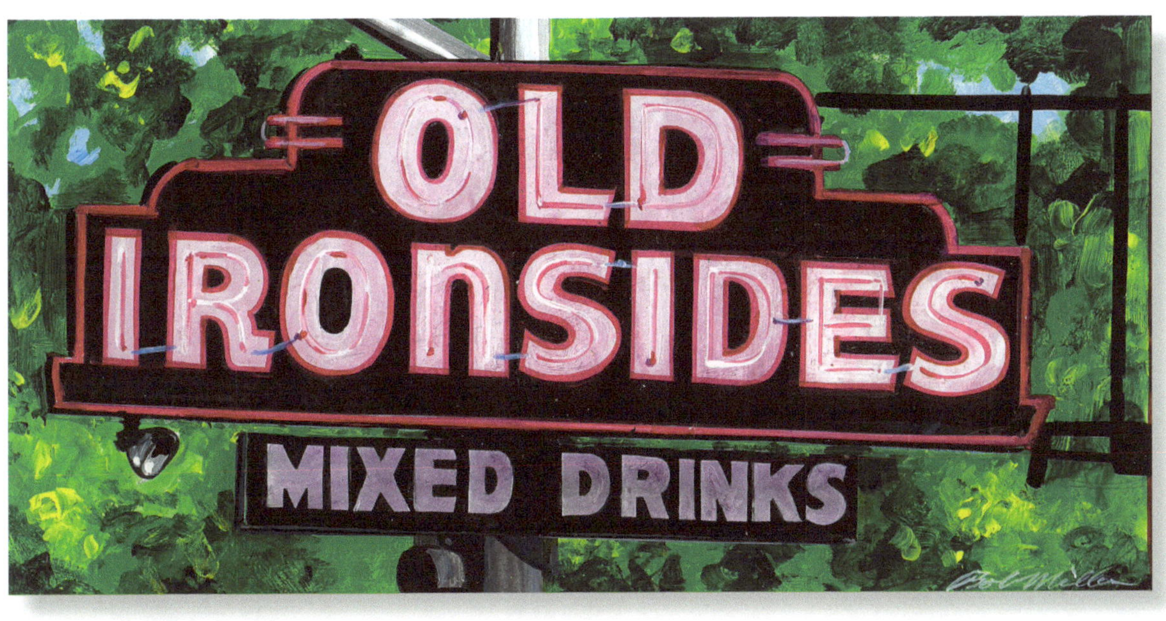
OLD
IRONSIDES
MIXED DRINKS

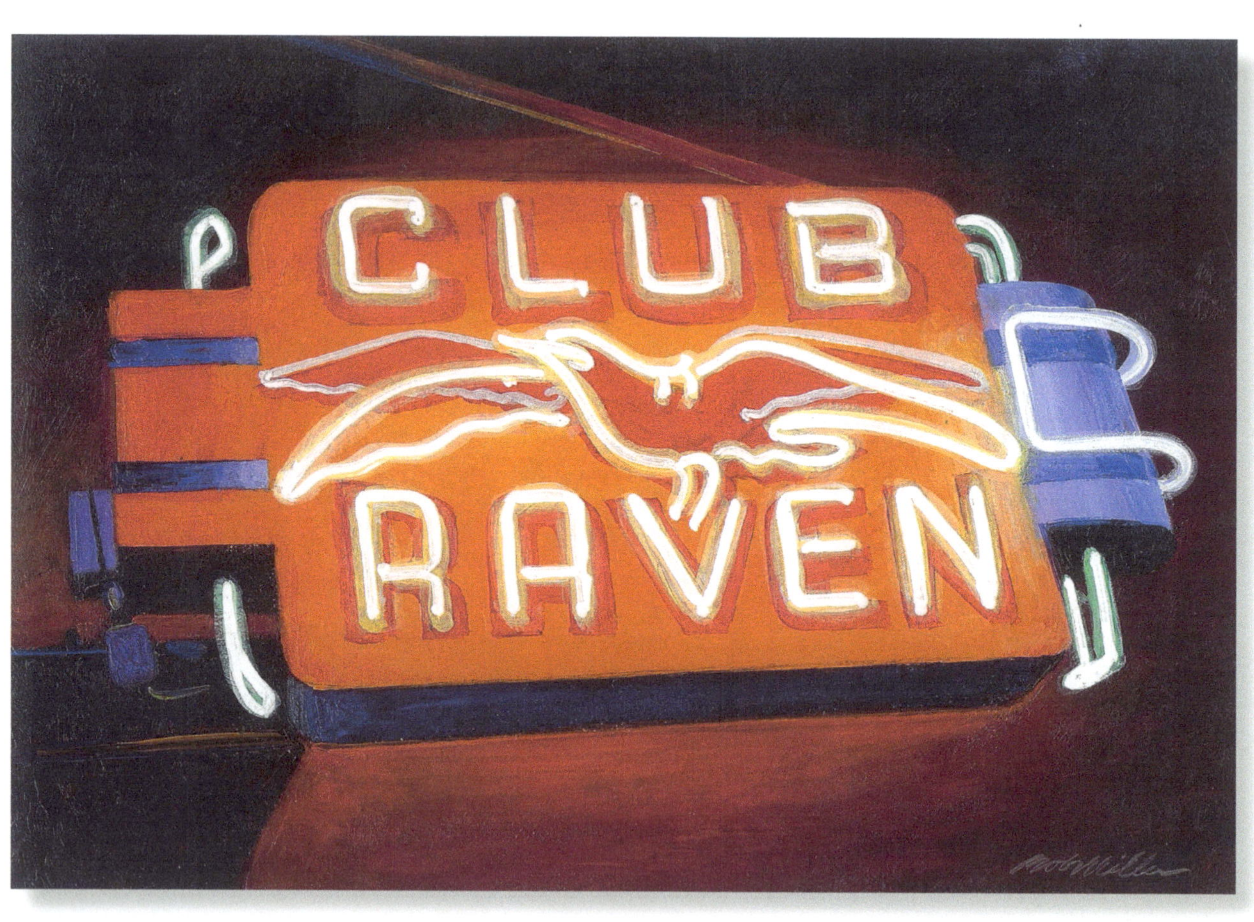
CLUB
RAVEN

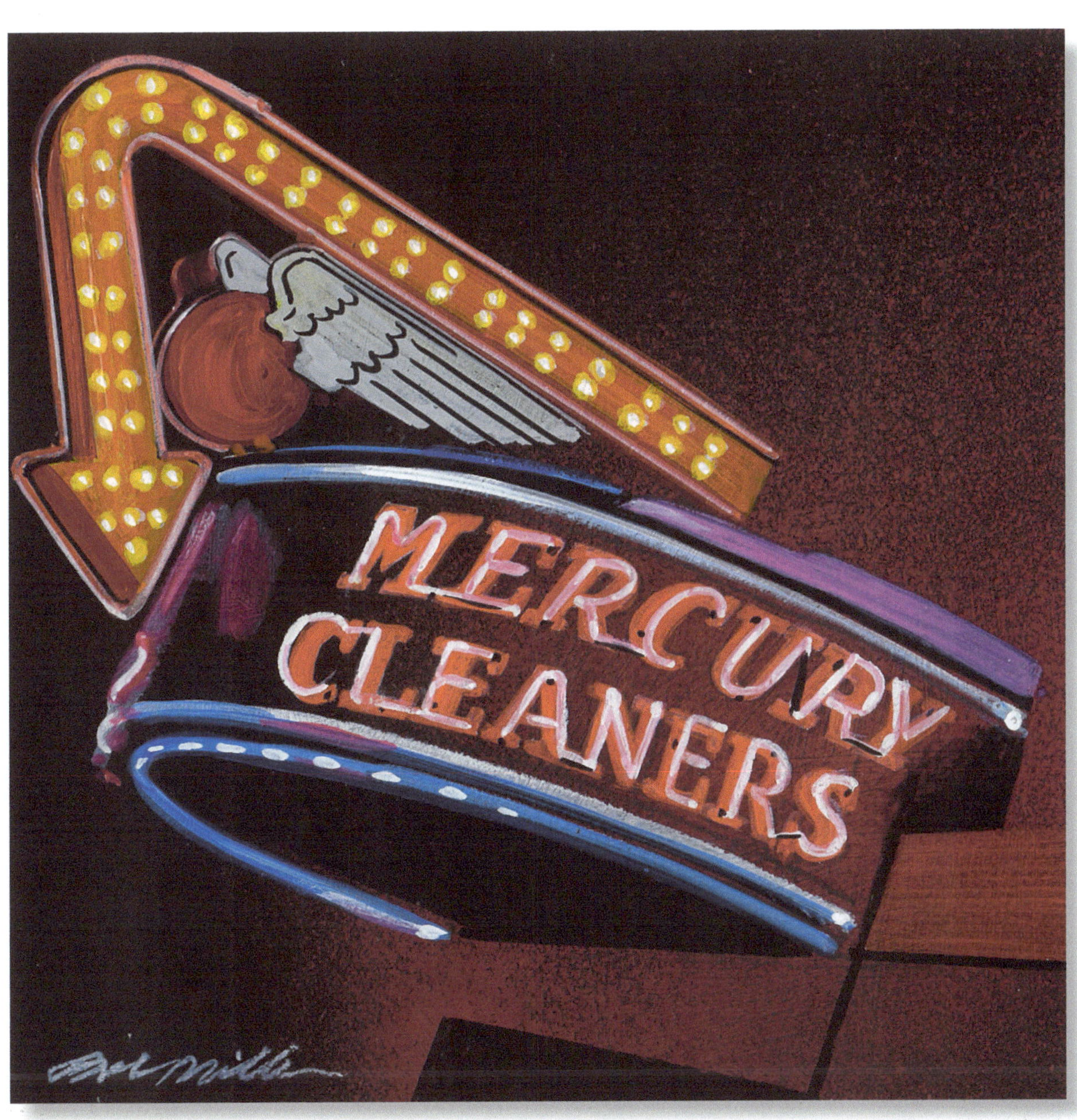
MERCURY
CLEANERS

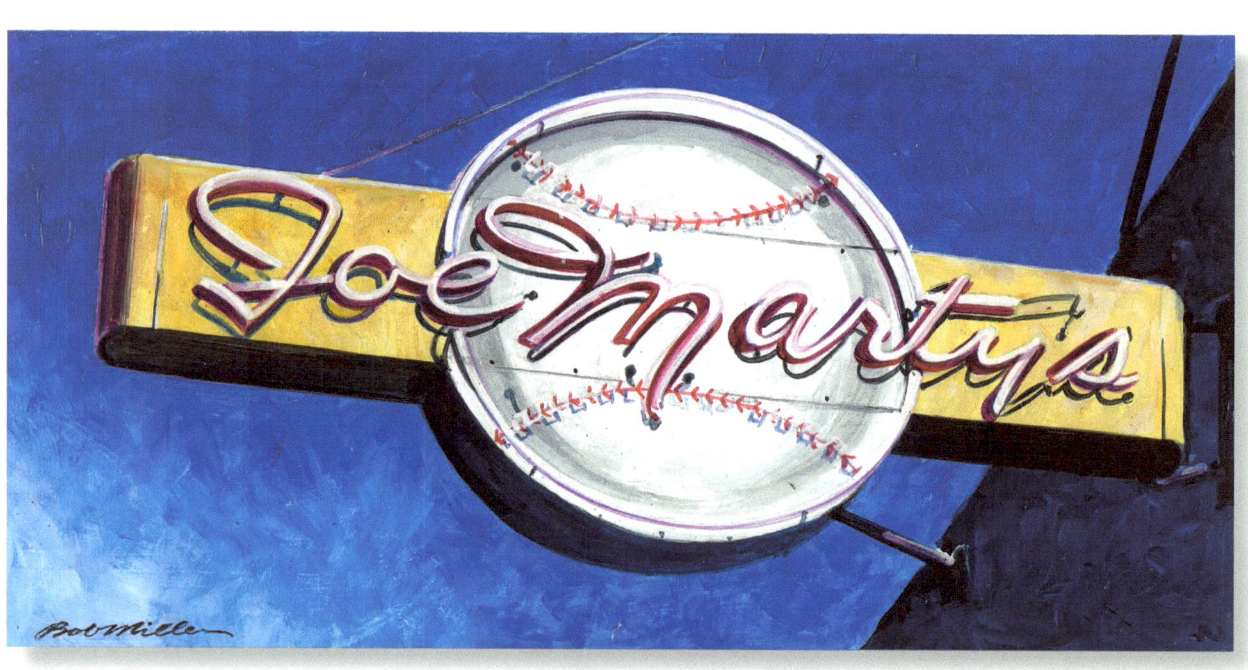
Joe Martys

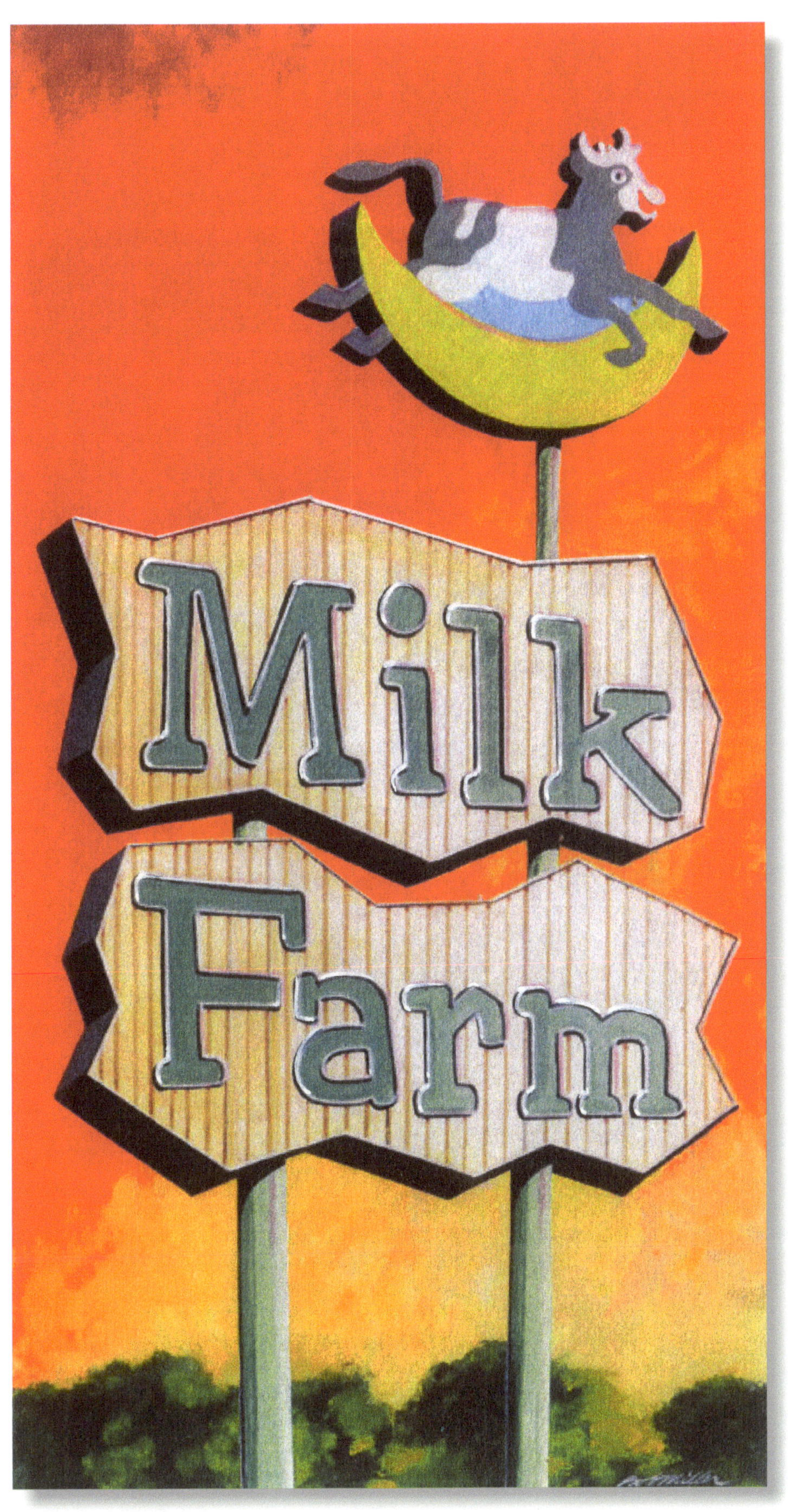
Milk
Farm

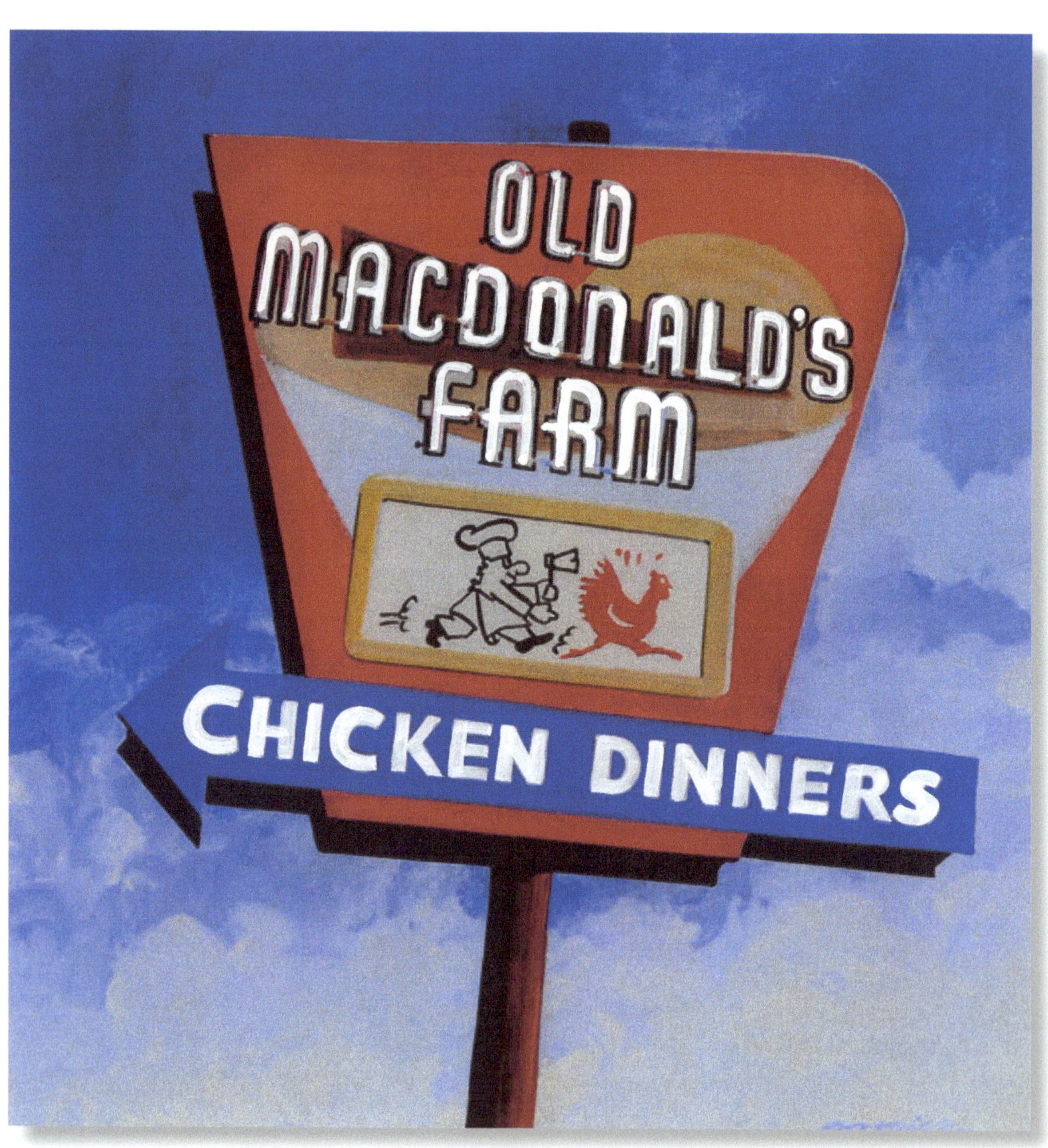
OLD
MACDONALD'S
FARM
CHICKEN DINNERS

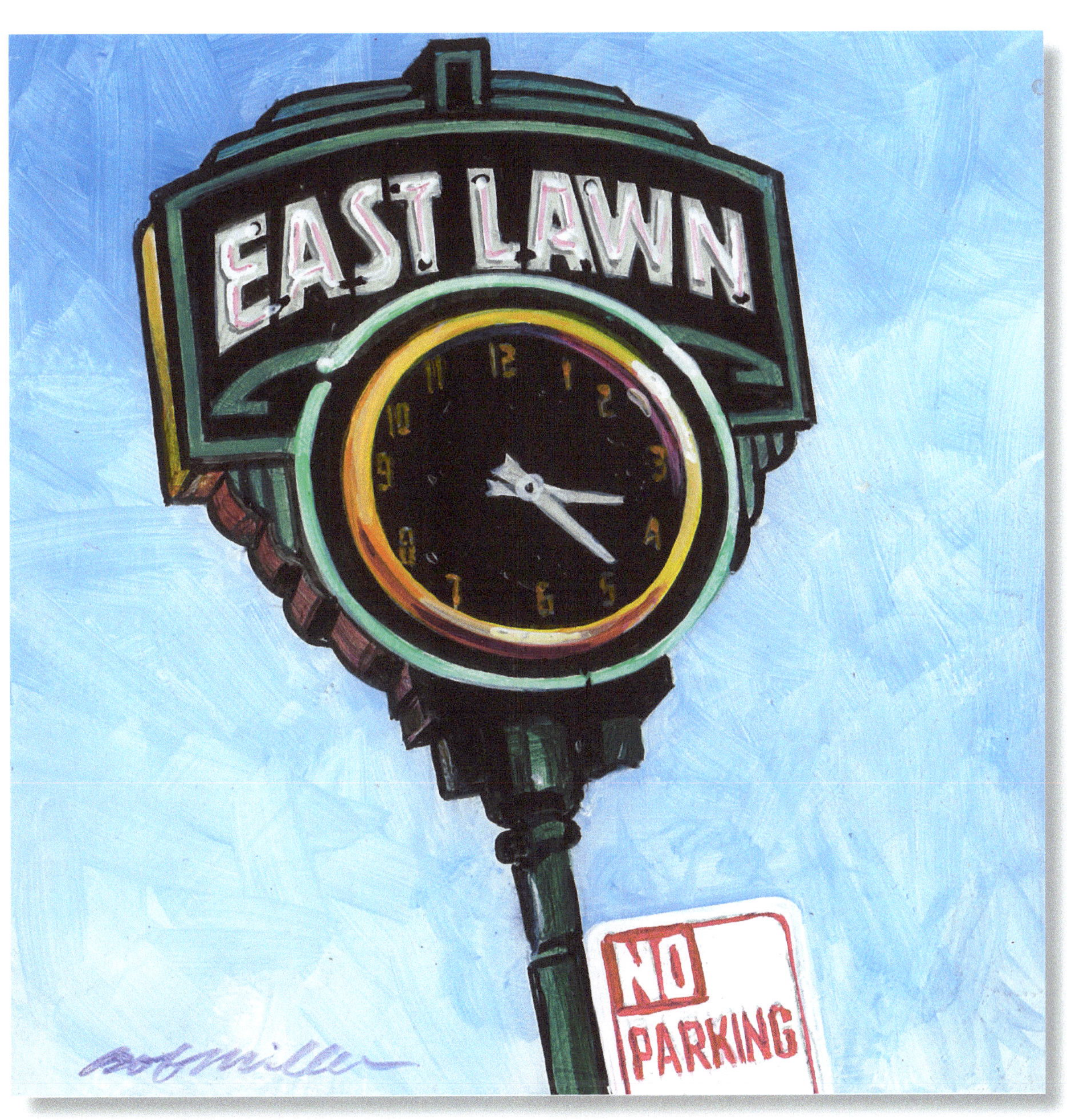
EAST LAWN
NO
PARKING

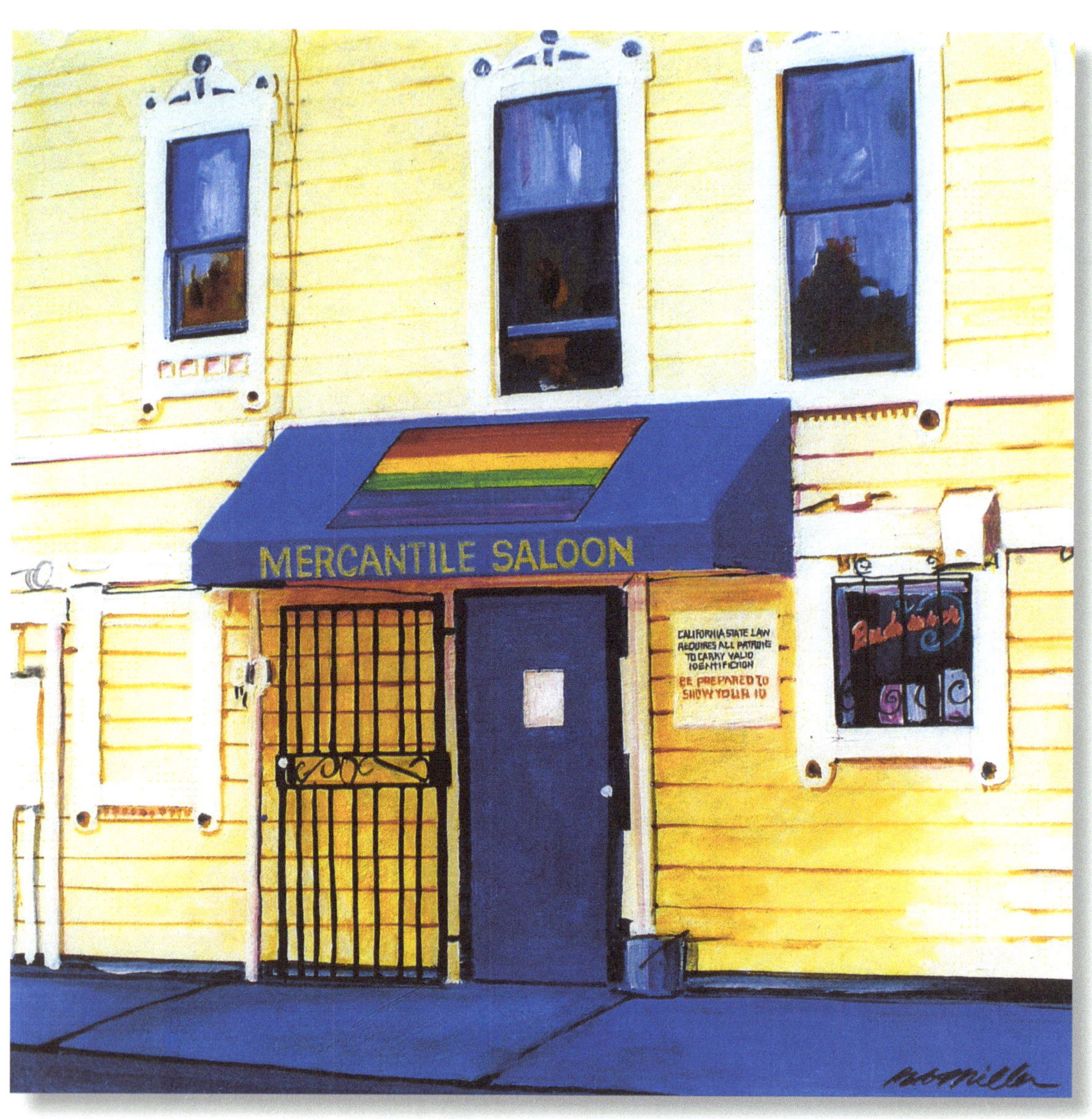
MERCANTILE SALOON
CALIFORNIA STATE LAW
BE PREPARED TO
SHOW YOUR ID

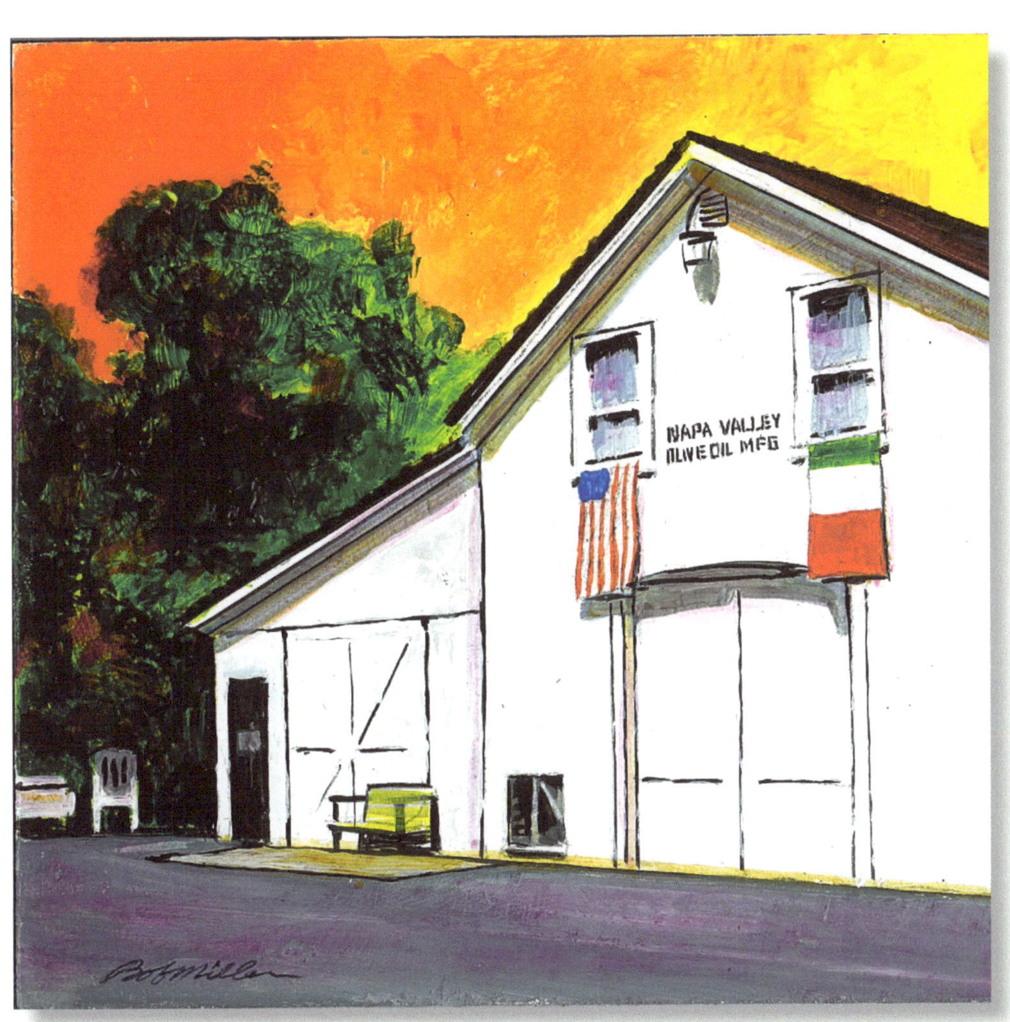
NAPA VALLEY
OLIVE OIL MFG

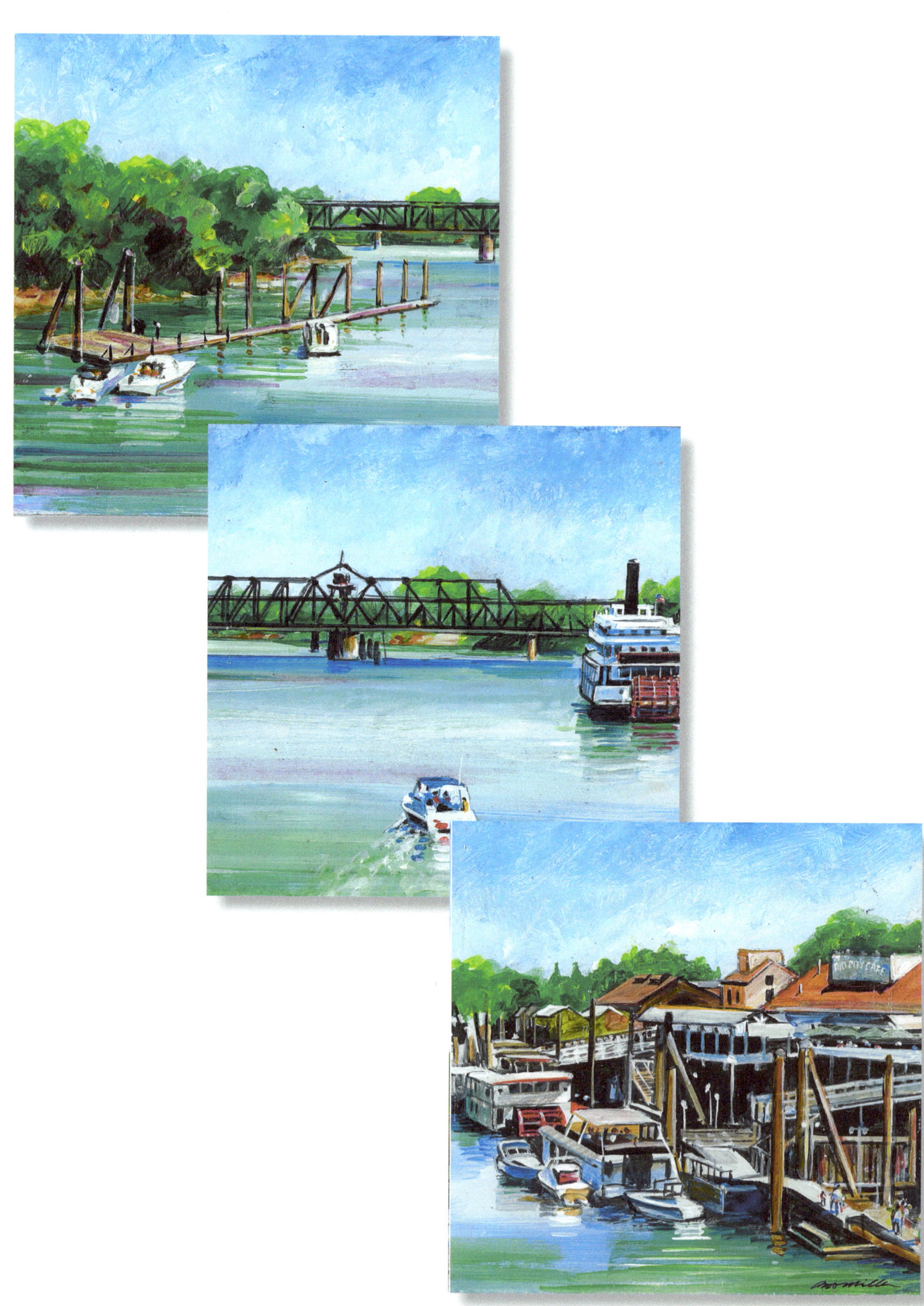

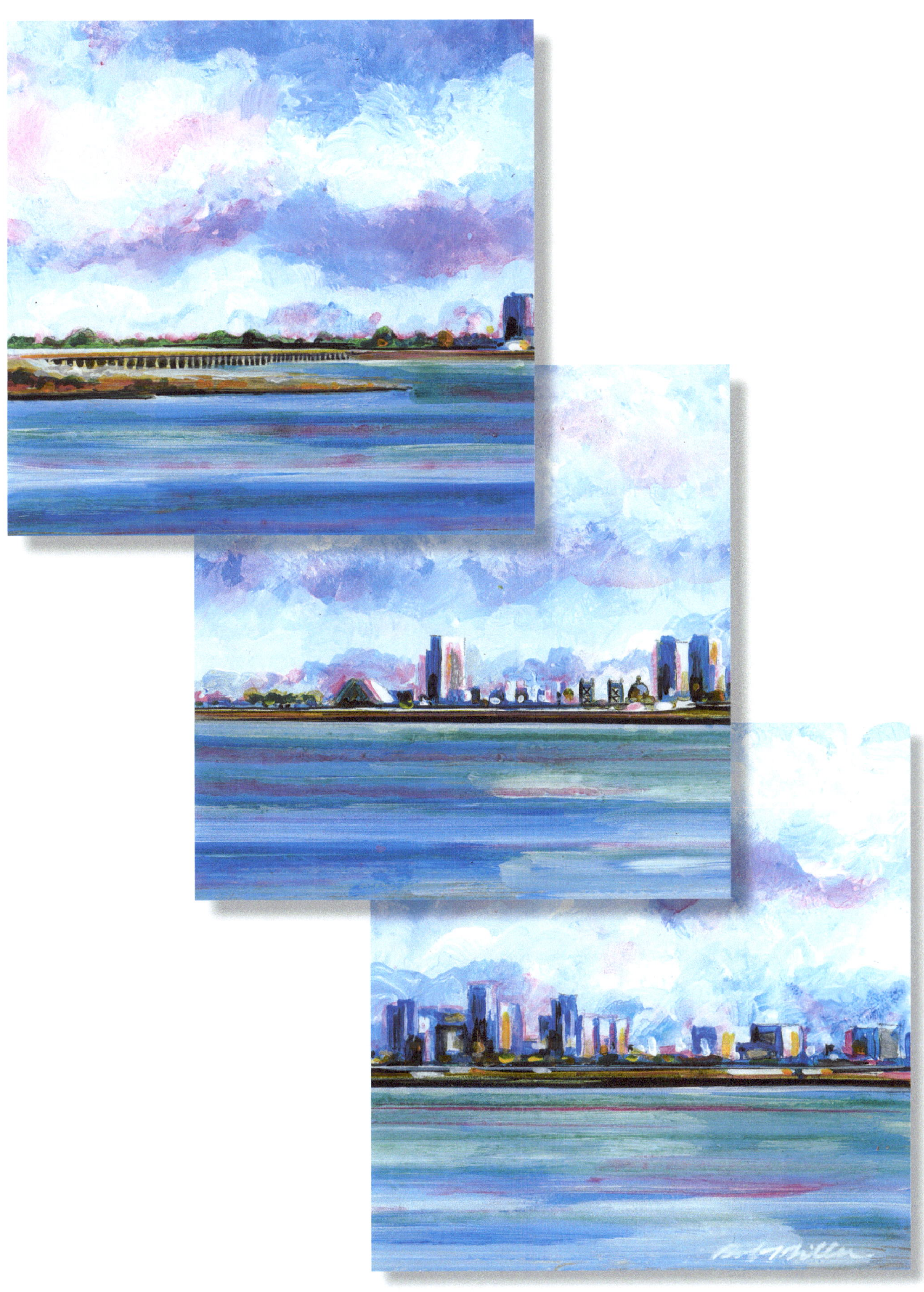

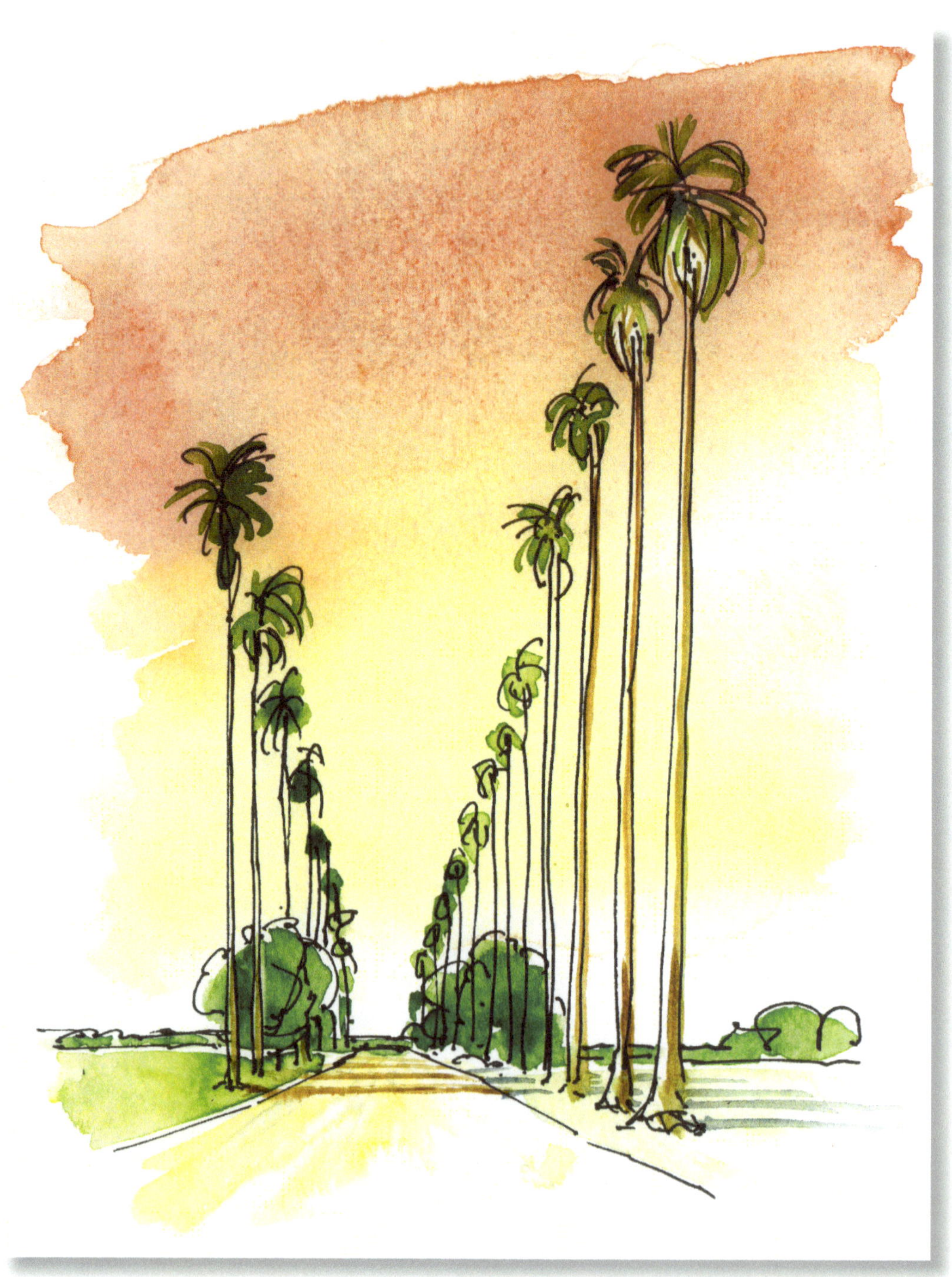

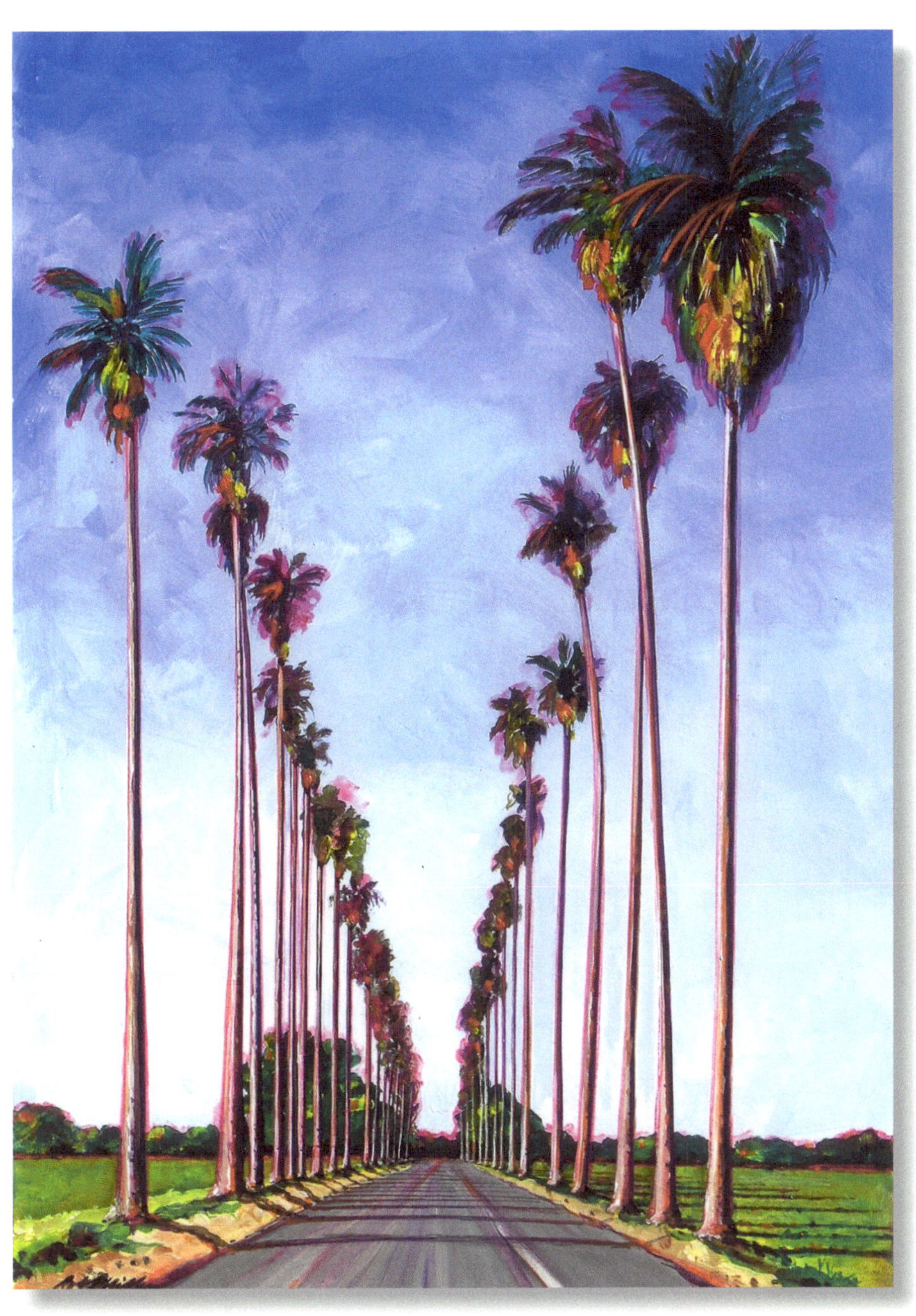

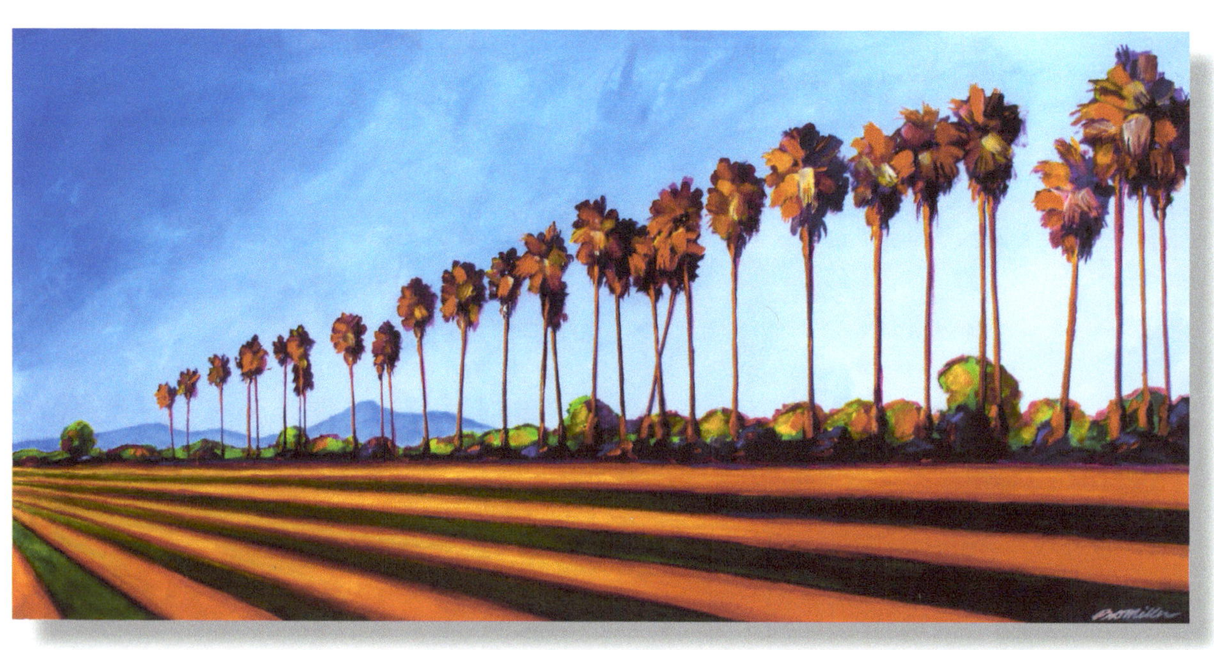

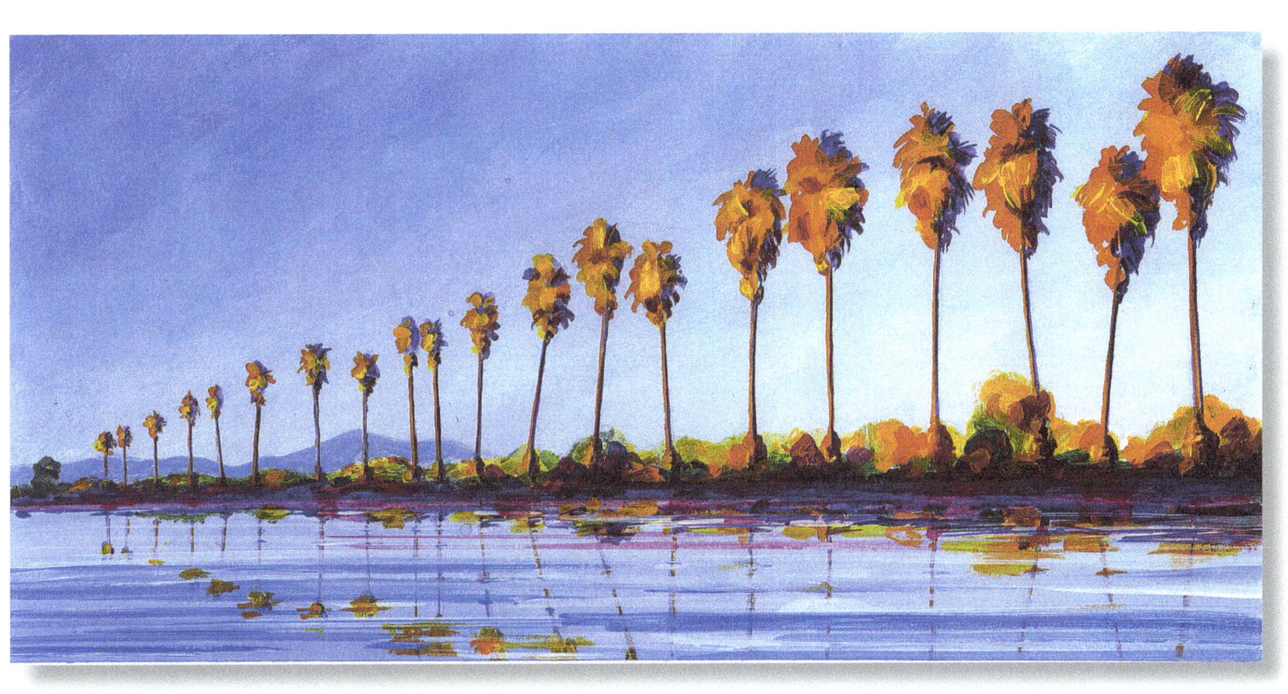

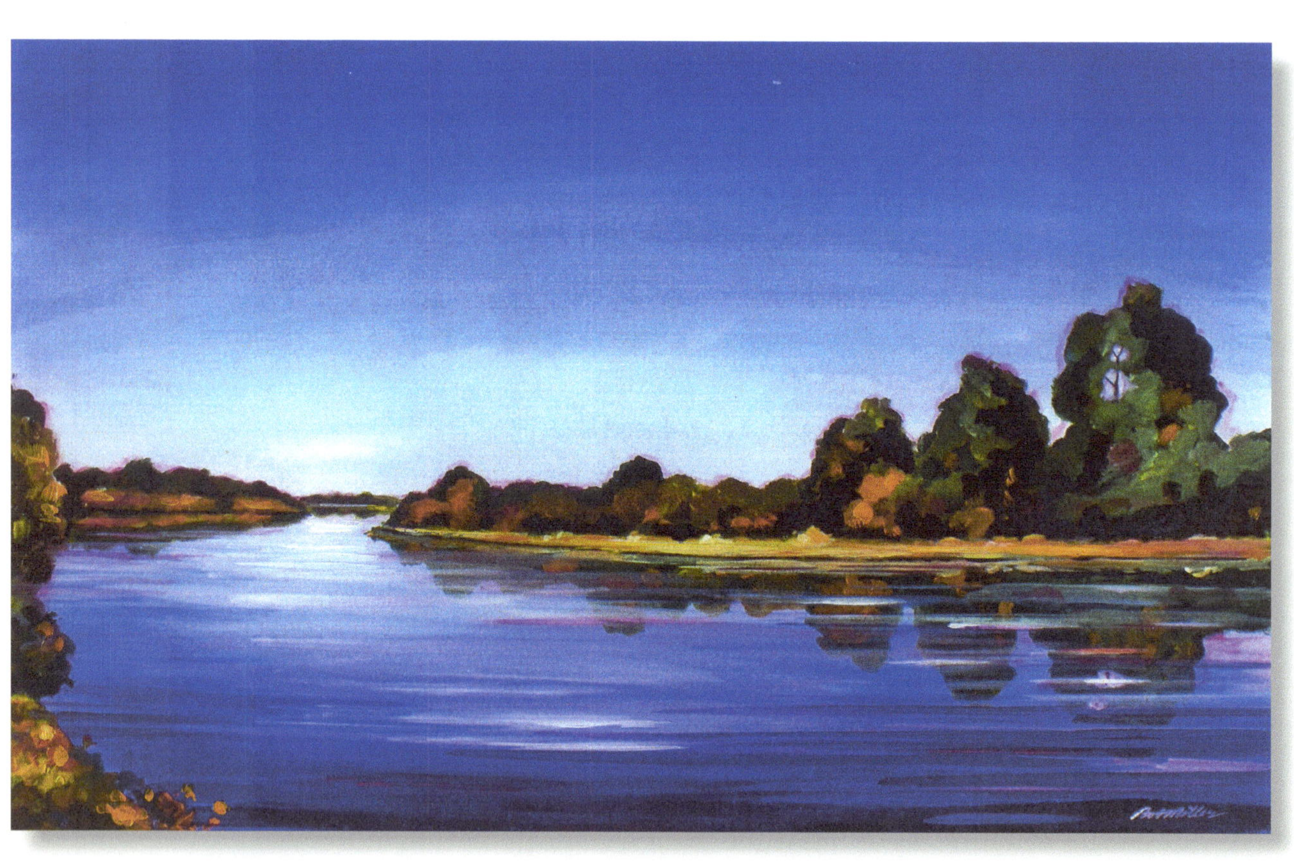

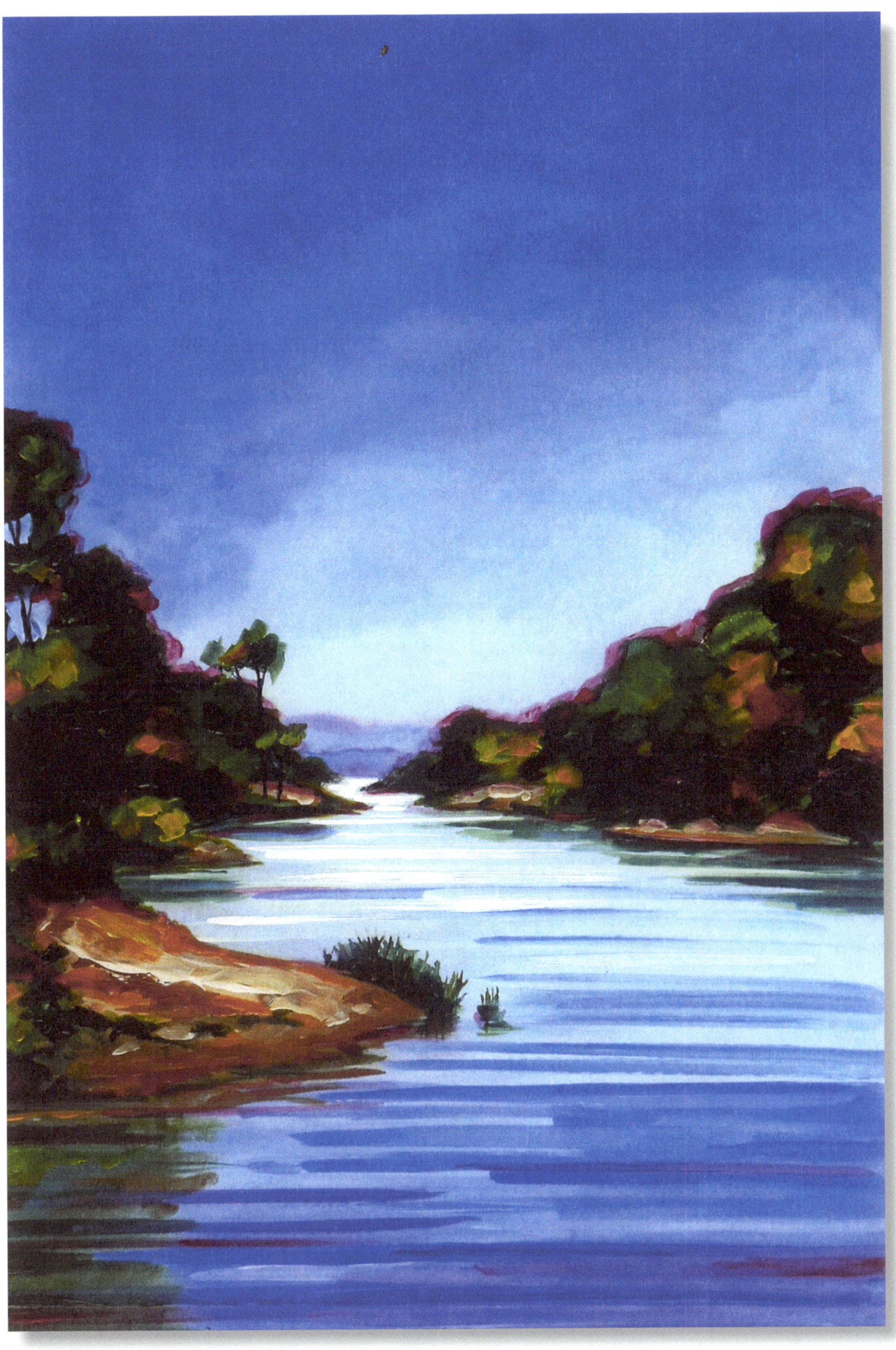

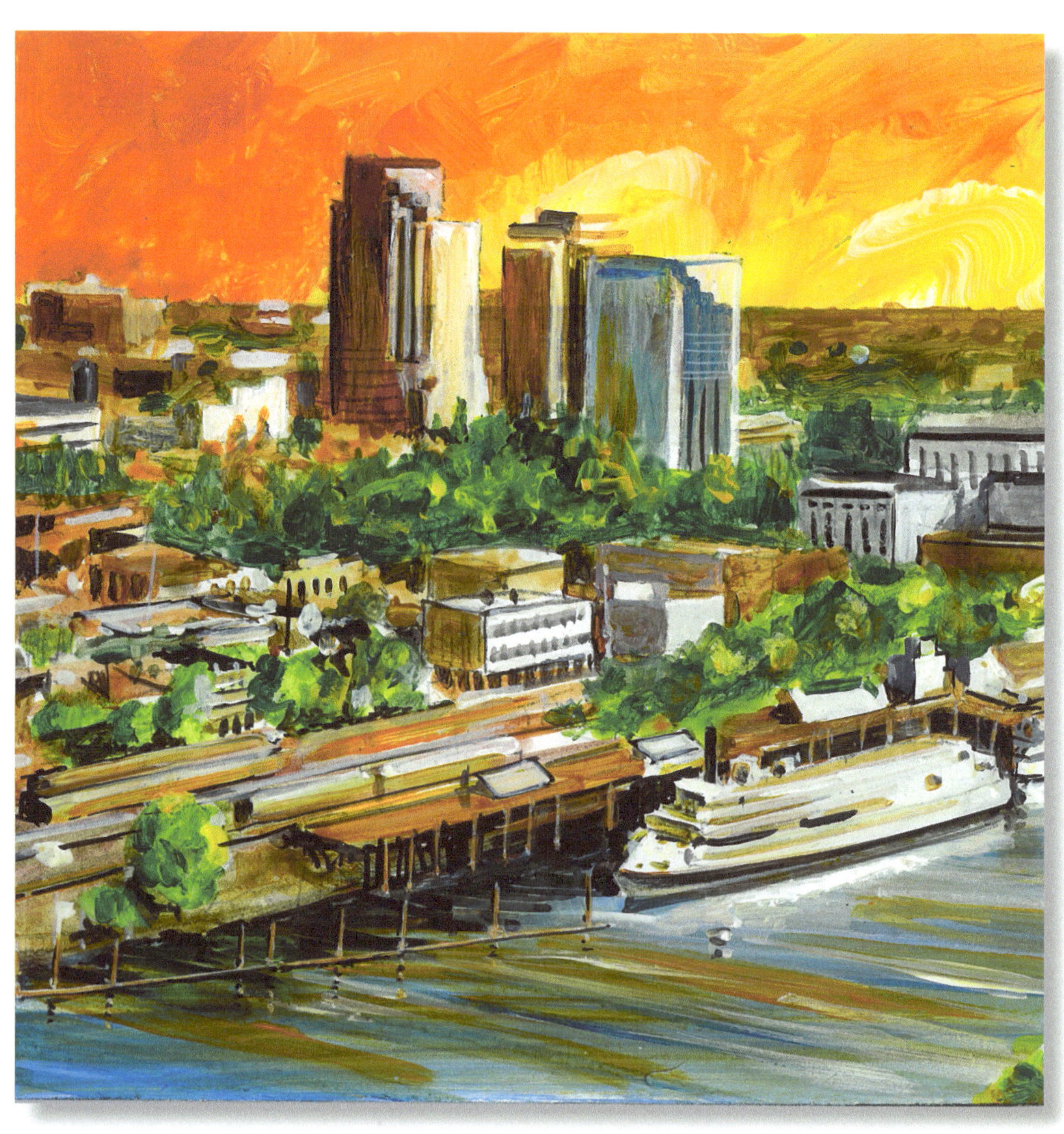

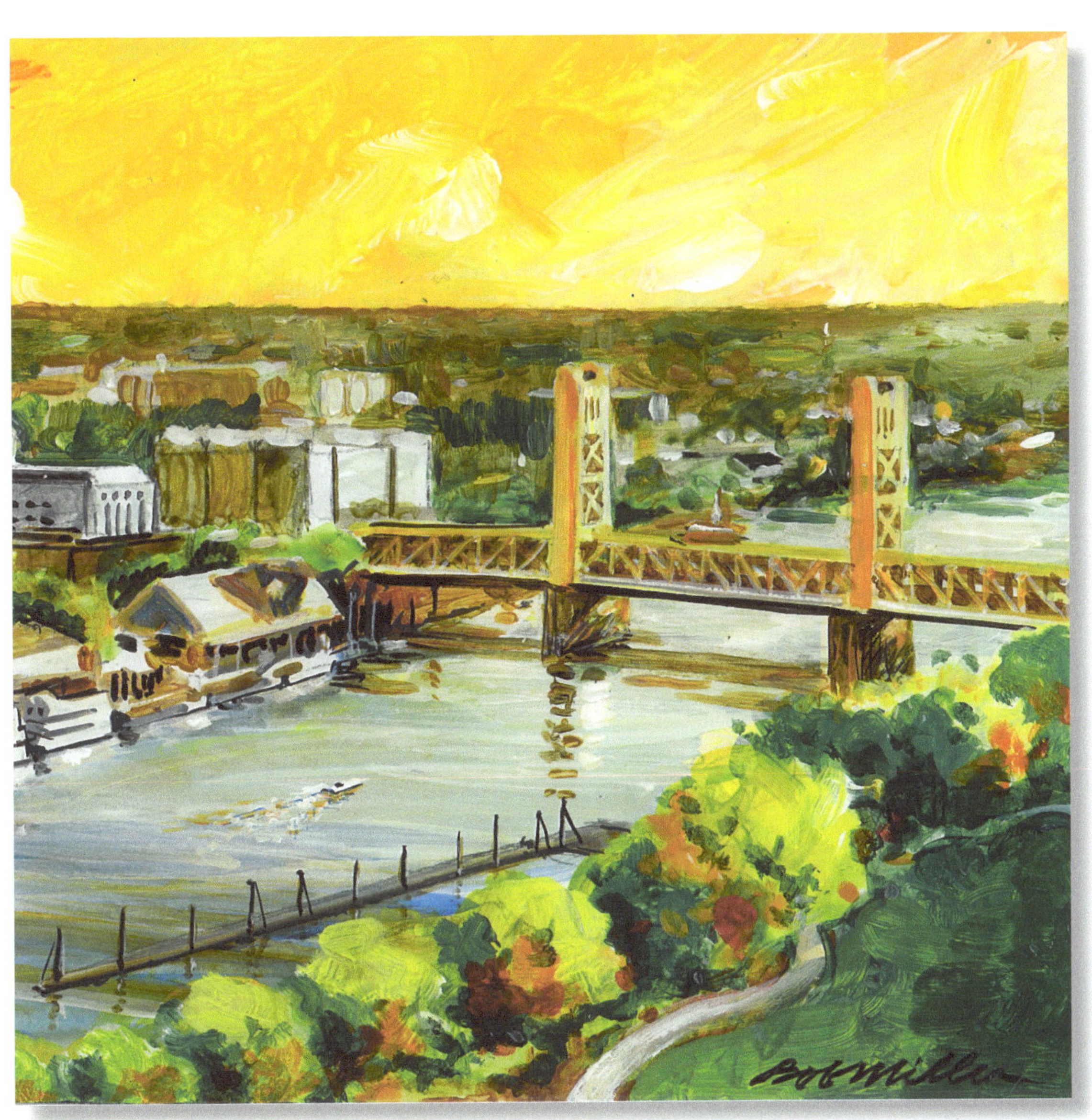
Bob Miller

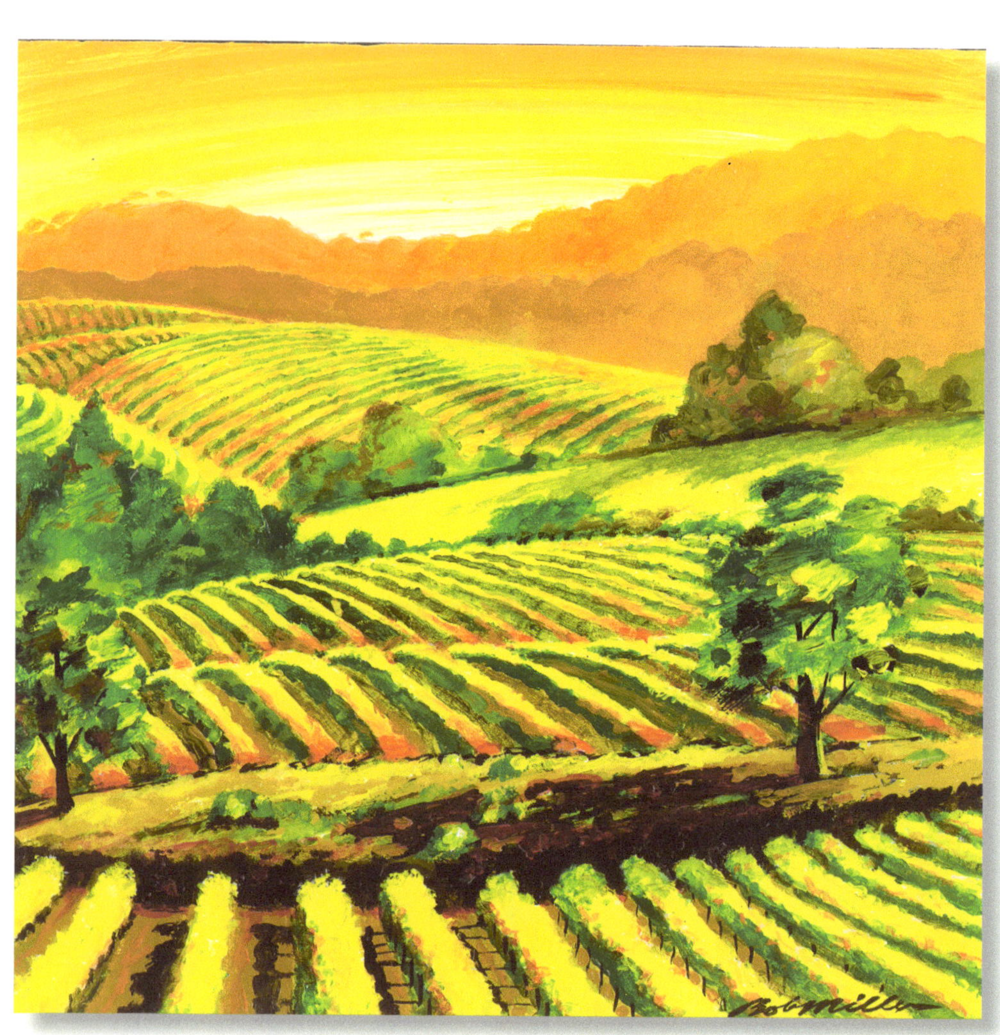

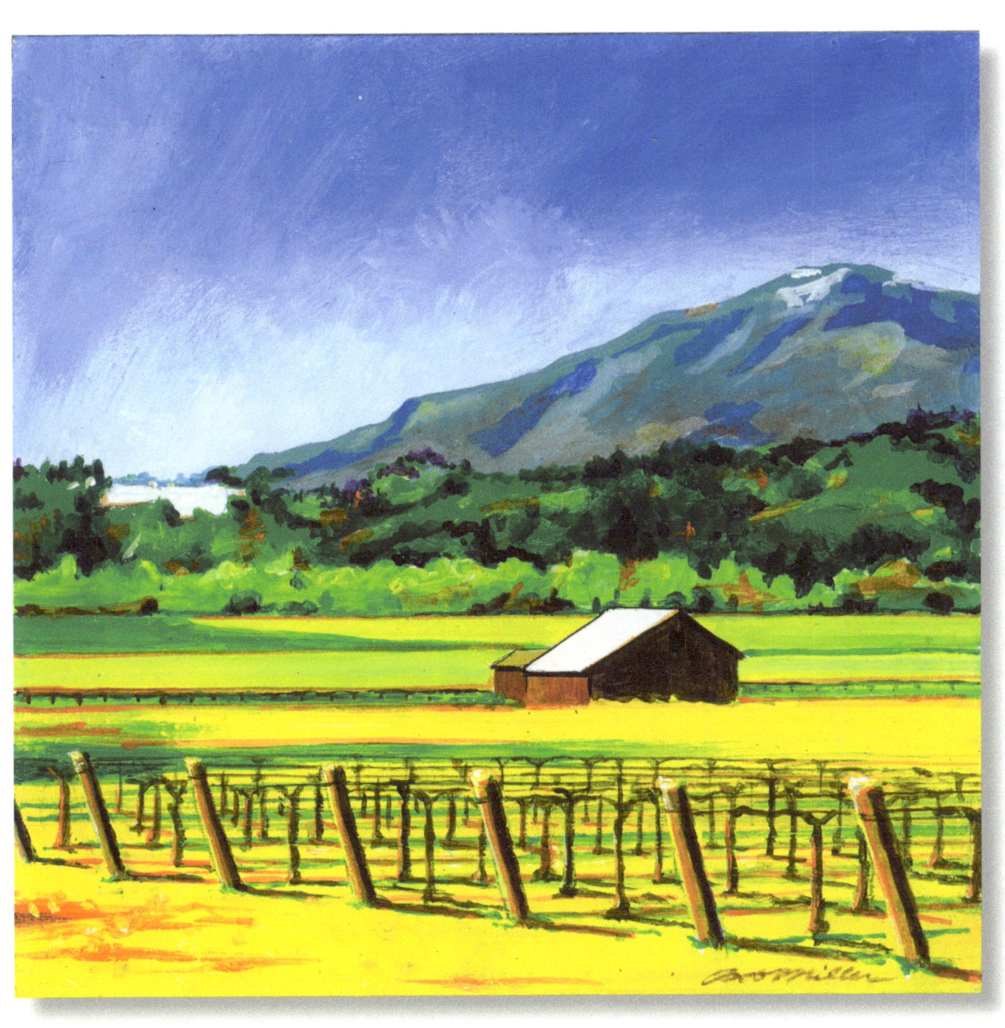

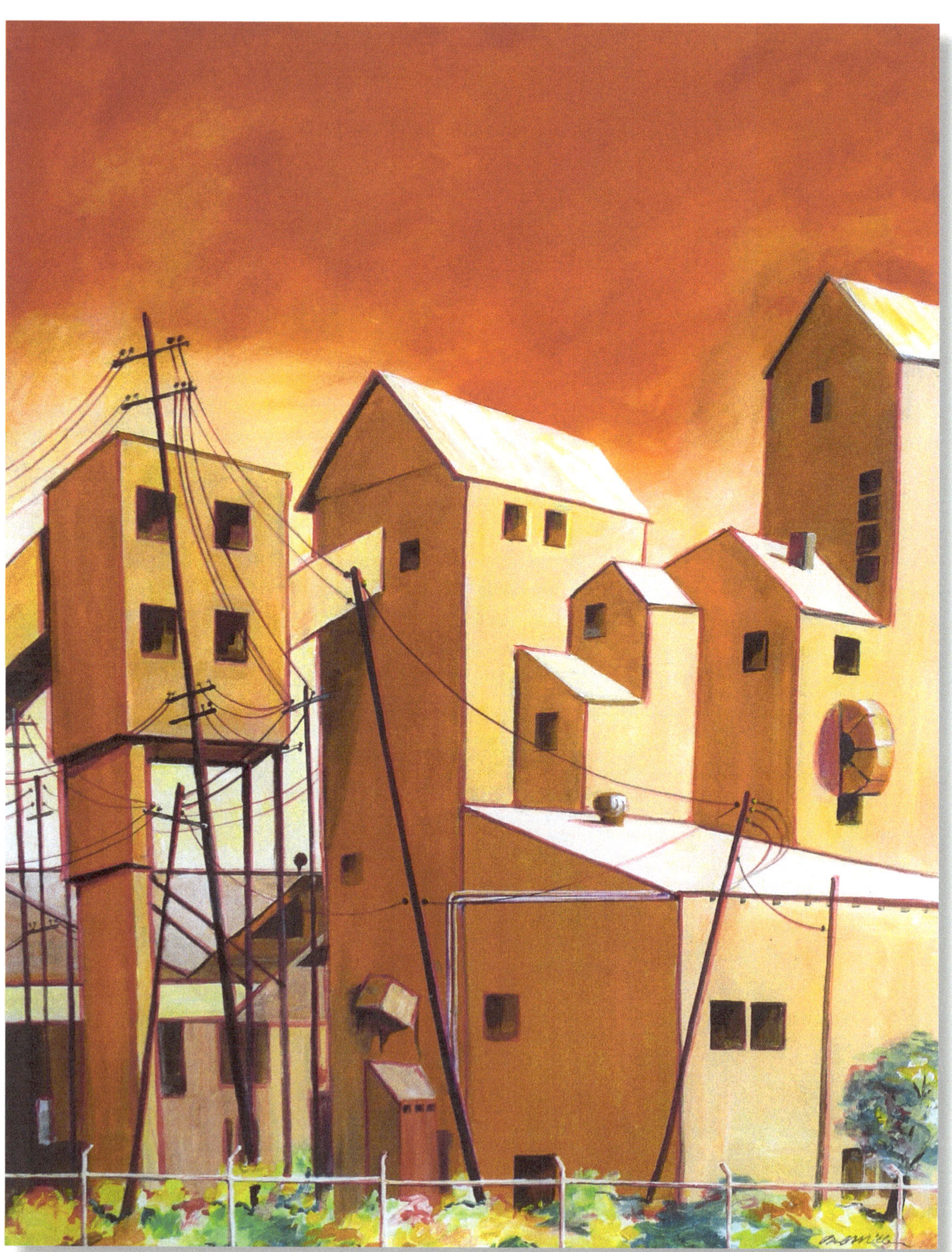

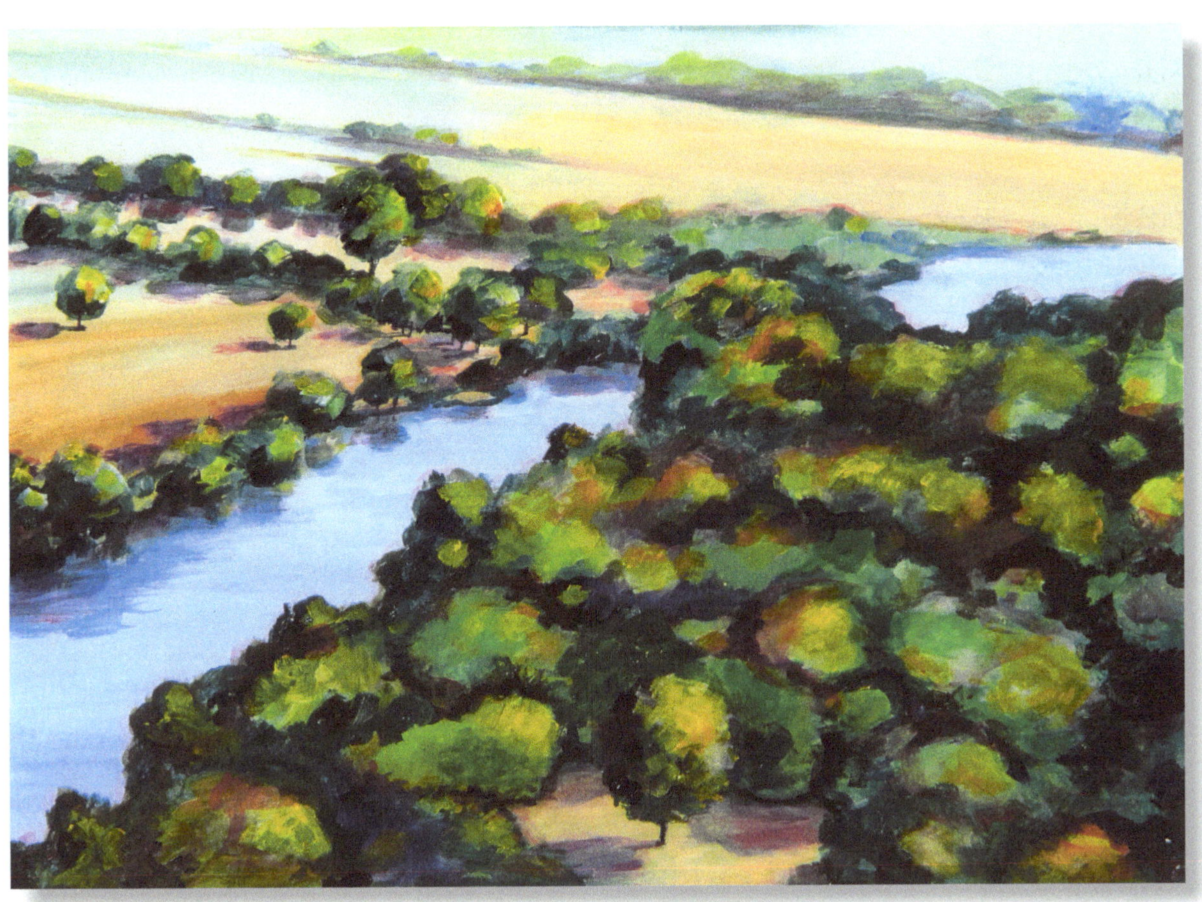

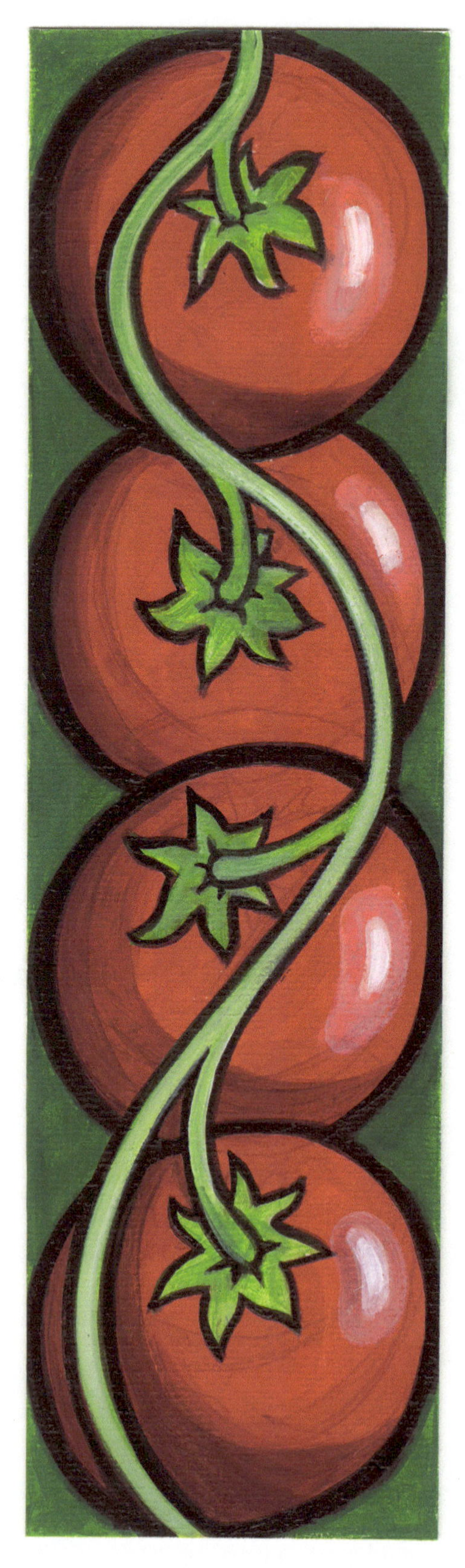

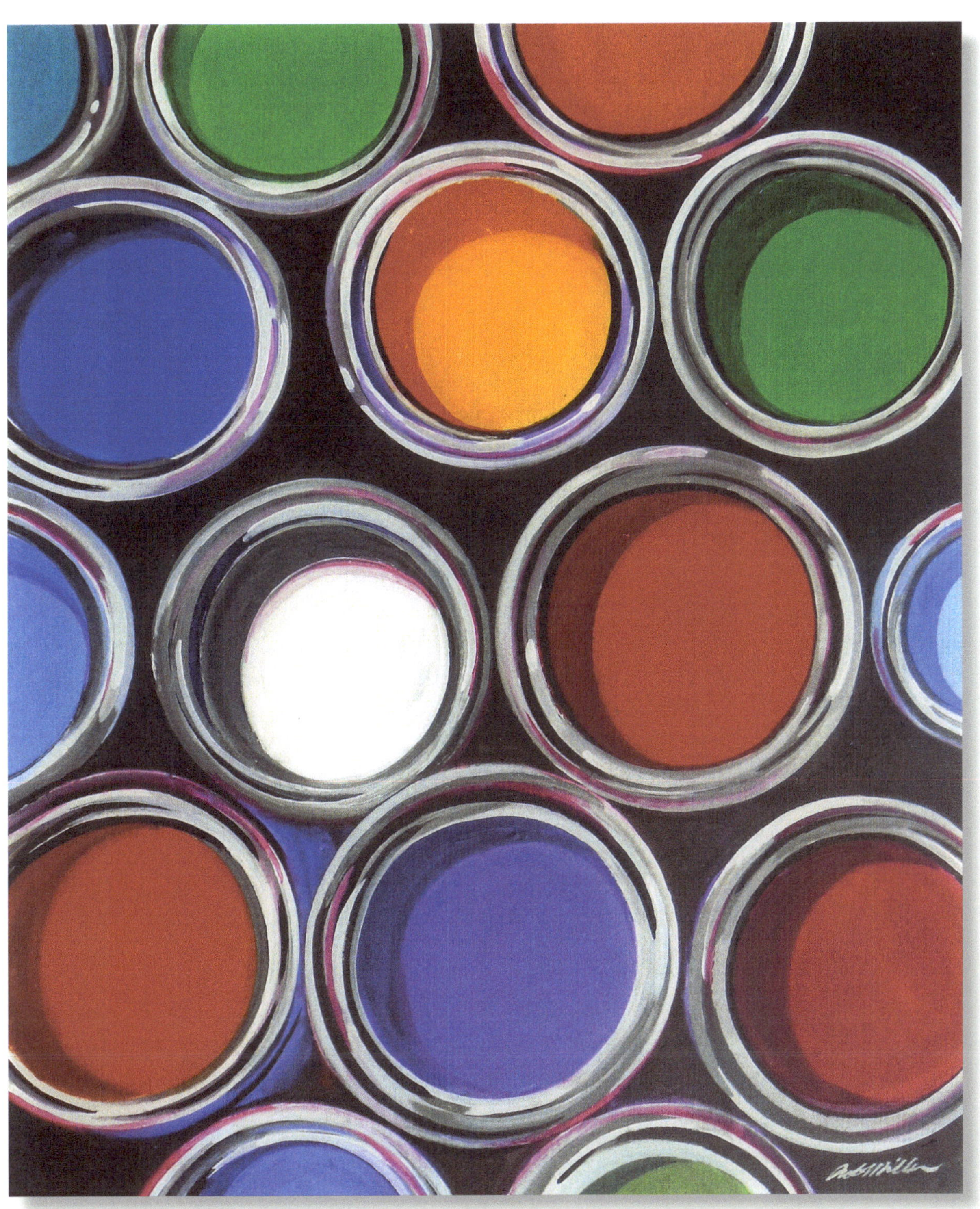

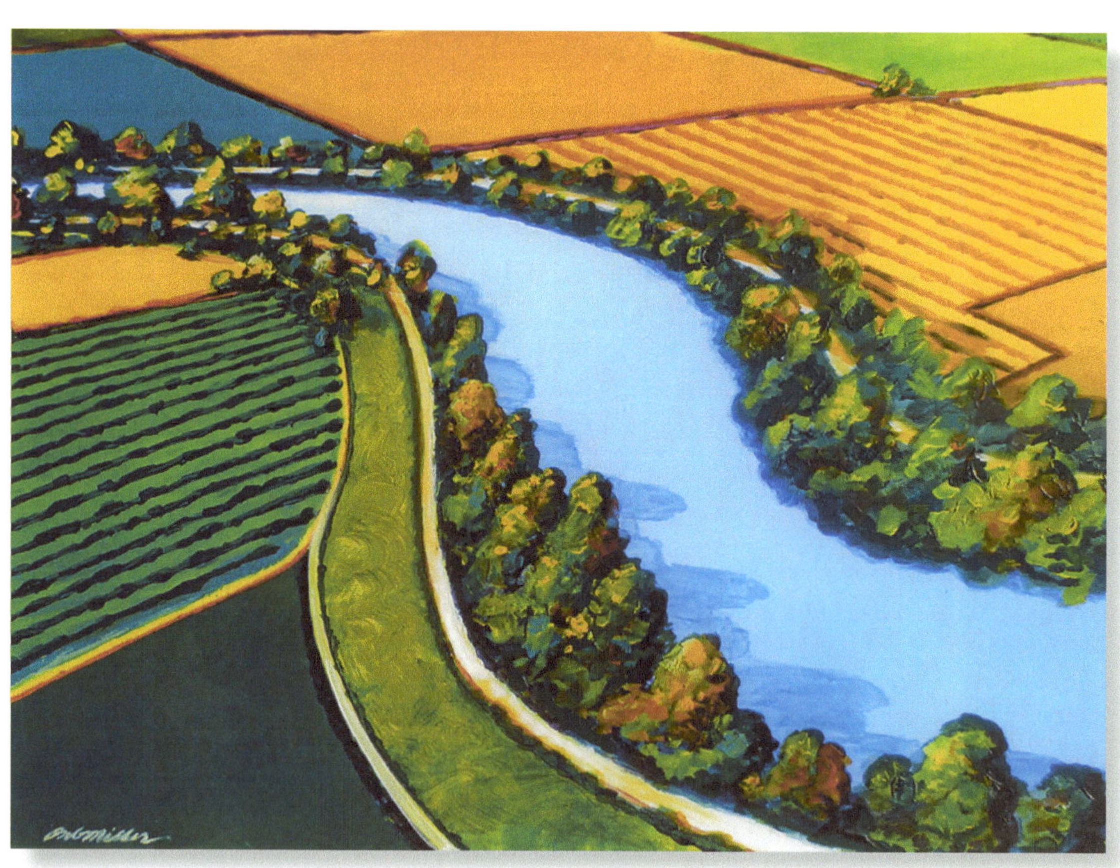

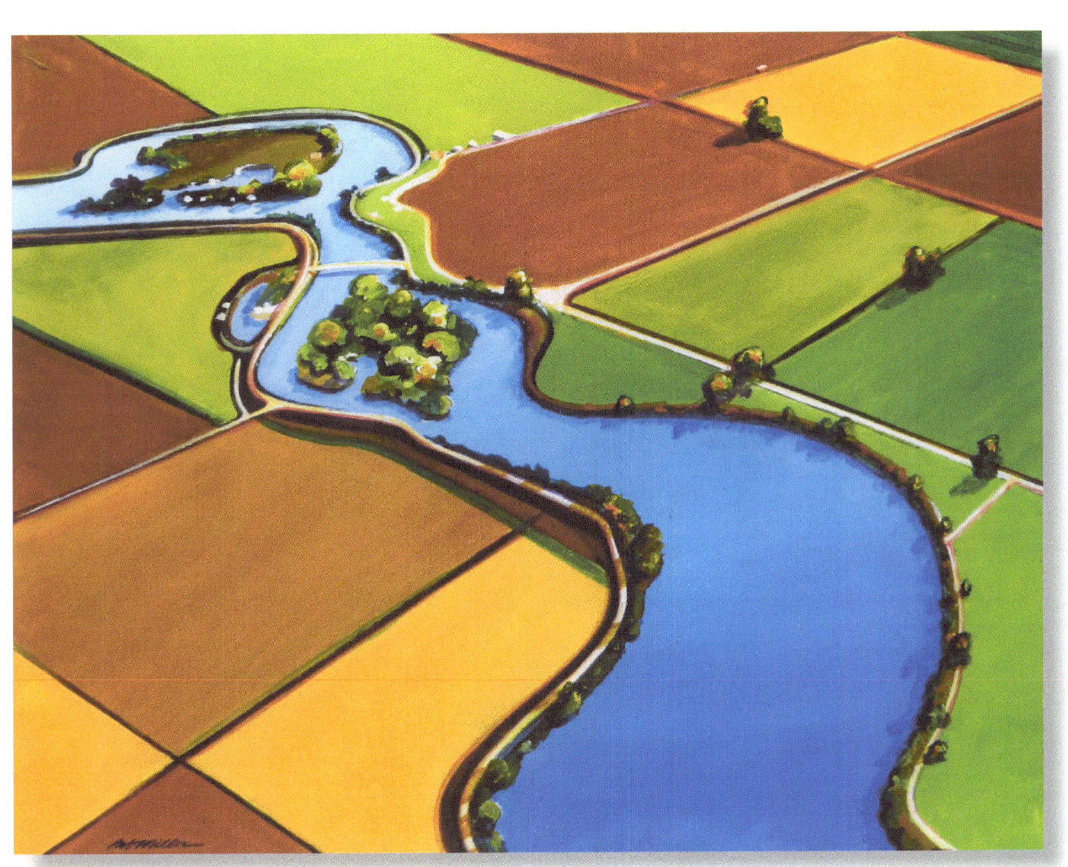

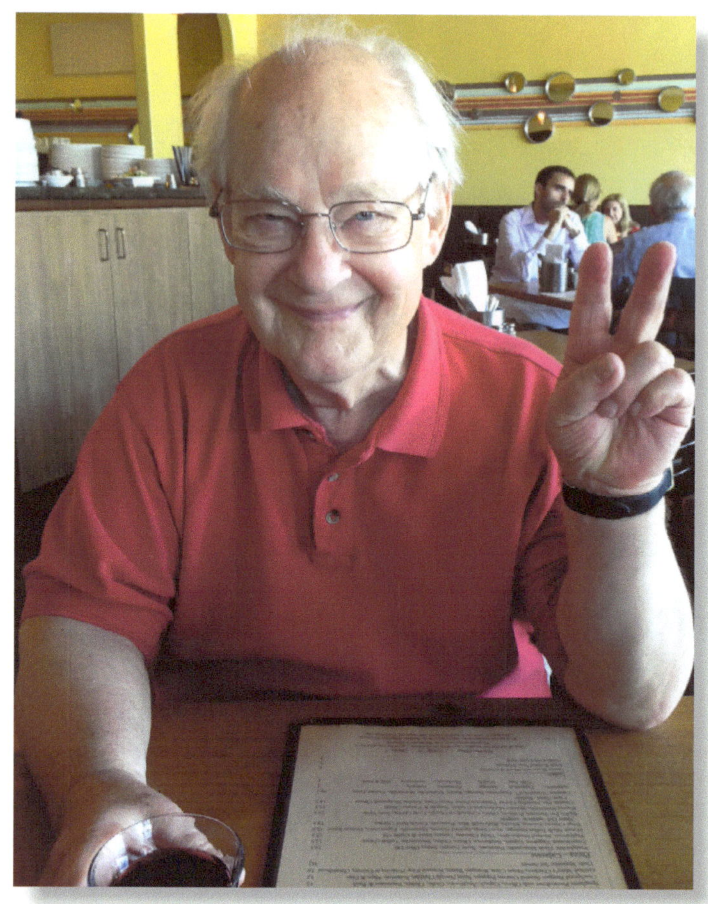

I am 85 years old. My health is relatively good. I have aches and pains that I did not have a few years ago. My lower back hurts when I stand for long periods of time. My sciatica is annoying, but ordinarily I don't notice it. I pee a lot. I know every bathroom in Northern California. And, if I think I may be caught in a long traffic jam on the Bay Bridge I wear a "Depends." Yes, I admit it, Bob occasionally wears a diaper.

I find I need naps in the afternoon. I eat a light lunch, then drowse off in my lounge chair for an hour or so. It's difficult for me to contine to work without my nap. Then I get a second wind and can function well til midnight. I go to bed at midnight and sleep until about 7:30. I sleep very well and dream well.

Sleeping is an adventure for me. It's like entering another world. Every night there are dreams. Some are like the old "short subjects" films, but with no beginnings or endings. Others are complete stories. Many I do not remember but I have written down some that I have remembered. It's like the "midnight movies" and I relish going to sleep.

I have been fortunate in my life not to have lost many close friends that were taken at their zenith. Tragedy, for the most part, has avoided me. Most relatives,

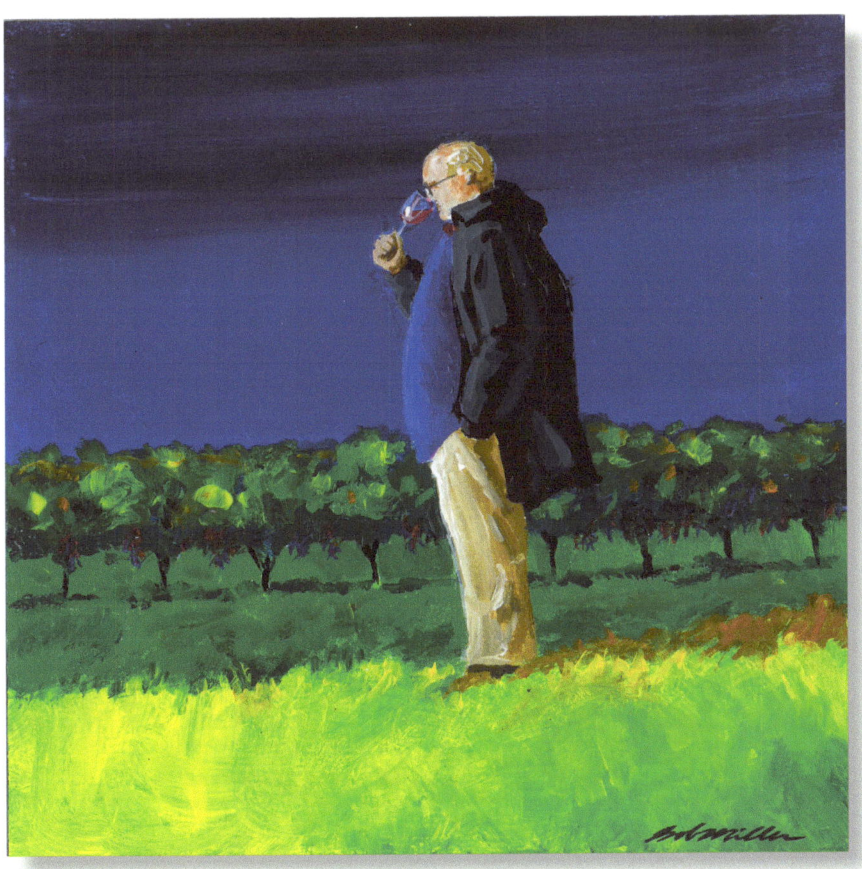

friends and lovers lives ended in old age; however, losing a close friend even in old age can hurt. My good friend Audrey Tsuruda died at 83. She lived a full, long productive life; nevertheless, I miss her. I think of her every day. I still have the impulse to call her when I see something that strikes my fancy. One makes new friends but they are unique to themselves and cannot replace those that are lost.

As I get older I think of death often. I don't want to die. Life has been a great deal of fun and I hope I can continue on this path for a long time. I don't believe in an afterlife. I don't remember anything before 1931 and I don't think I'll witness anything after my death date.

I am not religious. I don't believe there is an all-seeing God. I don't know how all of this amazing and wonderful universe was created. I look up and I can see forever. I am awed by what I see but for me it's beyond explanation.

So, I have had a rich and full life here on earth. That will have to be enough. I leave behind a legacy I am proud of. We have had joy and loss. The joy has exceeded the loss.

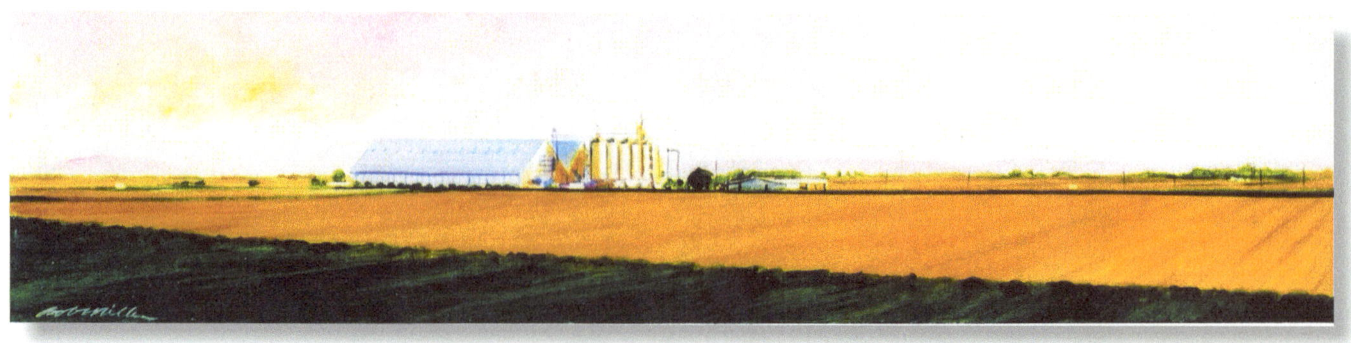

A final word from Bob Androvich

As a child of television the Channel 3 logo was burned into my brain by the time I was 7 years old. One Saturday at my dad's printing business, he was "shooting photostats" of the logo and some other original artwork. I was mezmerized, thrilled I would see it later on TV. When I asked him who at Channel 3 made it he told me Bob Miller.

From that moment on, as a television nut and commercial art fan, Bob Miller took on near legendary status in my mind. He created Channel 3's logo. He did all of Crystal Creamery's stuff. As I grew up and eventually took over and built up my dad's business, Bob Miller kept getting "bigger and bigger."

From KCRA to Wade Advertising and then out on his own, Bob Miller was everywhere, but impossible to meet. Everyone I knew knew Bob. I didn't.

As a printer, I wanted his business. I could never even get an appointment with him or speak to him on the telephone. He had a solid wall of good women employees who sealed him off from unneeded meetings and kept him on track. I stopped after ten years of trying.

Fifteen years later, although Bob's paintings were popping up everywhere, I still had never met him until Mother's Day, 2012.

It was at a crowded garden party. The hostess said Bob was in attendance. Knowing Bob's reputation as a pioneer of television art direction, a noted survivor of the MadMen era, and painter of all these cool images, I began scanning the crowd for a suave, gray haired version of Dan Draper.

"Where is he?" I asked.

Pointing to the top of a head about twenty feet away, barely visible among the crowd, she said,"There he is!"

Like everyone who meets Bob for the first time, you expect a giant and discover the opposite: a truly diminutive man. But like everyone who gets to know Bob, he grows on you.

Since that day, we have met nearly every Wednesday for a long lunch. At the very first lunch he broke out a copy of a book I had produced and showered me with compliments on its design. After just minutes--or possibly a couple glasses of wine--it seems I was volunteering to produce a similar book about his life and work.

Being Bob Miller, he produced a hand written manuscript in short order. One day when I suggested a custom alphabet of initial caps to lead off paragraphs might be a cool feature, he designed a set by the next day! He jumped into the project wholeheartedly, in true Bob Miller fashion.

The book didn't take three and a half years to create, produce and publish. I should have finished it sooner, really. But how could I? The luncheons with Bob morphed into a three year salon of sorts. Bob graciously introduced me to every person he knows, from famous artists and political fatcats to school teachers and restaurateurs. Our chats inspired me to create more art of my own and eventually open a gallery in my home where I feature Bob's art and many of the terrific artists he has brought into my life.

So now, the book is finished. There's a lot in it. There's a lot left out. The story is Bob's as he chose to tell it.

Bob and I have become dear friends since the Mother's Day when I couldn't quite find that little guy at the party. And I've learned he really is a giant.

See you at lunch Wednesday.

Thanks to Carol Davydova for the suggestions when I was stuck and the first edit; my darling Debbie for her patience (and a near-final edit!); Bob's family and friends for putting up with hearing about "The Book" while wondering if I was ever going to produce it!

Thanks to the contributors for sharing your memories of Bob; and to all those who shared stories with us at lunch.

Thanks also to Aaron, Riva, Sam, Nicole and Rick at OneSpeed for taking such good care of us during those lunches!

And thanks to Bob for being Bob!

www.ingramcontent.com/pod-product-compliance
Lightning Source LLC
LaVergne TN
LVHW070122110826
845147LV00002B/174